Young Peop s
and Domest

Maria Mellins · Rachael Wheatley ·
Caroline Flowers
Editors

Young People, Stalking Awareness and Domestic Abuse

In Partnership with The Alice Ruggles Trust

palgrave
macmillan

Editors
Maria Mellins
St Mary's University
Twickenham, UK

Rachael Wheatley
University of Derby
Derby, UK

Caroline Flowers
Nottingham Trent University
Nottingham, UK

ISBN 978-3-031-32378-2 ISBN 978-3-031-32379-9 (eBook)
https://doi.org/10.1007/978-3-031-32379-9

Cover credit: eStudioCalamar

This Palgrave Macmillan imprint is published by the registered company Springer Nature Switzerland AG
The registered company address is: Gewerbestrasse 11, 6330 Cham, Switzerland

Foreword

"Mum, I think he's the one."

But our daughter Alice's new boyfriend did not turn out to be the perfect partner she had imagined early in their relationship. He turned out to be the one who would seek to coerce and control her during their short relationship, the one who would stalk her relentlessly after she finished it, and the one who would ultimately break into her flat and brutally kill her.[1]

We now know that Trimaan ('Harry') Dhillon wasn't an irritating ex-boyfriend who would eventually accept Alice's decision and move on. He was a dangerous stalker whose subsequent actions could have been anticipated and quite possibly prevented if the appropriate action had been taken. Alice should not have died. Her death might not have happened if she and her friends and family had had more understanding of the dangers of controlling behaviour and stalking; if she had been persuaded to go to the police far sooner and if the police and other agencies (including Dhillon's employers) had had sufficient professional training and awareness and acted in the right way when they were contacted. Alice's 101 calls should have triggered a robust criminal justice response together with the involvement of specialist advocates and relevant agencies (such as social services, healthcare and prison and probation services). It is essential that these key players work together to immediately safeguard the victim, manage the perpetrator and most importantly to mitigate the risk as effectively as possible going forward.

We founded the Alice Ruggles Trust in 2017 to help prevent what happened to Alice happening to others. We work to raise awareness of stalking and coercive control, to ensure that relevant legislation is effective and adhered to and to bring about lasting improvements in the management of perpetrators and the protection of victims. Our long-term goal is to equip a generation with the confidence to recognise coercive control and stalking, and a criminal justice system and support services that have a thorough understanding of the issues involved. We need to empower stalking victims to seek help much sooner, and to build a society that reacts in the right way when they do.

A particular focus of the Trust is to work with young people, alerting them to the dangers of stalking and relationship abuse, helping them to recognise and call out stalking and giving them the confidence to seek support for themselves or a friend. We do this through both statutory education and less formal channels such as youth groups and social media. Our Relationship Safety Resource, a package of quality-assured teaching materials and lesson plans on stalking and coercive behaviour aimed primarily at Key Stage 4 (14- to 16-year-old) students, has been freely available to secondary teachers throughout the UK since 2019 as part of the PSHE (Personal, Social, Health and Economic) curriculum. These lessons are being delivered around England and Wales not only by PSHE teachers but also by police community support teams. Additionally, we speak to students at school assemblies and train school staff to understand the issues so that they too can present assemblies and lessons.

Professionals working with young people also need to recognise stalking and respond appropriately. Working together with St Mary's University, Twickenham, London, we have developed Ofqual-registered qualifications and short courses aiming to upskill professionals working with young people in education environments. In cooperation with other agencies and charities, we deliver training for social care and health professionals and workshops for domestic abuse caseworkers across England and Wales and have produced comprehensive packages of training materials for use in the NHS.

Our annual Alice Ruggles Trust conferences bring together academics and practitioners to highlight current research and best practice and to explore better ways of linking them in the future. The 2020 conference focused on stalking among young people and revealed how little was known about stalking victimisation and perpetration among adolescents. It highlighted the need for further research and professional understanding in this area, and so provided the impetus that has resulted in the publication of this book.

The issue of stalking among young people deserves our attention for three important reasons. First, adolescents are at greater risk than adults of being stalked yet understand the risks less well. Better-trained professionals and improved personal awareness mean better outcomes for young stalking victims. Second, identifying perpetrator behaviours among young people at an early stage raises the possibility of psychological interventions that can prevent those behaviours developing into something much more serious. A viable strategy for tackling stalking in the longer term has to be to stop people developing into perpetrators. The third, and perhaps most fundamental, reason is that focusing on today's young people provides our best hope of changing the mindset of a generation with regard to stalking.

We are confident that this book will be of value to students, academics and professional practitioners alike.

Leicester, UK
January 2023

Clive Ruggles
Sue Hills

Note

1. Alice's story is told more fully at https://alicerugglestrust.org/alices-story. It has also been the subject of various television and internet documentaries.

Contents

Notes on Contributors

Dr. Catrin Andersson is a Senior Lecturer in Criminology in the Department of Law and Criminology at Sheffield Hallam University. She holds degrees in Forensic Psychology (B.A., M.A.) and Criminal Justice (M.Phil., Ph.D.) from the City University of New York, USA. She has co-authored papers on substance abuse recovery, homicide statistics and gambling addiction. Her current primary research interests revolve around violence at both micro and macro levels, cybercrime, comparative research and research methods.

Ms. Rachel Austin is a Ph.D. Student in the Criminology and Criminal Justice Department at Nottingham Trent University. Rachel Austin's research interest is adolescents' understanding of personally motivated cybercrime and the level of cyber education they receive in schools.

Prof. James Banks is a Professor of Criminology at Sheffield Hallam University. His research is focused on gambling-related crime and technology, although he continues to publish in other areas. To date, he has authored two research monographs—Online Gambling and Crime: Causes, Controls and Controversies and Gambling, Crime and Society—while his research has been published in high-ranking journals such as International Gambling Studies, the European Journal of Criminology, the International Journal of Comparative Criminology and Offender Therapy, Crime, Media, Culture and Critical Criminology.

Dr. Sadiq Bhanbhro is a Senior Research Fellow at Sheffield Hallam University, UK. He is an anthropologist, public health professional and experienced interdisciplinary researcher. He has a Ph.D. in the political economy of community notions of honour and honour killings of women and girls in the UK and Pakistan. He primarily focuses on global public health, gender, sexuality, violence (particularly honour crimes and honour killings), equality, diversity, inclusion and anti-racism.

Eloise Bovill is a first-class Bio-Medical graduate of St Mary's University, London. Eloise identifies as autistic and has a keen interest in autism and studies related to this.

Dr. Helen Bovill is an Associate Professor at the University of the West of England, Bristol, in the College of Health, Science and Society and the School of Education and Childhood. Helen's research interests include Relationships, Health and Sex Education Provision within schools, and prevention of gender-based violence within education and society, her publications in these areas can be found at https://people.uwe.ac.uk/Person/Helen2Bovill.

Julie Buckland is an Associate Head of Department for Initial Teacher Education at the University of the West of England, Bristol, (UK) in the College of Health, Science and Society and the School of Education and Childhood. She is also a Doctoral Student with an interest in curriculum design and delivery and a Trustee and Governor of a local all through SEND school.

Dr. Sarah Chicken is a neurodivergent academic working as a Senior Lecturer at the University of the West of England, Bristol, in the College of Health, Science and Society and the School of Education and Childhood. Sarah's research aims to amplify the voices of often marginalised groups in society and is underpinned by a rights-based approach, her publications in these areas can be found at https://people.uwe.ac.uk/Person/SarahChicken.

Dr. Rahmanara Chowdhury is a Chartered Psychologist and Course Lead of the B.A. and M.A. Islam and Pastoral Care programmes at the Markfield Institute of Higher Education (MIHE). She completed her doctoral research at Brunel University London (funded by the ESRC). She has authored several books on the topic of domestic abuse. Her research interests include domestic violence and abuse, spiritual abuse, forensic mental health, intersectionality and holistic approaches to wellbeing. She is the Head of the Markfield Centre for the Study of Wellbeing which seeks to showcase and support grassroots wellbeing expertise.

Fiona Drouet MBE is the Founder and CEO of charity EmilyTest, a Scottish Government-funded charity with a specialist focus on GBV prevention, intervention and support specifically in the further education (FE) and higher education (HE) sectors.

Dr. Caroline Flowers is a British Psychological Society chartered forensic psychologist and Health and Care Professions Council registered (practitioner) psychologist. Caroline is a full member of the Division of Forensic Psychology. Caroline has worked for Her Majesty's Prison and Probation Services (UK) Psychology Services Group for 14 years in various roles. Caroline is currently a Senior Lecturer in psychology at Nottingham Trent University (NTU) and is the course leader for the Doctorate in Forensic Psychology, where she is involved in a range of research projects and consultancy which focuses on intimate partner violence and stalking. Caroline is also an independent forensic practitioner and is a psychologist member of the parole board for England and Wales. Caroline completed her Doctor of Psychology in Forensic Psychology degree on *A qualitative exploration of intimate partner stalking: Current issues for risk and intervention* in September 2019. Caroline has developed and delivered training packages and acts as a consultant to the police and continues to publish papers in this area and is keen to continue to raise awareness of stalking and partner abuse through both consultancy and ongoing research.

Poppy Gerrard-Abbott is a Ph.D. in sociology and social policy at the University of Edinburgh researching gender-based violence (GBV) in UK higher education (HE) and is the co-author of EmilyTest's *GBV Charter for universities and colleges,* the first Charter of its kind.

Dr. Mohammad Mazher Idriss LL.B. (Hons.), LL.M., Cert. Ed., Ph.D. is a Senior Lecturer in Law and LL.M. Programme Director at Manchester Metropolitan University. He completed his Ph.D. thesis on 'Honour-Based Violence in Ethnic Communities in England and Wales', which was externally examined by Professor Lynn Welchman (of SOAS, University of London). He is author of a number of articles on HBA and his most recent publications include: "Abused by the Patriarchy': Male Victims, Masculinity, Honor-Based Abuse and Forced Marriages' (2021) 37(13–14) *Journal of Interpersonal Violence* NP11905-NP11932; 'Key Agent and Survivor Recommendations for Intervention in Honor-Based Violence in the UK' [2018] *International Journal of Comparative and Applied Criminal Justice*, 42(4) 321–339; 'The Mosques Are the Biggest Problem We've Got Right Now'—'Key Agent and Survivor Accounts of Engaging Mosques with Domestic and Honor-Based Violence in the United Kingdom' [2017] *Journal of Interpersonal Violence*, 35(13–14) 2464–2491; 'Not Domestic Violence or Cultural Tradition: Is Honour-Based Violence Distinct from Domestic Violence?' [2017] *Journal of Social Welfare and Family Law*, 39(1), 3–21; 'Forced Marriages—The Need for Criminalisation?' [2015] *Criminal Law Review*, 663 and 'Sentencing Guidelines for HBV and Honour Killings' [2015] *Journal of Criminal Law*, 79(3), 198–210. He was also co-editor (with T. Abbas) of *Honour, Violence, Women and Islam* (Routledge-Cavendish, 2010) and was general editor of *Men, Masculinities and Honour-Based Abuse* (Routledge, 2020).

Dr. Morag Claire Kennedy is a Senior Lecturer in Criminology who leads the M.A. Criminology course at Nottingham Trent University. She researches and writes on topics such as intimate partner abuse/homicide, digital coercive control and feminism. Her current research considers the emotional labour of Ph.D. research.

Dr. Michael Lewis, Ph.D., is a Registered Forensic Psychologist, Chartered Psychologist, Chartered Scientist and Associate Fellow of the British Psychological Society. Dr. Lewis is the Course Director for the M.Sc. Applied Forensic Psychology programme at the University of Central Lancashire. He also works clinically for a therapeutic service, providing specialist psychological input at a forensic step-down unit. Dr. Lewis is a Editor-In-Chief of the *Journal of Criminological Research, Policy and Practice*, and an active researcher in personality, aggression and psychological trauma.

Saeeda Mayat is the Chief Operating Officer at Paladin National Stalking Advocacy Service and has overseen the strategic and operational direction of the service since 2018. A passionate advocate for the EVAWG sector she has worked within the sector for 18 years in roles including refuge young people's worker and IDVA. For the last 10 years she has used her front line delivery experience to develop and lead trauma-informed, needs-led services that keep service users at the heart of their function, most recently at Paladin. Saeeda has been involved in a number of research projects, including 'They speak for you when you can't speak' An Evaluation of the Paladin Service. 'Consequences of the COVID-19 Lockdown on Stalking Victimisation'. 'The Evaluation of the Lancashire Safer Together Transition Project'. Saeeda is a board member for a number of local VAWG charities, serving as a chair for two years. She also has 7 years of experience in leadership and management in the private sector. Saeeda has extensive experience in writing and delivering training, public speaking and developing/leading innovative services within the EVAWG and stalking advocacy sector. Qualifications include Master in Business Administration (M.B.A.).

Prof. Kieran McCartan is a Professor of Criminology at the University of the West of England Bristol, (UK) in the College of Health, Science and Society and the School of Social Sciences. He has a track record of public, academic and professional engagement on criminological issues, including the origins and causes of sex offending, and societal responses to sex offenders. Professor McCartan has advised the HMPPS, Confederation of European Probation, European Commission, Council of Europe, New Zealand Police, End Child Prostitution in Asian Tourism, Bravehearts as well as the Department of the Prime Minister and Cabinet, Australia, to name a few, his publications can be found at https://people.uwe.ac.uk/Person/KieranMccartan.

Dr. Maria Mellins is an Associate Professor in Criminology at St Mary's University. Maria is also a trained Independent Stalking Advocacy Caseworker (ISAC) and Sexual Violence Liaison Officer for Universities (SVLO) which underpins her undergraduate and postgraduate teaching in the area of gender-based violence. Together with the Alice Ruggles Trust, where she holds the position of Trustee, Maria has written a suite of stalking and abuse awareness qualifications (SAfEE) that are Ofqual accredited and offered to education providers throughout the UK, she also manages a One Stop Shop for domestic abuse, stalking and sexual violence. In terms of research, Maria has written sociological monographs, novels, research papers and articles including *Critiquing Violent Crime in the Media* (co-edited with Sarah Moore, Palgrave Macmillan, 2022) and also supervises Ph.D. students in the areas of stalking, abuse and the media.

Dr. Tine Munk is a Senior Lecturer in Criminology and Criminal Justice Department at Nottingham Trent University. Tine Munk's research interest is cybercrime and cybersecurity in relation to governance, power, strategies, resilience and preparedness.

Louise Neville is the Young Peoples Coordinator and Senior ISAC, at Paladin National Stalking Advocacy Service. Louise is a qualified Youth and Community worker (PGDip), has a post-grad certificate in Safeguarding children & young people and a Masters in Informal and Community Education. With experience of working with young people for 23 years, Louise has experience working with young people through statutory and third-sector organisations, including generic youth work settings, schools, young people in care, homeless young people and for the last 16 years she has specialised in working and developing services for young people who have experienced domestic abuse and more recently stalking. Throughout her work with young people she has always promoted young people's rights and the voice of young people and worked within a participatory framework, to best support and safeguard. Louise is an experienced trainer and public speaker, around stalking, domestic abuse, working with young people and safeguarding young people.

Dr. Catherine O'Sullivan is a Vice Dean of Learning, Teaching Curriculum at the School of Law, UCC, is a graduate of UCC (B.C.L., LL.M.) and completed a Ph.D. at Osgoode Hall Law School, Canada. Her main research interests lie in Criminal Law, Criminology, Gender and the Law, Children's Rights and Law and Popular Culture. She is the Chair of the Sexual Violence Centre Cork (SVCC) Board of Directors and has trained to provide Bystander Intervention workshops and Consent workshops to third-level students. She is a co-author of a leading student and practitioner text, *Criminal Law in Ireland: Cases and Materials*, 2nd ed (2021), and of *Fundamentals of the Irish Legal System* (2016). She has authored articles in a variety of national and international publications including the *Irish Jurist*, the *Dublin University Law Journal*, the *Northern Ireland Legal Quarterly*, *Legal Studies* and *Human Rights Quarterly*.

Prof. Clive Ruggles is Alice's father and a co-founder of the Trust. Clive has spoken at numerous training and development sessions for the police, CPS and judiciary as well as to social and healthcare services, academic colleagues and students. He manages the Trust's administrative services and plays a leading role in its public awareness raising and campaigning work.

Laura Scarr works as a Vulnerability Operational Support Officer with Manchester Police. Her M.A. in Criminology was completed at Nottingham Trent University in 2021 and this chapter showcases her M.A. research with the focus being on stalking in hands-on occupations.

Dr. Ciara Staunton has been lecturing on the topics of forensic psychology and criminality for over 15 years at University College Cork, Ireland. She holds an M.Sc. in Forensic and Legal Psychology (Leicester University) and a Ph.D. in Forensic Psychology from UCC. While her doctoral studies focused on psychophysiological forms of assessment of deviant sexual arousal patterns, her research interests pertain to gender-based violence in the main. Ciara's courses on forensic psychology and criminal behaviour are popular with law enforcement personnel as well as those who work within the criminal justice system and allied health and social care settings. Her short courses on the Criminal Mind are ideal for those who are simply true crime fanatics and Ciara is a regular contributor to the radio and print media regarding high-profile cases in Ireland.

Dr. Rachael Wheatley is a British Psychological Society chartered forensic psychologist and Health and Care Professions Council registered (practitioner) psychologist. Rachael is a full member of the Division of Forensic Psychology, a BPS chartered scientist, an associate fellow of the BPS, holds a European Certificate in Psychology and has an expert witness qualification. Rachael has worked for Her Majesty's Prison and Probation Services (UK) Psychology Services Group for 21 years and now manages a forensic psychology professional practice postgraduate diploma at the University of Derby, where she remains active in research. She is also an independent practitioner, continuing to provide psychological risk assessments, individual interventions, supervision, training and consultancy related to addressing stalking (and related VAWG offending). Rachael was the lead author of the recently published BPS practitioner guide for psychologists working with those who have engaged in stalking, and co-developer of the Early Awareness Stalking Intervention (EASI), targeting whose charged with stalking offences. Rachael has specialised in working with people who have stalked for the last 13 years and completed her Doctor of Psychology degree on *what drives men who stalk and how practitioners can best respond to their needs*, publishing widely on this topic. Rachael is particularly interested in raising awareness of stalking behaviours and in working to improve (early) interventions with those who stalk and is a proud trustee of the Alice Ruggles Trust.

Dr. Rachel Worthington is a Chartered Psychologist, and a full member of the Division of Forensic Psychology, including holding Associate Fellow status. She is also a Chartered Scientist, holds European Psychologist status and a registered Forensic Psychologist with the HCPC. She is also a Senior Lecturer at both Manchester Metropolitan University and the University of Central Lancashire and works in private practice. She has published a range of peer-reviewed articles and she has presented both nationally and internationally on working positively with people with complex needs to improve their quality of life and reduce behaviours of concern.

List of Figures

List of Tables

Part I

Recognising Stalking & Relationship Abuse in Young People

Introduction

1

Caroline Flowers, Maria Mellins, and Rachael Wheatley

Key Points This introduction chapter aims to provide the context of the book and in particular aims to:

- Raise awareness of stalking and domestic abuse that occurs amongst, by and towards young people within the UK and Ireland.
- Highlight the nuances, diversity and complexities surrounding the ways that stalking and abusive behaviours exist in our society.
- Signposts to the wide range of chapters within this book by a diverse group of authors that addresses related issues within different settings, for example within our education system, and to more recent behaviours of focus such as so-called honour-based stalking and strangulation.

Stalking and relationship abuse are two forms of interpersonal violence, which unfortunately continue to need a united, multi-agency focus to impel improvements and pivotal change in our society. Both stalking and relationship abuse are deemed widespread criminal, social and public health problems that disproportionately affect women and girls and have a profound, long-lasting impact on victims. Recent years have seen renewed attention from the criminal justice arena

C. Flowers
Nottingham Trent University, Nottingham, UK
e-mail: caroline.flowers02@ntu.ac.uk

M. Mellins (✉)
St Mary's University, London, UK
e-mail: Maria.mellins@stmarys.ac.uk

R. Wheatley
University of Derby, Derby, UK
e-mail: R.Wheatley@derby.ac.uk

M. Mellins et al. (eds.), *Young People, Stalking Awareness and Domestic Abuse*,
https://doi.org/10.1007/978-3-031-32379-9_1

and both stalking and relationship abuse (for example, coercive and controlling behaviours) have been the subject of evolving legislation, research and political interest. Nonetheless, despite the increased interest and attempts to educate professionals and the public on the catastrophic impact and serious consequences of stalking and relationship abuse, they continue to be crimes that are not adequately addressed, both within the public and professional arena and yet are rife.

Victims of these forms of interpersonal violence do not represent homogenous groups. Similarly, those who stalk have varying motivations for their behaviours and target different victims (for example, some will more likely target an ex-partner, whilst others an acquaintance; usually the person stalking is known to the person being stalked). Many victims and perpetrators of these types of offences are unlikely to fit the stereotypical bill based on their outward appearances and presenting characteristics and behaviours. Our unconscious biases about the typical or 'ideal' victim and perpetrator profiles (Christie 1986) can hinder efforts to attain proportionate justice.

Concerningly, stalking and relationship abuse perpetrated by and affecting young people is a significant social and legal problem, affecting the health and psychological well-being of this generation, at such a critical emotional and vocational stage in their lives (Mullen et al. 2009). A large body of international literature highlights the high prevalence of stalking victimisation in young people, particularly so in samples of college and university students (Björklundet al. 2010; Grangeia and Matos 2018; Ravensberg and Miller 2004; Spitzberg et al. 2010). This also aligns with wider data collected by digital media and broadcast company *VICE* in collaboration with Paladin National Stalking Advocacy Service and the Alice Ruggles Trust, during their 'Unfollow Me' campaign. *VICE* carried out a survey of 12,000 young people aged 13–24, which found that 35 per cent of this group had personally been subjected to stalking, whilst 56 per cent knew someone who had been a victim.

Our Aims

The overarching aim of this book is to describe and discuss some of the contemporary issues within research and practice on stalking and relationship abuse with a particular focus on young people, a group that is impacted more than any other life stage. This book approaches stalking as a gender-based crime, which aligns with the majority of stalking literature that reports males who stalk and females as victims. We feel that acknowledging the centrality of violence against women and girls within stalking and domestic abuse is vital in order to understand and address this public health issue, however it is also important to note that stalking motivations do vary and not all cases of stalking are carried out by men on women. This book therefore recognises *all* victims and the additional barriers that are present relating to people from various ethnic minority backgrounds and LGBTQ + communities, as well as people who are neurodiverse and have health conditions.

Whilst the contents of this book tackle stalking and domestic abuse in general, a further aim is to raise awareness of stalking and domestic abuse within the context of the UK and Ireland and to ensure that light is shed on the complexities and varied ways that stalking and abusive behaviours exist in our society. For instance, we include chapters that explore stalking in relation to so-called 'honour'-based crimes. We consider our education system and particularly the role of universities as a context for gender-based violence. Discussions also focus on strangulation awareness and the impacts of pornography amongst young people, as well as exposing the more hidden victims of domestic abuse and stalking by considering the links with suicide (Monckton-Smith et al. 2017). By publishing this book, that includes contributions from professionals working across diverse areas—including those with lived experience, charities, frontline advocacy services, academic researchers, and forensic psychologists who work with those who stalk—we hope to identify important gaps that need to be addressed so that we can gain a fuller understanding and safeguard young people.

We wanted this book to culminate in a discussion of priorities going forward. The final chapter is co-authored with Clive Ruggles, co-founder of the Alice Ruggles Trust, and accounts for our recommendations and a *vision for the future.*

The Issue of Definition

Consideration is firstly given to exploring the complexities of defining both stalking behaviour and relationship abuse. With regards to language, throughout the book we will use the terms *stalking* and *relationship abuse*. The term *relationship abuse* is used interchangeably with *domestic abuse*, *domestic violence* and *intimate partner violence* within the academic literature and forensic practice. Historically, there has been international debate and a lack of consensus on what behaviours constitute relationship abuse. The *Domestic Abuse Act 2021* has now introduced a statutory definition of domestic abuse that places emphasis on the fact that domestic abuse is not just physical violence, but also includes emotional, psychological, sexual and economic abuse, controlling or coercive behaviours, as well as recognising children as victims of domestic abuse in their own right. An overarching factsheet of the Domestic Abuse Act legislation is provided in Chapter 13 of this book and full details of the legislation are available at legislation.gov.uk. Whilst this is an important step forward in broadening the definition of domestic abuse, there is a great deal of work to be done raising societal and cultural awareness in this area.

Stalking is a prevalent and complex, pattern-based crime against a person(s) that can be life-threatening for victims (Dreßing et al. 2020). The Suzy Lamplugh Trust, which runs the National Stalking Helpline, defines stalking as 'a pattern of fixated and obsessive behaviour which is repeated, persistent, intrusive and causes fear of violence or engenders alarm and distress in the victim'. The term *stalking* has traditionally described the hunting activities of animals (Mullen et al. 2009), and the term *stalking* originated from the United States in the late 1980s to describe *star stalkers* who were fans obsessively pursuing celebrities (Cosgrove 1990; Lowney and Best 1995). Following the murder of actress Rebecca Schaeffer in 1989, killed by an obsessed fan, there was increased attention on stalking, however it also skewed society's notion that stalking only affects celebrities or public figures (Palarea et al 1999).

Historically, the legal, academic and clinical definition of stalking has been the subject of ongoing debate. Stalking has been explored internationally from a diverse range of disciplines. Within and between disciplines, such as criminology, psychiatry, psychology, clinical practitioners, legal professionals, policymakers and legal academics, there is inconsistency in how stalking is defined (Fox et al. 2011). This remains a crucial and unresolved issue (Owens 2016). Yet it is noticeable that descriptions for stalking do largely share three key features; (1) that the stalking is intentional; (2) that the stalking causes the victim reasonable fear and/or distress and (3) that the behaviours constituting stalking are unwanted (Logan and Walker 2017).

Recognising Harmful Behaviours

Research on stalking victimisation reveals that stalking is a common crime (Logan et al. 2007; Sheridan and Roberts 2011). What is currently known about the prevalence of stalking in the United Kingdom, is that approximately one in five women, and one in ten men, will be stalked in their lifetime (ONS 2019). However, obtaining accurate prevalence estimates of stalking is challenging. This is due to a number of factors including varied definitions of stalking (both in the UK and internationally). Many stalking cases may not enter the criminal justice process as they are not recognised or reported, and if they are, there are crucial barriers to law enforcement identifying and correctly *criming*, charging and investigating stalking offences. Subsequently, arrest rates, prosecutions and convictions remain low and there are challenges in gathering evidence for a successful prosecution. Therefore, the true number of cases is not reflected within the official data indicating a 'dark figure' of stalking and relationship abuse (Brady and Nobles 2017). A critical challenge for all professionals across the criminal justice system is the importance of identifying and managing this population swiftly and robustly before more fixated and entrenched patterns bed in and escalate in seriousness. Without correctly identifying and classifying stalking behaviour, those who stalk will not come to the attention of the criminal justice system and the impacts and risks will increase for victims. Those who stalk will not receive appropriate case management and access to effective intervention, leaving them to continue their stalking campaign and create further victims.

The methods of stalking are extremely varied; a list of stalking 'behaviours' is presented in the stalking legislation, the *Protections of Freedoms Act 2012*, which was an amendment to the *Protection from Harassment Act 1997* (this is not an exhaustive list). Stalking behaviours include repeated and unwanted direct, indirect, offline and online methods such as making telephone calls, sending text messages, emails, letters, sending or leaving unwanted items, using social media, surveillance, loitering, proxy stalking, property damage or invasion, threats and interfering with personal items, as well as other criminal acts as part of the stalking episode. Advances in technology have introduced a new wave of stalking methods that facilitate constant and instant forms of contact, enabling perpetrators to track victims' movements, monitor them online and attempt to isolate them by restricting their contact with others (Woodlock 2017). Research exploring online stalking (also known as *cyberstalking* or *digitally enabled stalking*) has found that those who engage in stalking tend to use a variety of tactics, such as online surveillance and contact through social media (Reyns et al. 2012) and for ex-intimate partner stalking, the use of private accounts and home security systems to track movements (Dimond et al. 2011).

Relationship abuse can include behaviours that are closely linked with stalking behaviours, but the behaviours are enacted during an intact relationship. Therefore this is better defined as controlling and coercive behaviour, and can also involve emotional, psychological, sexual, financial, and image-based sexual abuse (colloquially known as *revenge porn*, a term to avoid due to its connotations of victim blaming). Coercive control was made an offence under Sect. 76 of the *Serious Crime Act 2015* and has recently been extended to post-separation abuse through the *Domestic Abuse Act 2021*. Both coercive control and stalking are pattern-based, as opposed to incident-based, offences (Scott et al. 2020) and are often undetected by family, friends, law enforcement and even the person who is being subjected to these behaviours. The independent behaviours may not appear threatening in isolation, but when examined as part of a pattern carry a very high risk and are tantamount to what Evan Stark (2007) has called a hostage situation. In his seminal work, *Coercive Control. How Men Dominate Women in Personal Life,* Stark states that whilst coercive control may be interweaved with physical assault which, in the worst cases, can lead to fatality, 'the primary harm abusive men inflict is political, not physical, and reflects the deprivation of rights and resources that are critical to personhood and citizenship' (2007, 5). Stark underlines that control is the aim of the offender, and is achieved over time through micro-regulation of everyday routine roles, such as withholding access to money, food, transport and communication (2007, 5). Amongst young people, coercive and controlling behaviour can present in a number of ways, but some examples include: using threats and intimidation to take control over their everyday life such as who they are allowed to see or choosing their clothes; tracking and monitoring their time and asking for 'evidence' of where they are (e.g. 'send me a picture' or 'share your map location so that I know where you are'); humiliating them and making them feel subordinate; isolating them and not allowing them to see their friends or family; being cruel and demeaning about them and eroding their self-esteem; gaslighting and manipulating them and/or others to believe things that are false; causing reputational damage; taking control of their finances; limiting their basic human rights such as access to food, water, sanitary products; controlling light and temperature settings within the home; forcing them to take part in criminal activity; threatening, coercing and humiliating them to have sex/during sex and forcing them to attend to the offender's needs; threatening to share private images or personal information (such as 'outing' them); assaulting them and threatening to hurt or kill them or their loved ones (including pets); perpetrating abusive acts associated with so-called family 'honour'.

In her book *See What You Made Me Do: Power Control and Domestic Abuse* (2020) Jess Hill draws on Albert Biderman (1957) and highlights links between the pattern of coercive and controlling behaviour in domestic abuse cases and techniques used to torture prisoners of war. Both situations include an offender that lives alongside their captive for a significant amount of time, who gradually isolates them from others and becomes the most important person in their life. It is this gradual take-over that causes the captive person to experience a shift in attitudes and beliefs. In this way, the captors gain control of their captive so they become compliant, dependent and begin to share their worldview. But as psychiatrist and trauma specialist Judith Herman explains, control is not gained immediately, instead victims-survivors are 'taken prisoner gradually, by courtship' (Herman 2001, 82).

Crucially, the perceptions of those working in the criminal justice system play a significant role in recognising and managing stalking behaviour. Within the stalking perception literature, research has focused on establishing attitudes and perceptions of stalking, spanning across university samples, community samples and police professionals (for example, Dennison 2007; Duff and Scott 2013; Kamphuis et al. 2005; Phillips et al. 2004; Sheridan et al. 2003, 2019; Scott et al. 2014). This research has highlighted there is frequently a discrepancy between the perceptions held by the samples explored and the reality of what is known about stalking behaviour. For example, whilst research suggests that ex-intimate partner stalking perpetrators present as the most persistent and potentially dangerous subtype (James and Farnham 2003; Mullen et al. 1999), perception research has identified that stalking behaviour is portrayed as being more serious if this is committed by a stranger (for example, Hills and Taplin 1998; Phillips et al. 2004; Scott and Sheridan 2011). Critically, misperceptions have a significant impact on the reporting of stalking and radiate to those working in the criminal justice system, which may influence how stalking is recognised and managed.

Structure of the Book

This book is divided into three separate but interlinked parts. Part One: *Recognising Stalking and Relationship Abuse in Young People*, Part Two: *Methods and Behaviours of Stalking and Coercive Control* and Part Three: *Stalking Support Services and Healthy Relationship Education.*

Part One: Recognising Stalking and Relationship Abuse in Young People

Within this section there are three distinct chapters. Chapter 2 is written by Michael Lewis and Rachael Wheatley and discusses classifying adolescent stalking exploring preliminary considerations for investigation in intervention and risk assessment. This chapter attends to the academic literature on stalking classification systems, reviewing key similarities and differences in stalking patterns and behaviours between adults and adolescents. In doing so, the chapter aims to discuss underpinning motives and the context within which adolescent stalking takes place, whilst also introducing integral theory to provide explanation for the behaviour exhibited. Links are made to forensic practice to ensure that the chapter remains informative and relevant to professionals, as well as providing insight for students studying this topic at degree level. The chapter argues there is a need for intervention and risk management attempts to be idiosyncratic, focusing on individual psychological needs whilst also accounting for responsivity issues and insight of this population.

Chapter 3 is written by Rachel Worthington. The chapter focuses on challenging bias in the assessment and treatment of adolescent stalking. The chapter aims to explore the role of bias in relation to the protected characteristics in terms of the assessment and treatment of adolescent stalking. Specifically, this work focuses on how bias impacts on victim reporting, victim vulnerability, victim selection, police responding and perpetration. The chapter will provide practical recommendations for how these may be overcome.

Chapter 4 is written by Tine Munk and Rachel Austin. The focus of this chapter is on adolescent perceptions of stalking and the interplay between the role of adolescents' use of popular media to learn relationship behaviours and the dangers of portraying stalking positively in movies. The chapter argues that adolescents and children may not be aware of the real consequences of stalking, for both victims and perpetrators, due to a lack of holistic understanding of popular movies and TV shows. The chapter discusses how adolescents are particularly vulnerable to the influence of popular movies and that during this phase of life, young people will search for information from various sources about life, relationships and behaviours.

Part Two: Methods and Behaviours of Stalking and Coercive Control

There are four chapters within this Part. Chapter 5 is written by Catherine O'Sullivan and Ciara Staunton and explores stalking methods and behaviours, and the results of the stalking survey in Ireland. The chapter considers the international literature concerning those who stalk, who they tend to stalk and the types of behaviours they tend to engage in. Consideration is given to identifying and discussing the psychological, physical, economic and social impacts of stalking on those who are stalked. Finally, the chapter discusses the European trend towards criminalising stalking in addition to criminalising harassment and considers recent developments in Ireland.

Chapter 6 is written by James Banks and Catrin Andersson and explores the role of technology in stalking and coercive control amongst young people. This chapter introduces readers to the role of technology in facilitating and enhancing stalking and coercive and controlling practices. The chapter details how a growing range of internet-enabled digital devices has facilitated greater interconnectivity that transcends physical boundaries. The chapter demonstrates the increased centrality of ICT in the lives of young people and how such technology may act as a conduit for stalking and coercive behaviours. The authors argue how it is only through a combination of law, technology, education, the telecommunications industry, social media organisations, criminal justice and domestic violence professionals, that coercive control, stalking and other abusive behaviour can be effectively responded to.

Chapter 7 is written by Sadiq Bhanbhro and explores stalking and coercive control in terms of the commonly used strategies in so-called 'honour'-based abuse (HBA) against young people. This chapter draws on primary and secondary research that discusses coercive control and stalking in honour-based abuse against young people in the United Kingdom. The author discusses how the family honour is, at root, male honour, which works at different levels—in a social group, community or nation through the patriarchal system called the honour system. Thus, the perpetrators of honour abuse are the victims' male family members. The families employ various methods to exercise power and control over young people, mainly girls, to maintain family honour. The research suggests stalking actions are used to track the victims and their activities, in which coercive control is often used to maintain that control. The chapter concludes that coercive control and stalking are key strategies the perpetrators employ in honour-related abuse against young people.

Chapter 8 is written by Mohammad Mazher Idriss and Rahmanara Chowdhury and also focuses on honour-based stalking. This chapter provides an original contribution to the understanding of HBA and honour-based stalking, through providing case details of young people, in particular young women, and a more holistic lens currently lacking within academia and practice. The author discusses the web model of domestic violence and abuse (DVA) which focuses on placing the victim at the heart of interventions. Its unique feature is its ability to support practitioners in developing a more holistic understanding of the circumstances specific to each victim, without losing the centrality of the victim voice, regardless of which community is discussed.

Part Three: Stalking Support Services and Healthy Relationship Education

This part has five chapters. Chapter 9 is written by Saeeda Mayat and Louise Neville from Paladin National Stalking Advocacy Service. The chapter explores how support is given to young people who are experiencing stalking and what services are available. Consideration is given to identifying why specific young people's services are needed and how supporting young victims of stalking is different to supporting adults. The chapter also discusses some of the additional barriers and risks, that young victims of stalking face. The barriers include accessing support, availability of specific services and professionals' misunderstandings of young people. The importance of young people's voices being central to service development and delivery to effectively engage with young people is also highlighted, alongside how to ensure young people are involved in the service from the start.

Chapter 10 is written by Laura Scarr and Morag Claire Kennedy and critically discusses the existent literature in the context of hands-on occupations. The chapter explores the responses to stalking experiences from both a legislative and workplace point of view, accompanied by analysis of areas requiring change. The authors, together with Nick Gazzard, Founder and CEO of the Hollie Gazzard Trust, argue that stalking in hands-on occupations is an under-researched area that needs urgent attention. The chapter also highlights the gap in the literature related to the LGBTQ + community and people from various ethnic minority backgrounds, highlighting how this is failing stalking survivors.

Chapter 11 is written by Fiona Drouet and Poppy Gerrard. The first section of this chapter is written by Fiona Drouet about her daughter Emily. During this section Fiona outlines the EmilyTest, which is the world's first Gender-Based Violence (GBV) Charter for colleges and universities. The chapter discusses how the charter is a comprehensive, research-based guide to getting GBV prevention, intervention and support for students. The second part of the chapter is written by Poppy Gerrard who surveys research and literature in the field to address 'the education sector in crisis'.

Chapter 12 is written by Helen Bovill, Sarah Chicken, Eloise Bovill, Julie Buckland and Kieran McCartan and explores stalking and relationship sex and health education (RHSE) for young people on the Autistic Spectrum. This chapter presents findings demonstrating many young people do not have a strong understanding of stalking. The chapter discusses the characteristics associated with Autistic Spectrum Disorder (ASD) and how these can put people with ASD at a higher risk of (or perception of) engaging in stalking behaviour. The chapter will assess the scant extant literature and argues how RSHE could be shaped, to inform and equip young people with ASD with the tools and knowledge to develop healthy relationships.

Chapter 13 is written by Maria Mellins and Clive Ruggles and discusses the critical issue of improving public awareness of stalking and domestic abuse in young people. The chapter explores how concerningly young people are impacted by stalking and domestic abuse, and highlights that sadly, there is still a great deal of work to do in this area. The chapter revisits the key messages within the book which relate to issues with the criminal justice system; victim support services; employment; the education system and the media. Finally, this chapter turns to our partner, The Alice Ruggles Trust, who outline their recommendations for future work in this area.

Conclusion

It is our ambition that this book continues to raise awareness of stalking and relationship abuse and that it highlights how we can work together to impact meaningful, sustainable change. We hope that the valuable chapters within this collection make their way into schools, colleges and universities; into workplaces; media studios, and on to the desks of those who govern, write policy and enforce the law. Going forward we need a joined-up approach to enhance public identification and recognition of stalking and domestic abuse so they do not remain hidden crimes.

Discussion Questions

- What are the diverse areas that most require our attention as professionals, advocates, policymakers, and where should we start?
- Where do you see important gaps in our knowledge that need to be addressed so that we can gain a fuller understanding of these issues and safeguard young people?

Bibliography

Biderman, A. 1957. Communist Attempts to Elicit False Confessions From Air Force Prisoners of War. *Bulletin of the New York Academy of Medicine*, September, 33, no. 9: 616–625.

Brady, Patrick Q. and Matt R. Nobles. 2017. The Dark Figure of Stalking: Examining Law Enforcement Response. *Journal of Interpersonal Violence; J Interpers Violence* 32, no. 20: 3149–3173. https://doi.org/10.1177/0886260515596979.

Björklund, Katja, Helinä Häkkänen-Nyholm, Lorraine Sheridan, Karl Roberts, and Asko Tolvanen. 2010. Latent Profile Approach to Duration of Stalking: Stalking Duration. *Journal of Forensic Sciences* 55, no. 4: 1008–1014. https://doi.org/10.1111/j.1556-4029.2010.01421.x

Chan, Heng Choon and Lorraine Sheridan. 2020. *Psycho-Criminological Approaches to Stalking Behavior : An International Perspective*. Hoboken, NJ: Wiley.

Cosgrove, Stuart. 1990. Erotomania-star-stalking Obsessively Pursuing the Rich and Famous is One of the More Sinister by-products of the Media Age. *New Statesman & Society* 3, no. 111: 31–32.

Christie, N. 1986. The Ideal Victim. In E.A. Fattah (Ed), *From Crime Policy to Victim Policy*. London: Palgrave Macmillan.

Dennison, Susan M. 2007. Interpersonal Relationships and Stalking: Identifying When to Intervene. *Law and Human Behavior; Law Hum Behav* 31, no. 4: 353–367. https://doi.org/10.1007/s10979-006-9067-3.

Dimond, Jill P., Casey Fiesler, and Amy S. Bruckman. 2011. Domestic Violence and Information Communication Technologies. *Interacting with Computers* 23, no. 5: 413–421. https://doi.org/10.1016/j.intcom.2011.04.006.

Dreßing Harald, Gass Peter, Schultz Katharina, Kuehner Christine. 2020. The Prevalence and Effects of Stalking—a replication study. *Dtsch Arztebl Int* 117: 347–353. https://doi.org/10.3238/arztebl.2020.0347.

Duff, Simon C., and Adrian J. Scott. 2013. Understanding Perceptions of Stalking: the Impact of Additional Contextual Information Regarding the Breakdown of Relationships. *Journal of Criminal Psychology* 3, no. 2: 136–144.

Edwards, Katie M., Emily E. Camp, Stephanie Lim, T. K. Logan, Ryan C. Shorey, and Wayne Babchuk. 2022. Stalking among Sexual and Gender Minorities: A Systematic Literature Review. *Aggression and Violent Behavior* 66: 101777. https://doi.org/10.1016/j.avb.2022.101777.

Fissel, Erica R., Bradford W. Reyns, and Bonnie S. Fisher. 2020. Stalking and Cyberstalking Victimization Research: Taking Stock of Key Conceptual, Definitional, Prevalence, and Theoretical Issues. *Psycho-criminological Approaches to Stalking Behavior: the International Perspective*: 11–36.

Fox, Kathleen A., Matt R. Nobles, and Bonnie S. Fisher. 2011. Method Behind the Madness: An Examination of Stalking Measurements. *Aggression and Violent Behavior* 16, no. 1: 74–84. https://doi.org/10.1016/j.avb.2010.12.004.

Grangeia, Helena, and Marlene Matos. 2018. Persistent Harassment: Targets and Perpetrators among Young Adults. *Victims & Offenders* 13, no. 1: 102–121. https://doi.org/10.1080/15564886.2016.1268987.

Gruenewald, Jeff and Kristin Kelley. 2014. Exploring Anti-LGBT Homicide by Mode of Victim Selection. *Criminal Justice and Behavior* 41, no. 9: 1130–1152. https://doi.org/10.1177/0093854814541259.

Herman, J. L. 2001. *Trauma and Recovery*. New York: Pandora.

Hill, Jess. 2020. *See What You Made Me Do*. London: C Hurst and Co. Publishing LTD.

Hills, Adelma M., and Jacqueline L. Taplin. 1998. Anticipated Responses to Stalking: Effect of Threat and Target-stalker Relationship. *Psychiatry, Psychology, and Law :An interdisciplinary journal of the Australian and New Zealand Association of Psychiatry, Psychology and Law*, 5: 139–146.

Hine, Benjamin A. 2019. "it Can't Be That Bad, I Mean, He's a Guy": Exploring Judgements Towards Domestic Violence Scenarios Varying on Perpetrator and Victim Gender, and Abuse Type. In *Intimate Partner Violence*, pp. 43–57. Routledge.

James, David V., and Frank R. Farnham. 2003. Stalking and Serious Violence. *Journal of the American Academy of Psychiatry and the Law Online* 31, no. 4: 432-439.

Kamphuis, Jan H., Gian M. Galeazzi, Laura De Fazio, Paul M. G. Emmelkamp, Frank Farnham, Anne Groenen, David James, and Geert Vervaeke. 2005. Stalking-Perceptions and Attitudes Amongst Helping Professions. an EU Cross-National Comparison. *Clinical Psychology and Psychotherapy; Clin.Psychol.Psychother* 12, no: 215–225. https://doi.org/10.1002/cpp.451.

Logan, T. K., and Robert Walker. 2017. Stalking: A Multidimensional Framework for Assessment and Safety Planning. *Trauma, Violence & Abuse; Trauma Violence Abuse* 18, no. 2: 200–222. https://doi.org/10.1177/1524838015603210.

Logan, T. K., Lisa Shannon, and Jennifer Cole. 2007. Stalking Victimization in the Context of Intimate Partner Violence. *Violence and Victims; Violence Vict* 22, no. 6: 669–683. https://doi.org/10.1891/088667007782793147.

Lowney, Kathleen S., and Joel Best. 1995. Stalking Strangers and Lovers: Changing Media Typifications of a New Crime Problem. In *Images of issues*, pp. 33–58. Routledge.

Mullen, Paul E., Michele Pathé, and Rosemary Purcell. 2009. *Stalkers and their Victims*. Cambridge: Cambridge University Press.

MacKenzie, Rachel, Troy Erin McEwan, Michele Pathe, David V. James, James Robert Ogloff, and Paul Edward Mullen. 2009. Stalking Risk Profile: Guidelines for the Assessment and Management of Stalkers.

McFarlane, Judith, Jacquelyn C. Campbell, and Kathy Watson. 2002. Intimate Partner Stalking and Femicide: Urgent Implications for Women's Safety. *Behavioral sciences & the law* 20, nos. 1–2: 51–68.

Monckton-Smith, Jane, Karolina Szymanska, and Sue Haile. 2017. Exploring the Relationship Between Stalking and Homicide. *Suzy Lamplugh Trust.*

Mullen, Paul E., Michele Pathe, Rosemary Purcell, and Geoffrey W. Stuart. 1999. Study of Stalkers. *The American Journal of Psychiatry; Am J Psychiatry* 156, no. 8: 1244–1249. https://doi.org/10.1176/ajp.156.8.1244.

Office for National Statistics (ONS). 2019. *Stalking: Findings from the Crime Survey for England and Wales.* London.

Owens, Jennifer Gatewood. 2016. Why Definitions Matter: Stalking Victimization in the United States. *Journal of Interpersonal Violence; J Interpers Violence* 31, no. 12: 2196–2226. https://doi.org/10.1177/0886260515573577.

Palarea, R. E., Scalora, M. J., & Langhinrichsen-Rohling, J. 1999. Risk assessment inventory for stalking. Unpublished measure.

Phillips, Lorraine, Ryan Quirk, Barry Rosenfeld, and Maureen O'Connor. Is it Stalking?: Perceptions of Stalking among College Undergraduates. *Criminal Justice and Behavior* 31, no. 1: 73–96. https://doi.org/10.1177/0093854803259251.

Ravensberg, Victoria, and Catherine Miller. 2004. Stalking among Young Adults: A Review of the Preliminary Research. *Aggression and Violent Behavior* 8, no. 4 (2003): 455–469. https://doi.org/10.1016/S1359-1789(02)00075-7.

Reyns, Bradford W., Billy Henson, and Bonnie S. Fisher. 2012. Stalking in the Twilight Zone: Extent of Cyberstalking Victimization and Offending Among College Students. *Deviant Behavior* 33, no. 1: 1–25. https://doi.org/10.1080/01639625.2010.538364.

Schuyler, Ashley C., Cary Klemmer, Mary Rose Mamey, Sheree M. Schrager, Jeremy T. Goldbach, Ian W. Holloway, and Carl Andrew Castro. 2012. Experiences of Sexual Harassment, Stalking, and Sexual Assault during Military Service among LGBT and Non-LGBT Service Members. *Journal of Traumatic Stress; J Trauma Stress* 33, no. 3: 257–266. https://doi.org/10.1002/jts.22506.

Scott, A., Rajakaruna, N., and Handscomb, N. A. and Waterworth, G.A.H. 2020. Public Familiarity and Understanding of Stalking/Harassment Legislation. In H. Chan and L. Sheridan (eds.), *Psycho-Criminological Approaches To Stalking Behavior*. London: John Wiley and Sons.

Scott, Adrian J., Nikki Rajakaruna, and Lorraine Sheridan. 2014. Framing and Perceptions of Stalking: The Influence of Conduct Severity and the Perpetrator-Target Relationship. *Psychology, Crime & Law* 20, no. 3: 242–260. https://doi.org/10.1080/1068316X.2013.770856.

Scott, Adrian J., and Lorraine Sheridan. 2011. 'reasonable Perceptions of Stalking: The Influence of Conduct Severity and the Perpetrator–target Relationship. *Psychology, Crime & Law* 17, no. 4: 331-343.

Sheridan, Lorraine, Raphael Gillett, Graham M. Davies, Eric Blaauw, and Darshana Patel. 2013. 'There's No Smoke Without Fire': Are Male Ex-partners Perceived as More 'Entitled' to Stalk Than Acquaintance or Stranger Stalkers?. *British Journal of Psychology* 94, no. 1: 87–98.

Sheridan, Lorraine, and Karl Roberts. 2011. Key Questions to Consider in Stalking Cases. *Behavioral Sciences & the Law; Behav.Sci.Law* 29, no. 2: 255–270. https://doi.org/10.1002/bsl.966.

Sheridan, Lorraine P., Adrian J. Scott, and Amy M. Campbell. 2019. Perceptions and Experiences of Intrusive Behavior and Stalking: Comparing Lgbtiq and Heterosexual Groups. *Journal of Interpersonal Violence* 34, no. 7: 1388–1409.

Spitzberg, Brian H., William R. Cupach, and Lea DL Ciceraro. 2010. "Sex differences in stalking and obsessive relational intrusion: Two meta-analyses." *Partner Abuse* 1, no. 3: 259-285.

Spitzberg, Brian H. and William R. Cupach. 2004. *The Dark Side of Relationship Pursuit: From Attraction to Obsession and Stalking.* Mahwah: Routledge. doi:https://doi.org/10.4324/9781410609908.

Stark, Evan. 2007. *Coercive Control. How Men Entrap Women in Personal Life*. Oxford: Oxford University Press.
Woodlock, Delanie. 2017. The Abuse of Technology in Domestic Violence and Stalking. *Violence Against Women; Violence Against Women* 23, no. 5: 584–602. https://doi.org/10.1177/1077801216646277.

Classifying Stalking Among Adolescents: Preliminary Considerations for Risk Management

2

Michael Lewis and Rachael Wheatley

Key Points

- Stalking by adolescents is prevalent and the harm caused to victims and to oneself by victimising others is potentially even more detrimental than adult stalking.
- Stalking by adolescents is different to stalking by adults because of identified motivations and contexts.
- Stalking classifications can be useful in certain contexts but cannot be singly applied to both adult and adolescent stalking cases.

Introduction

Young people have been stalked and do stalk others. Despite research findings highlighting that adult stalking is a significant social problem, there has been relatively little investigation into stalking by, and perpetrated towards, young people. Whilst stalking by adolescents does occur (Purcell et al. 2014; Smith-Dardenet al. 2016), there is limited research into this phenomenon, particularly with a focus on, and in the context of, the rapid developmental changes during these years (Leitz and Theriot 2005; Smith-Darden et al. 2016), and the potential longer-term harms caused by experiences of victimisation and perpetration. An increased focus on

M. Lewis (✉)
University of Central Lancashire, Preston, UK
e-mail: MLewis9@uclan.ac.uk

R. Wheatley
University of Derby, Derby, UK
e-mail: R.Wheatley@derby.ac.uk

M. Mellins et al. (eds.), *Young People, Stalking Awareness and Domestic Abuse*,
https://doi.org/10.1007/978-3-031-32379-9_2

this more recently is noted, and one proposal for the dearth of attention is the misconception that young people are not capable of engaging in extreme behaviours such as stalking (Purcell et al. 2009). The neglect regarding young people and stalking is concerning given the crucial stage at which this behaviour occurs; that is, the significant psychosocial development and sexual changes of the perpetrator and their victims, who are usually also young people.

Research has highlighted that there is a high prevalence of stalking among this age group (Brady et al. 2017). One study, for example, found that the prevalence rate for college and university students over the age of eighteen was larger than that found among adults, with around 52.6% of females and 34.9% of males stating that they were stalked before the age of 25 (Black et al. 2011). In a large-scale survey, Reidy et al. (2016) found that the annual prevalence of stalking victimisation was 14% for females and 13% for males; all aged between 11 and 15 years, whereas in high school students, the annual prevalence was around 18% for females and 14% for males (Fisher et al. 2014). Based on a survey completed with 27 US colleges and universities, Cantor et al. (2018) reported that 4.2% of the sample indicated they had been stalked following their enrolment, and highlighted findings that those identifying as transgender, gender non-conforming, or questioning their gender, experienced much higher rates of victimisation than those identifying as male or female. These figures emphasise adolescent stalking as a prevalent issue, though given the lack of empirical investigation, a more accurate measure of the problem is needed.

Young people are constantly navigating and learning about themselves and others, particularly in a relational sense. They are in a period where they will experience many new scenarios and 'firsts', even infatuations (informally known as 'crushes' during this developmental phase) on those familiar to them. However, having a 'crush' is not the same as stalking, although for some it can lead to such, and associated risks may remain unseen and masked by notions of innocent 'puppy love' (Brewster 2003; Mullen et al. 2008b). Stalking by adolescents has also been viewed in the context of bullying beyond the school gates (Evans and Meloy 2011). Existing literature suggests that stalking by adolescents may share some similarities as well as differences with that exhibited by adults (Purcell et al. 2014), and thus it is vital to understand and raise awareness of the prevalence, nature and motivations of adolescent stalking, as well as the associated risks and psychosocial needs. By neglecting to attend to the scale of the problem, opportunities to intervene early and safeguard young people, as well as prevent stalking and other related interpersonal offences, will continue to be missed (Purcell et al. 2005a, b).

This chapter will provide an overview of adult stalking classification systems, present a current understanding of stalking by adolescents as well as propose adolescent stalking classifications, and highlight the bespoke issues relevant to stalking by this population. It will conclude with implications for risk management and signposting to future research needs.

Classifying Stalking Behaviour

In the case of stalking, literature focusses on both classification and typology; however, the degree to which the two terms are used correctly remains questionable. Often, 'typology' and 'classification' are two terms used interchangeably in the Social Sciences to account for how a group may relate based on their characteristics. Characteristics in this context may include those that relate to an offence, or indeed, the attributes of those who offend or are victims. According to Barrow et al. (2014), typology is distinct from classification in that it involves the formation of groups according to an empirical criteria or similarity. Classification, however, comprises a set of attributes or variables that are linked in a conceptual way to form logical classes. Nevertheless, it is to be acknowledged that over the years various classifications, and to some extent, typologies, of those who stalk have been proposed that differ according to the professional needs and priorities of their respective authors.

Despite differing priorities, the overall goal of classifying stalking behaviour is to delineate key differences between the groups that underlie the perpetrator population. The focus is then on utilising the identified differences to inform management and subsequent intervention by predicting certain behaviours, such as violence, intimidation, harassment, or threats, occurring in the context of stalking (Racine et al. 2014). It is these behaviours that arguably cause physical and/or psychological harm to those to whom they are directed and are therefore of concern. There is thus some merit in having a classification system for stalking; however, it is to be acknowledged that such systems are predominantly descriptive and limited in their explanatory power. Whilst classification systems are helpful in guiding initial hypotheses, multi-factor theories (i.e., theories that consider a range of contributory mechanisms when explaining a phenomenon) are likely to have greater utility in accounting for stalking behaviour (Parkhill et al. 2022). However, multi-factor theories of stalking remain underdeveloped, hence the focus on classification systems as an initial attempt at capturing the complexity of this behaviour.

Research is yet to agree on a uniform classification that can be applied, and which likely relates to the complexity and heterogeneity of stalking behaviour (Parkhill et al. 2022). Of the classifications proposed, most can be mapped onto one or more of the following categories: (1) those that classify according to an underlying mental disorder; (2) those that classify according to the existence of a prior relationship with a victim; and (3) those that classify according to the primary motivation for stalking (Mullenet al. 2008b, p. 58). Classification systems that utilise aspects from all three categories are thought to hold the most promise in facilitating a more comprehensive understanding of stalking; one that enables professionals to make sense of the offence information and pose hypotheses surrounding the function of the stalking behaviour (McEwan and Davis 2020).

It is to be noted that the more contemporary classification systems of stalking have begun to focus on motivation and the context within which stalking occurs, as opposed to solely attending to the type of stalking or series of interpersonal behaviours exhibited (Racine and Billick 2014). Indeed, this shift mirrors developments in the aggression literature, where there is a drive to focus less on the nature of aggression and more on its motivation (Ireland 2018). Attending to motivation allows for intent and the underlying reasons for enacting a given behaviour to be considered. Its inclusion in classification systems holds promise for understanding common elements of stalking behaviour that go beyond mere nature to capture the underlying causal mechanism(s) compelling a perpetrator to act.

To date, classification systems of stalking have focussed primarily on adults, particularly men, neglecting younger perpetrators within the 'adolescent' demographic; adolescence in this instance captures those between the ages of 13 and 18 (Leitz and Theriot 2005), though there does need to be recognition that cognitive and emotional maturity may vary on an individual basis. Stalking by adolescents has been viewed as rare and, as noted, has resultantly received minimal empirical attention (Evans and Meloy 2011; Leitz and Theriot 2005). This assumption, however, appears to be premature, as rates of adolescent stalking have tentatively been proposed as being greater than those found among adult perpetrators (Fisher et al. 2014). Adolescents have also been noted to stalk peers of a comparable age (Cloonan-Thomas et al. 2022), as well as adults (Roberts et al. 2016), and exhibit similar patterns and levels of violence to their adult counterparts (Leitz and Theriot 2005; McCann 1998, 2001). Based on these findings, it would be rash to dismiss adolescent stalking and the harm that may arise from it.

Although existing findings are dated and based predominantly on case studies, important similarities and differences are thought to exist between adult and adolescent perpetrators of stalking (Mullen et al. 2008a). There is thus value in attending to existing classification systems on adult stalking when looking to advance understanding of this behaviour among adolescents since the knowledge base on adult systems is arguably more robust by comparison. This chapter will move on to consider classification systems for adult stalking behaviour, presenting core models, which will form the context through which stalking among adolescents will then be discussed.

Adult Stalking: A Review of Classification Systems

According to Purcell et al. (2003), over twenty different classification systems have been proposed to capture adult stalking. Such systems are thought to have flourished in the absence of an explanatory theoretical framework that attends specifically to stalking behaviour. However, they are not without limitations. In addition to their limited explanatory function, classification systems of stalking have been generally criticised for overlapping with one another (Racine and Billick 2014), for failing to recognise that those who commit stalking may exhibit changes in victim preference (Zorza 2009), and for overly emphasising the role of psychopathology (Nijdam-Joneset al. 2018). The latter relates to a sampling bias, with early research focussing predominantly on psychiatric populations (Wheatley et al. 2020).

Zona's Offender-Victim Types

Adopting a psychiatric approach to classification, Zona et al. (1993) reviewed 74 case files processed by the Los Angeles Police Department's (LAPD) Threat Management Unit and delineated three stalking groups: (1) simple obsessional; (2) love obsessional; and (3) erotomanic. Whilst their initial sample of 74 cases focussed predominantly on convicted adults with a mental disorder, further data was sourced that comprised 341 cases argued to represent a 'community population' (Zona et al. 1998).

Simple obsessional followers are referred to as the most prevalent. Zona et al. (1998) indicated that, by definition, these cases do not need to be based on a prior intimate relationship, but if one has occurred, stalking tends to emerge following a one-sided termination, with intimidation, harassment, and/or violence utilised to coerce the victim back into a relationship (Schlesinger 2002), or to seek revenge for rejection (De Smet et al. 2015; Racine and Billick 2014; Zona et al. 1998). Among simple obsessional followers, rejection is thought to induce narcissistic injury as their interpersonal entitlement is challenged (Zonaet al. 1993), and which conveys a role for personality pathology among this stalking group. When considering a non-intimate scenario, such as in the case of a client stalking their therapist or doctor, violence may present through an individual pursuing intimacy, or where they perceive mistreatment by the victim and seek retribution for this (Purcell et al. 2005a, b; Zona et al. 1998).

Cases fitting the love obsessional category have no relationship to the victim. Instead, victims tend to be those projected through media outlets. Those who fit within this category are thought to often present with severe and persistent mental health concerns (Racine and Billick 2014). These conditions make it more likely for an individual to unrealistically believe that if they could make themselves known to the victim, then the victim would likely be attracted to them. Significant effort is therefore made to obtain the attention of the victim, and if no response is received, or one that is perceived as negative, frustration and anger may arise, though not to the same extent as that exhibited by the simple obsessional group.

The final category, erotomanic, overlaps with a rare delusional disorder, known as erotomania. In the fifth edition of the Diagnostic and Statistical Manual of Mental Disorders (DSM-5; American Psychiatric Association 2013), erotomania features under the delusional disorder—'erotomanic type', which applies when the central theme of the delusion (i.e., a fixed false belief; Kelly 2018) is that another person is in love with them. Despite its chronicity, the onset of the delusion tends to be sudden and thought to occur in the context of loneliness and social isolation, serving as a compensatory strategy for self-esteem, shame, and disappointment (Kelly 2018). It is noted that cases will often cite improbable proof of the victim's affections for them and view rejection as a declaration of love, and thus aggression is rare. Erotomanic is the least common classification posed by Zona et al. (1993) and is thought to relate more to women than men (Kelly 2018).

Mullen's Study of Stalkers

In 1999, Mullen and colleagues built on previous classification systems to account for motivation and the context within which stalking occurs, including the nature of the relationship with the victim and the presence of psychopathology. A review of 145 cases (115 of which were male) referred to a forensic psychiatric service elucidated five non-mutually exclusive categories: (1) rejected; (2) intimacy-seeker; (3) incompetent suitor; (4) resentful; and (5) predatory.

Rejected stalking cases (n = 52; 36%) were the most prevalent grouping and mirrored the simple obsessional classification delineated by Zona et al. (1993, 1998). Rejected stalking cases (i.e., stalking that involved ex-intimate partners) were characterised by their sense of loss, which co-occurred with negative emotion. Individuals within this group were reported to oscillate between a desire for reconciliation and a desire for revenge. Personality challenges were dominant among this group (Mullen et al. 1999).

Forty-nine (34%) of the stalking cases comprised the intimacy-seeker group whose primary objective was to establish a relationship, though isolation and deficits in social skills inhibited this (Racine and Billick 2014). Many cases presented with a psychotic disorder and found themselves prey to jealousy and enraged by a partner's indifference, with incidents of aggression noted (Mullen et al. 1999). It is this behaviour that differentiates those in the intimacy-seeker classification from the preoccupied and delusional individuals captured within Zona's love obsessional and erotomanic groupings. Whilst the incompetent suitor group of stalkers, consisting of 22 (15%) cases, overlapped with the intimacy-stalking classification, in that they saw their victims as potential partners, they were not infatuated and recognised that feelings were not reciprocated. Instead, their motivation for stalking is centred around a sense of entitlement to a relationship with the chosen victim (Racine and Billick 2014).

The remaining two groups, resentful (n = 16; 11%) and predatory (n = 6; 4%), were the least prevalent in Mullen's classification system. Cases in the predatory group possessed convictions for sexual offences and presented with paraphilias, and therefore thought to pose a heightened risk. Predatory individuals enjoyed planning and preparing an attack, getting to know the victim, and fantasising about their intentions. Mullen et al. (1999) do, however, warn that this classification requires further clarification as it was tentatively proposed given its sample size and restrictions when determining its predictive value.

Resentful cases, like those in the rejected category, evidenced certain characteristics captured within Zona's simple obsessional grouping. Half of the individuals within this group pursued a vendetta against a victim, driven by a sense that they had wronged them. The remainder pursued victims at random, motivated by some form of grievance. Verbal threats are likely to manifest among this stalking group, and which serves a functional purpose by providing a sense of control by instilling fear in the victim (Racine and Billick 2014).

The RECON Classification System

Referring to their classification system as RECON (RE-lationship and pursuit CON-text), Mohandie and colleagues (2006) defined two broad static categories based on the connection with a victim and the private versus public figure context of pursuit. They excluded motivation and mental illness on the notion that they are dynamic factors and may impact classification stability. Category one, also known as type one, comprised of those who had a previous relationship with the victim, whereas category two, or type two, involved those with no (or limited) previous contact. Individuals classified as 'type one' were subdivided into those who had had an intimate relationship with the victim and those whose victim represented more of an acquaintance. Cases in 'type two' were also subdivided, and as such, consisted of those who pursued a victim identified as a public figure, and those who pursued a victim in a private figure context. Thus, the RECON classification system generates four groups: (1) intimate; (2) acquaintance; (3) public figure; and (4) private stranger.

Utilising a large (n = 1,005; 86% male and 14% female) non-random sample of North American stalking cases, Mohandie and colleagues established high levels of inter-rater reliability for group assignment, as well as discriminant validity between the four groups. However, it is to be acknowledged that cases of domestic violence were included in Mohandie's sample, and which gives rise to criticism, as stalking and domestic violence should ideally be considered as separate behaviours, particularly as not all cases of stalking involve an intimate relationship or family member.

The intimacy category consisted of 50% (n = 502) of the cases and was the most dominant class, yet this may represent a sampling bias with the presence of domestic abuse cases influencing this. It is perhaps not surprising based on its label, that individuals within this grouping held a previous intimate relationship with the victim. Intimate cases were thought to be characterised predominantly by men who exhibit violence, make threats, use weapons, abuse substances, and feature suicidal ideation. They were therefore considered dangerous and a concern for public protection. Aggression among these cases manifested in the absence of a severe and enduring mental illness, such as schizophrenia. Whilst not directly assessed for, personality challenges, however, were hypothesised as prevalent among this category (Mohandie et al. 2006).

Acquaintance stalking comprised 13% (n = 129) of the overall sample. Interestingly, 21% of the cases in this group were women, which is consistent with more general understanding of adult females who stalk (e.g., Brooks et al. 2021; Purcell et al. 2001), in that their efforts tend to be indirect and target friends or colleagues as opposed to previous partners. Individuals within this classification were significantly less violent than intimate cases, but violence was not ruled out completely. However, it was argued that a lesser attachment with the victim buffered against violence risk, though pursuit behaviour remained enduring. DSM axis I (mental illness) and axis II (personality disorder) symptoms were reported among members of this group.

A greater number of women also featured in the public figure stalking category, with these representing 27% of the 271 (27% of the overall sample) cases comprising the group, and who were found to target male victims. However, Mohandie et al. (2006) indicated that the 'normal' gender disparity remained, with men being responsible for most stalking across groupings. Public figure stalkers pursued known personalities whom they had no prior relationship with (Racine and Billick 2014). They were more likely to be psychotic, of an older age, and to not have a criminal history of violence. Although public figure cases may articulate a desire for love, their behaviour was deemed unlikely to escalate, and they were identified as preferring non-proximity-based contact (Mohandie et al. 2006).

The fourth category delineated by Mohandie and colleagues relates to private stranger stalking. Individuals within this category (n = 103; 10% of the overall sample) are thought to consist predominantly of men with persistent major mental illness. Whilst individuals in this category can be violent towards an unknown victim, this is significantly less frequent than violence enacted by those in the intimate group. Unlike intimate cases, they are thought not to abuse substances; rather, it is their mental illness that is presumed to increase the risk of violence.

Although the RECON classification system claims not to focus on motivation and to differ in content and form, there is overlap with earlier models outlined in this chapter. Mohandie and colleagues (2006) do recognise, for instance, that many intimate cases would represent simple obsessional followers outlined in Zona's model. It would also not be unreasonable to speculate that specific characteristics of erotomanic and love obsessional groupings feature among public figure stalking. In the case of RECON, there was a particular drive to assign cases based on behaviour as opposed to mental illness; however, mental illness featured across type two groupings, and which somewhat verifies its role among those who target others unknown to them. Yet, this does not consider progressive psychopathological deterioration and the notion that the presence of stalking itself may give rise to the restriction of experience, including limitations to behaviour, cognition, and affect, that may result in diagnostic psychiatric morbidity (Dressing et al. 2011).

Summary

Adult stalking appears to be heterogenous, with classifications differing based on the presence of psychopathology, nature of the relationship with the victim, and motive. The motivations underpinning adult stalking are diverse and range from attempts to restore a failed intimate relationship to a need to instil fear or distress. Attempts have been made to differentiate behaviour from motive; however, one would argue that this is not possible as behavioural expression is largely underpinned by motivation or intent. Despite the effort, no one classification system appears to be superior; rather, given the conceptual overlap identified within this review, the models could be said to complement one another and offer concurrent validity.

All models have some utility in informing risk management through their consideration of case characteristics and psychological needs. However, there remains scope for enhancing understanding of adult stalking by going beyond case information and obtaining data directly from professionals, those who stalk, and victims. This suggestion also extends to the study of adolescent stalking, which by comparison has received minimal empirical attention. This chapter will now move on to discuss classification systems for stalking behaviour among adolescents, determining the extent to which adult systems can be meaningfully applied.

Adolescent Stalking and Classification

Adolescence marks the slow transitional period between childhood and adulthood, characterised by social, emotional, and vocational development (Mullen et al. 2008a). It is a period of vulnerability (Dahl 2004), as well as 'firsts', as young people seek out ways of asserting their independence. Indeed, for many young people, adolescence involves navigating an intimate relationship having not experienced one previously. This brings about new challenges, which according to Mullen et al. (2008a), are complicated due to differing levels of cognitive and affective maturity, as well as social competence. Whilst engaging in an intimate relationship during adolescence is considered customary and somewhat a 'normal' experience, not all infatuations result in a relationship, and a young person must instead learn to contain their often-powerful emotions. In more extreme cases, however, a 'crush' may lead to stalking-type behaviour, particularly in the context of social ineptitude (Mullen et al. 2008a), emotional dysregulation (Cloonan-Thomas et al. 2022), and emerging psychopathology (McCann 1998). It is to be recognised that infatuations can range in intensity and frequency (Leitz and Theriot 2005), and like with adults, it is when an infatuation becomes obsessional, fixated, and characterised by a pattern of unwanted and intrusive contact, that it becomes a concern.

An explanation for the high prevalence of stalking among young people is that romantic relationships, peer-friendships, and groups, play a key role in identity formation and provide a sense of belonging (Zarrett and Eccles 2006). During this life period, it is likely that young people will also have their first experiences of heartbreak and rejection (Baumeister et al. 1993). Young people, perhaps more so than some adults, will likely lack experience with these situations, and their resultant feelings may serve to overwhelm them and could lead to negative behaviours, including stalking (Ruvolo et al. 2001). The individual that has been rejected, slighted, or heartbroken may try to remain connected to their ex-partner, love interest, or perceived antagonist, whilst adjusting to their experience. It has been suggested that the primary motivation for stalking among young people is the individual's desire for intimacy or sexual contact with the victim following a rebuff or relationship breakdown (rejection), oftentimes intermittently motivated by revenge and resentment (Purcell et al. 2009; Zarrett and Eccles 2006). With exponential technological advances and a growing reliance on fast-changing platforms for social connection among young people, it is important to note the common use of technology within stalking episodes. Stalking and cyberstalking have long been understood to co-occur, with some older studies suggesting that between 25–48% of stalking victims reported elements of cyberstalking (Baum et al. 2009; Sheridan and Grant 2007). For clarity, cyberstalking, or digitally enabled stalking, involves the use of electronic or internet-capable devices to engage in stalking behaviours (Reyns et al. 2012). Commencing stalking of an individual, whichever methods are used, will then likely have a detrimental effect on the young individuals involved.

There are at least two studies examining the relationship between ex-partner stalking among young people and intimate partner abuse during the relationship. This is important information to consider given the social, cognitive, and sexual developmental stages of both victims and perpetrators, and the need for preventative intervention. Borges and Dell'aglio (2019) identified that one-third of their sample of adolescents (total sample, n = 527) aged between 14 and 19 years had experienced intimate partner abuse in a relationship that had ended, and which was subsequently ensued by stalking behaviour. Similar work took place in Australia, with Daff and colleagues (2018) exploring youth intimate partner abuse (YIPA) and stalking among 423 adolescents aged between 14 and 18 years. Just under half of the sample were reportedly female. Findings indicated that stalking behaviour was not uncommon and present in one in six adolescent relationship break-ups. A significant portion of the sample also included elements of reciprocal stalking. For the most part, stalking behaviour was found to be similar to that exhibited by adults; however, digital methods were commonly used, with less violence noted. Victim experiences of fear and distress were deemed to be low despite the presence of violence, threats, or previous YIPA, and which was thought to be representative of lower levels of risk perception among young people. Daff et al. (2018) concluded that whilst in their sample most stalking episodes had been preceded by YIPA, most of those who had experienced YIPA did not then become victim to stalking post-relationship. Specifically, it was found that the use of threats (determined as psychological abuse) within the intact relationship significantly predicted stalking post-relationship. The researchers also illuminated the conclusion that rumination about relationships was a crucial factor relevant to adolescent stalking, and which, in turn, conveys a clear role for emotion processing skills training at an early age.

Case Study Examples of Adolescent Stalking

In the absence of robust data, attempts have been made to classify stalking behaviour among adolescents based on case information. Whilst helpful in generating initial interest, case studies are limiting in terms of their generalisability and application. In most instances, case studies tend to be based on a single case (n = 1), and whilst offering a unique insight into that specific individual, there is no scope for comparison or statistical analysis, which would serve to enhance the reliability of findings. Nevertheless, this section of the chapter will present content on case studies featuring in the academic literature as a means of conveying early attempts at classifying adolescent stalking.

The first case study presented by Urbach and colleagues (1992), and then cited by McCann (1998), introduced a 13-year-old black female. The young person exhibited a delusional erotomanic fixation on her teacher, and following this, her treating psychiatrist. Interestingly, the young person perpetrated violent behaviour thought to stem from frustration relating to unmet erotomanic needs. This presentation is in stark contrast to adult erotomanics, who Zona et al. (1993, 1998) found rarely to be aggressive. Further to this, the young female was noted to transfer her erotomanic preoccupation, which again differed to the adult variant where object constancy was demonstrated. It was concluded by McCann (1998) that perhaps adolescent erotomanics were more violent than their adult counterparts and were able to transfer their fixation, thus evidencing poor impulse control and gender identity diffusion.

A 15-year-old white male was utilised as the second case study and found to possess many of the same traits as the love obsessional follower portrayed by Zona et al. (1993). The young male presented with schizophrenia characterised by delusions that were not purely erotomanic. It is reported that he did not believe that the female victims were in love with him; rather, he would stalk them to make his presence known in an attempt to develop a relationship, though did not present with any aggressive or threatening behaviour. However, in contrast to Zona's depiction of the love obsessional follower, the young male pursued females that were known to him but perhaps unattainable given the situation engendered by his mental illness (McCann 1998).

The third case comprised a white male aged 15 years thought to present with conduct disorder and emerging personality challenges. The male was described as exhibiting a pattern of dysfunctional behaviour that saw him becoming angry at his parents for interfering in his relationship, running away from home, and then being located by the police outside of the residence of his ex-partner, breaching an order of protection taken out by his ex-partner's family. He is said to have interpreted the one-sided termination of the relationship as rejection. Whilst attempts were made to repair the relationship, the young male also sent threatening letters to his ex-partner, and which mirrors the presentation of a simple obsessional follower defined by Zona and colleagues (1993). However, in this instance, the threat of harm extended beyond the ex-intimate partner to a third party, notably his caregivers (adopted parents). This is thought to be rare among simple obsessional stalkers; yet may be a defining feature of adolescent stalking.

McCann's findings offer some promise in utilising Zona's classification system to capture adolescent stalking. However, several factors emerged that distinguished adolescent stalking from that manifesting in adulthood, and which have practical implications for risk management. There may be more than one victim, for example, with adolescent stalkers shifting their obsession, as well as targeting those perceived to be preventing their pursuit. Victims therefore do not always relate to an intimate partner and may capture casual acquaintances, including professionals, and parents/caregivers, and which would therefore distinguish them from

Mohandie's type two perpetrator. Aggression is also thought to be likely, and measures therefore need to be taken to prevent harm. In this instance, adolescent stalking is also associated with severe and enduring psychopathology, as well as impairment in attachment and identity. Whilst this may reflect a sampling bias given that two out of the three cases were made available through contact with mental health services, it would suggest a role for psychiatric intervention.

Based on clinical interviews with two adolescent males, Evans and Meloy (2011) tentatively suggested that there was evidence for a group of socially awkward individuals who stalk, as well as an angry/disgruntled group. There was hesitation in proposing a classification system due to the limited information available, though the authors did note that both cases differed on object relations, motivation, stalking modality, and risk of violence. The socially awkward case was characterised by poor social and intimacy skills. However, there was a desire to form relationships with others driven by a preoccupied attachment style and dependency on others to enhance self-esteem and worth (Evans and Meloy 2011). It was postulated that the victim was likely to be an acquaintance, with obsessive following, surveillance, and repeated harassment (i.e., via telephone calls, letters, emails, etc.) likely. Direct face-to-face contact was deemed rare, thus limiting the opportunity for violence.

In contrast, the angry/disgruntled case captured a 'popular' youth, with an exaggerated self-esteem and narcissistic tendencies. The young person in this case was sensitive to criticism and reacted with anger to feelings of humiliation. In this instance, the victim was a previous intimate partner, and despite the young person moving on, they remained fixated, using threats, intimidation, and violence to control the victim and seek revenge, with violence also being directed at the victim's new partner. Thus, violence among angry/disgruntled cases is likely to be prevalent, with a moderate-to-high risk noted (Evans and Meloy 2011). Bullying may also occur as the perpetrator seeks to demean their victim, enlisting others to support their efforts.

Overlap was noted with Mullen et al's (1999) classification of adult stalkers, with rejected stalkers resembling the angry/disgruntled case, and the intimacy-seeker and incompetent stalkers capturing elements of the socially awkward case. The RECON model also shared commonalities in that prior sexual intimates and acquaintance stalkers mapped onto angry/disgruntled and socially awkward cases, respectively.

In both case studies, Evans and Meloy (2011) identified adverse parent–child relations. Developmental experiences, particularly those pertaining to attachment, could therefore be proposed as influencing the nature of stalking exhibited (Creamer and Hand 2022; MacKenzie et al. 2008), and thus, the category or classification to which cases are assigned. This is not a new suggestion but does nevertheless highlight the importance of considering developmental profiles as part of early intervention when tackling stalking behaviour.

Classifying Adolescent Stalking Based on Motivation

Purcell et al. (2009) reviewed 299 Australian stalking case files of male and female adolescents aged between nine and 18 years, selected from applications made for restraining orders. Their sample comprised 64% male perpetrators (Mean age = 15 years), highlighting a greater prevalence of female perpetrators when compared to adult studies of stalking behaviour. They delineated a classification system comprising six groups that focussed primarily on motive: (1) stalking as an extension to bullying; (2) retaliating stalkers; (3) rejected stalkers; (4) disorganised and disturbed stalkers; (5) predatory stalkers; and (6) intimacy-seeking stalkers. The most prevalent category, and which attended to stalking occurring in the context of bullying, was unique to adolescents and captured cases (n = 84; 28%) who exposed their victims to threats, assaults, and intimidation over several months. Interestingly, males and females both represented perpetrators and victims, and it was not uncommon for a victim to be of the same sex as the perpetrator. According to Purcell et al. (2009), stalking among these cases occurred mainly at school, but there was no obvious trigger to the behaviour.

Those in the retaliatory group (n = 65; 22%) were distinguished from those who bullied others in that there was an identifiable grievance triggering their behaviour, thus reflecting the resentful stalking cases outlined by Mullen et al. (1999). Individuals in this group were motivated by perceived injury or slight and targeted acquaintances and estranged peers, as opposed to fellow pupils. Males and females were represented among perpetrators, indicating that female adolescents tended to involve themselves in individual and group-based harassment, and bullying that included relational forms of aggression, as well as malicious gossip and ostracism (Purcell et al. 2010). Adolescent males, in comparison, were represented across all six categories and thus exhibited a broader range of motivations for stalking.

With the exception of disorganised and disturbed stalkers (n = 58; 20%), which comprised of perpetrators with longstanding conduct problems, targeting multiple victims including adults; the remainder of the groups, consisting of rejected stalkers (n = 64; 22%), predatory stalkers (n = 15; 5%), and intimacy-seeking stalkers (n = 6; 2%), all resembled the categories proposed by Mullen et al. (1999) and will not be repeated here. It is worth noting, however, that male adolescents across these groups demonstrated a greater propensity to target female victims, and which compares to their adult counterparts (Mullen et al. 1999). Incompetent suitor stalking did not feature among adolescents. Rather, it is thought that incompetent suitor stalking may reflect a relational intrusion normalised among this age group and viewed as an inconvenience as opposed to something more serious, and thus unlikely to be reported (Purcell et al. 2010), allowing the stalking behaviour to progress into adulthood unchallenged. Table 2.1 provides a summary of the study findings in regard to perceived motivations and key characteristics across categories.

Interestingly, the researchers concluded that these stalking episodes were largely contextual to bullying and some form of perceived retaliation, targeting a same-sex victim and frequently employing others in attempts to stalk their victim. Threats

Table 2.1 Perceived motivations and key characteristics (Purcell et al. 2009)

Perceived motivation (Sample prevalence in %)	Key characteristics
Extension of bullying (28%)	Commenced in school; Extended beyond the school boundaries; No clear trigger but desire was to persecute/torment victim; Victims were a school peer (56%) or estranged friend (21%); Males/females equally represented as perpetrators and victims; Same-gender stalking and stalking by proxy were most likely to occur in this context
Retaliatory (22%)	Distinguished from bullying as triggering incident/grievance could be identified in every case; Males/females equally represented amongst perpetrators; Commonly targeted acquaintances (48%) and estranged friends (29%)
Rejected (22%)	Stalking following the termination of an intimate or dating relationship; Usually involved a male intruding upon a female, peer-aged victim (86% of cases)
Disorganised and disturbed (20%)	Harassed several people, with few (if any) links between them; Neighbours (47%) and acquaintances (22%) were the most common targets; No clear trigger for the behaviour, although frequently noted 'longstanding' conduct problems
Predatory (5%)	Aimed at imposing unwanted sexual contact on the victim; With the exception of one case, all perpetrators were male; Victim usually a younger child (31%) or an age-peer (62%)
Intimacy seeking (2%)	With the exception of one case, perpetrators were male; Cases were notable for a longer duration of their pursuit than all other groups; Notable for greater number of stalking methods, being one of the few to maintain surveillance (50%) and to loiter (33%)

issued were common among the whole sample, with violence resulting in 54% instances, and the sample employed stalking behaviours in a manner similar to adult samples (e.g., telephone calls, following, and unwanted approaches). However, adolescents also differed from adult samples as only 21% targeted ex-intimate partners within their stalking, although 98% had had a previous 'relationship' with victims, but crucially their motivations differed from those seen in adults (Purcell et al. 2009). One key finding of this study was that stalking among adolescents occurred most commonly in the context of an extension of bullying, which began at school (and would therefore be considered legitimate contact if ignoring the nature of the behaviour) and progressed beyond this environment, where not only the nature was harmful, but the legitimacy of contact would be too.

Summary

Research on adolescent stalking remains in its infancy. The models outlined here require evaluation utilising large data sets, allowing them to be empirically verified. However, this may not be realistic given the progress made thus far, and which would suggest difficulties in accessing a meaningful sample; one that is not restricted to those referred to mental health or Criminal Justice Services. Nevertheless, existing data tentatively indicates that adolescent perpetrators may engage in stalking for antisocial purposes, use aggression, target a range of victims including adults, and exhibit stalking in the context of bullying. In many of the cases, stalking occurred in the context of the school environment and which points to the educational establishment to identify emerging issues and refer these to relevant agencies (McCann 1998). Indeed, views of dangerousness should not be restricted to male adolescent perpetrators, as females also evidenced the potential to cause physical harm in regards to stalking. Early intervention is thus crucial to manage risk.

Implications for the Risk Management of Adolescent Stalkers

Stalking exhibited by, and perpetrated against young people is prevalent, as is intimate partner abuse. Whilst there are some similarities between adolescent stalking and adult stalking, there are also significant differences, with many aspects still to be investigated. The starting point for many risk management considerations is to review and be led by a robust risk assessment tool. In this instance, there is an absence of such a tool given that the Stalking Risk Profile and Stalking Assessment Manual were developed upon and intended to be used with those aged eighteen and above ('adults'). The other key issue is to understand the person's needs and the function of the stalking within the context of their social, relational, and intrapersonal experiences. Dating is common, needing to belong within the social group is common, and therefore the importance of interpersonal relationships during this time should not be underestimated. Yet, this is also a time when adolescents lack experience in intimacy and when applying conflict resolution skills in everyday peer relationships. They may, for example, have learnt or seen (and may replicate) poor examples of how to navigate relationships with others, resulting in them downplaying risk and harm (Roberts et al. 2016). Teaching fundamental principles and skills for conflict resolution, focussing on life goals and personal values, understanding the constituents of healthy relationships, and how to relate to oneself during difficult experiences is likely to prove beneficial at an early age in proactively preventing stalking behaviour.

Adolescent stalking is a particular concern given the likely impact on both victim and perpetrator at a crucial developmental stage in their life. Stalking experiences may negatively affect a young person's education (due to the emotional toll and/or risking suspension), early career prospects (similarly, but also risking a criminal record), sense of self and others in their relational world (and therefore personality development), and so on (Mullen et al. 2008a). Mullen and colleagues (2008a) draw attention to stalking in adolescence as potentially traumatic and abusive experiences, with such experiences in childhood commonly leading to difficult psychosocial outcomes during adulthood (Fergusson and Mullen 1999), and also that, 'intervening at the first signs of stalking offers the best chance of reducing stalking recidivism in the perpetrator, and arguably of stemming any progression to more entrenched or serious forms of interpersonal violence in later life' (p. 124). It would not be unreasonable to advocate for a more proactive stance; that of improved education and inter-/intra-personal skills training in schools, for parents and for teachers, and greater awareness in society. Yet before this, there would be value in equipping young people with the necessary and fundamental skills in navigating intense emotional experiences in response to their developing social worlds and interpersonal relationships.

Risk and needs assessments, as well as risk management interventions, need careful thought so as not to criminalise what can be normal emotional responses, and instead are to be robust in distinguishing such responses from more harmful behaviour, such as intimate partner abuse and stalking. Whilst authors have asserted views on psychological treatment interventions, for adolescents, the context, content, and delivery model require additional thought. For example, Larsen et al. (2020) assert that 'the most effective treatment of stalking behaviour is aimed at the client's underlying problems that cause the stalking. A common theme is learning to understand oneself and others and improving the ability to regulate one's own emotions' (p. 369). Whilst this may be equally true for adolescents, and studies have suggested rumination as common (e.g., Cloonan-Thomas et al. 2022), there is a need to learn more about responsivity issues relating to this age group. This recommendation also applies when determining the function, motivation, and skills deficits associated with adolescent stalking behaviour.

Conclusion

In conclusion, studies focussing on adolescent stalking to date highlight that stalking perpetrated and experienced by this age group is as common and problematic as adult stalking, and shares some commonality in terms of motivation and impact on victims. However, one key motivational and contextual difference relates to stalking emerging from bullying (Purcell et al. 2009). It has also been recognised that given most victims of adolescent stalking are children or adolescents themselves, thus developmentally experiencing a significant life phase, the long-term impact may be even more detrimental (Mullen et al. 1999). This therefore calls for further empirical study on adolescent stalking to inform early intervention and proactive risk management. Indeed, existing research points to emotion dysregulation and rumination as treatment targets among adolescent perpetrators, yet from a multi-factor theoretical perspective, intervention will likely need to be much broader than this, attending to relational aspects, including attachment and interpersonal skills. Regardless, given the heterogeneity among stalking cases observed in this chapter, there is a need for any intervention and risk management attempts to be idiosyncratic, focussing on individual psychological needs whilst also accounting for responsivity issues, education, developmental stage, and capacity for or level of insight.

Discussion Questions

- What are the common motivations and contexts for adolescent stalking as they are currently understood?
- What are the likely implications for educational institutions?
- Where should the focus be next on investigating adolescent stalking?

Bibliography

American Psychiatric Association. (2013). Diagnostic and Statistical Manual of Mental Disorders—Fifth Edition (DSM-5). Author.

Barrow, L. M., Rufo, R. A., and Arambula, S. (2014). Police and profiling in the United States: Applying theory to criminal investigations. Taylor and Francis.

Baum, K., Catalano, S., Rand, M., and Rose, K. (2009). Stalking victimisation in the United States. US Department of Justice.

Baumeister, R. F., Wotman, S. R., and Stillwell, A. M. (1993). Unrequited love: On heartbreak, anger, guilt, scriptlessness, and humiliation. *Journal of Personality and Social Psychology*, 64, 377–394.

Black, M. C., Basile, K. C., Breiding, M. J., Smith, S. G., Walters, M. L., Merrick, M. T., Chen, J., and Stevens, M. R. (2011). The national intimate partner and sexual violence survey: 2010 summary report. Accessed from: https://www.nsvrc.org/sites/default/files/2021-04/NISVS_Report 2010-a.pdf.

Borges, J. L., and Dell'Aglio, D. (2019). Stalking following the breakup of dating relationships in adolescence. *Trends in Psychology*, 27, 413–426.

Brady, Patrick Q., Matt R. Nobles, and Leana A. Bouffard. (2017). Are college students really at a higher risk for stalking?: Exploring the generalizability of student samples in victimization research. *Journal of Criminal Justice* 52, 12–21.

Brewster, M. (2003). Power and control dynamics in prestalking and stalking situations. *Journal of Family Violence*, 18, 207–217.

Brooks, N., Petherick, W., Kannan, A., Stapleton, P., and Davidson, S. (2021). Understanding female-perpetrated stalking. *Journal of Threat Assessment and Management*, 8, 65–76.

Cantor, D., Fisher, W. B., Chibnall, S., Townsend, R., Lee, H., Bruce, C., and Thomas, G. (2018). Report on the AAU campus climate survey on sexual assault and sexual misconduct. Accessed from: http://www.aau.edu/uploadedFiles/AAU_Publications/AAU_Reports/Sexual_Assault_Capus_Survey/AAU_Campus_Climate_Survey_12_14_15.pdf.

Cloonan-Thomas, S., Daff, E. S., and McEwan, T. E. (2022). Post-relationship stalking and intimate partner abuse in a sample of Australian adolescents. *Legal and Criminological Psychology*, 27, 194–215.

Creamer, C. J., and Hand, C. J. (2022). Intimate partner stalking/pursuit: A pathophysiology of attachment style. *International Journal of Offender Therapy and Comparative Criminology*, 66, 604–624.

Daff, E. S., McEwan, T. E., and Luebbers, S. (2018). Australian adolescents' experiences of aggression and abuse by intimate partners. *Journal of Interpersonal Violence*, 36, e1–e24.

Dahl, R. E. (2004). Adolescent brain development: A period of vulnerabilities and opportunities. *Annals of the New York Academy of Sciences*, 1021, 1–22.
De Smet, O., Uzieblo, K., Loeys, T., Buysse, A., and Onraedt, T. (2015). Unwanted pursuit behavior after breakup: Occurrence, risk factors, and gender differences. *Journal of Family Violence*, 30, 753–767.
Dressing, H., Foerster, K., and Gass, P. (2011). Are stalkers disordered or criminal? Thoughts on the psychopathology of stalking. *Psychopathology*, 44, 277–282.
Evans, T. M., and Meloy, J. R. (2011). Identifying and classifying juvenile stalking behavior. *Journal of Forensic Sciences*, 56, 266–270.
Fergusson, David M., and Paul E. Mullen. (1999). *Childhood sexual abuse*. Vol. 40. Sage.
Fisher, B. S., Coker, A. L., Garcia, L. S., Williams, C. M., Clear, E. R., and Cook-Craig, P. G. (2014). Statewide estimates of stalking among high school students in Kentucky: Demographic profile and sex differences. *Violence Against Women*, 20, 1258–1279.
Ireland, J. L. (2018). Individual assessments of aggression: Accounting for core factors. In J. L. Ireland, C. A. Ireland, and P. Birch (Eds.), Violent and sexual offenders: Assessment, treatment, and management (2nd ed., pp. 203–227). Routledge.
Kelly, B. D. (2018). Love as delusion, delusions of love: Erotomania, narcissism and shame. *Medical Humanities*, 44, 15–19.
Larsen, L. L., Bomholdt, D., and Hundahl, H. (2020). The Danish stalking centre, 2019. In H. C. Chan and L. Sheridan (Eds.), Psycho-criminological approaches to stalking behavior: The international perspective (pp. 351–380). Wiley.
Leitz, M. A., and Theriot, M. T. (2005). Adolescent stalking: A review. *Journal of Evidence-Based Social Work*, 3–4, 97–112.
MacKenzie, R. D., Mullen, P. E., Ogloff, J. R. P., McEwan, T. R., and James, D. V. (2008). Parental bonding and adult attachment styles in different types of stalker. *Journal of Forensic Sciences*, 53, 1443–1449.
McCann, J. T. (1998). Subtypes of stalking (obsessional following) in adolescents. *Journal of Adolescence*, 21, 667–675.
McCann, J. T. (2000). A descriptive study of child and adolescent obsessional followers. *Journal of Forensic Sciences*, 45, 195–199.
McCann, J. T. (2001). Stalking in children and adolescents: The primitive bond. American Psychological Association.
McEwan, T. E., and Davis, M. D. (2020). Is there a 'best' stalking typology? Parsing the heterogeneity of stalking and stalkers in an Australian sample. In H. C. Chan and L. Sheridan (Eds.), Psycho-criminological approaches to stalking behavior: An international perspective (pp. 119–139). Wiley.
McGuire, B., and Wraith, A. (2000). Legal and psychological aspects of stalking: A review. *The Journal of Forensic Psychiatry*, 11, 316–327.
Mohandie, K., Meloy, R., Green McGowan, M., and Williams, J. (2006). The RECON typology of stalking: Reliability and validity based upon a large sample of North American stalkers. *Journal of Forensic Sciences*, 51, 147–155.
Mullen, P. E., Pathé, M., and Purcell, R. (2008a). Stalking among juveniles. Cambridge University Press.
Mullen, P. E., Pathé, M., and Purcell, R. (2008b). Stalkers and their victims. Cambridge University Press.
Mullen, P. E., Pathé, M., Purcell, R., and Stuart, G. W. (1999). Study of stalkers. *American Journal of Psychiatry*, 156, 1244–1249.
Nijdam-Jones, A., Rosenfeld, B., Germband, J., Quick, E., and Galietta, M. (2018). Psychopathology of stalking offenders: Examining the clinical, demographic, and stalking characteristics of a community-based sample. *Criminal Justice and Behavior*, 45, 712–731.
Parkhill, A. J., Nixon, M., and McEwan, T. E. (2022). A critical analysis of stalking theory and implications for research and practice. *Behavioral Science and the Law*, 40, 562–583.

Purcell, R., Gennady N. Baksheev, and Paul E. Mullen. (2014). A descriptive study of juvenile family violence: Data from intervention order applications in a Childrens Court. *International journal of law and psychiatry*, 37 6, 558–563.
Purcell, R., Moller, B., Flower, T., and Mullen, P. E. (2009). Stalking among juveniles. *The British Journal of Psychiatry*, 194, 451–455.
Purcell, R., Pathé, M., and Mullen, P., E. (2001). A study of women who stalk. *American Journal of Psychiatry*, 158, 2056–2060.
Purcell, R., Pathé, M., and Mullen, P. E. (2003). Classification of stalkers. In M. P. Brewster (Ed.), Stalking: Psychology, risk factors, interventions, and the Law (1st ed., pp. 6-1–6-21). Civil Rsearch Institute.
Purcell, R., Pathé, M., and Mullen, P. E. (2005). Association between stalking victimisation and psychiatric morbidity in a random community sample. *British Journal of Psychiatry*, 187, 416–420.
Purcell, R., Pathé, M., and Mullen, P. E. (2010). Gender differences in staling behaviour among juveniles. *The Journal of Forensic Psychiatry and Psychology*, 21, 555–568.
Purcell, R., Powell, M. B., and Mullen, P. E. (2005). Clients who stalk psychologists: Prevalence, methods, and motives. *Professional Psychology: Research and Practice*, 36, 537–543.
Racine, C., and Billick, S. (2014). Classification systems for stalking behavior. *Journal of Forensic Sciences*, 59, 250–254.
Reidy, D. E., Smith-Darden, J. P., and Kernsmith, P. D. (2016). Behavioral and mental health correlates of youth stalking victimisation: A latent class approach. *American Journal of Preventative Medicine*, 51, 1007–1014.
Reyns, B. W., Henson, B., and Fisher, B. S. (2012). Stalking in the twilight zone: Extent of cyberstalking victimisation and offending among college students. *Deviant Behavior*, 33, 1–25.
Roberts, K., Tolou-Shams, M., and Madera, K. (2016). Adolescent versus adult stalking: A brief review. *Journal of Forensic Psychology Practice*, 16, 236–252.
Ruvolo, A. P., Fabin, L. A., and Ruvolo, C. M. (2001). Relationship experience and change in attachment characteristics of young adults: The role of relationship breakups and conflict avoidance. *Personal Relationships*, 8, 265–281.
Schlesinger, L. (2002). Stalking, homicide, and catathymic process: A case study. *International Journal of Offender Therapy and Comparative Criminology*, 46, 64–74.
Sheridan, L. P., and Grant, T. (2007). Is cyberstalking different? *Psychology, Crime, and Law*, 13, 627–640.
Smith-Darden, J. P., Reidy, D. E., and Kernsmith, P. D. (2016). Adolescent stalking and risk of violence. *Journal of Adolescence*, 52, 1–10.
Urbach, J. R., Khalily, C., and Mitchell, P. P. (1992). Erotomania in an adolescent: Clinical and theoretical considerations. *Journal of Adolescence*, 15, 231–240.
Wheatley, R., Winder, B., and Kuss, D. J. (2020). What are the features of psychopathology for men who commit stalking offences? A systematic review. *Aggression and Violent Behavior*, 55, e1–e15.
Zarrett, N., and Eccles, J. (2006). The passage to adulthood: Challenge of late adolescence. *New Directions for Youth Development*, 111, 13–28.
Zona, M., Palarea, R. E., and Lane, J. C. (1998). Psychiatric diagnosis and the offender-victim typology of stalking. In J. R. Meloy (Ed.), The psychology of stalking (pp. 69–84). Academic Press.
Zona, M., Sharma, K., and Lane, J. (1993). A comparative study of erotomanic and obsessional subjects in a forensic sample. *Journal of Forensic Sciences*, 38, 894–903.
Zorza, J. (2009). Some controversies concerning classifying and treating stalkers. *Family and Intimate Partner Violence Quarterly*, 2, 155–162.

3 Understanding Adolescent Stalking: Challenging Adult Bias Through a Developmental Lens

Rachel Worthington

Key Points

- Adult definitions and measurements of stalking behaviour are considered in terms of their applicability to adolescents and how this may skew findings in the research.
- Mislabelling adolescents as engaging in 'stalking' behaviour could pose serious implications in terms of the development of their self-concept and developmental pathway.
- When exploring stalking behaviours in adolescents these should be considered within the cultural and societal structure in which the adolescent exists.

This chapter will begin by defining adolescence, stalking and bias before considering the research in relation to adolescent stalking, the impact of bias and ways in which this could be reduced. Recommendations for future research and practice are made.

What Is Bias?

Bias is a personal judgement or prejudice in favour of or against a certain thing, person or group that is considered to be unfair (Fitzgerald and Hurst 2017). Bias may happen at an individual, group or societal level (Fadus et al. 2020) and can be both conscious (explicit) or unconscious (implicit). However, both can lead to differences in decision-making (Kahneman et al. 2021). Furthermore, it is noted that

R. Worthington (✉)
Manchester Metropolitan University, Manchester, UK
e-mail: r.worthington@mmu.ac.uk

M. Mellins et al. (eds.), *Young People, Stalking Awareness and Domestic Abuse*,
https://doi.org/10.1007/978-3-031-32379-9_3

these biases exist equally in healthcare professions compared to the general public (Fitzgerald and Hurst 2017) even when professionals state they are not biased and opposes this (Fadus et al. 2020) due to unconscious pejorative stereotypes (Devine et al. 2012).

The purpose of this chapter is to consider in what way bias may exist in relation to the current assessment and treatment of adolescent stalking by applying the knowledge and tools used to understand adult stalking. Exploring how to reduce this bias is then discussed. For example, this includes understanding what is meant by the term 'stalking' and what tools may be suitable for assessing adolescents to establish if their behaviour constitutes stalking as well as what therapies or interventions may be most effective for reducing a young person's risk of engaging in stalking behaviour.

What Is Adolescence?

The World Health Organisation (2022) conceptualises adolescence as the phase of life between childhood and adulthood and it is considered to be a time when individuals experience rapid physical, cognitive and psychosocial growth which may impact on how they feel, think, make decisions and interact with the world around them. This is important because it acknowledges that thinking and behaviour may fluctuate during this period because of changes in the young person's brain, biology and emotional functioning and that these should not be considered as a static phenomenon as would be expected in adulthood.

When adolescence begins and ends have changed throughout history (Sawyer et al. 2018). The UN Convention on the rights of a child and the WHO define adolescence as ranging from 10 to 19 but others suggest this should end between the ages of 18–26 (Patton et al. 2016). These differences exist due to individual and cultural variations when defining the onset and cessation of adolescence as this is comprised of both a social construct (stages between childhood and adulthood) as well as a biological construct (e.g. puberty).

The biological construct of puberty is marked by changes to the release of hormones regulating sexual maturation and fertility (Child Growth Foundation 2003). However, changes to the brain have also been noted during adolescence, such as re-modelling of the frontal cortex (Blakemore 2012) which is responsible for decision-making, consequential thinking and impulsivity (Choudhury et al. 2008) as well as changes that cause a reduced capacity for regulating emotional reactivity (Heller and Casey 2016). Thus, it is argued that labelling adolescent risk-taking behaviour (which breaks social norms) as 'offending behaviour' may be too simplistic. This is especially the case given risk-taking behaviour is considered a natural neurological process (Dumontheil 2016) which is necessary for social and psychological development. Pandey et al. (2017a, b) note that at the same time adolescent capacity for social interactions develops. Thus, adolescence is a time when people may have an increased capacity for social interactions and impulsivity, but have a reduced capacity for emotional regulation and consequential thinking and a reduced capacity for coping with stress (Romeo 2013). As a result this can leave adolescents vulnerable to adopting a negative trajectory (Best and Ban 2021) if they are not exposed to positive environmental influences during a time when they are questioning their identity and autonomy (Steinber and Silverberg 1986) with increased independent thinking (Stefanou et al. 2004). In addition, the plasticity of the developing adolescent brain means it is shaped more by life experiences than adults (Giedd 2003) by exposure to social environments within specific cultures (Blakemore and Mills 2014). This happens not just in terms of synaptic pruning in the brain, but also through the shifting cognitive and emotional neural systems maturing at a different pace (Choudhury et al. 2008). In other words, the adolescent brain is changing with increased sensitivity in emotional neural systems but with a reduced cognitive capacity to logically reason through these. In addition, networks of the frontal lobe also develop at different ages. For example, research has shown that basic abilities, such as those involving memory, attention and logical reasoning, can develop by the age of 15 however skills such as thinking ahead and balancing risks and rewards are not developed until the mid-20s (Giedd 2008). Therefore the adolescent brain is undertaking a period of development unlike that in adults.

Within the stalking research, the age of adolescence has similarly varied. It has been noted that adulthood has generally been regarded as anyone of the age of 18 or over (Mullen et al. 2000) which is below the WHO (2022) cut-off of 19. In addition, other research has regarded 12 years old to be the cut-off for childhood with adolescence therefore ranging from 13 to 17 years (Leitz and Theriot 2005). This is important because tools validated for the assessment of stalking are based on specific age ranges. For example, the Stalking Risk Profile (SRP) is validated on people aged 18 and over and so would be valid using the WHO definition for adolescents aged 18–19 but would not be acceptable if adhering to the age of 17. It would also not be acceptable using either definition for adolescents 17 and below. In addition, tools such as the SRP are designed on the five typologies of stalking in adults and the risk factors associated with these typologies (McEwan et al. 2018). These do not take into account the motivations and functions of adolescent stalking. In addition, scoring items on adult stalking risk assessment tools may be over or under-inflated for adolescents because of their stage of development. For example, they are less likely to have employment and financial stability which would result in inflation when scoring this item in comparison to adults. Therefore, the use of adult risk assessment tools with adolescents (even when they are over 18) should be considered very carefully.

In summary, 'although one may define puberty in specific neuroendocrinological terms,… adolescence is, of its essence, a period of transition rather than a moment of attainment, and so, it is difficult to distinguish its beginning or end' (Spear 2000, 417). Thus, it is important to remember the ways in which the adolescent brain is still developing and the impact this may have on understanding stalking behaviour when considering prior and future research.

What Is Stalking?

Historically in the adult literature, stalking has been defined as a course of conduct consisting of unwanted attention directed by one individual towards another that induces fear in the victim (Mullen et al. 2000). However, this has been regarded as being ambiguous in terms of the frequency of the unwanted contact which has subsequently been debated. For example, in *Stalkers and their Victims*, Mullen et al. (2000) proposed this should comprise of two or more separate acts whereas others have suggested this should consist of at least five unwanted intrusions (McEwan et al. 2020) because research has shown that engaging in five or more intrusions is associated with threats and violence (Thompson and Dennison 2008). In addition, the duration of behaviour has also been debated. Purcell et al. (2004) suggested a duration of two weeks meaningfully distinguishes shorter, self-limiting bursts of harassment from persistent patterns of stalking. This led to the 'five plus two' (five unwanted intrusions over two weeks) criteria of stalking (McEwan et al. 2020) but with the caveat that the behaviour should also cause fear or distress to the victim. This is reflected in UK law which identifies stalking as a course of conduct which causes fear or distress to the victim.

It should also be noted that definitions of stalking vary across the world and as noted by Chan and Sheridan (2021) stalking is not regarded as a crime in a majority of countries, particularly in most non-Western countries (Sheridan et al. 2016). Some countries do not have laws in relation to stalking but this may be dealt with through laws in relation to partner violence in the form of restraining orders, trespass or nuisance (Chan and Sheridan 2021). The wording used in criminal codes to define stalking also vary substantially, for example, whether the victim experienced fear as a result of the behaviour. This is important to consider when understanding the literature pertaining to adolescent stalking both in terms of the frequency of the behaviour and the victim's interpretation of this. For example, Rothman et al. (2021) explored the prevalence of both stalking victimisation and perpetration in a sample of 12–18-year olds. However, the sample consisted of participants who stated they were either currently in a dating relationship or had been in the past year. In the UK if this behaviour was occurring in a relationship it would not be classified as stalking but coercive control. Thus, generalising adolescent 'stalking' research across countries is met with complexities in the definitions of stalking. In the UK, for a behaviour to be classified as stalking it has to be deemed to cause fear or distress to the victim. This raises questions as to the perception of the victim as well as the intent of the behaviour.

Adolescent Intent

In their study of 10–15-year olds Ybarra et al. (2017) found 64% of those that met the criteria for engaging in stalking behaviours reported benign intent. 22% reported their intent as malicious and 14% were unsure. In addition, the odds of reporting malicious intent were 64% lower for males than females and increased with age and alcohol use, but decreased as empathy increased. This is important because empathy (the ability to understand the emotional states of others) has an impact on how people act in social situations (Overgaauw et al. 2017). Empathy is also known to change in adolescence where this increases in females but decreases in males which it is thought may be due to both changes in testosterone levels (Hermans et al. 2006) and the ways in which females may be socialised within the social environment known as the gender identification hypothesis (Hill and Lynch 1983). Therefore when considering intent in adolescent stalking it is important to consider the capacity of young people to empathise with others and how this may differ in this age group in comparison to adults.

Howard et al. (2019) also found in their study that females described seeing stalking behaviour as a positive mechanism for protecting themselves from harm. For example, they described how before dating a partner they used friends to 'stalk' the person and that they would *'do their homework'* (p. 781) on potential partners and monitor them to see if there were any signs they would be unfaithful. This was done without their knowledge or permission, hence whether they would have been fearful of this had they known is unclear. It could be argued that this behaviour would not meet the threshold for stalking because it was not undertaken with the intent to cause fear or distress to the victim. Nonetheless, the participants called their behaviour 'stalking' seeing it as a positive way of gathering information as to their potential compatibility with a partner. As a result, it is noted by the authors that the narratives adolescents use to describe behaviour in adolescence should be considered more carefully by clinicians. This was also replicated in the research conducted by Spitzberg (2017) who found that some college students over-acknowledged their experiences of victimisation as 'stalking' when these did not meet the threshold using the adult criteria for stalking. This could have implications in terms of reporting behaviour but also the narratives young people use to describe behaviour. Labelling adolescents as engaging in 'stalking' behaviour could pose serious implications in terms of the development of their self-concept and developmental pathway, particularly if their behaviour does not meet the threshold for stalking.

Adolescent Perceptions of Fear

Perceptions of fear or distress may also differ in adolescents. In their study Cloonan-Thomas et al. (2022) found that although adolescents in their sample reported experiencing at least five unwanted intrusions over at least two weeks by an ex-partner, only 5.7% of these reported this behaviour to cause significant fear or distress. This replicated the findings of Purcell et al. (2009) who suggested that this type of behaviour may be normalised by adolescents in comparison to adults using the same scale whereby the prevalence of fear or distress was 30% (McEwan et al. 2020).

What constitutes 'fear or distress' is also open to interpretation given the different types of measures that could be used for this and variances in individual perception of what makes the victim feel frightened or distressed (Owens 2016). In the US this is acknowledged through the 'reasonable person standard' (National Center for Victims of Crime 2007, 48) which states that behaviour can constitute stalking if a reasonable person would have experienced emotional distress from it. This alleviates the burden of the prosecution to demonstrate the victim was frightened or distressed. However, in the UK without evidence of fear or distress the same behaviour only amounts to harassment and not stalking. Thus, how fear or distress measured is important for prosecution.

The reasonable person test relies on the assumption that a person should have the capacity to understand that their behaviour would cause any reasonable person fear or distress. Whilst this may be applicable to adults with mental capacity, the ability to understand how another may feel may differ in adolescence. Research has shown that the more complex social processes, such as understanding the mental states of others (Blakemore et al. 2007), social emotional processing (Burnett et al. 2009) and negotiating complex interpersonal decisions (Crone 2013), continue to develop throughout adolescence (Apperly 2010; Blakemore 2012). For example, adolescents differ in their capacity to read and understand the emotions in the faces of others (Yurgelun-Todd and Killgore 2006). Specifically, in their study they showed adolescents (aged 11–17) and adults, images of people with fearful expressions whilst at the same time scanning their brains using fMRI. The results showed that in comparison to adults, the adolescents had less activity in the amygdala (which is responsible for identifying fear and other emotions) and frontal lobes. Only 50% of the adolescents could identify fearful expressions in comparison to 100% of adults. Thus, even the capacity for an adolescent to identify the potential for fear in another is not the same as the ability of adults.

It has also been noted that fear is a poor marker of what constitutes legitimate stalking and the risk of violence in young people (Smith-Darden et al. 2016) and that regardless of whether the victim reports feeling fearful, they are still at risk of violent victimisation. Spitzberg (2017) found that 18% of adolescents who reported being victims of stalking behaviour stated they were not fearful of this and females were more likely to under-acknowledge stalking behaviour (not label this as stalking even though it met the threshold). However, Smith-Darden et al. (2016) found that adolescents who engaged in stalking are violent in their behaviour and that the rate of reported fear of the victim is 'irrelevant' (p. 198) because regardless of the victim's perception of harm, adolescents pose a risk of violent stalking. In addition, research shows people misjudge/underestimate the threat towards them due to naivety or victim resiliency but the consequence of this is exposure to repeated stalking tactics (van der Aa 2018). For example, victims may report that a person is repeatedly following them or contacting them (either online or in-person) over a period of 4 weeks when they have told them not to (unwanted) but they do not perceive the individual poses a risk of harm. This is particularly relevant in adolescence whereby the invincibility fable is more active than in adults (Elkind 1996) leading them to feel nothing bad will happen to them and bad things only happen to others. This invincibility phase in adolescence has been associated with risk-taking behaviour and exposure to harm. Research has shown that the illusion of invincibility results in a decreased perceived risk of harm to the self and increased involvement in risk behaviours (Casey et al. 2008; Leone et al. 2005; Monneuse et al. 2008). This is concerning as the ability of victims to assess stalking risk accurately is poor, potentially placing them at risk of harm (Smith-Darden et al. 2016). Furthermore, if the victim does not report fear or distress (as they feel infallible) the stalking behaviour would not be recognised under UK law but this may not reflect the risk posed to them (van der Aa 2018; Smith-Darden et al. 2016).

The concept of fear is complex and additionally so when considering fear in adolescents compared to adults. Fear of crime is comprised of two parts: an emotional reaction to a crime; and the cognitive perception of risk (Ferraro and LaGrange 1987). This then influences behavioural responses to fear (Doran and Burgess 2012) designed to reduce their risk of victimisation which is known as constrained behaviour (e.g. avoiding dark places at night or arming themselves with a weapon). However, when measuring 'fear' in the adolescent stalking literature this is limited to simple single-item questions such as asking if the person was scared or frightened. For example, 'Did this unwanted pursuit occur in a manner that you personally felt was threatening, or placed you in fear of your safety, or the safety of your family, friends, pets, or property?' with the option of yes/no or no response (Spitzberg 2017, p. 3). As noted, the infallibility effect which attends to cognitive perceptions of risk may mask the impact of emotional reactions to stalking. In addition, single-item questions of 'fear' fail to identify the impact of stalking on constrained behaviour in adolescents. Future research exploring the impact of stalking on young people would benefit from attending to the more complex ways in which fear may manifest in adolescents.

Adult findings in relation to stalking have previously identified males to be more likely to be the offenders and females most likely to be the victims (Mullen et al. 2000). Spitzberg's (2002) meta-analysis of adults which found that over 70% of people who stalk are male and over 80% of victims are female. Research also shows that older people are more fearful than younger people (LaGrange and Ferraro 1989; Russo et al. 2013; Tseloni and Zarafonitou 2008; Weinrath and Gartrell 1996). In addition, men are less like to admit to fear and underestimate their potential victimisation risk (Agnew 1985; Gilchrist et al. 1998; Sutton and Farrall 2005). Victims of cyberstalking have also been found to be less likely to feel fear when they were stalked by a female compared to a male (Dietz and Martin 2007; Gatewood-Owens 2017; Pondana and Imriskova 2014). This is important because in the adolescent literature Purcell et al. (2009) found that 57% of adolescents in their sample engaged in stalking behaviour towards someone of the same gender with this being most common in females [86.1% females compared to 40.3% in males] (Purcell et al. 2010). As a result it is possible that the nature of adolescent stalking behaviour and perceptions of fear of harm are influenced by biases in perpetrator gender. Furthermore, research also shows that victims of cyberstalking are significantly less likely to experience fear if the offender was a previous intimate partner, friend or classmate (Fissel 2021). The most common typology of adolescent stalking (28%) was stalking as an extension of bullying whereby the victim was usually a school peer (56%) or an estranged friend (21%).

(Purcell et al. 2009). Therefore, the way in which fear is reported may differ in adolescents compared to adults because of the differences in perpetrator gender and typology. Purcell et al. (2010) also noted that of those who had come to the attention of the courts, males and females may engage in different tactics. For example, females favoured harassing telephone calls and spreading malicious rumours, but were significantly less likely than males to loiter or to damage property. They were also more likely to engage in stalking by proxy (getting someone else to stalk the victim). However, males and females did not differ in the rates of threats or physical assault to the victim. Therefore it is also possible that the ways in which male and female adolescents engage in stalking may also influence the likelihood of experiencing fear. This is something that warrants further research.

Studies into adolescent victimisation from crime also show that generally the majority of crimes against children and young people are not reported to the police. Only 13% of violent offences and 15% of thefts are reported by young victims (ONS 2014). The reasons for this are that young people may not realise that what they have experienced constitutes a crime or other form of victimisation (Beckett and Warrington 2014) and this can be more so where forms of criminal behaviour have been normalised within a peer group or a community. This is important given in the adolescent stalking literature Pereira et al. (2016) found that 66.1% of victims of cyber-harassment and stalking were also perpetrators. Thus, it is possible that adolescent stalking is normalised as a behaviour, young people are likely to be exposed to and as a result of the frequency of this young people may not report fear as a legitimate response. Research shows that young people are also reluctant to report offences due to the risk of reputational damage and unwritten group 'rules' in certain social contexts which result in a silencing power over young people's likelihood of reporting a crime (Beckett and Warrington 2014). Hence, the combination of the infallibility effect, peer normalisation of stalking and the risk of reputational damage by acknowledging behaviour as inducing negative emotions, may result in a combined effect of under-reporting of fear in young people. Thus, bias exists in the adult stalking literature in terms of defining stalking and it is unclear how applicable such definitions may be to adolescents in terms of the concept of fear.

'Five Plus Two' in Adolescence

Moshman (2020) noted the capacity of the adolescent to cope with relationship conflict (be it with peers or in a relationship) during a time of already significant emotional and behavioural dysregulation may be significantly lower than that of an adult. This may apply not just to the perpetrator but also to the victim given some of the findings that only 5.7% of adolescents report the 'five plus two' intrusions to cause them fear or distress in comparison to 30% in adults (McEwan et al. 2020). In addition, the methods of stalking used by adolescents may also impact on the utility of the 'five plus two' criteria.

Stalking behaviour used by adolescents may take different forms such as in-person or online. Cloonan-Thomas et al. (2022) noted that the most common form of 'unwanted pursuit behaviours' for those involved in ex-partner relationship stalking included the use of technology such as phone calls (victims = 91.2% and perpetrators = 93.5%) and social media (victims = 88.2% and perpetrators = 100%). Furthermore, Ybarra et al. (2017) noted that adolescents use social media to initiate and maintain relationships with others, but that technology also facilitates the potential for online monitoring of others because of the ease and speed with which information can be obtained (Sheridan and Grant 2007). For example, Borges and Dell'Aglio (2019) found in their study of 14–19-year olds experiences of stalking following the break-up of a relationship most of the stalking victims in the study suffered more than ten incidents during the post-breakup period of a romantic relationship which is a much greater frequency than that in adults (De Smet et al. 2015; Edwards and Gidycz 2014). Most of the adolescents suffered stalking via messages sent by their ex-partners and via their ex-partner's attempts to obtain information about them from their friends and family or through the internet. This was also replicated in the findings of Fisher et al. (2014) who found that 89% of stalking victims reported they received unwanted communication via media in comparison to 50% who reported the person 'showed up at places when not wanted'. This included school, work or home.

The introduction of online stalking which has been referred to as 'cyber-harassment', 'cyber-abuse', 'technological stalking' and 'stalking with technology' (Davies 2013) may have implications for the 'five plus two' criteria in adolescents. For example, Howard et al. (2019) suggested that the use of social media to gather information on others does not necessarily constitute antisocial behaviour and instead serves a self-protective function. In their study young people justified what they themselves called 'stalking' behaviour towards potential future partners by stating this was to ensure the individual was safe and would not cause them harm. They described activating social networks on social media to get feedback on the individual without their knowledge. They also described enlisting their friends to help in this quest and adopting different ways of checking the individual's profile online and friend requests without their knowledge. In this study the victim was unaware of the person engaging in this behaviour and so it was difficult to establish if the victim would have been frightened or distressed by this had they known. It would also have been difficult to measure the frequency of behaviour as this was conducted online with the assistance of friends. Thus, although the individual labelled their behaviour as 'stalking', under UK law it would be difficult to establish if this was stalking or if it was a means by which the person was attempting to ensure their safety. It would also be difficult to establish if this behaviour would be replicated in an offline space or if the use of technology provides a separate mental space in which behaviour may be excused. For example, Fernet (2019) noted how the emergence of technology in the last 10 years has facilitated both positive and negative communication whereby the impersonal nature of communication online can lead to de-individuation (not seeing the other as human) and hence increases the propensity for expressions of aggression (Aoyama et al. 2011). Therefore the ways in which adolescents may use social media may differ to that of adults.

The American Academy of Child and Adolescent Psychiatry (2022) also noted that 90% of adolescents aged 13–17 have used social media with 51% reporting they use it at least daily with an average of nine hours per day spent online (excluding time for homework). In addition, Teen users of Snapchat check the app an average of 30 times daily (Anderson and Jiang, 2021) with the use of snapchat/instagram alone accounting for nearly an hour and a half a day. This is in comparison to an average of 30 minutes per day in adults (Shepherd 2022). Furthermore, one in three adolescents send more than 100 text messages a day or more than 3000 text messages per month (Anderson and Jiang, 2021) with females aged 14–17 being the most active. This is in comparison to adults who send 13 texts on their personal cell phones every day (Anderson and Jiang, 2021). Hence, it is possible that the use of 'five plus two' criteria in relation to technological stalking may result in an inflation of adolescents being identified as engaging in stalking because of the very nature of technological communication being greater in comparison to in-person communication. In addition, adolescents may be more vulnerable to such inflation due to their increased use of social media in comparison to adults.

As noted by Howard et al. (2019) the role of technology and adolescent stalking behaviour is under-researched. Furthermore, the nature through which adolescents use technology may also lead to a naturally higher number of online communications generally in comparison to adults, thus when communicating in a potential stalking dyad (victim–perpetrator), five instances of communication may not be unusual. The ways in which adolescents communicate with each other via social media may differ to adults whereby adolescents may not wait for a reply before sending another message (Ehrenreich et al. 2020) and on average send 400 messages to peers and another 435 messages to romantic partners in a four day period. In addition, they may send multiple messages before receiving a reply. Furthermore, they respond faster to peers (14.5 minutes) and romantic partners (9.27 minutes) than they do to their parents (50.39 minutes) (Ehrenreich et al. 2020). This may have implications for what criteria may be used to measure adolescent stalking because they communicate in a different way to adults. As a result, Mullen et al. (2001) suggested based on their experience the criteria for adolescent stalking could be 10 or more intrusions rather than five. However, this was based on research over 20 years ago and the ways in which people (including adolescents) communicate have changed since this time. Therefore the precise number of intrusions which may be suitable to adolescents is unknown, but it would seem that the adult use of 'five plus two' may not appear suitable for young people. Future research should look to consider this more precisely.

It is also important to consider adolescent communication in relationships more generally when considering the frequency and intent of behaviour. Research shows that adolescence is a time when young people are becoming more sexually active resulting in them developing questions about sexual morality and sexual identity (Steinberg 2011). Furthermore, this occurs at a time when they are also expected to be more independent from adults but at a time when their capacity for consequential thinking and problem-solving has not fully developed. Thus, how people may navigate these social complexities in adolescence may differ compared to adults. For example, they may be at a greater risk of making mistakes in navigating social communication in relationships than adults as they have less experience of these. Pereira et al. (2016) found that 66.1% of adolescent victims of cyber-harassment and stalking were also perpetrators suggesting that adolescents generally find navigating the online social space challenging.

Adolescence is associated with increased reactivity to emotional cues as a result of physiological changes in the limbic circuitry of the brain (Spear 2009; Patwell et al. 2013). This can result in faster life history strategies (Brumbach et al. 2009; Blakemore and Mills 2014) making them more prone to focus on present-orientated and impulsive decision-making in relationships with others rather than deliberate and future-orientated behaviour. This is thought to be because the pleasure-seeking reward system of the adolescent brain develops faster than the part of the brain which is responsible for planning ahead and judgement. This in turn makes them more prone to engage in risky impulsive behaviours (Chein et al. 2011; Somerville et al. 2010) because they weight risk and reward differently (Steinberg 2011), preferring social rewards in relationships and short-term immediate rewards over long-term gains (Darby et al. 2015). Thus, the adolescent brain may influence the frequency and type of communication they engage in due to impulsivity and reduced consequential thinking which is not comparable to adults.

The question remains as to how applicable adult definitions of stalking are to adolescents. Studies citing the prevalence of adolescent stalking often include behaviours such as harassment, relationship coercive control and victimisation related to sexual harassment rather than stalking per se (Curtis 2012). Furthermore, other studies have included behaviours to measure 'stalking' using concepts such as 'hyper-intimacy' and 'intrusive pursuit' (Ybarra et al. 2017). These included statements on a scale where they were asked if they engaged in the following behaviours: Tried to get someone's attention by doing something 'over the top'. This includes things like calling them multiple times a day, buying a big gift for them when a small one would do or Tried to 'talk with someone when it seemed like they did not want you to. This includes things like calling, texting, posting on their profile on a social networking site' (Ybarra et al. 2017, p. 3). Helpfully the authors note that these behaviours should not be considered direct representations of legally prosecutable stalking and refer to them as stalking-like behaviours. Within the context of adolescence and the complexities of attempting to navigate social relationships it would seem developmentally feasible that a person aged 10–15 might misjudge whether a person wants to talk to them and then afterwards realise they had tried to talk to someone when maybe they did not want them to. Clearly, this would not constitute 'stalking' and constraints in the tools used to measure adolescent 'stalking' have also been noted by Exner-Cortens (2018). For example, researchers using the Safe Dates Scale which is a 16 item tool designed to measure physical violence (e.g. kicked, choked) measured stalking by simply adding the term 'stalked'. Obviously this does not meet the threshold for establishing if five instances of behaviour occurred over a period of two weeks ('five plus two').

In summary, as noted by Mullen et al. (2001) stalking behaviour should be clearly differentiated from bullying or occasional irritating and undesirable behaviours that are part of most people's everyday experience when their relationship has come to an end (Mullen et al. 2001). Furthermore, this should be considered within the context of adolescent development.

Legitimacy of Contact

The nature of the relationship to the victim is of extreme importance. Fisher et al. (2014) noted that in their sample, 50% of adolescent stalking victims reported the perpetrator tactics included 'showing up at places'. However, as noted by Purcell et al. (2009) the majority of stalking behaviour in their sample commenced in the school setting and was perpetrated towards school peers even though in their study they excluded stalking which occurred within school. Thus, given the very limited geographical nature of adolescent education it is likely that 'showing up at places' where the victim was present would likely be inflated if they simply attended the same school or lived within close proximity. As a result, the limited social mobility of adolescents should be considered when exploring the tactics used such as coming into close proximity to the victim because if the victim and perpetrator go to the same school/college then such contact could be deemed legitimate. Ozaki (2020) noted this raises issues as to how schools can be places of safety for both victims and perpetrators. For example, the routine activities of adolescents may exist within a smaller geographical sphere but with a greater exposure to larger numbers of other adolescents in comparison to the social exposure of adults to other adults (Roberts et al. 2016). This may explain the increased likelihood of stalking acquaintances compared to former partners (Roberts et al. 2016) but may also account for a higher number of stalking-type behaviours because of the smaller geographical sphere. This should be considered when considering the frequency of behaviour and 'five plus two' criteria.

Purcell et al. (2009) proposed that stalking involved 'imposing oneself on another person in a context where the perpetrator has no legitimate right' (p. 451) deeming some authors to conclude that stalking could not be classified as occurring within the school (Purcell et al. 2009, 2010). However, it was identified that students who reported being stalked by their peers or ex-partners who attended the same school experienced depression, suicidal ideation and were 'sick with fear' (Purcell et al. 2009). This close proximity raises questions about how stalking behaviour in adolescents should be managed. Borges and Dell'Aglio (2019) found that adolescent victims of stalking by an ex-partner exhibited significantly higher mean scores for depression, anxiety and stress symptoms than did non-victims; and female victims presented greater symptomatology than did male victims. PTSD symptoms, mood changes and a higher risk of involvement in abusive relationships have also been found in adolescent victims of stalking (Smith-Darden et al. 2016). Victims in the Purcell et al. (2009) study also reported experiencing extreme anxiety, being unable to concentrate at school and absenteeism with some being removed from the school or educated at home as a result of stalking victimisation. Hence, future research should establish how peer stalking could be managed in a way that ensures the safety of both the victim and the perpetrator but at the same time navigates legitimacy of contact within a limited geographical sphere.

Identifying who are victims and who are perpetrators in such a sphere may also be a complex task. Cloonan-Thomas et al. (2022) found in their study of 14–18-year olds that 6.6.% of participants in their study reported being both a victim and perpetrator of stalking, this accounts for approximately a third of stalking perpetration and victimisation in their sample. This study only included victimisation and perpetration during their 'most difficult relationship' thus it did not include friendship stalking. This was also replicated in the findings of Rothman et al. (2021) who found one-third of their sample of 12–18-year olds who experienced stalking in a relationship were both victims and perpetrators of stalking behaviour. This was also the case for Pereira et al. (2016) exploring cyberstalking in adolescents in Portugal. Thus, it is possible that adolescent stalking may also mirror the IPV (Intimate Partner Violence) literature in that an individual may be both a perpetrator and victim of adolescent stalking and may engage in both dual perpetration and victimisation. In the IPV literature, this is referred to as the victim–perpetrator overlap model (Park and Kim 2019) whereby it is thought that victims of IPV may observe aggression and adopt this behaviour through social learning (Bandura 1971) or they mirror the aggression strategies adopted by perpetrators towards them as a means of coping. Jang (2013) observed this in victims of school violence and found that the more victimised students became the more violent they became towards others. Thus, it is possible that this victim–perpetrator overlap model may also apply to adolescent stalking. For example, Cloonan-Thomas et al. (2022) noted that at least half of stalking was preceded by Youth Intimate Partner Abuse (YIPA) and that this was mutual whereby 68% of stalking perpetrators reported prior YIPA victimisation whilst 53% of stalking victims reported prior YIPA perpetration.

Whilst it is clear that not all YIPA results in stalking, the mutuality of YIPA and stalking behaviour should be considered and explored further. Pereira et al. (2016) found that 66.1% of victims of cyber-harassment and stalking were also perpetrators and that this was more common in males than females. However, the psychological process that underpins why an adolescent may begin to engage in stalking behaviour is unknown. For example, it is unclear if young people are victims of stalking by others and then adopt this behaviour as a form of coping, social learning or retaliation as is seen in the bullying literature on dual victim-bully role formation (Sung et al. 2018). Or, if they engage in this behaviour towards others first but suffered rejection or criticism from their peers as a result and thus became a victim (Sung et al. 2018). Hence, this double-involvement in stalking in adolescents is an area for future research. Understanding the process of how this evolves (e.g. which comes first—stalking victimisation or stalking perpetration) could have important implications for treatment (Pereira et al. 2016). Sung et al. (2018) found in the bullying literature that initial victims who seek help from adults but found this ineffective may be more likely to adopt a bully-victim role. In addition, reversing or terminating the bully-victim role was not a simple process and increased the risk of the individual returning back to either a pure victim or pure bully role. Therefore, the complex processes which underpin dual victim–perpetrator adolescent stalking behaviour requires more intensive research to ensure that the process through which this occurs is understood and so interventions to target this can be successful.

The potential for a victim–perpetrator dyad to be in a close environment also warrants careful consideration of how this can be managed. For example, the impact on both the victim and/or perpetrator of their education being disrupted as a mechanism for managing this behaviour could be significant. In addition, the complexity of navigating group or peer-facilitated stalking should also be considered.

Typologies of Adolescent Stalking

Research into adult stalking typologies is based on the form of their behaviours and the differing functions for this (Mullen et al. 1999). This has enabled complex risk assessment tools to be developed based on the factors associated with stalking risks such as the nature of the stalking behaviour, the perpetrator risk and victim vulnerability (Dearn et al. 2021). This includes tools such as the Stalking and Assessment and Management (SAM) guide (Kropp et al. 2008) and the Stalking Risk Profile (SRP) (Mackenzie et al. 2009). However, these tools were developed in the literature in relation to adults, and hence are only validated for their use on adolescents 18 and over (using the WHO definition) and are not validated on younger adolescents.

In their systematic review, Roberts et al. (2016) identified only three peer-reviewed empirical studies of stalking that reported on adolescent samples (Fisher et al. 2014; Purcell et al. 2009, 2010), two of which reported on the same sample. Fisher et al. (2014) conducted a study of 18,013 students aged 14–18. It found that 5.3% of their sample reported engaging in stalking behaviour and 16.5% had been victims of stalking. However, the study did not specify that the unwanted intrusions had to be perpetrated by the same person and as a result these figures could be inflated. In addition, the study did not meet the 'five plus two' threshold. The study also identified people as having engaged in stalking by asking if they had engaged in stalking behaviour towards 'someone that you may have been interested in hooking up with in the past or now' (Fisher et al. 2014, p. 1264). Thus, the perpetration questions related to stalking-type behaviours within the context of intimate relationships excluding peer or stranger interactions. However, the question asking if they had been a victim of stalking simply asked if they had been exposed to the list of behaviours. Thus, it is possible that this may explain the difference in perpetration and victimisation frequencies because not all stalking is undertaken by someone within the context of intimate relationships. For example, it is possible that of the 16.5% who reported being victims of stalking this could have been perpetrated by peers or people unknown to them and not just in the context of intimate partners.

Studies attempting to identify typologies of adolescent stalking have also been limited to samples using small forensic case studies (e.g. N = 13, McCann 2000; N = 2, Evans and Meloy 2011). In their larger study of 299 juvenile court records, Purcell et al. (2009) were able to identify five typologies of adolescent stalking (see Graph 3.1). Although it should be noted these were based solely on people who had come to the attention of the courts for consecutive applications for a restraining order against them. Hence, this research may not generalise to adolescent stalking in the community (i.e. stalking that has not been reported or considered as criminal offending). However, the most common typology (28%) was stalking as an extension of bullying whereby the victim was usually a school peer (56%) or an estranged friend (21%). This is particularly interesting given the sample excluded behaviours which happened within the premises of a school. 22% of participants were classed as engaging in 'Retaliating' stalking who sought revenge for a perceived wrong against them. No differences were found in gender in the retaliatory group. Only 22% were classified as engaging in stalking towards a former romantic partner ('Rejected' Typology) with 86% of these being perpetrated by a male towards a female victim. 20% were classified as a 'Disorganised' typology consisting of what was described as angry and delinquent youth who were at 'war with the environment' and 47% of these involved harassments of neighbours including threats and property damage. Only 2% of the sample engaged in stalking behaviour motivated by infatuation (intimacy seeking) and 5% were classed as predatory, whereby the function of the behaviour was sexual.

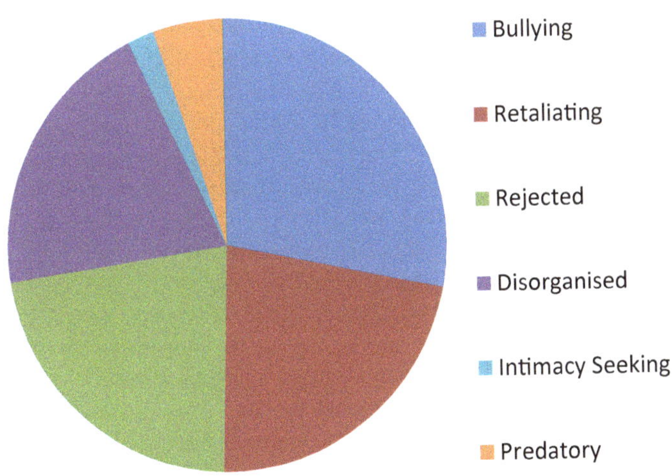

Graph 3.1 Frequency of adolescent stalking typologies

As a result, this study concluded that adolescents differed to adults in that stalking by ex-partners was much less common and that adolescent stalking was predominantly an extension of bullying or as a means of exhibiting retaliation. In addition, this has been replicated in the cyberstalking literature whereby only 4.7% of cyberstalking was undertaken by a former or current romantic partner in comparison to 43.6% who were friends (Pereira et al. 2016).

Research has also noted that bully-related stalking may be perpetrated by a group and not just an individual (Roberts et al. 2016; Purcell et al. 2009) and that bullying and stalking both involve more than one incident of threat, harassment or intimidation and involve fear in the victim (McCann 2001). This is particularly relevant given that research has demonstrated adolescents are more likely to engage in risk-taking behaviour in the presence of their peers (Silva et al. 2016). This also replicates the cyberbullying research which has found that bystanders may join in online behaviour as a result of de-individuation (Chan et al. 2022).

Research has also shown that adolescents predominantly engage in stalking behaviours towards other adolescents (Roberts et al. 2016; Purcell et al. 2009; Haugaard and Seri 2004). Examples of adolescents who have stalked adults do exist but these are based on small forensic case studies rather than community samples and so may be biased in their applicability (McCann 2000; Vaidya et al. 2005). In addition, despite evidence suggesting that adolescents are more likely to stalk casual acquaintances than (ex)dating partners (Fisher et al. 2014; McCann 2000; Purcell et al. 2009) research has continued to focus on stalking in adolescents within the context of relationships ending only. For example, Smith-Darden et al. (2016) explored adolescent stalking by asking 1,236 participants to report if they had experienced or engaged in 14 stalking behavioural indicators by asking 'How often have you pursued, or has someone else pursued you, in order to start or continue a relationship that wasn't wanted' (p. 193). The questionnaire included items such as 'saying I love you after only a short time together' and 'doing favours they didn't ask for'. Half of the males engaged in little to no stalking and were identified as the non-perpetrator group, a quarter fell into the hyper-intimacy group engaging in unwanted expressions of affection and the final group comprising of 6% of males who had significantly higher scores on all 14 stalking indicators. These were referred to as the comprehensive stalking group. In comparison, three quarter of the females fell into the non-perpetrator group and approximately one quarter fell into the hyper-intimacy category. However, females in the HIP group were more violent than HIP boys in terms of threats/intimidation and physical harm to stalking victims. Therefore, based on these findings it could be assumed that adolescents engaging in stalking do so predominantly due to a desire for hyper-intimacy. However, the relationship between the perpetrator and the victim was not included in this study nor was the motivation for offending. In addition, the design of the study required (as an inclusion criteria) that the stalking related to starting or continuing a relationship. Thus, research findings in relation to adolescent stalking have been biased by using stalking behavioural indicators within the context of (ex) intimate relationships.

Similarly, Borges and Dell-Aglio (2019) explored the stalking experiences of 527 adolescents (aged between 14 and 19) who were in a relationship. They found that 22% of their sample reported experiencing stalking and of these 15% reported that their ex-partner had kept them under observation or had followed them down the street more than five times, 13% reported that they had been pursued more than five times and 15% reported that their ex-partner had grabbed them or had impeded them from walking down the street more than three times. In 26% of cases this behaviour had lasted longer than six months. This has led to the conclusion that adolescent stalking amongst ex-partners is common. However, it should be noted that 77.8% of the sample of 527 adolescents were classified as non-victims suggesting they had not been a victim of stalking but the study only asked participants if they were victims of stalking in a relationship. Hence, it is unclear how many of the 527 participants may have been victims of non-intimate partner stalking. For example, in their study which included stalking victimisation by both friends and partners and using the 'five plus two' criteria, Ybarra et al. (2017) found that 36% of adolescents reported they had engaged in at least one type of behaviour. Therefore, the prevalence of adolescent stalking literature has been biased by attending to stalking within the context of intimate relationships.

Developing typologies of adolescent stalking has also been made more complicated due to the functions of behaviour differing across gender. For example, Roberts et al. (2016) note that same-gender stalking was more prevalent in adolescents than adults, and Purcell et al. (2009) found that 57% of adolescents in their sample engaged in stalking behaviour towards someone of the same gender with this being most common in females [86.1% females compared to 40.3% in males] (Purcell et al. 2010). Given only 21% of their sample involved stalking of an ex-partner it would seem reasonable to conclude that some of the same gender stalking was perpetrated towards peers or estranged friends who comprised 72% of the sample. Thus, same gender stalking cannot be assumed to be in the context of ex-partner relationships. Furthermore, the function of stalking in females was noted to be motivated by bullying and retaliation in comparison to males.

One area of particular concern was the findings of Niolon et al. (2015) who found that for females in their sample, the risk of perpetrating stalking was 7.8 times higher for those who reported weapon carrying than those that did not. In addition, Smith-Darden et al. (2016) found that males who engaged in hyper-intimacy pursuit engaged in more threatening and aggressive behaviour towards the target of their stalking alongside higher weapon carrying. Thus, there appears to be a potential link between weapon use and stalking although this needs further exploration. For example, previous research has linked weapon carrying with instrumental violence and psychopathic traits (Reidy et al. 2011) and longer persistence in offending. Lu et al. (2019) also found that young people who engaged in cyberbullying were 1.97 times more likely to carry a weapon. However, weapon carrying was also associated with being a victim of cyberbullying. Therefore, it is possible that some adolescent stalking may be associated with a more dissocial typology. For example, Purcell et al. (2009) found that disorganised or disturbed stalking was perpetrated by juveniles with more general conduct problems who engaged in prolonged harassment of neighbours and property damage. They were described as being 'at war with the environment' (p. 453) and had prior offences unrelated to stalking. Hence, stalking for this particular group of adolescents may represent an overall pattern of dissocial behaviour in which stalking is one of a number of illegal behaviours. The function of stalking in this instance does not appear to be related to intimacy seeking but appears as more of a pattern of dissocial behaviour. Thus, interventions for this typology of adolescent may benefit from attending to literature in relation to reducing dissocial behaviour rather than stalking per se.

In summary, adolescent stalking behaviour appears to differ to that used by adults and in order to develop reliable risk assessment tools, research needs to establish the precise frequency and nature of adolescent stalking behaviour. This should also include attending to individual differences which may contribute to this risk (e.g. relationship to the victim, legitimacy of contact) and victim vulnerability factors (e.g. close proximity to perpetrator in school). Measurements of 'fear' in adolescent victims of stalking also need to be developed to include the wide variety of ways in which victims may be impacted by a behaviour beyond single item constructs. The lack of research into adolescent stalking (Roberts et al. 2016) has made this task difficult which has been further compounded by different thresholds being used to define 'stalking' behaviour in the research that has been undertaken.

Areas for Future Research

Sexuality

Fisher et al. (2014) found that 27% of adolescents who reported being attracted to someone of the same sex reported being victims of stalking in comparison to 15% of students who reported being attracted to the opposite sex. In addition, for those who had engaged in intimate relationship partner stalking, 10% of adolescents who reported being attracted to someone of the same sex reported engaging in stalking in comparison to 5% of students who reported being attracted to the opposite sex. This is important because sexual orientation expression in adolescents differs across gender and is more fluid in comparison to adults (Bailey et al. 2016).

Sexual orientation refers to the degree to which a person is attracted to same or opposite sex members (Bailey et al. 2016). Research on sexual orientation stability patterns suggests adolescence to early adulthood poses important milestones. The mean age of self-reported first awareness of same-sex attraction has been reported to be at about 15 years of age or even earlier (Calzo et al. 2011; Floyd and Bakeman 2006). According to Xu et al. (2021) many of these individuals report changes in their sexual orientation around mid-adolescence but by later adolescence (approximately 20 years) sexuality is more stable with some of those who reported same-sex attraction later self-identifying as non-heterosexual in later adolescence or early adulthood (Calzo et al. 2011; Floyd and Bakeman 2006). In adolescence, Xu et al. (2021) noted that heterosexuality and being 'gay' were equally stable and relatively more stable compared to bisexuality for boys. However, in girls this was less stable, with adolescent females reporting being 'lesbian' and bisexual being more likely to change than heterosexuality. Female adolescents who reported being 'lesbian' were more likely to report changes in their sexual orientation than 'gay' adolescent boys (Xu et al. 2021) but few people changed their sexual orientation between the ages of 21–23. Therefore, consideration of sexual orientation in adolescence changes over time and this may have implications for understanding adolescent stalking.

Mennicke et al. (2021) studied 16,243 adolescents aged 14–18 years old. Stalking was measured using the following three questions 'you were followed, spied on or monitored using computer software, cameras, listening tools, or global positioning system (GPS); someone showed up at your home, school or work or waited for you when you did not want them to; you received unwanted phone calls, gifts, emails, text messages, or notes/pictures posted on social networking sites for example, Facebook, MySpace, or Twitter'. Therefore this did not meet the 'five plus two' criteria because participants were not asked how many times they experiences this behaviour and over what time period. Students who identified as non-heterosexual reported significantly higher levels of stalking victimisation in comparison to heterosexual participants. This led the authors to postulate that sexual minority adolescents may be victims of stalking behaviour because of their sexual identity rather than due to gender. However, amongst the non-heterosexual group, females reported significantly less stalking victimisation than males. Heterosexual girls reported the lowest number of events of stalking across groups. Hence, whilst this study has constraints, it raises important questions about the function of stalking and sexuality. For example, non-heterosexual participants were also statistically more likely to be victims of bullying, adding to the theory that adolescent stalking may be considered as an extension of this with implications for prevention and intervention programmes.

Future research would also benefit from exploring the duality of stalking perpetration and victimisation in adolescents who identify as non-heterosexual. This is because it has been noted that youth who identify as LGBTQ + (32%) are more likely to be bullied online than non-LGBTQ + youth (22%). LGBTQ + youth (7%) are also more likely to report that they have bullied others than heterosexual youth (4%) (Hinduja 2021). Thus, given the potential of stalking being an extension of bullying it will be important to explore the frequency of perpetration of stalking in adolescents who identify as LGBTQ + . In addition, no research has explored transgender adolescent experiences of stalking perpetration or victimisation. However, research has shown that teens who identify as transgender are more likely to be bullied online (35% compared to 24% girls and 22% boys) (Hinduja 2021). Thus, given the potential for adolescent stalking to be an extension of bullying this is something that would benefit from further research in the future.

Race, Ethnicity and Culture

Most of the research exploring adolescent stalking behaviours has been conducted in predominantly individualist cultures where it is regarded that the findings may not be generalisable in collectivist countries due to different attitudes towards courtship behaviour (Chan and Sheridan 2019). Thus, caution should be used when generalising research across cultures. Furthermore, even within cultures, variances may exist in adolescent experiences of stalking perpetration and victimisation. For example, research has found that being exposed to racial discrimination is associated with relational aggression (Wright and Wachs 2019), peer aggression and PTSD (Chen and Foshee 2015). Thus, it is important that racial and cultural factors are considered when understanding adolescent stalking.

Fisher et al. (2014) found that 20% of adolescents who identified as 'non-white' reported being victims of stalking in comparison to 16% of adolescents who identified as 'white'. Rothman et al. (2021) explored stalking victimisation and perpetration in 12–18-year-old youth either currently or previously in a dating relationship. 62% identified as White, 15% Black and 17% Latinx.[1] As previously noted, behaviours whilst still in a relationship with the person would not be classified as stalking in the UK but coercive controlling behaviour. In addition, 'stalking' was measured based on 3 questions ('Has [Partner's Name] ever done any of the following to you? Followed or spied on you; Damaged something that belonged to you; Gone through your online accounts (Instagram, Facebook, etc.)?'. Whilst this would not meet the threshold of 'five plus two', the findings provide some insight into potential differences across groups. One-third (36.5%) of white male participants perpetrated stalking and harassment and 39.1% had experienced it. Amongst Latinx male participants, 70.6% had perpetrated stalking and harassment whilst 70.7% had been victimised by it and Latinx males were significantly more likely to engage in male perpetration even when factors such as neighbourhood disadvantage, neighbourhood crime and substance misuse were controlled. In addition, females were significantly more likely to report both victimisation if they were younger than 15, used marijuana and identified as Black. Thus, it would seem that differences existed in this sample, but the reasons for this were unclear. For example, the authors noted that this could be due to the Latinx males being more honest about their behaviour or it could be that these findings reflect cultural differences in dating behaviour (Rothman et al. 2021). Fenimore et al. (2019) noted that factors such as acculturation, coercive discipline by their parents, exposure to violence, sensation seeking and alcohol use contributed towards Latinx males risk of using violence. Thus, it is possible that adolescent stalking behaviours are reflective of a more overall risk of violence within the context of multi-systemic factors. For example, minority stress theory suggests that marginalised populations are exposed to a multitude of chronic stressors (Mennicke et al. 2021) and vulnerability. For example, experiencing stigma, prejudice and discrimination may contribute to stress and negative mental health outcomes and make the individual more vulnerable in society in multiple ways. Hence, any attribution of adolescent stalking victimisation or perpetration in relation to race should consider the wider context in which the individual exists. As noted by Mennicke et al. (2021) other factors such as culture, region and political climates may influence stalking in adolescence and this may have implications for treatment or interventions in relation to adolescent stalking. For example, person-centred cultural formulations should be used in the treatment planning for young people. A tool such as the Cultural Formulation Interview (CFI) (Aggarwal et al. 2020) could assist with understanding the young person's stalking behaviour within the wider context of their culture.

Treatment

There is currently a severely limited evidence base for the efficacy of the psychological treatment of stalking behaviours in adults (Leigh and Davies 2021) where the stalking research is more advanced than in relation to adolescents. As noted by Niolon et al. (2015) understanding the risk factors that influence the occurrence of adolescent stalking is critical for developing evidence-based prevention and treatment interventions. However, to date interventions that have been identified relate to programmes such as 'Dating Matters' which teaches 11–14-year olds healthy relationship skills before they start dating and reducing behaviours that increase the risk for dating violence. It is unclear how such interventions would target adolescent stalking outside of the context of intimate relationships.

In addition, research has noted the use of legal measures to reduce stalking such as intervention orders (Thomas et al. 2008) however a lack of research exists in relation to preventative or treatment options for adolescents engaging in stalking. Future research would benefit from considering if treatments targeted at bullying behaviours may have some benefit for those where the function is an extension of bullying. For example, Byers et al. (2021) identified clinical guidelines for working with bullying and cyberbullying which could be applied to adolescent stalking. Specifically, they recommended that practitioners should work multi-systemically to understand the system in which the behaviour is occurring. In addition, they also emphasise the importance of providing a place where victims can express their feelings about being bullied and identifying ways for them to cope not only with feelings of fear, but to also reduce the risk of reactive aggression (retaliation). Given the noted duality between being both a victim and a perpetrator of adolescent stalking, this approach could have significance. In addition, Byers et al. (2021) suggest the use of culture-specific social skills groups and noting the common trauma dynamics which may exist in terms of adolescents being exposed to bullying across contexts. Finally, they also suggest the importance of building empathy, problem-solving and communication skills. This could have significant implications given the noted deficits in these areas for adolescents generally. Future research would benefit from exploring the efficacy of interventions for adolescent stalking, as well as the role of factors such as empathy, problem-solving and communication. This is consistent with the adult stalking literature whereby it is noted that a significant absence exists in terms of evaluations of the efficacy of interventions to reduce stalking behaviour (Purcell and McEwan 2018).

In the interim it is recommended that interventions for adolescents who engage in stalking should include:

1. An assessment of the function, typology, frequency and nature of the behaviour. This should be undertaken with consideration to the person's age and attend to the cognitive and emotional development of the adolescent.
2. The formulation of behaviour should include consideration of wider systems surrounding the young person such as their peer relationships, family and culture. This could include the cultural formulation interview.
3. Consideration should be given to the young person's mental health given these difficulties may begin to emerge in adolescence. Formulations should attend to the potential for mental health difficulties using tools which are validated on young people. These should be undertaken sensitively given the young person may not have discussed these previously with people due to their age and perceived stigma associated with mental health difficulties.
4. Professionals undertaking assessments with young people should consider the communication challenges young people may face. For example, people with Speech Language and Communication Needs (SLCN) are 50% more likely to be involved in criminal activity and juveniles who engaged in stalking have been found to have communication challenges which are a risk factor for stalking (Purcell and McEwan 2018). Therefore interventions for young people should attend to the potential for communication challenges. This could include screening for SLCN in young people by a Speech and Language Therapist (SLT) and seeking consultancy on how interventions for adolescents could be adapted to enhance efficacy.

Conclusions and Recommendations for Future Practice and Research

Labelling adolescents as engaging in 'stalking' behaviour could pose serious implications in terms of the development of their self-concept and developmental pathway. Furthermore, this review has revealed serious concerns about the ways in which adolescent stalking is measured, defined and conceptualised. Adult research and concepts in relation to stalking do not appear to easily generalise onto adolescents both in terms of the demographics of who engages in this behaviour, the prevalence and function.

The prevalence of adolescent stalking through technology also requires attention in terms of how young people could be supported to navigate media environments. For example, concepts such as de-individuation have been found to contribute to moral disengagement and online harmful behaviours.in cyberbullying research (Chan et al. 2022). Given the links between bullying and stalking in adolescents, it is possible that bullying interventions could have some utility in interventions for adolescent stalking.

Clinicians working with adolescents should also be mindful of the potential for adolescents to be both victims and perpetrators of stalking. Furthermore, whilst this behaviour may have taken place online or through technology it is likely that the individuals in a victim–perpetrator dyad may have limited geographical mobility. This may lead to inflated estimations of stalking based on the 'five plus two' definition because it may be difficult for adolescents to avoid contact with each other and avoid 'unwanted' intrusions, contact or communication. Furthermore, the nature through which adolescents use technology may also lead to a naturally higher number of online communications generally in comparison to adults, thus when communicating in a potential stalking dyad, five instances of communication may not be unusual.

This review has also noted that when exploring stalking behaviours these should be considered within the cultural and societal structure in which the adolescent exists. Individualised formulations should be used to understand the function of the behaviour with consideration of both individual factors and the environmental context in which the adolescent resides. This is because there are currently no standardised risk assessment tools for adolescents and the adult tools do not easily generalise to this client group. A summary of the recommendations for practitioners and researchers working with clients at risk of stalking is made below.

- Practitioners working with adolescents should be mindful of the age of their clients when reviewing the literature in terms of its applicability to their individual biological and social development.
- Standardised risk assessment tools could be developed to support individualised formulations of the adolescents at risk of being a victim or perpetrator of adolescent stalking based on the function of their behaviour and the risk, severity and frequency of the behaviour (Borges and Dell'Aglio 2019). This should include consideration of the client's social mobility and the risk of stalking by proxy.
- Formulations and interventions designed to reduce adolescent stalking vulnerability and risk should take into account the complex multi-systemic factors surrounding stalking behaviour.
- Interventions to reduce stalking vulnerability need to be developed based on the literature. These could consider some of the literature in relation to bullying as well as educating students about stalking and the disregard of boundaries in partnerships and the criminal consequences of stalking should be explained (Kliem et al. 2021).
- Future research would benefit from reviewing the threshold for what constitutes stalking behaviours within the context of adolescence (e.g. the frequency and duration of behaviour) and the applicability of these for in-person versus technological stalking behaviour.
- Standardised tools should be developed to measure adolescent 'stalking' behaviours based on the threshold for adolescents in order for research in the field to be more consistent and reliable.

- Tools such as the DSM-5 Cultural Formulation Interview (Aggarwal et al. 2016) could be adapted for adolescents to assist practitioners to improve their cultural competence when understanding stalking behaviour. Cultural formulations take into account cultural and ethnic differences in reporting of behaviours and experiences and facilitate culturally informed interviewing.
- Studies of the long-term effects of stalking victimisation for adolescents have not been carried out. This should be undertaken using tools which are validated for adolescents.
- Researchers are encouraged to include questions about perpetrator intent in adolescent stalking-focused studies because of problems sometimes encountered when relying on victim fear as a benchmark of behaviour (Ybarra et al. 2017).
- The role of social media in adolescent stalking needs to be further understood in terms of the process through which this extends into stalking and the frequency and intensity of adolescent technology use (Roberts et al. 2016).
- There is a need for more research to understand adolescent stalking behaviour outside of westernised individualist cultures.
- More research is needed to understand the duality of being both a victim and perpetrator of adolescent stalking and the processes that underpin this.
- Understanding the risk factors and processes for how adolescent IPV may extend into adolescent stalking would be of benefit to inform future interventions and assessments.
- Given the prevalence of stalking as an extension of bullying, more research is needed to understand the process of how this develops and what differentiates adolescents who engage in bullying only in comparison to those that also engage in stalking.
- Future research should explore the narratives that adolescents use to describe stalking behaviour within the context of seeing this as not harmful or being self-protective.
- Research into adolescent stalking should be undertaken 'with' young people rather than 'to' them. It should use an inclusive methodology which facilitates the experiences of young people from their view taking into account their diverse and rich experiences which are relevant to their developmental period.
- The links between stalking and general aggression warrant further exploration, particularly in relation to factors such as generalised dissocial behaviour (harassment, property damage) as well as weapon carrying.
- There is a need for greater research into adolescent stalking in clients who identify as LGBTQ + and transgender.
- Interventions to reduce adolescent stalking should ensure they are designed within an 'adolescent lens'. This should include attending to how the adolescent brain experiences rewards, making learning a rewarding experience through increasing novelty and by linking teaching content to their interests. This should include providing teaching environments that facilitate positive

social interactions between peers, provide a sense of community and teach emotional regulation (Feinstein 2011; Hinton et al. 2012).

Discussion Questions

- What is 'stalking' in adolescence?
- How do adolescents who engage in 'stalking' differ from those that engage in bullying?
- What interventions may help young people at risk of being both a victim and/or a perpetrator of adolescent stalking behaviour?

Note

1. Latinx is a neologism in American English, sometimes used to refer to people of Latin American cultural or ethnic identity in the United States.

References

Aggarwal, Neil Krishan, Peter Lam, Enrico G. Castillo, Mitchell G. Weiss, Esperanza Diaz, Renato D. Alarcón, Rob Van Dijk et al. 2016. How do clinicians prefer cultural competence training? Findings from the DSM-5 cultural formulation interview field trial. *Academic Psychiatry* 40, no. 4: 584–591.

Aggarwal, Neil Krishan, G. Eric Jarvis, Ana Gómez-Carrillo, Laurence J. Kirmayer, and Roberto Lewis-Fernández. 2020. The cultural formulation interview since DSM-5: Prospects for training, research, and clinical practice. *Transcultural Psychiatry*57, no: 4: 496–514.

Agnew, Robert S. 1985. Neutralizing the impact of crime. *Criminal Justice and Behavior* 12, no. 2: 221–239.

Anderson, Monica, and Jingjing Jiang. 2021, May 27. Teens, social media & technology 2018. Pew Research Center: Internet, Science & Tech. https://www.pewresearch.org/internet/2018/05/31/teens-social-media-technology-2018/.

Aoyama, Ikuko, Lucy Barnard-Brak, and Tony L. Talbert. 2011. Cyberbullying among high school students: Cluster analysis of sex and age differences and the level of parental monitoring. *International Journal of Cyber Behavior, Psychology and Learning (IJCBPL)* 1, no. 1: 25–35.

Apperly, Ian. 2010. *Mindreaders: the cognitive basis of" theory of mind"*. Psychology Press.

Bailey, J. Michael, Paul L. Vasey, Lisa M. Diamond, S. Marc Breedlove, Eric Vilain, and Marc Epprecht. 2016. Sexual orientation, controversy, and science. *Psychological Science in the Public Interest* 17: 45–101. https://doi.org/10.1177/1529100616637616.

Beckett, Helen, and Camille Warrington. 2014. *Suffering in silence: Children and unreported crime.* Victim Support/University of Bedfordshire.

Best, Olivia, and Sasha Ban. 2021. Adolescence: Physical changes and neurological development. *British Journal of Nursing* 30, no. 5: 272–275.

Blakemore, Sarah-Jayne. 2012. Imaging brain development: The adolescent brain. *Neuroimage* 61, no. 2: 397–406.

Blakemore, Sarah-Jayne, Hanneke den Ouden, Suparna Choudhury, and Chris Frith. 2007. Adolescent development of the neural circuitry for thinking about intentions. 130–139.

Blakemore, S. J., & Mills, K. L. (2014). Is adolescence a sensitive period for sociocultural processing?. *Annual Review of Psychology, 65*, 187–207.

Borges, Jeane Lessinger, and Débora Dalbosco Dell'Aglio. 2019. Stalking following the breakup of dating relationships in adolescence. *Trends in Psychology* 27: 413–426.

Brumbach, Barbara Hagenah, Aurelio José Figueredo, and Bruce J. Ellis. 2009. Effects of harsh and unpredictable environments in adolescence on development of life history strategies: A longitudinal test of an evolutionary model. *Human Nature* 20: 25–51.

Burnett, Stephanie, Geoffrey Bird, Jorge Moll, Chris Frith, and Sarah-Jayne Blakemore. 2009. Development during adolescence of the neural processing of social emotion. *Journal of cognitive neuroscience* 21, no. 9: 1736–1750.

Bush, Kevin Ray. 2000. Separatedness and connectedness in the parent-adolescent relationship as predictors of adolescent self-esteem in US and Chinese samples. *Marriage & Family Review* 30, nos. 1–2: 153–178.

Byers, David S., Faye Mishna, and Carolyn Solo. 2021. Clinical practice with children and adolescents involved in bullying and cyberbullying: Gleaning guidelines from the literature. *Clinical Social Work Journal* 49, no. 1: 20–34.

Calzo, Jerel P., Toni C. Antonucci, Vickie M. Mays, and Susan D. Cochran. 2011. Retrospective recall of sexual orientation identity development among gay, lesbian, and bisexual adults. *Developmental Psychology* 47, no. 6: 1658.

Casey, Betty Jo, Sarah Getz, and Adriana Galvan. 2008. The adolescent brain. *Developmental Review* 28, no. 1: 62–77.

Chan, Heng Choon, and Lorraine Sheridan. 2019. Who are the stalking victims? Exploring the victimization experiences and psychosocial characteristics of young male and female adults in Hong Kong. *Journal of Interpersonal Violence.* Advance online publication. https://doi.org/10.1177/0886260519889938.

Chan, Heng Choon, and Lorraine Sheridan. 2021. Who are the stalking victims? Exploring the victimisation experiences and psychosocial characteristics of young male and female adults in Hong Kong. *Journal of interpersonal violence* 36, no. 21–22: NP11994-NP12015.

Chan, Tommy K. H., Christy M. K., Cheung, Izak Benbasat, Bo Xiao, and Zach W. Y. Lee. 2022. Bystanders Join In Cyberbullying on Social Networking Sites: The Deindividuation and Moral Disengagement Perspectives. *Information Systems Research.*

Chein, Jason, Dustin Albert, Lia O'Brien, Kaitlyn Uckert, and Laurence Steinberg. 2011. Peers increase adolescent risk taking by enhancing activity in the brain's reward circuitry. F1–F10.

Chen, May S., and Vangie A. Foshee. 2015. Stressful life events and the perpetration of adolescent dating abuse. *Journal of Youth and Adolescence* 44, no. 3: 696–707.

Child Growth Foundation. 2003. Premature sexual maturation (including precocious puberty. https://tinyurl.com/y6vq7hk9

Choudhury, Suparna, Tony Charman, and Sarah-Jayne Blakemore. 2008. Development of the teenage brain. *Mind, Brain, and Education* 2, no. 3: 142–147.

Cloonan-Thomas, Sinead, Elizabeth S. Daff, and Troy E. McEwan. 2022. Post-relationship stalking and intimate partner abuse in a sample of Australian adolescents. *Legal and Criminological Psychology.*

Crone, Eveline A. 2013. Considerations of fairness in the adolescent brain. *Child Development Perspectives* 7, no. 2: 97–103.

Curtis, Laura F. 2012. Virtual vs. reality: An examination of the nature of stalking and cyberstalking. PhD diss. San Diego State University.

Darby, S., Del Piero, L. Immordino-Yang, M. H., Kaplan, J., & Margolin, G. 2015. Neural correlates of adolescents' viewing of parents' and peers' emotions: Associations with risk-taking behavior and risky peer affiliations. Social Neuroscience, 10(6), 592–604. https://doi.org/10.1080/17470919.2015.1022216

Davies, E. L. 2013. The lived experiences of individuals who have been technologically stalked by a past intimate: A hermeneutic phenomenological study through a communication privacy manangement theory lens. University of Missouri-Columbia. https://mospace.umsystem.edu/xmlui/bitstream/handle/10355/42942/research.pdf?sequence=1&isAllowed=y.

Dearn, G., Whatson, C. & Wheatley, R. 2021. Stalking risk assessment tools: A brief critical review. In Forensic Update Issue, 138 (pp. 58–63). British Psychological Society.
Devine, Patricia G., Patrick S. Forscher, Anthony J. Austin, and William TL Cox. 2012. Long-term reduction in implicit race bias: A prejudice habit-breaking intervention. *Journal of experimental social psychology* 48, no. 6: 1267–1278.
De Smet, Olivia, Kasia Uzieblo, Tom Loeys, Ann Buysse, and Thomas Onraedt. 2015. Unwanted pursuit behavior after breakup: Occurrence, risk factors, and gender differences. *Journal of family violence* 30, no. 6: 753–767.
Dietz, Noella A., and Patricia Yancey Martin. 2007. Women who are stalked: Questioning the fear standard. *Violence Against Women* 13, no. 7: 750–776.
Doran, B. J., & Burgess, M. B. 2012. Putting fear of crime on the map. Springer, New York.
Dumontheil, Iroise. 2016. Adolescent brain development. *Current Opinion in Behavioral Sciences* 10: 39–44.
Edwards, Katie M., and Christine A. Gidycz. 2014. Stalking and psychosocial distress following the termination of an abusive dating relationship: A prospective analysis. *Violence Against Women* 20, no. 11: 1383–1397.
Ehrenreich, Samuel E., Kurt J. Beron, Kaitlyn Burnell, Diana J. Meter, and Marion K. Underwood. 2020. "How adolescents use text messaging through their high school years." *Journal of Research on Adolescence* 30, no. 2: 521–540.
Elkind, David. 1996. Inhelder and Piaget on adolescence and adulthood: A postmodern appraisal. *Psychological Science* 7, no. 4: 216–220.
Evans, Thomas M., and J. Reid Meloy. 2011. Identifying and classifying juvenile stalking behavior. *Journal of Forensic Sciences* 56: S266–S270.
Exner-Cortens, Deinera. 2018. Measuring adolescent dating violence. *Adolescent Dating Violence*: 315–340.
Fadus, Matthew C., Kenneth R. Ginsburg, Kunmi Sobowale, Colleen A. Halliday-Boykins, Brittany E. Bryant, Kevin M. Gray, and Lindsay M. Squeglia. 2020. Unconscious bias and the diagnosis of disruptive behavior disorders and ADHD in African American and Hispanic youth. *Academic Psychiatry* 44, no. 1: 95–102.
Feinstein, Sheryl. 2011. The Teenage brain and technology. *Learning Landscapes* 5, no. 1: 71–84.
Fenimore, Danielle M., Nicholas Perez, and Wesley G. Jennings. 2019. Early risk factors for violence among Hispanic youth: Evidence from a systematic review. *Aggression and violent behavior* 49 (2019): 101305.
Fernet, Mylene, Andreanne Lapierre, Martine Hebert, and Marie-Marthe Cousineau. 2019. A systematic review of literature on cyber intimate partner victimisation in adolescent girls and women. *Computers in Human Behavior* 100: 11–25.
Ferraro, Kenneth, F., and Randy LaGrange. 1987. The Measurement of Fear of Crime. *Sociological Enquiry* 57:70–101.
Fisher, Bonnie S., Ann L. Coker, Lisandra S. Garcia, Corrine M. Williams, Emily R. Clear, and Patricia G. Cook-Craig. 2014. Statewide estimates of stalking among high school students in Kentucky: Demographic profile and sex differences. *Violence Against Women* 20, no. 10: 1258–1279.
Fissel, Erica R. 2021. Victims' perceptions of cyberstalking: An examination of perceived offender motivation. *American Journal of Criminal Justice*. Advance online publication. https://doi.org/10.1007/s12103-021-09608-x.
Fissel, Erica R., Bradford W. Reyns, Matt R. Nobles, Bonnie S. Fisher, and Kathleen A. Fox. 2022. Cyberstalking Victims' Experiences With Fear Versus Other Emotional Responses to Repeated Online Pursuit: Revisiting the Fear Standard Among a National Sample of Young Adults. *Crime & Delinquency*: 00111287221096374.
FitzGerald, Chloë, and Samia Hurst. 2017. Implicit bias in healthcare professionals: a systematic review. *BMC medical ethics* 18, no. 1: 1–18.
Floyd, Frank J., and Roger Bakeman. Coming-out across the life course: Implications of age and historical context. *Archives of Sexual Behavior* 35, no. 3 (2006): 287–296.

Gatewood-Owens, Jennifer. A gender-biased definition: Unintended impacts of the fear requirement in stalking victimisation. *Crime & Delinquency* 63, no. 11 (2017): 1339–1362.
Giedd, Jay N. 2003. The anatomy of mentalization: A view from developmental neuroimaging. *Bulletin of the Menninger Clinic* 67, no. 2: Special Issue: 132.
Giedd, Jay N. 2008. The teen brain: insights from neuroimaging. *Journal of adolescent health* 42, no. 4: 335–343.
Gilchrist, Elizabeth, Jon Bannister, Jason Ditton, and Stephen Farrall. WOMEN AND THE 'FEAR OF CRIME' Challenging the Accepted Stereotype. 1998. *The British Journal of Criminology* 38, no. 2: 283–298.
Haugaard, Jeffrey J., and Lisa G. Seri. 2004. Stalking and other forms of intrusive contact among adolescents and young adults from the perspective of the person initiating the intrusive contact. *Criminal Justice and Behavior* 31, no. 1: 37–54.
Heller, Aaron S., and B. J. Casey. 2016. The neurodynamics of emotion: Delineating typical and atypical emotional processes during adolescence. *Developmental science* 19, no. 1: 3–18.
Helwig, Charles C. 2006. The development of personal autonomy throughout cultures. *Cognitive Development* 21, no. 4: 458–473.
Hermans, E. J., P. Putman, and J. van Honk. Testosterone reduces empathetic mimicking in healthy young women. *Psychoneuroendocrinology* 31 (2006): 859–866.
Hill, John P., and Mary Ellen Lynch. 1983. The intensification of gender-related role expectations during early adolescence. In *Girls at puberty*, pp. 201–228. Springer, Boston, MA, .
Hinduja, S. 2021. Cyberbullying in 2021 by age, gender, sexual orientation, and race. Cyberbullying Research Center. https://cyberbullying.org/cyberbullying-statistics-age-gender-sexual-orientation-race.
Hinton, C., Fischer, K. W., and Catherine Glennon. 2012. Mind, brain, and education. *Mind.*
Howard, Donna E., Katrina J. Debnam, and Amanda Strausser. 2019. I'm a stalker and proud of it: Adolescent girls' perceptions of the mixed utilities associated with internet and social networking use in their dating relationships.*Youth & Society* 51, no. 6: 773–792.
Jaffray, Piper, and T. Sandven. 2015. Taking stock with teens. *Spring2013* http://www.whiteboardadvisors.com/files/Taking_Stock_Teachin_Spring_2013_MV_2.pdf.
Jang, Y. O. 2013. Moderating effects of adolescents' family healthy on the relation between experience of school violence and coping behaviors. *Middle School Education* 60: 231–260.
Kahneman, Daniel, Olivier Sibony, and Cass R. Sunstein 2021. *Noise: A flaw in human judgment.* Little, Brown.
Kliem, Sören, Yvonne Krieg, and Dirk Baier. 2021. Stalking im Jugendalter: Prävalenz und Zusammenhänge mit psychischer Befindlichkeit. *Kindheit und Entwicklung* 30, no. 4: 244–253.
Kropp, P. Randall, S. D. Hart, and D. R. Lyon. 2008. Guidelines for Stalking Assessment and Management (SAM). User manual. Vancouver, Canada: ProActive ReSolutions Inc.
LaGrange, Randy L., and Kenneth F. Ferraro. 1989. Assessing age and gender differences in perceived risk and fear of crime. *Criminology* 27, no. 4: 697–719.
LaGrange, Randy L., Kenneth F. Ferraro, and Michael Supancic. 1992. Perceived risk and fear of crime: Role of social and physical incivilities. *Journal of research in crime and delinquency* 29, no. 3: 311–334.
Lee, Chien-Ti, Troy E. Beckert, and Thane R. Goodrich. 2010. The relationship between individualistic, collectivistic, and transitional cultural value orientations and adolescents' autonomy and identity status. *Journal of Youth and Adolescence* 39, no. 8: 882–893.
Leigh, Shonagh, and Jason Davies. 2021. A rapid evidence assessment of psychological treatment approaches for stalking behaviour. *The Journal of Forensic Practice*, December.
Leitz, Mary Ann, and Matthew T. Theriot. 2005. Adolescent stalking: A review. *Journal of Evidence-Based Social Work* 2, no. 3–4: 97–112.
Lu, Yu, Flor Avellaneda, Elizabeth D. Torres, Emily F. Rothman, and Jeff R. Temple. 2019. Adolescent cyberbullying and weapon carrying: Cross-sectional and longitudinal associations. *Cyberpsychology, Behavior, and Social Networking* 22, no: 3: 173–179.
Leone, P., A. Adimora, E. Foust, D. Williams, M. Buie, J. Peebles, L. Fitzpatrick et al. 2005. "HIV transmission among black women-North Carolina, 2004 (Reprinted from MMWR, vol 54, pg

89–94, 2005). *JAMA-JOURNAL OF THE AMERICAN MEDICAL ASSOCIATION* 293, no. 11: 1317–1319.

MacKenzie, Rachel, Troy Erin McEwan, Michele Pathe, David V. James, James Robert Ogloff, and Paul Edward Mullen. 2009. Stalking risk profile: Guidelines for the assessment and management of stalkers.

Madden, Mary, Amanda Lenhart, Sandra Cortesi, Urs Gasser, Maeve Duggan, Aaron Smith, and Meredith Beaton. 2013. Part 1: Teens and social media use. Pew Research Center. Washington DC.

Marcia, James E. 1966. Development and validation of ego-identity status. *Journal of Personality and Social Psychology* 3, no. 5: 551.

McCann, J. T. 2000. A descriptive study of child and adolescent obsessional followers. *Journal of Forensic Science* 45, no. 1: 195–199.

McEwan, Troy E., Lianne Harder, Cleo Brandt, and Vivienne de Vogel. 2020. Risk factors for stalking recidivism in a Dutch community forensic mental health sample. *IInternational Journal of Forensic Mental Health* 19, no. 2: 127–141.

McEwan, Troy E., Daniel E. Shea, Michael Daffern, Rachel D. MacKenzie, James RP Ogloff, and Paul E. Mullen. 2018. The reliability and predictive validity of the Stalking Risk Profile. *Assessment* 25, no. 2: 259–276.

Mennicke, Annelise, Constance Austin Coates, Bridget Jules, and Jennifer Langhinrichsen-Rohling. 2021. Who do they tell? College students' formal and informal disclosure of sexual violence, sexual harassment, stalking, and dating violence by gender, sexual identity, and race. *Journal of Interpersonal Violence*: 08862605211050107.

Monneuse, Olivier JY, Avery B. Nathens, Nicole N. Woods, Julie L. Mauceri, Sonya L. Canzian, Wei Xiong, and Najma A. Ahmed. 2008. Attitudes about injury among high school students. *Journal of the American College of Surgeons* 207, no. 2: 179–184.

Moshman, David. 2020. Adolescent reasoning and rationality. In *Critical Thinking and Reasoning*, pp. 99–113. Brill.

Mullen, Paul E., Michele Pathé, and Rosemary Purcell. 2001. Stalking: New constructions of human behaviour. *Australian & New Zealand Journal of Psychiatry* 35, no. 1: 9–16.

Mullen, Paul E., Rosemary Purcell, and Geoffrey W. Stuart. 1999. Study of stalkers. *American Journal of Psychiatry* 156, no. 8: 1244–1249.

Mullen, Paul E., Michele Pathé, and Rosemary Purcell. 2000. *Stalkers and their victims*. Cambridge University Press.

National Center for Victims of Crime. 2007. Potential effects of cyberstalking. http://www.ncvc.org/ncvc/main.aspx?dbName=DocumentViewer&DocumentID=32458.

National Criminal Justice Association. 1993. *Project to develop a model anti-stalking code for states*. National Institute of Justice.

Niolon, Phyllis Holditch, Alana M. Vivolo-Kantor, Natasha E. Latzman, Linda Anne Valle, Henrietta Kuoh, Tessa Burton, Bruce G. Taylor, and Andra T. Tharp. 2015. Prevalence of teen dating violence and co-occurring risk factors among middle school youth in high-risk urban communities. *Journal of Adolescent Health* 56, no. 2: S5–S13.

ONS. 2014. Crime in England and Wales, Year ending March 2014. http://www.ons.gov.uk/ons/rel/crime-stats/crime-statistics/period-ending-march-2014/stb-crime-stats.html.

Overgaauw, Sandy, Carolien Rieffe, Evelien Broekhof, Eveline A. Crone, and Berna Güroğlu. 2017. Assessing empathy across childhood and adolescence: Validation of the empathy questionnaire for children and adolescents (EmQue-CA). *Frontiers in Psychology* 8: 870.

Owens, Jennifer Gatewood. 2016. Why definitions matter: Stalking victimisation in the United States. *Journal of Interpersonal Violence* 31, no. 12 (2016): 2196–2226.

Ozaki, Reiko. 2020. Preventing dating violence, sexual violence, and stalking in high schools to support the whole child. *Leadership and Research in Education* 5, no. 1: 10–32.

Pandey, Anuja, Daniel Hale, Anne-Lise Goddings, Sarah-Jayne Blakemore, and Russell Viner. 2017a. Systematic review of effectiveness of universal self-regulation-based interventions and their effects on distal health and social outcomes in children and adolescents: review protocol. *Systematic Reviews* 6, no. 1: 1–5.

Pandey, Anuja, Daniel Hale, Anne-Lise Goddings, Sarah-Jayne Blakemore, and Russell Viner. 2017b. Systematic review of effectiveness of universal self-regulation-based interventions and their effects on distal health and social outcomes in children and adolescents: review protocol. *Systematic Reviews* 6, no. 1: 1–5.

Patton, George C., Susan M. Sawyer, John S. Santelli, David A. Ross, Rima Afifi, Nicholas B. Allen, Monika Arora et al. 2016. Our future: A Lancet commission on adolescent health and wellbeing. *The Lancet* 387, no. 10036: 2423–2478.

Park, Sihyun, and Sin-Hyang Kim. 2019. Who are the victims and who are the perpetrators in dating violence? Sharing the role of victim and perpetrator. *Trauma, Violence, & Abuse* 20, no. 5: 732–741.

Pattwell, Siobhan S., Francis S. Lee, and BJ3761221 Casey. 2013. Fear learning and memory across adolescent development: Hormones and Behavior Special Issue: Puberty and Adolescence. *Hormones and Behavior* 64, no. 2: 380–389.

Pereira, Filipa, Brian H. Spitzberg, and Marlene Matos. 2016. Cyber-harassment victimisation in Portugal: Prevalence, fear and help-seeking among adolescents. *Computers in Human Behavior* 62: 136–146.

Pondana, Zuzana, and Romana Imrîšková. 2014. Victims' responses to stalking: An examination of fear levels and coping strategies. *Journal of Interpersonal Violence* 31, no. 5: 792–809.

Purcell, R., & McEwan, T. E. 2018. Treatment approaches for stalking. In In J. L. Ireland, C. A. Ireland, & P. Birch (Eds.), *Violent and sexual offenders: Assessment, treatment and management* (2nd ed., pp. 400–416). Routledge.

Purcell, Rosemary, Michele Pathe, and Paul Mullen. 2004. When do repeated intrusions become stalking?. *Journal of Forensic Psychiatry & Psychology* 15, no. 4: 571–583.

Purcell, Rosemary, Bridget Moller, Teresa Flower, and Paul E. Mullen. 2009. Stalking among juveniles. *The British Journal of Psychiatry* 194, no. 5: 451–455.

Purcell, Rosemary, Michele Pathé, and Paul Mullen. 2010. Gender differences in stalking behaviour among juveniles. *The Journal of Forensic Psychiatry & Psychology* 21, no. 4: 555–568.

Reidy, Dennis E., John F. Shelley-Tremblay, and Scott O. Lilienfeld. 2011. Psychopathy, reactive aggression, and precarious proclamations: A review of behavioral, cognitive, and biological research. *Aggression and Violent Behavior* 16, no. 6: 512–524.

Roberts, Karl, Marina Tolou-Shams, and Kaila Madera. 2016. Adolescent versus adult stalking: A brief review. *Journal of Forensic Psychology Practice* 16, no. 4: 236–252.

Romeo, Russell D. 2013. The teenage brain: The stress response and the adolescent brain. *Current Directions in Psychological Science* 22, no. 2: 140–145.

Rothman, Emily F., Eva Bahrami, Nnenna Okeke, and Elizabeth Mumford. 2021. Prevalence of and risk markers for dating abuse–related stalking and harassment victimisation and perpetration in a nationally representative sample of US adolescents. *Youth & Society* 53, no. 6: 955–978.

Russo, S., M. Roccato, and A. Vieno. 2013. Criminal victimisation and crime risk perception: A multilevel longitudinal study. *Social Indicators Research* 112: 535–548.

Sawyer, Susan M., Peter S. Azzopardi, Dakshitha Wickremarathne, and George C. Patton. 2018. The age of adolescence. *The Lancet Child & Adolescent Health* 2, no. 3: 223–228.

Shepherd, J. (2022). https://thesocialshepherd.com/blog/snapchat-statistics

Sheridan, Lorraine P., and Tim Grant. 2007. Is cyberstalking different? *Psychology, Crime & Law* 13: 627–640. https://doi.org/10.1080/10683160701340528.

Sheridan, Lorraine, Adrian J. Scott, and Karl Roberts. 2016. Young women's experiences of intrusive behavior in 12 countries. *Aggressive behavior* 42, no. 1: 41–53.

Silva, Karol, Elizabeth P. Shulman, Jason Chein, and Laurence Steinberg. 2016. Peers increase late adolescents' exploratory behavior and sensitivity to positive and negative feedback. *Journal of Research on Adolescence* 26, no. 4: 696–705.

Smith-Darden, Joanne P., Dennis E. Reidy, and Poco D. Kernsmith. 2016. Adolescent stalking and risk of violence. *Journal of Adolescence* 52: 191–200.

Somerville, Leah H., Rebecca M. Jones, and B. J. Casey. 2010. A time of change: behavioral and neural correlates of adolescent sensitivity to appetitive and aversive environmental cues. *Brain and cognition* 72, no. 1: 124–133.
Spear, Linda P. 2000. The adolescent brain and age-related behavioral manifestations. *Neuroscience & biobehavioral reviews* 24, no. 4: 417–463.
Spear, Linda Patia. 2009. Heightened stress responsivity and emotional reactivity during pubertal maturation: Implications for psychopathology. *Development and psychopathology* 21, no. 1: 87–97.
Spitzberg, Brian H. 2002. The tactical topography of stalking victimisation and management. *Trauma, Violence, & Abuse* 3, no. 4: 261–288.
Spitzberg, Brian H. 2017. Acknowledgment of unwanted pursuit, threats, assault, and stalking in a college population. *Psychology of Violence* 7, no. 2: 265.
Stefanou, Candice R., Kathleen C. Perencevich, Matthew DiCintio, and Julianne C. Turner. 2004. Supporting autonomy in the classroom: Ways teachers encourage student decision making and ownership. *Educational psychologist* 39, no. 2: 97–110.
Steinberg, Laurence, and Kathryn C. Monahan. Adolescents' exposure to sexy media does not hasten the initiation of sexual intercourse. *Developmental Psychology* 47, no. 2 (2011): 562.
Steinberg, Laurence, and Amanda Sheffield Morris. 2001. Adolescent development. *Journal of Cognitive Education and Psychology* 2, no. 1: 55–87.
Steinberg, Laurence, and Susan B. Silverberg. 1986. The vicissitudes of autonomy in early adolescence. *Child development*: 841–851.
Sung, Y. H., Chen, L. M., Yen, C. F., & Valcke, M. 2018. Double trouble: The developmental process of school bully-victims. *Children and Youth Services Review*, 91, 279–288.
Sutton, Robbie M., and Stephen Farrall. 2005. Gender, socially desirable responding and the fear of crime: Are women really more anxious about crime?. *British Journal of Criminology* 45, no. 2: 212–224.
Thomas, Stuart DM, Rosemary Purcell, Michele Pathe, and Paul E. Mullen. 2008. Harm associated with stalking victimization. *Australian and New Zealand Journal of Psychiatry* 42, no. 9: 800–806.
Thompson, Carleen M., and Susan M. Dennison. 2008. Defining relational stalking in research: Understanding sample composition in relation to repetition and duration of harassment. *Psychiatry, Psychology and Law* 15, no. 3: 482–499.
Tseloni, Andromachi, and Christina Zarafonitou. 2008. Fear of crime and victimisation: A multivariate multilevel analysis of competing measurements. *European Journal of Criminology* 5, no. 4: 387–409.
Vaidya, Girish, Nevyne Chalhoub, and Jo Newing. 2005. Stalking in adolescence: A case report. *Child and adolescent mental health* 10, no. 1: 23–25.
van der Aa, Suzan. 2018. New trends in the criminalization of stalking in the EU member states. *European Journal on Criminal Policy and Research* 24, no. 3: 315–333.
Weinrath, Michael, and John Gartrell. 1996. Victimisation and fear of crime. *Violence and Victims* 11, no. 3: 187–197.
Wright, Michelle F., and Sebastian Wachs. 2019. Does social support moderate the relationship between racial discrimination and aggression among Latinx adolescents? A longitudinal study. *Journal of adolescence* 73: 85–94.
World Health Organisation [WHO] (2022). https://www.who.int/health-topics/adolescent-health#tab=tab_12.
Xu, Yin, Sam Norton, and Qazi Rahman. 2021. Childhood gender nonconformity and the stability of self-reported sexual orientation from adolescence to young adulthood in a birth cohort. *Developmental Psychology* 57, no. 4: 557.
Ybarra, Michele L., Jennifer Langhinrichsen-Rohling, and Kimberly J. Mitchell. 2017. Stalking-like behavior in adolescence: Prevalence, intent, and associated characteristics. *Psychology of violence* 7, no. 2: 192.
Yurgelun-Todd, D. A., & Killgore, W. D. (2006). Fear-related activity in the prefrontal cortex increases with age during adolescence: A preliminary fMRI study. *Neuroscience Letters*, 406, 194–199.

4 Stalking in Movies: Could You Be a Victim?

Tine Munk and Rachel Austin

Key Points

- This chapter explores the definitional problems related to defining stalking behaviours.
- This chapter examines the role of adolescents' use of popular media to learn. relationship behaviours and the dangers of portraying stalking positively in movies.
- This chapter provides a systematic review of how direct and indirect stalking is described by the Internet Movie Database (IMDb), such as plot keywords, plot synopsis and movie descriptions.

Introduction

There is a fascination with stalking movies and series that do not mirror reality. In the award-winning Netflix drama, *You* (2018), the actor Badgley rose to fame playing the main character, Joe Goldberg. Goldberg is a dark and sinister stalker admired by the show's fans. The show develops from his point of view (PCADV 2021). According to Goldberg, he does nothing wrong, as he 'just' wants to protect his love interest. The character and show have been described as: 'A dangerously charming, intensely obsessive young man goes to extreme measures to insert himself into the lives of those he is transfixed by' (IMDb 2018b; Netflix 2018). In popular media, a leading man's obsessive, coercive or stalking behaviour is portrayed as an expression of his love and devotion. Examples of these behaviours

T. Munk (✉) · R. Austin
Nottingham Trent University, Nottingham, UK
e-mail: tine.munk@ntu.ac.uk

M. Mellins et al. (eds.), *Young People, Stalking Awareness and Domestic Abuse*,
https://doi.org/10.1007/978-3-031-32379-9_4

are showing up unwanted at a person's workplace, home or school, repetitive and unwelcome communications and following the love interest (Liez 2021). Many movies and shows have integrated stalking elements into the storyline directly or indirectly. The stalking features prove that 'no, does not mean no'. Instead, it wrongly signals 'try harder' to pursue the end goal and win the love of your life. This show signals to the audience that it is okay to stalk without consideration for its harmful and objectifying impact on the victim. The current legislation criminalising stalking is already problematic, and a universal definition of stalking is missing. When much-loved movies like *Twilight* (2008), *Stranger Things* (2016), and *Love Actually* (2003) have included a stalking storyline (featuring direct or indirect stalking), they create a notion that stalking is not something the audience should worry about (Liez 2021; IMDb 2003, 2008, 2016a). When popular media glamourise stalking, they devalue the experience of the victims, and they blur the lines between what is the acceptable pursuit and what is stalking.

Stalking is not a new phenomenon. Popular media will often depict the violent extremes of stalking without considering the psychological effects. However, depictions of stalking in popular media are not openly labelled as stalking or stalker-like behaviour. This chapter will focus on the problems of identifying stalking in movie plots and how this behaviour is being normalised. The main focus is the potential impact these stalking movie plots can have on adolescents and their understanding of certain behaviours. This chapter systematically assesses movies available on popular video streaming services where a stalking element is included. Empirical research is conducted to investigate how thrillers and romance movies are described in plot keywords, movie synopsis and by the IMDb. The aim is to gain an in-depth understanding of these stalking movies streamed to a broad audience on services like Netflix, Amazon Video, Disney+ and Apple Video. Data were collected at the beginning of September 2022, where researchers identified the 50 most popular movies appearing using the Google Search engine.

Stalking's Scope

Stalking Characteristics

At the beginning of the 1990s, stalking became criminalised in different jurisdictions where California adopted the first stalking legislation. Subsequently, the US criminalised stalking on the federal level, and other western countries followed (Taylor-Dunn et al. 2018, NP5966). At that time, stalking was an unknown entity, which caused trouble with identifying the nature of the crime (Sheridan and Davies 2001, 133; Sheridan et al. 2003, 148). The term refers to intentional pattern of terrorising behaviours aimed at a specific individual, which causes them to feel emotions of panic and anxiety (Logan and Walker 2017; Miller 2012; Lippman 2018, 395, Spitzberg and Cupach 2014). Stalking includes a broad range of repeated behaviours, means and methods, such as using phones, letters, or surveillance (Westrup and Fermouwa 1998). According to Holin (2016), 'Stalking is a form of sexual harassment that includes obscene and threatening communications either by writing, telephone or email; following, watching, or waiting at the victim's home or place of work; or tampering with personal property' (Holin 2016, 128). The UK Crown Prosecution Service (CPS) includes this definition to assist in reviewing and preparing cases recognising the reoccurrence of electronic communications, social media and the Internet in stalking cases (CPS 2022). Stalking activities and behaviours must be considered in conjunction with an ongoing, intrusive campaign. In isolation, the behaviours might be parts of everyday life. Still, there is a cumulative effect when the behaviours are considered in conjunction with other actions (Quinn-Evans et al. 2021).

It is widely recognised that stalking is a social problem, and despite several legislations adopted worldwide, there is no consensus on how stalking should be defined (Sheridan and Davies 2001, 133). Despite the problems with the legislative definitions, which differ from country to country, some characteristics still emerge in most of them. Stalking is linked to a persistent and unwanted following of a person, which causes the victim of stalking to feel unsafe (Eterovic-Soric et al. 2017, 279). The nature of stalking is repetitive or systematic, directed towards a specific person (Mullen et al. 2001; Van der Aa 2018). Mullen et al. (1999) defined stalking as 'part of a spectrum of activities that merge into normal behaviour, often around aspirations as initiating or re-establishing a relationship' (Mullen et al. 1999, 1244). Stalking and cyberstalking are both interpersonal crimes, and due to the Internet and virtual spaces, there is no need for physical proximity for harm to occur. Today, stalking can efficiently be conducted from a distance using the online environment to harass, cause fear and terrorise the victim (Lavrogna 2020, 91).

Previous studies of stalking are predominately about adults, whereas stalking among children and adolescents is rare and uncommon. There is a misinterpretation in understanding the particular parameters included in adolescent stalkings, such as age and maturity. This lack of insight led to the assumption that children and adolescents cannot engage in stalking behaviour. According to Purcell et al. (2009), and Juarez (2019) this is a naïve perception. Although the adult behaviour is mirrored by the younger age group, i.e., initiating and terminating relationships or dealing with the different aspects of behaviours in friendships. Navigating relationships among adults can be reflected in the challenges young people face. On top of managing these challenges, adolescents have new experiences, such as their first format of sexual experiences (Purcell et al. 2009, 451; Juarez 2019). This study also outlines a crossover between stalking and bullying. With adolescents, the behaviours are often seen as bullying. This argument is supported by Roberts et al. (2016), who argued that there is a lack of awareness regarding adolescents' experience and understanding of stalking behaviours. School programmes include bullying as a topic, but they fail to include stalking behaviour despite its distinct cause and motivation (Roberts et al. 2016, 250). Smith-Darden et al. (2016) expanded the research area from a direct focus on stalking to include stalking preparations and the different risks of violence associated with stalkings, such as physical assault, instrumental violence and the use of weapons (Smith-Darden et al. 2016). A study by Waterman et al. (2019) included similar areas, where they focused on adolescents and their experience with adult behaviours and risks. They identified stalking problems related to binge drinking, interpersonal violence (stalking), sexual harassment, sexual assault and dating violence (Waterman et al. 2019). According to Juarez (2019), there is a correlation between several risk factors linked to interpersonal violence, such as homicide, fighting, family violence, dating violence, sexual violence, gang violence, bullying and cyberbullying (Juarez 2019).

Behaviours

Stalking is not likely to be defined by one particular behaviour. Instead, stalking can include several actions (Sheridan and Davies 2001, 136). Some of the definitions developed around the time stalking were criminalisation varied, and most focused solely on the offender. Mullen et al. (2001) defined stalking as 'persistent harassment in which one person repeatedly imposes on other unwanted communications and/or contacts' (Mullen et al. 2001, 9). Sometimes stalking might appear harmless on the surface, but it can still devastate the victims. Therefore, some legislation refers to victim impact to determine whether the behaviour constitutes an offence. This is principally done through the concept of fear. However, fear is subjective, so one person's perception of fear might not apply to others (Taylor-Dunn et al. 2018). Sinclair and Frieze (2000) have described staking 'as a continuum of behaviours ranging from seemingly harmless courtship attempts to physical assault and homicide. While crimes like theft can be established after one episode, stalking, by definition, cannot' (Sinclair and Frieze 2000; Boehnlein et al. 2020, 756). Therefore, it is essential to establish a staking pattern, which can often span weeks or months with a significant impact on the victim (Boehnlein et al. 2020, 756).

The effect of stalking is considered a public health priority due to the severe social, emotional, physical and psychological impact on the victim (Breiding et al. 2014; Dressing et al. 2006; Owens 2016). Victims of stalking have reported adverse mental and physical health effects such as depression, post-traumatic stress and substance abuse (Blaauw et al. 2002; Davis et al. 2002; DuMonthier et al. 2017; Geistmann et al. 2012; Purcell et al. 2004). Victims of post-intimate stalking often feel fear, shame and a sense of loss, lack trust in other people, and an increased sense of alienation, isolation and self-blame (Kamphuis et al. 2003, 153). Stalking can make victims feel they are losing control over their own lives and makes victims enforce restrictions on their typical day-to-day activities and lifestyle to avoid interactions with the perpetrator (Davis et al. 2002). Mullen et al. (2009) found that stalking can disrupt the victims' sense of control over their own lives and that the world is fair (Mullen et al. 2009). Similarly, victims of stalking have acknowledged that they 'feel as if they are living in a prison of the stalkers' making' (Morewitz 2003, 39). Victims might end up with financial problems, as they have lost wages due to lengthy processes like restraining orders. In other instances, the stalker has arrived at the victim's place of work, which can impact the victim's employment and productivity (DuMonthier et al. 2017; Logan et al. 2007).

Post-Traumatic Stress Disorder (PTSD), an anxiety disorder caused by traumatic events or situations, is also linked to the impact of stalking. PTSD is characterised by various behaviours, such as reoccurring nightmares, anxieties, irritability, decreased responsiveness to the external world and depression (Roberts and Dziegielewski 1996; Wallace and Silverman 1996; Pathé and Mullen 1997). Stalking often affects beyond the immediate target, where it affects co-victims, such as family members and friends. These co-victims experience stress on the victim's behalf and from being unable to protect the victim from further victimisation (Spitzberg and Cupach 2007; Lippman 2018, 369).

Legal Definitions

The criminalisation of stalking is relatively new, and there are still problems defining stalking in opposition to other behaviours. Most of the issues are related to the victim's experiences and what constitutes a case that can be legally prosecuted. Baseline academic definitions are developed from precedents, including quantification of harassment and unreasonable behaviour, whereas the legal definitions are not harmonised and vary between justifications. Yet, a general definition is linked to a '*wilful form* of continued pursuit of harassment which is unwarranted, often with *malicious* intent, and causes of fear through repeated intrusive behaviours' (Quinn-Evans et al. 2021).

The legal definition of stalking varies across the US states. Therefore, the legislation is constantly being updated. In the US, legislations frequently derive from each state's anti-harassment laws, which creates an inconsistent framework across the US. This means that the criminal definitions of stalking are interlinked with behaviours defined in a precinct or within local and state laws (Messing et al. 2020, 694; Owens 2016, 2197). In 1996, the US Congress passed an anti-stalking law, which is a part of the Violence Against Women Act (VAWA). This Federal Law, 18 US Code 2261A, criminalises cross-state stalking. Article 1 includes 'travels in interstate or foreign commerce or is present within the special maritime and territorial jurisdiction of the United States or enters or leaves Indian country, with the intent to kill, injure, harass, intimidate, or place under surveillance with intent to kill, injure, harass, or intimidate another person, and in the course of, or as a result of, such travel or presence engages in conduct that…' (US Department of Justice 2021; GovInfo 1996). This legislation is linked to whether a 'reasonable person would consider the actions threatening or fear-inducing (Sheridan et al. 2003, 149).

In the European region, the Council of Europe Convention on Preventing and Combating Violence against Women (Istanbul Convention, CETS No. 210) includes stalking as a part of gender-based violence because it is about control and dominance (CoE 2018, 2019, 3). The Istanbul Convention does not explicitly include any provisions about stalking. But the offence is mentioned in Article 3, covering gender-based violence that results/or is likely to result in physical, sexual, psychological or economic harm and/or suffering. In this context, the offence includes threats of such acts, coercion and arbitrary deprivation of liberty in public or private places (CoE 2011).

Stalking does not have a specific definition according to legislation in England, Wales and Northern Ireland. However, in the Protection Against Harassment Act 1997, there is a generalised list of behaviours associated with stalking (CPS 2018; Legislation.gov.uk 1997, 2012; Sheridan et al. 2003, 150). The Stalking Bill was processed through Parliament in 1996 as it was recognised that stalking was not criminalised. During the legislative process, concerns about the legislation's scope were raised, which led to changes including a broader spectrum of harassment (Taylor-Dunn et al. 2018, NP5967; Legislation.gov.uk 2012). Section 2A(3) of the Protection against Harassment Act 1997 provides and non-exhaustive list indicating the types of behaviours included in the act, i.e. Following someone, contacting or attempting to contact the person, public or private loitering, watching/spying, or publishing statements or material on the Internet (CPS 2018; Legislation.gov.uk 1997; Taylor-Dunn et al. 2018, NP5967). The stalking offences in Sections 2A and 4A of the Protection of Freedoms Act 2012 extend the provisions in the Protection against Harassment Act 1997. Sections 4 and 4a establish that it is an offence to put people in fear of violence or serious alarm or distress as a part of stalking. A potential racial or religious motive behind the stalking is also an aggravating factor. These factors will often classify stalking as a hate crime (CPS 2018, 2022; Legislation.gov.uk 2012). Key features to prosecuting stalking offences in most jurisdictions are (1) there is a 'course of conduct' that typically is defined as two or more incidents; (2) the offender or 'a reasonable person' should know that the intentional 'course of conduct' would instil fear in the target—or a 'reasonable person' (Lippman 2018, 395; CPS 2018; Spitzberg and Cupach 2014).

Popular Culture and Stalking

Popular Media

As demonstrated above, research into stalking has been conducted since the area was criminalised in the 1990s. However, less research has explored the link between the impact of stalking in popular culture and the audience's perception of stalking in these storylines. Books, music and movies have been made with direct and indirect links to stalking (Nicol 2006, 44). At the time of the criminalisation of stalking, several staking movies were released in cinemas that today are considered to be classic movies, such as *Fatal Attraction* (1989), *Sleeping with the Enemy* (1991), *Pacific Heights* (1990), *Single White Female* (1992), *Fear* (1996) (Nicol 2006; IMDb 1987, 1990, 1991, 1992a, 1996). Hollywood portrayals of stalking are linked to a stereotyping scenario enacted by a crazed or mentally disturbed person or an unwanted pursuit or harassing behaviour before or during a romantic relationship. These two scenarios will likely give the audience a wrong interpretation of stalking in real life (Schultz et al. 2014, 614). Obsessional following, obsessional relational intrusion, and obsessional harassment are all terms that have been used to describe stalking. According to Muellen et al. (2006), there are more factors to consider, such as the stalker's 'cognitive function, experience and expression of anger, personality traits, self-image, acceptance of behavioural responsibility, and interpersonal attachment' (Mullen et al. 2006, 242). The problem with these typologies is often linked to persistent pursuit. Still, they are less valuable to describe stalking in a non-romantic relationship, where the context goes beyond 'being pursued' (Birch et al. 2018). In movies, there is a common perception that love endures all obstacles that necessitate tensions. These tensions are often portrayed as volatile and abusive (Hayes 2014). For example, in *Say Anything* (1989), the male lead shows up on the lawn belonging to the female lead after an argument playing ear-spitting loud music from a boombox (IMDb 1989). The male character in *The Notebook* (2004) threatens to jump off a Ferris wheel if the female character does not agree to date (Maas and Bonomi 2021, 512; IMDb 2004a).

People's primary source of information about crime comes from popular media, which invest in cultivating fandom, identification and para-social relationships with fictional characters and personalities. The media, television and magazines are essential sources for young people to be educated about sexual relationships and behaviours (Maas and Bonomi 2021, 511, Ward 2003, 348). One part of the cultivation of the audience relates to their ability to fudge external realism (Schultz et al. 2014). Busselle and Bilandziz (2008) argue that it is a factor "to the extent to which fictional content is consistent with the actual world" (Busselle and Bilandzic 2008, 267). Characteristics and qualities of romantic relationships are constantly being distributed through several sources, such as parents, peers and media. These are known as 'romantic relationship norms' widely reflected in popular culture, for example, in fairy tales, books, movies and television. Popular media present the audience with a particular, not necessarily realistic, understanding of romantic relationships (Tudor 2013; Maas and Bonomi 2021).

Relationships, romance and sexual content are portrayed in media, from shows, sitcoms and dramas to feature films. Therefore, media is essential for adolescents who observe countless verbal and visual examples of social norms and rules around dating, intimacy, sex and relationships (Ward 2003, 348). The Sexual Media Practice Model developed by Shafer et al. (2012) shows a cyclical process of how media use affects attitudes, and individual attitudes affect media selection. Popular media transmit new romance and sexual norms to a broader audience. The norms are then incorporated into everyday life, and new media are selected based on internalised norms. Popular movies, like the *Fifty Shades* trilogy (IMDb 2015, 2017, 2018a) and the *Twilight* saga (IMDb 2008, 2009, 2010, 2012), tap into the way popular media glorify controlling and obsessive behaviour. So, the media have a significant influence on the whole cycle and by the behaviour of the individuals to ensure that they choose media aligning with them (Shafer et al. 2012; Maas and Bonomi 2021, 511; Bonomi et al. 2016; Collins and Carmody 2011).

Perceptions of Stalking

Perceptions of stalking can be considered as learned behaviour. Individuals within society will use tools at their disposal, such as daily newspapers, social media and media outlets like TV shows and movies, to explore these unknown aspects of life. Adolescents, more than adults, are susceptible to the influence of the media, friends and video games (Leitz and Theriot 2005). Therefore, it is essential to include Social Learning Theories to explain perceptions of stalking. According to the theory, crime is caused by social forces, such as differential associations (other people's behaviours), modelling (imitating behaviours), differential reinforcement (cost-benefit analysis) and definitions (beliefs and values) (Akers 1973, 27; Fissel et al. 2020, 27; Fox et al. 2011, 41). Although this theory was initially developed to explain offending, it can also be linked to victims. According to Fox et al. (2011), victims can have a similar experience as offenders as 'victims can also learn to adopt beliefs, behaviours, and perceptions that may put them at risk of victimisation' (Fox et al. 2011, 41; Fissel et al. 2020, 28). In Bandura's Social Cognitive Theory from 2001, 'the "psychological matching processes" describe how an observer changes his or her thought patterns, emotional responses, and/or behaviours to match those of another person' (Hoffner and Buchanan 2005, 326, Bandura 2001).

To understand the potential impact stalking in movies can have on the audience, they must consider their age groups. Young children can rely on physical characteristics, and different movie genre makes it easy to identify particular aspects, such as being able to separate cartoon actors from real actors. As children mature, they would be able to separate the appearance of an object and the true nature of the object (Flavell 1986; Shapiro and Chock 2003, 166–167). Older children can perceive real characteristics. For example, the middle group of children may still focus on the physical characteristics and knowledge about different genres. Still, as a part of their development, they begin to understand more sophisticated categories linked to reality. These can, for example, be real events vs those constructed by popular media (Shapiro and Chock 2003, 167). The group with older children has developed an understanding where they can define reality as probable or plausible rather than possible, as younger children would do. However, children's experiences are drivers for this change of understanding of particular areas, as they will use their real-world and television experience to understand complex areas (Austin et al. 1990; Davies 1997; Shapiro and Chock 2003, 167). When reaching adulthood, young adults will have a more complex understanding of reality, making them capable of making a distinction between fiction and fact (Shapiro and Chock 2003, 167; Cohen et al. 1983; Adoni et al. 1984).

Adolescence is linked to the period where young people begin to explore their sexuality and develop an understanding of romantic and sexual relationships. During this period, the adolescent receives information from numerous sources. The formal information derives from school-based sex education and health practitioner programmes. At the same time, the informal sources of information come from parents/guardians, friends, television and movies (Bleakley et al. 2018, 15–16).

Adolescents often turn to mass media and popular media to learn about romantic relationships, how to love/be loved, how to date, and what a romantic relationship looks like. However, the way adolescent and adult relationships are portrayed in popular media does not necessarily give a nuanced picture of these areas—or an understanding of the difference between a legal and illegal pursuit. Movies often portray stereotypical relationships, glamorising crimes, abusive relationships and violence, which can lead adolescents to perceive this behaviour as an accepted love language (Wilson and Maloney 2019, 84; Collins and Carmody 2011).

Young people use the mass media similarly to their learning through communications with friends. Through observational learning, adolescents might adopt the behavioural scripts they see in entertainment material and explicitly choose material that teaches them about relationship behaviours (Bleakley et al. 2018, 16). Suppose a young person believes that persistent pursuit behaviours, romanticised in movies, are evidence of love. In that case, the person might struggle to identify this behaviour as being criminalised in real life. A female viewer might get the impression that if a man persistently pursues her, it is a sign that she is desirable. Therefore, she will consider the pursuit flattering rather than a course for concern. This perception would affect the likelihood of her becoming a victim of stalking in real life if she cannot identify this behaviour in fiction (Lippman 2018).

Key Indicators of Stalking in Movies (Popular Video Streaming Services September 2022)

The following section reviews how direct and indirect stalking is described by using plot keywords, plot synopsis and movie descriptions. These indicators are used to signpost whether the audience is being accurately informed about the level of stalking included in these moves.

Methodology

Based on the literature review above, people of all ages have moved to video streaming services during the Covid-19 pandemic lockdowns and continue using these services. However, it can be problematic to identify stalking elements in movie plots when they are often portrayed positively. Movies like the *Twilight* saga appeal to young people because the story and the characters are known from books and the actors playing these roles (IMDb 2009, 2010, 2012). However, many people would not recognise the stalking plot included in this trilogy as it is covered up with several different storylines—the question is whether adolescents would recognise stalking. Other popular movies, like *Love Actually*, have one straightforward stalking plot and some borderline stalking stories that undercut the central theme of love. This movie is loved across generations. Yet, the plot synopsis on IMDb's website does not mention stalking as a theme.

The research was conducted using the Internet Movie Database or IMDb, a website allowing users to find ratings and reviews on a vast collection of movies and TV shows (IMDb. 2022a). A frequent user of IMDb had compiled their list of the *Best Obsession/Stalker Movies and TV shows*, which was considered for this research. However, this list is mainly outdated as it was compiled in 2016 despite an update in May 2020 (IMDb 2020a). Another list on the IMDb's webpage, the *Best Stalker Movies All Time*, includes more updated material from July 2020 (IMDb 2020b). These two lists only provide a partial understanding of stalking movies assessable in 2022. Still, they do not include movies offered by video streaming services at a particular time. Moreover, how people use video streaming services has changed since the first pandemic lockdown.

Video Streaming Services

The world changed during the pandemic, with people staying in places with nowhere to go and nothing to do. During the Covid-19 pandemic lockdowns, rules and stay-at-home mandates, online learning, and social distancing requirements increased reliance on computer technologies, i.e., screens and the Internet (Nagata et al. 2022). The speciality of online streaming services became apparent as they enabled people to connect and provided a platform for people to communicate online and to be entertained. In nearly all areas of adolescents' lives, screen times went up, and new services and social media sites became a part of everyday life in the chase for entertainment, socialising and education (BBC News 2020; Nagata et al. 2022, 94).

Streaming services such as Netflix, Hulu, Disney+, Apple TV+, NBC's Peacock, and HBO Max have become household names, and global streaming consumption habits have stayed post-pandemic (Jia 2021, 815–816). Covid-19 lockdowns accelerated the demand and subscriber growth in using video streaming services. Not only is a large selection of movies available to the audience but several high-profile cinema movies were released directly on these platforms (Wroan 2021). In 2020, the number of people subscribing to online video streaming services reached 1.1 billion users worldwide. In UK Ofcom's 2021 Media Nations report, the highest gain of viewers during the Covid-19 pandemic was video streaming services, such as Amazon Video and Netflix (Newsflash 2021; Ofcom 2021). According to the UK Ofcom's Media Nation Report 2022, the market plateaued after returning to normality. However, it is predicted that the numbers would decrease slightly due to the cost-of-living crises, i.e., Netflix lost 210,000 subscribers in the UK in the first half of 2022 (Guerilla Scope 2022; Ofcom 2022a, 2022b, 3). In the UK, the subscription to streaming services like Netflix and Disney+ went down by 1%. These services were used by 67% of UK households in the second quarter of 2022. This percentage slightly declined from 68% in the first quarter (Ofcom 2022b, 2). In the UK's Ofcom's Media Use and Attitudes Report 2022, it was stated that children between 3 and 17 years used video-streaming

Table 4.1 Research areas and questions

Number	Research aim	Research question
1	Investigating whether the label provided by Google is consistent with the movie plot, i.e., thriller, romance or both	Are Google's labels of the movies being romantic or trillers consistent with the actual content?
2	Investigating the plot keywords of the selected movies, i.e., stalker, stalking, etc.	Does the list give any indications of stalking in the movies?
3	Investigate the movie descriptions from the IMDb webpage	Does this description indicate whether there is a stalking element in the movie?

services. 78% watch services like Netflix, Amazon Prime Video and Disney+, whereas only 47% watch live TV (Ofcom 2022a, 3, 25).

Research Aims

The research aims to gain insight into how stalking is labelled in popular movies and how portraying stalking positively in movies can affect adolescents' perceptions. To ensure that data is up-to-date and reflects the reality of movie streaming post-pandemic, a systematic review of staking movies was conducted at the beginning of September 2020, where two datasets were gathered to include popular movies on video streaming services. A systematic content data collection and analysis have subsequently been conducted to identify stalking in movies (Table 4.1).

The empirical research methodology is based on systematic secondary data collection using key search terms. The study is conducted online using Google's search engine and the movies displayed on key streaming services, such as Netflix, Amazon Video, Disney+and Apple TV. These video streaming services were selected due to their popularity among adolescents in the post-covid-19 environment. Google search was used systematically to identify the most watched moves within each streaming service. Unfortunately, the services cannot provide the age groups of the viewers as access to the video streaming services is often based on a family subscription. Therefore, it was impossible to identify the movies that mainly appealed to adolescents.

The Datasets

The movies are divided into two datasets: Thriller movies and Romance movies. To progress the research, two distinct keywords were used to ensure consistency across the two datasets (Table 4.2).

Table 4.2 Research keywords and streaming services

Dataset	Search words
Thriller movies	Popular Thriller movies on [Streaming service name]/ Thriller Dramas on [Streaming service name] (Netflix 2022, Amazon Video 2022, Disney Plus 2022, Apple TV 2022)
Romance movies	Popular Romantic movies on [Streaming service name]/ Romantic Dramas on [Streaming service name] (Netflix 2022, Amazon Video 2022, Disney Plus 2022, Apple TV 2022)

Table 4.3 Datasets of popular thriller and romance movies in September 2022

Dataset	The overall number of movies identified from the list
Thrillers	255 movie titles from the four streaming services were investigated
Romance	193 movie titles from the four streaming services were investigated

Table 4.4 Datasets narrowed down based on content analysis of movies in September 2022

Dataset	The final number of stalking movies identified
Triller movies	31 movies from the dataset were considered stalking-related movies
Romance movies	22 movies from the dataset were considered stalking-related movies

Using these keywords, 50 movies from each of these video streaming services were identified and selected. Some titles appeared simultaneously on different streaming services' platforms, and duplicates were excluded from the dataset (Table 4.3).

After collecting the entire dataset, each movie was investigated using IMDb's movie description, the plot keyword list, and the outline of the movie plot (plot synopsis). These are used to give a consistent understanding of key features in the movies that would qualify or disqualify them. This research is based on the legal and academic definitions of stalking to separate the movies into (1) 'clear stalking references' or (2) 'indications of stalking' (Table 4.4).

Labelling the Movies

After labelling the movies from the Google list, the plot is not as clean-cut as it appeared on the streaming lists on Google search. Several movies include both a thriller and a romance element. Figures one (Thriller movies) and two (Romance movies) show how these movies are categorised. In Figure one, 43% of the stalking movies have thriller and romance elements. Figure two (Romance movies) is different, with only 19% of the movies having both plots included (Figs. 4.1 and 4.2).

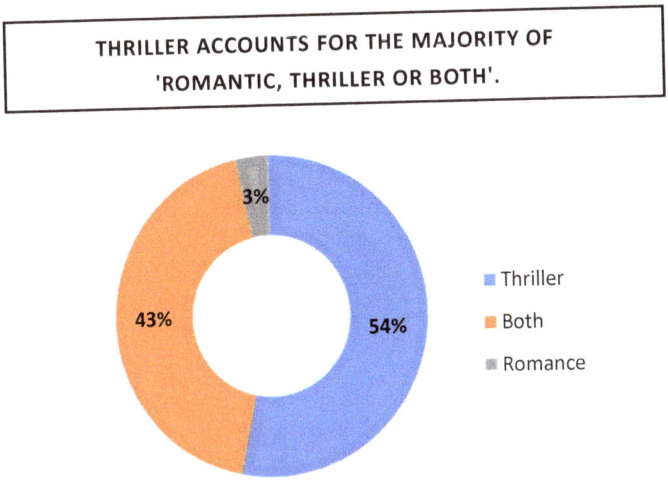

Fig. 4.1 Thriller movies dataset showing how the movies are labelled within each category

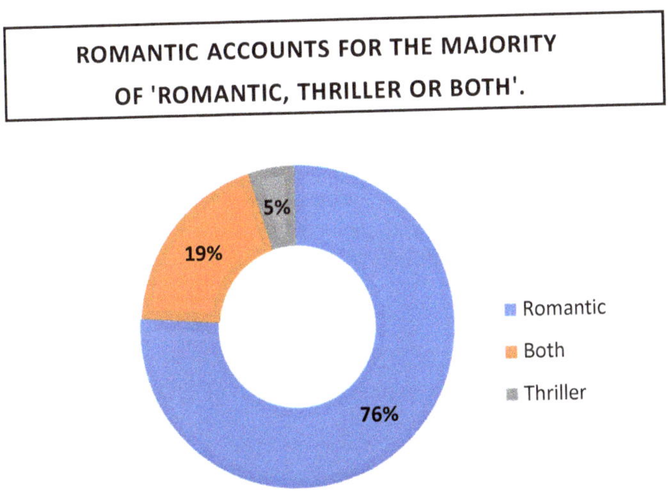

Fig. 4.2 Romance movies dataset showing the movies are labelled within each category

Stalking Movies and Plot Keywords

The film industry has for years stereotyped stalking as being enacted by mentally disturbed people, who often are a stranger or someone seeking revenge—as portrayed in the thrillers. These types are easier to identify than the nice guy who is deeply in love but is not being loved back. A basic plot in stalking movies is when there is no prior relationship between the leading characters. In this scenario, the leading male character persistently tries to get in contact with his love interest—who is not interested. Another theme emerging is stalking cases deriving from pre-existent relations or strangers engaged in unwanted pursuit or harassment, such as horror, slasher or serial killer movies (Spitzberg and Cupach 2007; Sides Schultz et al. 2014, 614) (Fig. 4.3).

There is a significant difference between the keywords uploaded by the audience concerning thriller movies and romance movies. The audience engaging with the outline of the movies on IMDb's website can include keywords describing the plot. According to the data, most movies are not labelled with 'stalking' or 'stalker' keywords or anything similar that can give the audience an impression of what they will watch.

The thriller movies contain plot keywords like: 'Stalker' (five movies); 'stalker, stalking' (five movies); 'stalking' (three movies), and 'none' (17 movies). Although 17 is a high number, there are still 13 movies with plot keywords that can give an understanding of elements included in the movie plot. It also shows that some viewers can identify staking, highlighting this as the plot keyword. The identification of romance movies is not as nuanced in using the keywords. The plot keywords in romance movies are: 'Stalker' (four movies), 'stalking' (zero movies), and none (17 movies) (Figs. 4.4 and 4.5).

Identifying stalking in relation to romance is a particular problem. It is an issue that there is no clear legislative definition of stalking. In particular, when movies do not promote stalking negatively in the storyline, it becomes confusing for the audience. Instead, it is integrated as a part of the romantic pursuit. Stalking romance movies are predominately considered in the realm of a persistent pursuit, which, contrary to thriller movies, is positively regarded as a part of a typical romantic courtship. Adolescent viewers are, therefore, likely to replicate the 'language of love' they identify in the movie and transfer the behaviour to real life (Lippman 2018). Often young people get information about relationships and reality mixed,

	Thriller	Thriller	Romance	Romance	
	No keywords	Keywords (stalking; stalking; stalking and stalker)	No keywords	Keywords (stalking; stalking; stalking and stalker)	
Indication of stalking	12	7	12	0	31
Clear stalking references	5	6	3	5	19
Clear stalking references/ indications of stalking	0	0	1	0	1
	17	13	16	5	51

Fig. 4.3 Movie plot keywords, categories and plot synopsis of the two different datasets

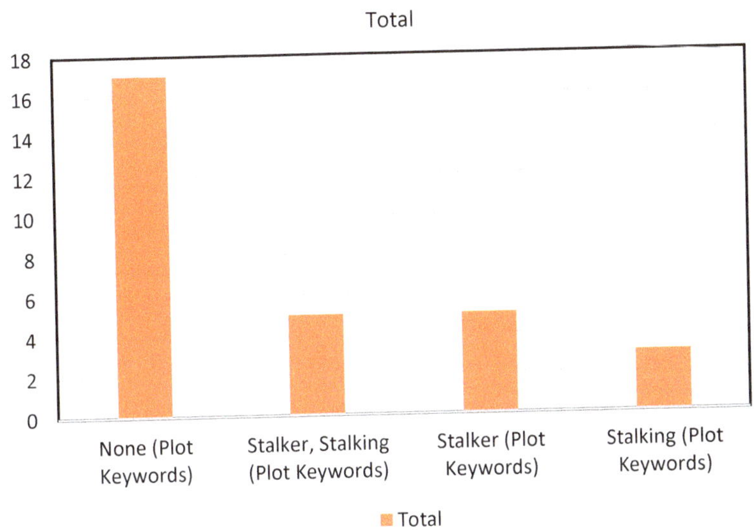

Fig. 4.4 Thriller movies identification of stalker and stalking being a part of the plot (Plot keywords)

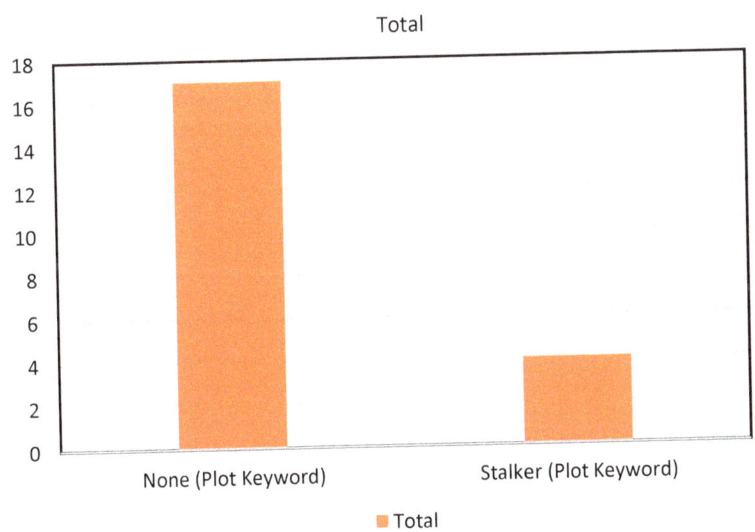

Fig. 4.5 Romance movies identification of stalker and stalking being a part of the plot (Plot keywords)

believing that this combination of love and persistent pursuit is part of a romantic relationship (Wilson and Maloney 2019, 84, Bonomi et al. 2016). To an audience inexperienced in relationships, this can be seen as evidence of true love (Lippman 2018).

Although stalking legislation is new compared to other crime types with more traditional forms of violence, aggression and control, they have still been in place since the 1990s (Sides Schultz et al. 2014, 613). The keywords used on IMDb's web pages demonstrate that it is easier for the audience to identify stalking in thriller movies than in romance movies. The behaviours portrayed as scary are more likely to be classified as stalking, for example, by featuring a man, with a clear psychologically troubled profile or a negatively loaded storyline pursuing a woman who is desperately trying to escape (Lippman 2018). Violence and aggression are often embedded in movies, and a rating system is in place to give a warning to the audience. However, certain forms of stalking violence and aggression are not specified or do receive much attention in popular media.

Stalking References in the Movie Synopsis

In the movie synopsis, the narrative related to stalking, direct and indirect stalking, is more explicit in both datasets compared with the plot keywords. In the thriller category, the different categorisations (thriller, both, romance) are more detailed than the movies that only have the romance plot included. Most of the movies in the Thriller dataset have indications of stalking (11 movies) and explicit stalking references (five movies). In the Romance movie dataset, most movies indicate stalking (10 movies) rather than an apparent stalking reference (five movies). There are many crossovers between the different plot categories in thriller movies. Eight movies containing both elements (thriller and romance) have indications of stalking, and five movies have an apparent stalking reference. In the Romance dataset, four movies include both categories (thriller and romance), where two movies had indications of stalking, and two movies had clear stalking references (Figs. 4.6 and 4.7).

The marketing of movies is based on a revenue-generating model. Popular media invest in different aspects of the process, such as cultivating fandom, identification and para-social relationships. Parts of the plots are created in a certain way to tap into the audience's preferences, experiences and likes. Therefore, the plot description contains vague references to the content with catchwords to gain the audience's attention without outlining the plot. This vagueness creates obstacles for the audience to assess the plot before watching the movie. The perceived realism plays into the audiences' level of knowledge, such as the familiarity with the typicality, events, emotions, personalities and actions (Shapiro and Chock 2003, 165). Stalking might not be the main storyline in the movie. Often there is a parallel or underlying story that contains stalking or links to stalking, but the main storyline follows another plot. By contrast, there might be a main stalking story in the movie, but other side stories in the scripts blur the identification or remove

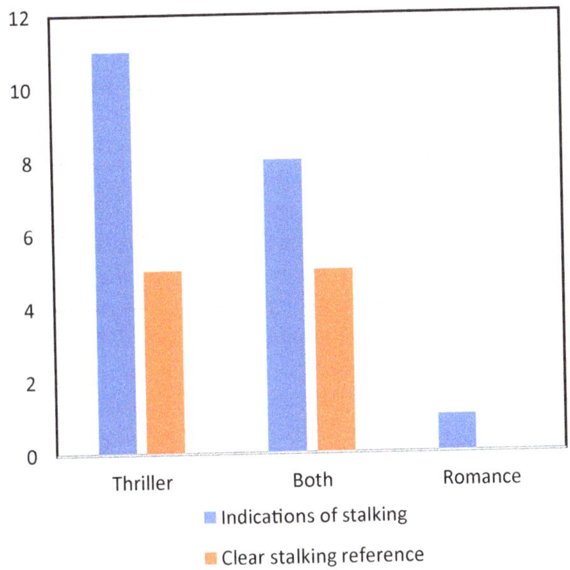

Fig. 4.6 Thriller movie dataset identification of the plot and the stalking level in the movie synopsis

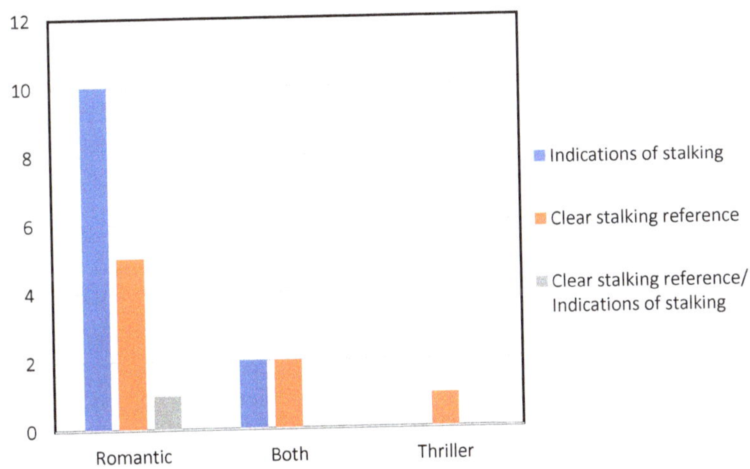

Fig. 4.7 Romance movie dataset identification of the plot and the stalking level in the movie synopsis

the focus from stalking. Therefore, these entangled stories can make interpreting the plots in the two datasets challenging, leaving some inconsistencies between the plot keywords and the synopsis (Thriller and Romance movies). The identification is not defined as an attitude, an emotion or a perception. Instead, it is a process linked to an increasing loss of self-awareness and the temporary replacement, where the viewer is emotionally and cognitively related to the character in the movie (Cohen 2001, 251, Hoffner and Buchanan 2005).

IMDb's Movie Descriptions

The plot of a typical romance movie shows 'the hero' (leading male character) is a nice guy that does not necessarily fit into the stereotypical masculine movie male. For different reasons, he has not found love, but one day he meets the perfect woman, is instantly fascinated by her and falls in love. Yet, there is a minor issue, the hero's love interest does not return these feelings. This setback does not stop the hero. Instead of giving up, he will do whatever is needed to win this woman. He might spy on her, prester her, and manipulate her until she sees the light (Stevens 2022). This scenario fits into legal stalking definitions that have developed since the criminalisation in the 1990s. The stalking myths are based on misconceptions that undermine the actual seriousness of stalking in real life. There is a notion that the alleged stalking victims are people playing hard to get, and they will change their minds due to the persistent pursuit or that the seriousness of the offence is downscaled. It also plays into the perception that stalking would stop if the victim explicitly told her/his stalker that they were not interested in a romantic relationship (Angyal 2016; Lippman 2018, 397, Haime 2020a). For example, in one of the side stories in *Crazy, Stupid, Love* (2011), the 13-years old character declares his love to his babysitter. This declaration of love happened even after the female love interest asked him in writing to stop this behaviour. After the teenage boy twice publicly humiliated her in front of her classmate, she caved in. She then gives him nude photos to tide him over until he is old enough to date her (Angyal 2016; IMDb 2011; Lippman 2018, 397) (Table 4.5).

The selection of movies in table five shows a sample of the movies from the Thriller dataset. Compared to the Romance dataset below, these IMDb descriptions contain more precise indications of an underlying stalking plot. *Sleeping with the Enemy* has a straightforward stalking plot in the description. The other movie descriptions indicate an underlying and unsettling plot likely to contain stalking. The precise identification can be linked to how stalking and stalkers are understood by the portrait of stalking as being largely aggressive and threatening, despite most stalking victims being subjected to physical violence and direct threats (McKeon et al. 2014, 292). Thrillers are similar to horror movies where it is much easier to identify the stalker when the plot is exaggerated and given beforehand due to the genre, i.e., movies like *Scream* where the plot is apparent 'the stalk-and-slash-them-up' franchise (Lee 2020; IMDb 2022a, 2022b) (Table 4.6).

This selection of movies from the Romance list shows a variety of storylines from IMDb's descriptions of the movies. Compared to the outline above, the descriptions and links to stalking are vaguer. The movies *Through my Windows* and *The Boy Next Door* outline indicate that something dangerous might happen, such as persistent pursuit and unwanted attention. It is not a surprise that adolescents

Table 4.5 IMDb descriptions of movie plots (Thriller movies)

Movie	IMDb description
Sleeping with the Enemy (1991)	*"A young woman fakes her own death in an attempt to escape her nightmarish marriage, but discovers it is impossible to elude her controlling husband"* (IMDb 1991)
One Hour Photo (2002)	*"A mentally unstable photo developer targets an upper middle-class family after his obsession with them becomes more sick and disturbing than any of them could imagine"* (IMDb 2002)
Enduring Love (2004)	*"Two strangers become connected by a tragedy, yet one dangerously feels that the connection goes much deeper than the other is willing to admit"* (IMDb 2004)
The Girl on the Train (2016)	*"A divorcee becomes entangled in a missing persons investigation that promises to send shockwaves throughout her life"* (IMDb 2016)
Greta (2018)	*"A young woman befriends a lonely widow who's harboring a dark and deadly agenda toward her"* (IMDb 2018)
The Woman in the Window (2021)	*"An agoraphobic woman living alone in New York begins spying on her new neighbors, only to witness a disturbing act of violence"* (IMDb 2021)

Note IMDb's Outline of Thriller Movie Plots (TM2022)

would struggle to understand the key elements included in stalking legislation to be able to identify stalking behaviour. Stalking is a crime type where troubling and annoying behaviour can quickly escalate into criminal activities with a significant impact on the victim (Campbell and Moore 2011, 507). The main characters fall in love in the *Twilight* sage and the *Fifty Shades of Grey* trilogy. Yet, by the movie's end, the female character has accepted different forms of violence and abusive behaviours to appease her partner (Wilson and Maloney 2019, 84). These movies can give adolescents a wrongful impression of stalking, which later can negatively impact their future dating relationships. Equally, by not being able to separate legal and illegal pursuits, the movies spread a narrative that normalises these behaviours (Collins and Carmody 2011; Bonomi et al. 2014).

In movies, the stalking (pursuit) often pays off, as the object of the stalker's affection realises that they are meant to be together, and the stalker's persistence is perceived as a positive indication (Haime 2020a, 2020b). Due to how popular media portrays romantic stalking, it becomes problematic for the viewers to understand what stalking is and what these movies try to show. It is essential to ascertain how interpersonal aggressions are represented and the potential impact of the agenda-setting impact that derives from these movies when there is an increase in screen hours among adolescence due to the widespread use of video streaming services' subscriptions (Schultz et al. 2014, 625–616).

Table 4.6 IMDb descriptions of movie plots (Romance movies)

Movie	IMDb description
The Bodyguard (1992)	*"A former Secret Service agent takes on the job of bodyguard to an R&B singer, whose lifestyle is most unlike a President's"* (IMDb 1992)
Love Actually (2003)	*"Follows the lives of eight very different couples in dealing with their love lives in various loosely interrelated tales all set during a frantic month before Christmas in London, England"* (IMDb 2003)
Twilight (2008):	*"When Bella Swan moves to a small town in the Pacific Northwest, she falls in love with Edward Cullen, a mysterious classmate who reveals himself to be a 108-year-old vampire"* (IMDb 2008).
Crazy, Stupid, Love (2011):	*"A middle-aged husband's life changes dramatically when his wife asks him for a divorce. He seeks to rediscover his manhood with the help of a newfound friend, Jacob, learning to pick up girls at bars"* (IMDb 2011).
Fifty Shades of Grey (2015):	*"Literature student Anastasia Steele's life changes forever when she meets handsome, yet tormented, billionaire Christian Grey"* (IMDb 2015).
The Boy Next Door (2015)	*"A woman, separated from her unfaithful husband, falls for a younger man who has moved in next door, but their torrid affair soon takes a dangerous turn"* (IMDb 2015)
West Side Story (2021):	*"An adaptation of the 1957 musical, West Side Story explores forbidden love and the rivalry between the Jets and the Sharks, two teenage street gangs of different ethnic backgrounds"* (IMDb 2021).
Through My Window (2022):	*"Raquel's longtime crush on her next-door neighbor turns into something more when he starts developing feelings for her, despite his family's objections"* (IMDb 2022).

Note IMDb's Outline of Romance Movie Plots (RM2022)

Closing Remarks and Considerations

Adolescents are particularly vulnerable to the influence of popular movies. During this phase of life, these young people will search for information from various sources about life, relationships and behaviours. Movies are one informal source, and the question is whether adolescents can identify stalking behaviours in real life when popular movies are romanticising persistent pursuit and unwanted attention. With constant access to movies on video streaming services, there is a need to consider whether stalking plots in movies can negatively affect young people. Particular plots in popular media should be acknowledged, such as the dynamic between victim and perpetrator, motivations for the stalking behaviour and the possibility of escalating violence in stalking. When adolescents learn about relationships and themselves as a part of their personal development, they can quickly gain the impression from movies that stalking behaviour is expected in a normal romantic relationship. Schultz, Moore and Spitzberg already highlighted in 2014 that the movie audience, particularly young people, might use movies to develop an understanding of relationships and interpersonal behaviour. Therefore, stalking portrayed might normalise certain behaviours (Schultz et al. 2014). Ybarra et al. (2017) research into stalking-like behaviour in adolescence is not directly related to movies and how these are being labelled. However, stalking among young people is increasing and stalking behaviour are perpetrated by young adolescents younger than pre-college age. This research also flags the benefits of early intervention covering a broad spectrum of behaviours and skills (Ybarra et al. 2017). Wilson and Maloney (2019) outline how confusing the representation of stalking in movies is for young adolescents who are learning how to love, be loved, date and be in a romantic relationship. However, the representation in media shows a different reality where the message of love is mixed with violence (Wilson and Maloney 2019). This argument is also supported by Maas and Bonomi (2021). More research is needed into how movies impact adolescents understanding of relationships and stalking behaviour to identify whether these are normalised. Popular movies like *Beauty and the Beast*, *Twilight* and *Fifty Shades of Grey* have shown that this behaviour is okay when the main characters fall happily in love by the end. Yet, questions need to be asked about how this stalking behaviour can impact adolescents during their young and adult years (Wilson and Maloney 2019; Maas and Bonomi 2021).

The way movies outline the plots have been displayed in this chapter, where the empirical research proves that the audience is not given any warnings about stalking plots and storylines. Adolescents are at a stage where they seek information about relationships, and they are increasingly using popular media to inform them. Since the Covid-19 pandemic, screen time has increased, and young people watch more movies unsupervised online. The movie industry and websites like IMDb should reconsider how they inform the audiences about the plots and take responsibility for providing detailed descriptions to guide their audience. One step forward is introducing a stalking rating system similar to the rating system developed by the Motion Picture Association. This system provides parents with ratings about movies appropriate for various age groups. This rating system would be a helpful tool for this age group, rather than relying on inconsistent reviews supplied by movie viewers. Finally, more research should be conducted into the adolescents' understanding of stalking definitions and the developmental and behavioural impact these movies have on the audience.

Lippmann's (2018) study into movies with romantic or thriller using stimuli showed a difference in incitement between romantic movies (persistent pursuit conditions) compared to the movies (scary persistent pursuit conditions). Therefore, women who are pursued respond differently to these two concepts (Lippman 2018). The data collected in this chapter shows similarities with Schultz, Moore and Spietzberg's findings from 2013. Schultz et al. (2014) highlighted issues with using the IMDb database in investigating stalking. The researchers argue that the public perceptions of stalking and the user-generated keywords used in the system may cause a disconnect between stalking research and media representation. Schultz, Moore and Spitzberg also identified a significant absence of 'stalking' keywords and descriptions in the movie narratives and plot synopsis. It is unclear whether this is because the audience cannot define stalking or is left out as the description could influence viewers previously affected by stalking (Schultz et al. 2014). This area opens up more up-to-date research as there is a significant knowledge gap. Although this research into the IMDb database is in line with previous research, primary research is needed to understand the impact of these descriptions and plot synopsis on the adolescent audience.

Discussion Questions

- How important is the role of 'persistent pursuit' in defining stalking?
- Stalking can affect people significantly; why are adolescents considered particularly vulnerable to stalking plots in movies?
- Do you think the movie industry does enough to warn the audience about the stalking plot in some movies? Do you believe it is easier to recognise stalking in thriller movies than in romance movies?

Bibliography

Adoni, H., A. A. Cohen, and S. Mane. 1984. Social Reality and Television News: Perceptual Dimensions of Social Conflicts in Selected Life Areas. *Journal of Broadcasting* 28 (1): 33–49. https://doi.org/10.1080/08838158409386513.

Akers, Ronald. L. 1973. *Deviant Behaviour—A Social Learning Approach*. Belmont: Wadsworth Publishing.

Amazon Video. 2022a. Popular Romantic Films on Amazon Video/Romantic Dramas on Amazon Video. Google, 05 09. https://www.google.com/search?rlz=1C1GCEA_enGB998GB998&sxsrf=ALiCzsYJ8Z0XboYNpfmjO3Gg4T6_EOfX7Q:1662398357188&q=Amazon+Prime+romantic+movies&sa=X&ved=2ahUKEwjyrbi8lP75AhWOgVwKHUPGAnwQ1QJ6BAhQEAE&biw=1920&bih=937&dpr=1#wxpd=:true. Accessed 30 Oct 2022.

———. 2022b. Popular Thrillers on Amazon Video/Thriller Dramas on Amazon Video. Google, 06 09. https://www.google.com/search?q=thriller+movies+on+Amazon+Video&rlz=1C1GCEA_enGB998GB998&sxsrf=ALiCzsaEt0Q_a4rXXK6vpD4v47ILf1cbFw%3A1662462369660&ei=oSkXY979J5frgQad0b6AAQ&ved=0ahUKEwie0vv3goD6AhWXdcAKHZ2oDxAQ4dUDCA4&uact=5&oq=thriller+movies+on+Amazon+Vi. Accessed 30 Oct 2022.

Angyal, Chloe. 2016. Romantic Comedies Teach Women That Stalking Is A Compliment. 28 01. https://www.huffingtonpost.co.uk/entry/romantic-comedies-teach-women-that-stalking-is-a-compliment_n_56a8fa1fe4b0f7179928a17d. Accessed 22 Aug 2022

Apple TV. 2022a. Popular Romantic Films on Apple TV/Romantic Dramas on Apple TV. Google, 05 09. https://www.google.com/search?q=Apple%2B++romantic+movies&rlz=1C1GCEA_enGB998GB998&biw=1920&bih=937&sxsrf=ALiCzsaxPPHlfRaluudcZRBRdU5rsWXZNg%3A1662399889915&ei=kTUWY-7FN6PB8gLUp7fYCg&ved=0ahUKEwiu0qaXmv75AhWjoFwKHdTTDasQ4dUDCA4&uact=5&oq=Apple%2B++romanti. Accessed 30 Oct 2022.

———. 2022b. Popular Thrillers on Apple TV/Thriller Drama on Apple TV. Google, 06 09. https://www.google.com/search?q=thriller+movies+on+Apple+TV&rlz=1C1GCEA_enGB998GB998&sxsrf=ALiCzsaJqYPUyOt3ncpkhH36vbpBRaIARQ%3A1662472353194&ei=oVAXY8G6C5SA8gK1_ZzAAw&ved=0ahUKEwiBj76QqID6AhUUgFwKHbU-BzgQ4dUDCA4&uact=5&oq=thriller+movies+on+Apple+TV&gs_l. Accessed 30 Oct 2022.

Austin, E. W., D. F. Roberts, and C. I. Nass. 1990. Influences of Family Communication on Children's Television-interpretation. *Communication Research* 17 (4): 545–564. https://doi.org/10.1177/009365090017004008.

Bandura, A. 2001. Social Cognitive Theory of Mass Communication. *Media Psychology* 3 (3): 265–299. https://doi.org/10.1207/S1532785XMEP0303_03.

BBC News. 2020. TV Watching and Online Streaming Surge During Lockdown. 05 08, August 5.

Birch, P., J. L. Ireland, and N. Ninaus. 2018. Treating Stalking Behavour: A Framework for Understanding Process Components. In *The Routledge International Handbook of Human Aggression: Current Issues and Perspectives*, by Jane L. Ireland, Philip Birch and Carol A. Ireland, 194–204. Abingdon: Routledge.

Blaauw, E., F. Winkel, W. Winkel, E. Arensman, L. Sheridenand, and A. Freeve. 2002. The Toll of Stalking: The Relationship Between Features of Stalking and Psychopathology of Victims. *Journal of Interpersonal Violence* 17(1): 50–63. https://doi.org/10.1177/088626050201700 1004

Bleakley, A., A. Khurana, M. Hennessy, and M. Ellithorpe. 2018. How Patterns of Learning About Sexual Information Among Adolescents Are Related to Sexual Behaviors. *Perspectives on Sexual and Reproductive Health* 50 (1): 15–23. https://doi.org/10.1363/psrh.12053.

Boehnlein, T., J. Kretschmar, W. Regooeczi, and J. Smialek. 2020. Responding to Stalking Victims: Perceptions, Barriers, and Directions for Future Research. *Journal of Family Violence* 36 (7): 755–768. https://doi.org/10.1007/s10896-020-00147-3.

Bonomi, A. E., J. M. Nemeth, L. E. Altenburger, M. L. Anderson, A. Snyder, and I. Dotto. 2014. Fiction or Not? Fifty Shades Is Associated with Health Risks in Adolescent and Young Adult Females. *Journal of Women's Health* 23 (9): 720–728. https://doi.org/10.1089/jwh.2014.4782.

Bonomi, A. E., E. M. Nichols, C. L. Carotta, Y. Kiuchi, and S. Perry. 2016. Young Women's Perceptions of the Relationship in Fifty Shades of Grey. *Journal of Women's Health* 25 (2): 139–148. https://doi.org/10.1089/jwh.2015.5318.

Breiding, M. J., J. Chen, and M. C. Black. 2014. Intimate Partner Violence in the United States—2010. CDC, National Centre for Injury Prevention and Control Centres for Disease Control and Prevention, Atlanta, 1–96. https://stacks.cdc.gov/view/cdc/21961#tabs-2. Accessed 8 Aug 2022.

Busselle, R., and H. Bilandzic. 2008. Fictionality and Perceived Realism in Experiencing Stories: A Model of Narrative Comprehension and Engagement. *Communication Theory* 18 (2): 255–280. https://doi.org/10.1111/j.1468-2885.2008.00322.x.

Campbell, J., and R. Moore. 2011. Self-perceptions of Stalking Victimisation and Impacts on Victim Reporting. *Police Practice and Research* 12 (6): 506–517. https://doi.org/10.1080/15614263.2011.607668?needAccess=true.

CoE. 2011. Council of Europe Convention on Preventing and Combating Violence Against Women and Domestic Violence. Vers. 210. CoE. 11 05. https://rm.coe.int/168008482e. Accessed 22 Aug 2022.

———. Istanbul Convention Factsheet. CoE. https://rm.coe.int/istanbul-convention-factsheet/168078ec5c. Accessed 22 Aug 2022.

———. 2019. Stalking. Safer from Fear. Safer from Violence. Convention on Preventing and Combatting Violence against Women and Domestic Violence (Istanbul Convention). https://rm.coe.int/stalking-istanbul-convention-web-a5/1680925867. Accessed 22 Aug 2022.

Cohen, A. A., H. Adoni, and G. Drori. 1983. Adolescents' Perceptions of Social Conflicts in Television News and Social Reality. *Human Communication Research* 10 (2): 203–225. https://doi.org/10.1111/j.1468-2958.1983.tb00011.x.

Cohen, J. 2001. Defining Identification: A Theoretical Look at the Identification of Audiences with Media Characters. *Mass Communication & Society* 4 (3): 245–264. https://www.tandfonline.com/doi/abs/10.1207/S15327825MCS0403_01.

Collins, V. E., and D. C. Carmody. 2011. Deadly Love: Images of Dating Violence in the Twilight Saga. *Affilia* 26 (4): 382–394. https://doi.org/10.1177/0886109911428425.

CPS. 2018. Stalking and Harassment. 23 05. https://www.cps.gov.uk/legal-guidance/stalking-and-harassment. Accessed 22 Aug 2022.

———. 2022. Social Media and Other Electronic Communications. https://www.cps.gov.uk/legal-guidance/social-media-and-other-electronic-communications. Accessed 12 Jan 2022.

Davies, Máire Messenger. 1997. *Fake, Fact, and Fantasy: Children's Interpretations of Television Reality*. Abingdon: Routledge.

Davis, K. E., A. L. Coker, and M. Sanderson. 2002. Physical and Mental Health Effects of Being Stalked for Men and Women. *Violence and Victims* 17 (4): 429–443. https://doi.org/10.1891/vivi.17.4.429.33682.

Disney Plus. 2022a. Popular Romantic Films on Disney Plus/Romantic Dramas on Disney Plus. Google, 05 10. https://www.google.com/search?q=Disney%2B++romantic+movies&rlz=1C1GCEA_enGB998GB998&biw=1920&bih=937&sxsrf=ALiCzsZ1pnAQ4JnussbeZiupTtbT_RGu9A%3A1662399179312&ei=yzIWY-nVEo2TgQax-KKABg&ved=0ahUKEwip57rEl_75AhWNScAKHTG8CGAQ4dUDCA4&uact=5&oq=Disney%2B++roman. Accessed 30 Oct 2022.

———. 2022b. Popular Thrillers on Disney Plus/Thriller Drama on Disney Plus. Google, 06 09. https://www.google.com/search?q=thriller+movies+on+disney+plus&rlz=1C1GCEA_enGB998GB998&sxsrf=ALiCzsaxyg-kLwzGu8NUR5mw-k1e7OXPcg%3A1662470271602&ei=f0gXY4umJJaAhbIP8ue5kA4&oq=thriller+movies+on+Disney+&gs_lcp=Cgdnd3Mtd2l6EAEYADIFCAAQgAQyBQgAEIAEMgYIABAeEB. Accessed 30 Oct 2022.

Dressing, H., C. Kuehner, and P. Bass. 2006. The Epidemiology and Characteristics of Stalking. *Current Opinion in Psychiatry* 19 (4): 395–399. https://doi.org/10.1097/01.yco.0000228760.95237.f5.

DuMonthier, A., M. Dusenbery, and S. Gonzalez. 2017. Intersections of Stalking and Economic Security. Briefing paper, Institute for Women's Policy Research, 1–11. https://www.ywca.org/wp-content/uploads/B365-STALKING_BRIEFING_PAPER.pdf. Accessed 7 November 2022.

Eterovic-Soric, B., K. R. Chooo, H. Ashman, and S. Mubarak. 2017. Stalking the Stalkers—Detecting and Deterring Stalking Behaviours Using Technology: A Review. *Computers & Security* 70: 278–289. https://doi.org/10.1016/j.cose.2017.06.008.

Fissel, E. R., B. R. Reyns, and B. S. Fisher. 2020. Stalking and Cyberstalking Vicitimization Research: Taking Stock of Key Conceptual, Definitional, Prevalence and Theoretical Issues. In *Psycho-Criminological Approaches to Stalking Behavior*: The International Perspective, by H. C. Chan and L. L. Sheridan. Hoboken: Wiley.

Flavell, J. H. 1986. Development of Children's Knowledge About the Appearance-reality Distinction. *American Psychologist* 41 (4): 418–425. https://doi.org/10.1037/0003-066X.41.4.418.

Fox, K. A., M. R. Nobles, and R. L. Akers. 2011. Is Stalking a Learned Phenomenon. An Empirical Test of Social Learning Theory. *Journal of Criminal Justice* 39 (1): 39–47. https://pdf.sciencedirectassets.com/271758/1-s2.0-S0047235210X00083/1-s2.0-S0047235210001911/main.pdf?X-Amz-Security-Token=IQoJb3JpZ2luX2VjEAIaCXVzLWVhc3QtMSJIMEYCIQDQnM7DuexGjBFFIMksLkKfuzbygN3gb1ZbpEu%2F5M83ugIhAO70M89p9vTm14SE8pL39tYSAYprmU6V%2BGHZmdH5. Accessed 22 Aug 2022.

Geistman, James, B. Smith, E. G. Lambert, and T. Cluse-Tolar. 2012. What to Do About Stalking: A Preliminary Study of How Stalking Victims Responded to Stalking and Their Perceptions of the Effectives of These Actions. *Criminal Justice Studies* 26 (1): 43–66. https://doi.org/10.1080/1478601X.2012.712534.

GovInfo. 1996. 18 US Code Title 2261A. https://www.govinfo.gov/content/pkg/USCODE-2013-title18/pdf/USCODE-2013-title18-partI-chap110A-sec2261A.pdf. Accessed 21 Aug 2022.

GOV.UK. 2022. 2 Years of COVID-19 on GOV.UK. 25 07. https://gds.blog.gov.uk/2022/07/25/2-years-of-covid-19-on-gov-uk/. Accessed 30 Oct 2022.

Guerilla Scope. 2022. Ofcom Media Nations 2022 Report: Key Takeaways. 30 08. https://www.guerillascope.co.uk/ofcom-media-nations-2022-report-key-takeaways/. Accessed 21 Aug 2022.

Haime, J. 2020a. Our Favorite Television Characters Are Still Stalkers. 16 01. https://www.unh.edu/unhtoday/2020/01/our-favorite-television-characters-are-still-stalkers. Accessed 22 Aug 2022.

———. 2020b. This Is Not Romantic. 16 01. https://www.unh.edu/unhtoday/2020/01/our-favorite-television-characters-are-still-stalkers. Accessed 4 Nov 2022.

Hayes, Sharon. 2014. *Sex, Love and Abuse: Discourses on Domestic Violence*. London: Palgrave Macmillan.
Hoffner, C., and M. Buchanan. 2005. Young Adults' Wishful Identification with Television Characters: The Role of Perceived Similarity and Character Attributes. *Media Psychology* 7 (4): 325–351. https://doi.org/10.1207/S1532785XMEP0704_2?needAccess=true.
Holin, Clive R. 2016. Sexual Violence. In *The Psychology of Interpersonal Violence*, 1st Edition, 119–146. New York: Wiley Blackwell
IMDb. 1987. Fatal Attraction. https://www.imdb.com/title/tt0093010/. Accessed 22 Aug 2022.
———. 1989. Say Anything. https://www.imdb.com/title/tt0098258/. Accessed 23 Aug 2022.
———. 1990. Pacific Heights. https://www.imdb.com/title/tt0100318/. Accessed 22 Aug 2022.
———. 1991. Sleeping with the Enemy. https://www.imdb.com/title/tt0102945/. Accessed 22 Aug 2022.
———. 1992a. Single White Female. https://www.imdb.com/title/tt0105414/. Accessed 22 Aug 2022.
———. 1992b. The Bodyguard. https://www.imdb.com/title/tt0103855/?ref_=fn_al_tt_2. Accessed 5 Sep 2022.
———. 1996. Fear. https://www.imdb.com/title/tt0116287/. Accessed 22 Aug 2022.
———. 2002. One Hour Photo. https://www.imdb.com/list/ls049332328/. Accessed 5 Sep 2022.
———. 2003. Love actually. https://www.imdb.com/title/tt0314331/. Accessed 22 Aug 2022.
———. 2004a. The Notebook. https://www.imdb.com/title/tt0332280/. Accessed 23 Aug 2022.
———. 2004b. Enduring Love. https://www.imdb.com/title/tt0375735/?ref_=fn_al_tt_1. Accessed 5 Sep 2022.
———. 2008. Twilight. https://www.imdb.com/title/tt1099212/. Accessed 5 Sep 2022.
———. 2009. The Twilight Saga: New Moon. https://www.imdb.com/title/tt1259571/. Accessed 23 Sep 2022.
———. 2010. The Twilight Saga: Eclipse. https://www.imdb.com/title/tt1325004/?ref_=tt_sims_tt_i_1. Accessed 23 Aug 2022.
———. 2011. Crazy, Stupid, Love. https://www.imdb.com/title/tt1570728/. Accessed 5 Sep 2022.
———. 2012. The Twilight Saga: Breaking Dawn—Part 2. https://www.imdb.com/title/tt1673434/. Accessed 23 Aug 2022.
———. 2015a. Fifty Shades of Grey. https://www.imdb.com/title/tt2322441/. Accessed 5 Sep 2022.
———. 2015b. The Boy Next Door. https://www.imdb.com/title/tt3181822/?ref_=fn_al_tt_1. Accessed 5 Sep 2022.
———. 2016a. Stranger Things. https://www.imdb.com/title/tt4574334/. Accessed 22 Aug 2022.
———. 2016b. The Girl on the Train. https://www.imdb.com/title/tt3631112/?ref_=fn_al_tt_1. Accessed 5 Sep 2022.
———. 2017. Fifty Shades Darker. https://www.imdb.com/title/tt4465564/. Accessed 23 Aug 2022.
———. 2018a. Fifty Shades Freed. https://www.imdb.com/title/tt4477536/. Accessed 22 Aug 2022.
———. 2018b. You. https://www.imdb.com/title/tt7335184/. Accessed 22 Aug 2022.
———. 2018c. Greta. https://www.imdb.com/title/tt2639336/?ref_=nv_sr_srsg_6. Accessed 5 Sep 2022.
———. 2020a. Stalker/Obsession Movies. 29 05. https://www.imdb.com/list/ls063469247/. Accessed 30 Oct 2022.
———. 2020b. Best Stalker Movies All Times. 27 07. https://www.imdb.com/list/ls085200305/. Accessed 30 Oct 2022.
———. 2021a. The Woman in the Window. https://www.imdb.com/title/tt6111574/?ref_=nv_sr_srsg_2. Accessed 5 Sep 2022.
———. 2021b. West Side Story. https://www.imdb.com/title/tt3581652/?ref_=ttpl_pl_tt. Accessed 5 Sep 2022.
———. 2022a. Through My Window.https://www.imdb.com/title/tt14463484/?ref_=nv_sr_srsg_0. Accessed 5 Sep 2022.

———. 2022b. Scream. https://www.imdb.com/title/tt11245972/?ref_=fn_al_tt_1. Accessed 1 Nov 2022.

Jia, Y. 2021. The Streaming Service Under Pandemic with the Example of Performance of Disney+. Edited by The 2021 International Conference on Social Development and Media Communication (SDMC 2021). *Advances in Social Science, Education and Humanities Research.* Atlantis Press. 815–818. https://www.atlantis-press.com/article/125968448.pdf. Accessed 5 Nov 2022.

Juarez, Paul D. 2019. Screening for Violent Tendencies in Adolescents. In *Adolescent Health Screening: An Update in the Age of Big Data.* Amsterdam, The Netherlands: Elsevier.

Kamphuis, J. H., P. M. G. Emmelkamp, and A. Bartak. 2003. Individual Differences in Post-traumatic Stress Following Post-intimate Stalking: Stalking Severity and Psychosocial Variables. *British Journal of Clinical Psychology* 42 (2): 145–156. https://doi.org/10.1348/014466503321903562?saml_referrer.

Lavrogna, Anita. 2020. *Cybercrimes. Critical Issues in a Global Context.* 1. London: Macmillan.

Lee, Benjamin. 2020. Look Who's Stalking: How the Slasher Movie Screamed Its Way Back. *The Guardian.* October 20.

Legislation.gov.uk. 1997. Protection from Harassment Act 1997. https://www.legislation.gov.uk/ukpga/1997/40/contents. Accessed 22 Aug 2022.

———. 2012. Protection of Freedoms Act 2012. https://www.legislation.gov.uk/ukpga/2012/9/part/7/crossheading/stalking/enacted. Accessed 22 Aug 2022.

Leitz. M. A., and M. T. Theriot. (2005) Adolescent Stalking. *Journal of Evidence-Based Social Work*, 2: 3–4, 97–112. https://doi.org/10.1300/J394v02n03_07

Liez, S. 2021. 'Stalking for Love' Needs to Stop. 17 09. https://pittnews.com/article/166977/opinions/opinion-stalking-for-love-needs-to-stop/. Accessed 21 Aug 2022.

Lippman, J. R. 2018. I Did It Because I Never Stopped Loving You: The Effects of Media Portrayals of Persistent Pursuit on Beliefs About Stalking. *Communication Research* 45 (3): 394–421. https://doi.org/10.1177/0093650215570653.

Logan T. K., L. Shannon, C. Cole, and J. Swanberg. 2007. Partner Stalking and Implications for Women's Employment. *Journal of Interpersonal Violence* 22 (3): 268–291. https://doi.org/10.1177/0886260506295380.

Logan, T. K., and R. Walker. 2017. Stalking: A Multidimensional Framework for Assessment and Safety Planning. *Trauma, Violence and Abuse* 18 (2): 200–222. https://doi.org/10.1177/1524838015603210.

Maas, M. K., and A. E. Bonomi. 2021. Love Hurts? Identifying Abuse in the Virgin-Beast Trope of Popular Romantic Fiction. *Journal of Family Violence* 36 (1): 511–522. https://link.springer.com/content/pdf/https://doi.org/10.1007/s10896-020-00206-9.pdf.

McKeon, B., T. E. McEwan, and S. Luebbers. 2014. "It's Not Really Stalking If You Know the Person": Measuring Community Attitudes That Normalise, Justify and Minimise Stalking. *Psychiatry, Psychology and Law* 22 (2): 291–306. https://www.tandfonline.com/doi/pdf/https://doi.org/10.1080/13218719.2014.945637?needAccess=true.

Messing, J., M. Bagwell-Gray, M. L. Brown, A. Kappas, and A. Durfee. 2020. Intersections of Stalking and Technology-based Abuse: Emerging Definitions, Conceptualisation, and Measurement. *Journal of Family Violence* 35 (7): 693–704. https://doi.org/10.1007/s10896-019-00114-7

Miller, L. 2012. Stalking: Patterns, Motives and Intervention Strategies. *Aggression and Violent Behaviour* 17 (6): 495–506. https://doi.org/10.1016/j.avb.2012.07.001

Morewitz, S. J. 2003. The Impact of Stalking. In: *Stalking and Violence: New Patterns of Trauma and Obsession.* Springer, Boston, MA. https://doi.org/10.1007/0-306-47943-5_4

Mullen, P. E., R. Mackenzie, J. R. Ogloff, M. Pathe´, T. McEwan, and R. Purcell, 2006. Assessing and Managing the Risks in the Stalking Situation. *Journal of the American Academy of Psychiatry and the Law Online* 34 (4): 439–450. https://citeseerx.ist.psu.edu/document?repid=rep1&type=pdf&doi=5c71605fa0b2cbb0a0fbe38ec6c7c9c96208b944. Accessed 12 Jan 2022.

Mullen, P. E., M. Pathé, and R. Purcell. 2001. Stalking: New Constructions of Human Behaviour. *Australian and New Zealand Journal of Psychiatry* 35 (1): 9–16. https://doi.org/10.1046/j.1440-1614.2001.00849.x.

———. 2009. Reducing the Impact of Stalking on Victims. In *Stalkers and Their Victims*, 2nd Edition, 262–281. Cambridge: Cambridge University Press.

Mullen, P. E., M. Pathé, R. Purcell, and G. W. Stuart. 1999. Study of Stalkers. *The American Journal of Psychiatry* 156 (8): 1244–1249. https://doi.org/10.1176/ajp.156.8.1244

Nagata, J. M., C. A. Cortez, C. J. Cattle, K. T. Ganson, P. Lyer, K. Bibbins-Domingo, and F. C. Baker. 2022. Screen Time Use Among US Adolescents During the COVID-19 Pandemic. *JAMA Pediatrics* 176 (1): 94–96. https://jamanetwork.com/journals/jamapediatrics/article-abstract/2785686.

Netflix. 2018. You. https://www.netflix.com/gb/title/80211991. Accessed 22 Aug 2022.

———. 2022a. Popular Romantic Films on Netflix/ Romantic Dramas on Netflix. Google, 05 09. https://www.google.com/search?q=Netflix+romantic+movies&rlz=1C1GCEA_enGB998GB998&biw=1920&bih=937&sxsrf=ALiCzsYetRnPZ7ad6727PA11pXmwSwOU_Q%3A1662398440970&ei=6C8WY_jwOrLC8gKd8Ij4AQ&ved=0ahUKEwj4hLLklP75AhUyoVwKHR04Ah8Q4dUDCA4&uact=5&oq=Netflix+romantic+mo. Accessed 30 Oct 2022.

———. 2022b. Popular Thrillers on Netflix/ Thriller Dramas on Netflix. Google, 05 09. https://www.google.com/search?q=+thriller+movies+on+netflix&rlz=1C1GCEA_enGB998GB998&sxsrf=ALiCzsZmHQ1hWvGWHYyLJeTv1NXAy3qsaA%3A1662462300235&ei=XCkXY_6BDsiP8gK90r_QBA&ved=0ahUKEwj-n-7WgoD6AhXIh1wKHT3pD0oQ4dUDCA4&uact=5&oq=+thriller+movies+on+netflix&gs_l. Accessed 6 Sep 2022.

Newsflash. 2021. Streaming Subscriptions Boom as Young People Turn Away from Traditional TV.. https://newsflash.tdsynnex.co.uk/news/streaming-subscriptions-boom-as-young-people-turn-away-from-traditional-tv/4616. Accessed 5 Nov 2022.

Nicol, Bran. 2006. *Stalking*. London: Reaktion Books.

Ofcom. 2021. Media Nations 2021: Interactive Report. Ofcom, 1–6. https://www.ofcom.org.uk/research-and-data/tv-radio-and-on-demand/media-nations-reports/media-nations-2021/interactive-report. Accessed 6 Nov 2022.

———. 2022a. Children and Parents: Media Use and Attitudes Report 2022. Ofcom, 1–80. https://www.ofcom.org.uk/__data/assets/pdf_file/0024/234609/childrens-media-use-and-attitudes-report-2022a.pdf. Accessed 5 Nov 2022

———. 2022b. Media Nations: UK 2022. Ofcom, 1–108. https://www.ofcom.org.uk/__data/assets/pdf_file/0016/242701/media-nations-report-2022b.pdf. Accessed 4 Nov 2022.

Office for National Statistics. 2020. Stalking: Findings from the Crime Survey for England and Wales. Edited by N Stripe. 25 11. https://www.ons.gov.uk/peoplepopulationandcommunity/crimeandjustice/datasets/stalkingfindingsfromthecrimesurveyforenglandandwales. Accessed 21 Sep 2022.

Owens, J. G. 2016. Why Definitions Matter: Stalking Victimisation in the United States. *Journal of Interpersonal Violence* 2196–2226. https://doi.org/10.1177/0886260515573577.

Pathé, M., and Mullen, P. E. 1997. The Impact of Stalkers on their Victims. *The British Journal of Psychiatry* 170 (1): 12–17. https://doi.org/10.1192/bjp.170.1.12.

PCADV. 2021. Stalking Isn't Romantic. 26 01. https://www.pcadv.org/blog/stalking-isnt-romantic/. Accessed 19 Aug 2022.

Purcell, R., B. Moller, T. Flower, and P. E. Mullen. 2009. Stalking Among Juveniles. *The British Journal of Psychiatry* 194 (50): 451–455. https://doi.org/10.1192/bjp.bp.108.054833.

Purcell, R., M. Pathé, P. E. Mullen. 2004. Editorial: When Do Repeated Intrusions Become Stalking? *The Journal of Forensic Psychiatry & Psychology* 15 (4): 571–583. https://doi.org/10.1080/14789940412331313368.

Quinn-Evans, L., D. A. Keatley, M. Arntfield, and L. Sheridan. 2021. A Behavior Sequence Analysis of Victims' Accounts of Stalking Behaviors. *Journal of Interpersonal Violence* 36 (15–16): 6979–6997. https://doi.org/10.1177/0886260519831389.

Roberts, A. R., and S. F. Dziegielewski. 1996. Assessment Typology and Intervention with the Survivors of Stalking. *Aggression and Violent Behaviour* 1 (4): 359–368. https://doi.org/10.1016/S1359-1789(96)00011-0.

Roberts, K., M. Tolou-Shams, and K. Madera. 2016. Adolescent Versus Adult Stalking: A Brief Review. *Journal of Forensic Psychology Practice* 16 (4): 236–252. https://doi.org/10.1080/15228932.2016.1192334.

Schultz, A. S., J. Moore, and B. H. Spitzberg. 2014. Once Upon a Midnight Stalker: A Content Analysis of Stalking in Films. *Western Journal of Communication* 78 (5): 612–635. Accessed August 22, 2022. https://doi.org/10.1080/10570314.2013.809475.

Shafer, Autumn, P. Bobkowski, and J. D. Brown. 2012. Sexual Media Practice: How Adolescents Select, Engage with, and Are Affected by Sexual Media. In *The Oxford Handbook of Media Psychology*, by K. E. Dill. Oxford: Oxford University Press.

Shapiro, M. A., and T. M. Chock. 2003. Psychological Processes in Perceiving Reality. *Media Psychology* 5 (2): 163–198. https://doi.org/10.1207/S1532785XMEP0502_3.

Sheridan, L. P., E. Blaauw, and G. M. Davies. 2003. Stalking: Knowns and Unknowns. *Trauma, Violence, & Abuse* 4 (2): 148–162. https://doi.org/10.1177/1524838002250766.

Sheridan, L., and G. M. Davies. 2001. Stalking: The Elusive Crime. *Legal and Criminological Psychology* 133–147. https://doi.org/10.1348/135532501168244.

Sides Schultz, A., J. Moore, and B. H. Spitzberg. 2014. Once Upon a Midnight Stalker: A Content Analysis of Stalking in Films. *Western Journal of Communication* 78 (5): 612–635. https://doi.org/10.1080/10570314.2013.809475.

Sinclair, H. C., and I. H. Frieze. 2000. Initial Courtship Behavior and Stalking: How Should We draw the Line. *Violence and Victims* 15 (1): 23–40. https://doi.org/10.1891/0886-6708.15.1.23

Smith-Darden, J. P., D. E. Reidy, and P. D. Kernsmith. 2016. Adolescent Stalking and Risk of Violence. *Journal of Adolescence* 52: 191–200. https://doi.org/10.1016/j.adolescence.2016.08.005

Spitzberg, B. H., and W. R. Cupach. 2007. The State of Art of Stalking: Taking Stock of the Emerging Literature. *Aggression Violent Behaviour* 12 (1): 64–86. https://doi.org/10.1016/j.avb.2006.05.001.

———. 2014. *The Dark Side of Relationship Pursuit: From Attraction to Obsession and Stalking*. New York: Routledge.

Stevens, H. 2022. Pop Culture Needs to Stop Romanticising Stalking. Movies Romanticise Stalking. https://digitaledition.chicagotribune.com/tribune/article_popover.aspx?guid=d3ee5490-4734-4881-8003-fd6f38f39052. Accessed 27 Aug 2022.

Taylor-Dunn, H., E. Bowen, and E. A. Gilchrist. 2018. Reporting Harassment and Stalking to the Police: A Qualitative Study of Victim's Experience. *Journal of Interpersonal Violence* 36 (11–12): NP5965-NP5992. https://doi.org/10.1177/0886260518811.

Tudor, Andrew. 2013. *Image and Influence: Studies in the Sociology of Film*. Abingdon: Routledge.

US Department of Justice. 2021. Interstate Stalking. 23 12. https://www.justice.gov/usao-ndga/victim-witness-assistance/interstate-stalking. Accessed 21 Aug 2022.

Van der Aa, S. 2018. New Trends in the Criminalisation of Stalking in the EU Member States. *European Journal of Criminal Policy and Research* 24 (1): 315–333. https://doi.org/10.1007/s10610-017-9359-9

Wallace, H., and Silverman, J. 1996. Stalking and Post Traumatic Stress Syndrome. *The Police Journal: Theory, Practice and Principles* 68 (3): 203–206. https://doi.org/10.1177/0032258X9606900

Ward, L. M. 2003. Understanding the Role of Entertainment Media in the Sexual Socialisation of American Youth: A Review of Empirical Research. *Developmental Review* 23 (3): 347–388. https://doi.org/10.1016/S0273-2297(03)00013-3.

Waterman, E. A., K. D. Lee, and K. M. Edwards. 2019. Longitudinal Associations of Binge Drinking with Interpersonal Violence Among Adolescents. *Journal of Youth and Adolescence* 48: 1342–1352. https://doi.org/10.1007/s10964-019-01035-w.

Westrup, D., and W. J. Fermouwa. 1998. Stalking Behaviour: A Literature Review and Suggested Functional Analytic Assessment Technology. *Aggression and Violent Behaviour* 3 (3): 255–274. https://doi.org/10.1016/S1359-1789(97)00023-2

Wilson, T., and M. Maloney. 2019. Dating Violence in Adolescent Relationships. *International Journal of the Whole Child* 4 (2): 82–88. https://libjournals.mtsu.edu/index.php/ijwc/article/view/1601. Accessed 27 Oct 2022.

Wroan, M. 2021. COVID-19 Accelerates Streaming Challenges as Well as Demand. https://info.kpmg.us/news-perspectives/technology-innovation/covid-19-accelerates-streaming-challenges-and-demand.html. Accessed 4 Nov 2022.

Ybarra, M. L., J. Langhinrichsen-Rohling, and K. J. Mitchell. 2017. Stalking-like Behaviour in Adolescence: Prevalence, Intent, and Associated Characteristics. *Psychology of Violence* 7 (2), 192–202. https://doi.org/10.1037/a0040145

Part II

Methods and Behaviours of Stalking and Coercive Control

Stalking in Ireland

5

Catherine O'Sullivan and Ciara Staunton

Key Points

- This chapter will consider the international literature on who tends to engage in stalking, who they tend to stalk, the types of behaviours they tend to engage in and examine if this fits with the Irish experience.
- The discussion will identify the psychological, physical, economic and social impacts of stalking on those who are stalked with reference to a study conducted in Ireland.
- This chapter will trace the European trend towards criminalising stalking in addition to criminalising harassment and consider recent developments in Ireland.

Introduction

In early February 2021 before Cork Circuit Court in Ireland, a 52-year-old man was sentenced to seven years in prison with two years suspended. A newspaper report at the time (Heylin 2021) described the perpetrator as having become obsessed with a woman who he harassed and threatened to rape. He was arrested as he was attempting to break into the woman's home, armed with what was described

C. O'Sullivan (✉) · C. Staunton
University College Cork (UCC), Cork, Ireland
e-mail: Catherine.OSullivan@ucc.ie

C. Staunton
e-mail: C.Staunton@ucc.ie

M. Mellins et al. (eds.), *Young People, Stalking Awareness and Domestic Abuse*,
https://doi.org/10.1007/978-3-031-32379-9_5

as a rape kit. Judge Seán Ó Donnabháin said the crime was 'dramatic' and 'horrific' and went significantly beyond a case of harassment, one of the offences with which the perpetrator was charged (Heylin 2021). That woman was Una Ring, one of two women whose experiences of stalking led them to campaign for the introduction of a new offence of stalking separate to that of harassment. The second is Eve McDowell, whose stalker was arrested and convicted after he attacked her roommate upon breaking into her apartment (Healy 2020). Their advocacy, supported initially by the Sexual Violence Centre Cork, has resulted in the inclusion of a new stalking offence in the *Criminal Justice (Miscellaneous Provisions) Bill 2022* (*2022 Bill*) which will be enacted in 2023. It also prompted us to conduct research into the experiences of stalking and harassment in Ireland. Although there had been some research on stalking and harassment in Ireland it focused on specific population subgroups or specific forms of harassment. There had been no general population studies with those who have been stalked or harassed. This chapter presents results from the first survey to be conducted in Ireland.

In this chapter we will chart the types of behaviours identified in the literature that may be included in the stalking process and how they impact those subjected to them with a particular focus on the course and nature of stalking as experienced by those who have been targeted in Ireland. Our online survey received ethical approval from University College Cork's Social Research Ethics Committee in November 2021, was launched on 25th November, and closed at the end of February 2022 with 1,018 responses. The survey explored: respondent demographic information; the behaviourally defined aspects of the stalking process, which included the categories of unwanted behaviours, threats and abuse, malicious communications and reputational damage; the impact of stalking from a financial, social, physical and psychological perspective; the identity of the person who was stalking; and the reaction of the respondent to the stalking behaviours. After screening the survey data, we were left 892 responses which are reported in this chapter.[1] In section "The Relationship Between the Person Engaging in the Stalking Behaviour and the Person Being Stalked" of this chapter we will look at what the literature tells us about who engages in stalking. In section "Stalking Behaviours" we will identify the types of behaviours that those who engage in stalking tend to perpetrate. In section "Impacts of Stalking" we look at the psychological, physical, social and economic effects of this behaviour on the person stalked. Finally, in section "Law in Ireland" we will discuss how growing awareness of the problem of stalking internationally has led to the introduction of targeted offences and situate recent Irish developments in that context.

The Relationship Between the Person Engaging in the Stalking Behaviour and the Person Being Stalked

Compared with many other intrusive crimes, stalking is difficult to classify and define. Who are the perpetrators or their targets likely to be? Can we identify a profile of a 'typical' case of stalking? The popular culture image of those who stalk is that they are strangers to the person they stalk who is sometimes a celebrity (Schultz et al. 2014). Indeed, the first anti-stalking legislation in the world was introduced in 1989 in California following public outcry after the murder of Rebecca Schaeffer, a TV actor, by her stalker (Purcell et al. 2004, 160). Stalking is also represented as a behaviour that is committed and experienced roughly equally by women and men (Schultz et al. 2014). Studies however tell us that while men and women stalk and are stalked the general profile of the person engaged in stalking is that they are male (e.g. Bjerregaard 2000; Meloy 1999; Sheridan et al. 2001) and the general profile of a person being stalked is that they are female, were in a relationship with and younger than the individual stalking them (Jones 1996). A meta-analysis of 175 studies on stalking involving 122,207 individuals was conducted by Spitzberg and Cupach (2007). Overall, they found that between 60 and 80% of victims in the relevant studies were female. From this they concluded that females were more likely to be victims than males with females having a 28.5% lifetime stalking victimisation risk as compared to an 11% risk for males.

Clinical studies of male perpetrators of stalking have found that common motivations are anger, jealousy, abandonment, rage and a need for power and control (Meloy and Gothard 1995). Individuals who engage in stalking and who have a diagnosis of a psychosis are significantly more likely to target a stranger or acquaintance than someone with whom they were previously intimately involved (Kienlen et al. 1997; Meloy 1996, 1998; Zona et al. 1993, 1998). Those who have been stalked perceive the most likely goal of the person stalking them is to control them (Tjaden and Thoennes 1997). A meta-analysis by Churcher and Nesca (2013) of 23 studies from six countries examined predictors of violence. When the datasets were combined, 35.4% (n = 1,059) of the 2,995 offenders (2,277 males, 668 females and 50 with unspecified gender) had been violent towards the person they were stalking. Of the 2,119 victims (285 males, 1,833 females and one married couple counted as a single participant), 28.4% (n = 604) had been physically harmed by the person stalking them (Churcher and Nesca 2013, 106). Eight risk factors were identified: gender, a prior intimate relationship, the presence of explicit threats, the presence of psychosis, presence of personality disorder, criminal history, violence history and a history of substance abuse. Other research has confirmed that a prior relationship with the person stalked is predictive of violence, with ex-intimates being the most likely to attack and strangers the least (Budd and Mattinson 2000; Purcell et al. 2002; Sheridan and Davies 2001; Thomas et al. 2008; Tjaden and Thoennes 1998).

The prevalence of post-relationship stalking (PRS) has led to a research focus on this form of stalking. PRS has been defined as a pattern of targeted, repeated and unwanted intrusive acts which occurs after a romantic relationship has dissolved that can be reasonably expected to cause apprehension, distress or fear in the person stalked (Douglas and Dutton 2001; McEwan et al. 2007; Mullen et al. 2009). In a survey of 95 self-defined victims of stalking in the United Kingdom, Sheridan et al. (2001) found that in 48% of cases (n = 46), the person engaged in the stalking behaviour was an ex-partner of the victim, and in 12% of cases (n = 11) there was no prior relationship between the victim and the person stalking them. In 37% of cases ($n = 35$), the person who was stalking was identified as a former acquaintance (Sheridan et al. 2001, 221). Spitzberg and Cupach's meta-analysis found that 79% of victims across 62 studies were acquainted with the person stalking them, and half ($n = 53$) of all stalking emerged from romantic relationships (2007, 64). Across 82 studies in which some estimate of violence was provided following the breakdown of an intimate relationship, there was physical violence in 32% of cases and sexual violence in 12%. Tjaden and Thoennes (1998) found that ex-husbands who stalked were significantly more likely than their non-stalking peers to have engaged in controlling and emotionally abusive behaviour towards their partner during the relationship. Stalking in this context can be understood as a form of male-perpetrated domestic abuse and coercive control (Mullen et al. 2009; Stark 2007; Walker and Meloy 1998). Ornstein and Rickne (2013) found that women who reported being subjected to controlling behaviour by their partners were more likely to be stalked later.

An extensive EU-wide survey on Violence Against Women was conducted across the then-28 member states with 42,000 women (European Agency for Fundamental Rights 2015). It reported that 18% of women have experienced stalking since the age of 15 and almost one in 10 women (9%) had been stalked by their previous partner. In England and Wales, the Crown Prosecution Service analysed a sample of stalking cases from 2019 and found that 84% involved complaints against ex-partners, three-quarters of whom had been abusive during the relationship (Crown Prosecution Service 2020). In Scotland, data from March 2019-March 2020 found that 65% of stalking charges originated in a domestic violence context (Scottish Government 2020). In 2020–2021, the figure was 57% (Scottish Government 2022).

In Ireland, of the resolved cases of 256 women who died violently between 1996 and January 2023, 55% were killed by a current or former intimate partner and almost nine in ten (87%) women knew their killer (Women's Aid Femicide Watch, 2023). A review by An Garda Síochána[2] of offences committed between 2019 and 2021 found a domestic abuse motive in 90% of the killings of women and girls and in 43% of all attempts/threats to murder, assaults, harassments and related offences (An Garda Síochána 2022, 8). Eleven percent of men were the victim of one of these offences in a domestic abuse context. It was also found that women were the victims of most harassment and related offences (67%) over this period (An Garda Síochána 2022, 10). The offence of coercive control was commenced in January 2019 and between 2019 and 2021, 259 incidents were reported to An Garda Síochána (An Garda Síochána 2022, 11).

The results of our survey are consistent with previous research in this area. The overwhelming majority of our respondents (88%, $n = 789$) identified themselves as female. Males represented 9% ($n = 78$) of our respondents and the remaining 3% ($n = 25$) declared themselves as non-binary, transgender MTF, Trans Male, or genderfluid. This 3% includes two participants who preferred not to say. The mean age of respondents was 35 years with an age range of 18–75 years.

Respondents were asked to describe the person who carried out the behaviour, focusing on their relationship to the respondent. More than one category could be selected, and many respondents identified more than one perpetrator. Consistent with international research, for a significant proportion of our respondents (52%, $n = 468$), the perpetrator was known to them as either a current or ex-partner. Twenty-three per cent ($n = 206$) of respondents reported that it was an acquaintance. A friend was identified 131 times, a work colleague 107 times and a neighbour 74 times. The high proportion of (ex-)partner perpetrators is evidence that popular culture images that it is strangers who stalk are largely inaccurate. However, 29% ($n = 257$) of respondents reported a stranger as the perpetrator while 0.3% ($n = 26$) of respondents did not know who was stalking them.

Stalking Behaviours

Little is known about the stalking process in its entirety given there is not a clear profile as to this kind of offence. The main issue is that the term 'stalking' does not apply to a single act or action which can be easily defined in legal terms. The person stalking may not be overtly threatening. Instead, they often engage in behaviours which are ostensibly routine, harmless and legal. However, it is the repetition of behaviour rather than the behaviour itself that constitutes stalking and this can explain why police fail to recognise the behaviour as stalking or the risk posed by the individual engaged in those behaviours. Drawing on research on coercive control, Taylor-Dunn, Bowen and Gilchrist note, 'that the incident-based nature of policing can result in officers missing "patterns of abuse that do not fit into traditional crime categories"' (2021).

It is accordingly important to investigate whether there are core behaviours which are common to the stalking process. This may help police to assess the future risk that those who report such behaviours may be under. Therefore, the question for us to address in this Part of the chapter is: what types of behaviours and activities constitute stalking? According to Meloy (1999), stalking is chronic behaviour that unfolds over time, from months to potentially years. While each behaviour on its own may not merit any cause for alarm, it is the compound effect of multiple nuisance, threatening and harassing behaviours which has a devasting impact on those who are subjected to them. Sheridan et al. (2003) concluded that those who stalk employ multiple tactics and that those tactics which tend to appear most often could be identified as common stalking behaviour. Research finds that some of the most common behaviours include loitering nearby the victim, following, harassing by telephone or mail, ordering goods on the victim's behalf, making threats, committing physical and sexual assaults and occasionally attempting or succeeding to kill (Harmon et al. 1995; Meloy and Gothard 1995; Mullen and Pathé 1994; Zona et al. 1998). Literature has also revealed certain patterns in behaviours. In a survey of 95 self-defined victims of stalking in the United Kingdom, Sheridan et al. found a pattern of repeated intrusions with being watched ($n = 86$) and followed ($n = 78$) emerging as the most frequently reported intrusions.

This led Sheridan et al. to conclude that these formed the basis of typical stalking cases (2001, 224).

The European Agency for Fundamental Rights survey on Violence Against Women indicated that 14% of women reported receiving repeated offensive or threatening messages or phone calls from the same person (European Agency for Fundamental Rights, 2015) while 23% of women reported changing their phone number or email address as a consequence of what they perceived to be a serious stalking episode. Cyberstalking was considered in the survey as stalking by means of email, text messages or the internet and this was reported by 4% of all 18–29-year-old women who participated in the survey.[3] Other findings from the survey revealed that 8% of the women who reported being the targets of stalking identified that they had been followed or that someone had loitered outside their house or workplace. Three per cent of women had their property repeatedly damaged by the same individual (European Agency for Fundamental Rights 2015, 85).

In a Higher Education Authority survey of Irish student experiences of sexual violence and harassment in the third level sector, almost one in four (24%) had sexual rumours spread about them via electronic means (MacNeela et al. 2022, 155). Approximately a fifth of female (19%), non-binary (20%) and those who preferred not to say (18%) respondents who chose to answer the question were subjected to unwelcome sexual comments, jokes or pictures by electronic means 'often' or 'many times' (MacNeela et al. 2022, 158). Five per cent of male respondents had this experience. One-fifth of the students who chose to answer a question about whether someone continued to ask them for a date after they said 'no' selected the 'often' or 'many times' options (MacNeela et al. 2022, 148). Those who preferred not to say their gender (28%) and females (26%) were the most likely to experience these levels of repeated unwanted attempts to establish a romantic sexual relationship, closely followed by a fifth (22%) of non-binary students. Seven per cent of male respondents had the same experience (MacNeela et al. 2022, 149).

Our survey asked respondents a series of questions about the types and frequency of unwanted behaviours, threats and abuse, malicious communications and reputational damage that they were subjected to. Most respondents experienced multiple behaviours. The data is presented in Tables 5.1–5.4 in count form based on the total final sample of 892 participants. What can be seen from the tables is the prevalence of myriad forms of nuisance behaviours at one end of the spectrum to stand-alone criminal acts such as physical and sexual assaults at the other.

Being approached and being followed were the two most common unwanted behaviours identified ($n = 509$ for both behaviours). Perpetrators loitering or spying on the respondents were the next most commonly reported unwanted behaviours ($n = 507$ and $n = 506$ respectively). More than a third of our 892 respondents experienced physical assaults ($n = 311$), and 44% sexual ($n = 391$) assaults and/or threats from the perpetrator to harm them or those close to them ($n = 393$). Property damage was reported 172 times with a further 74 reports of homes being broken into. There were also 367 reports of the perpetrator threatening to harm themselves around the respondent (Table 5.1 and 5.2).

Table 5.1 Unwanted behaviours

	Count
Made unwanted approaches to you (e.g. at home, at work, in public places)	509
Followed you (e.g. on foot, by car)	509
Loitered around your home or other places you frequent	507
Spied on you or tracked your movements whether online, using technology or in person	506
Made unwanted approaches to your friends, family or colleagues about you	431
Interfered with or damaged your property (e.g. car)	172
Broken into your home	74

Table 5.2 Threats and abuse

	Count
Threatened to harm you or those close to you, directly or indirectly	393
Sexually assaulted you	391
Threatened to harm themselves around you	367
Physically attacked or tried to attack you	311

Table 5.3 Malicious communication

	Count
Sent you inappropriate letters, faxes, texts, WhatsApps, or e-mails	623
Made inappropriate or malicious telephone calls to you	359
Sent or delivered unwanted gifts	234

Malicious communications in the form of inappropriate texts, WhatsApps or emails ($n = 623$) was the most common action identified by respondents. Social media also featured strongly in the reputational damage category. Being the target of inappropriate or malicious social media contacts (e.g. Twitter, Facebook) was mentioned 268 times, the second highest form in that category. Having pictures or recordings taken without consent was mentioned 270 times with 170 reports of private images of a very personal nature being shared. There were 130 reports of false complaints to agencies being made and 106 incidents of false legal action being instigated. The distribution of malicious material was identified by 90 respondents. All such actions are designed to undermine and intimidate the respondent and highlight the kinds of manipulations that perpetrators will instigate in order to exercise psychological power and control over their target. Such actions also highlight the lengths to which perpetrators will go as part of their campaign of stalking (Tables 5.3 and 5.4).

The extent to which respondents were subjected to criminal behaviours independent of a potential harassment charge—the current applicable offence in

Table 5.4 Reputational damage

	Count
Taken pictures/recordings of you without your consent	270
Engaged in inappropriate or malicious social media contacts (e.g. Twitter, Facebook)	268
Shared private images of you that are of a very personal nature (e.g. nude images, sexual images)	170
Made false complaints to agencies	130
Initiated false legal action against you	106
Distributed malicious material about you (e.g. flyers, web-sites, posters, newspaper ads)	90

Ireland—is an alarming finding. The most concerning findings pertain to the threats and abuse category. More than a third of our 892 respondents experienced physical assaults ($n = 311$) and 44% sexual ($n = 391$) assaults. The seriousness of the 393 reports that the perpetrator threatened to harm them or those close to them should also not be underestimated. Threats of harm are a serious indicator of risk of actual harm as highlighted in numerous studies (e.g. Budd and Mattinson 2000; Purcell et al. 2002; Tjaden and Thoennes 1998). Predictors of a physical attack for a victim were being threatened, being an ex-intimate and being younger at the time of the stalking incident (Purcell et al. 2002; Thomas et al. 2008).

Our study found that unwanted behaviours such as being followed, spied on or approached were more common than direct threats of harm towards the respondent or those known to them. These methods induce fear and impose control, hallmarks of stalking behaviour. Similarly, the use of indirect stalking and harassment methods, such as spreading untruthful information about the person being stalked or harassed, have the effect of jeopardising respondents' sense of security. The extent to which social media and modern technology are used as a means through which stalking and harassing behaviours are carried out is a worrying trend. It ranked highly in both the malicious communications (i.e. communications directed at the respondent) and reputational damage (i.e. communications about the respondent directed at or intended for a wider audience) categories of our study.

Generating a profile of the behaviours, acts and actions of those who stalk is extremely important and will be of use from a policing perspective. While the specific behaviour in isolation may not warrant investigation, an appreciation that the repetition of such behaviour changes its nature should encourage police to move beyond their narrow incident-based understanding of crime and recognise the potential seriousness of a pattern or repetition of apparently unserious actions (Taylor-Dunn et al. 2021). It may also help those who are being stalked to recognise the perpetrators' actions and report to authorities before the stalking results in serious physical, psychological, economic and social effects. As will be discussed in the next Part, these effects can have a very significant impact on the well-being of those being stalked.

Impacts of Stalking

It is often stated that stalking causes harm to those who are stalked (e.g. Fremouw et al. 1997; Jones 1996; Tjaden and Thoennes 1998), but only a few studies have considered the economic and social effects of stalking and fewer its psychological or psychiatric consequences. Those that have been conducted found that that almost all who are stalked suffer from deleterious psychological effects (Brewster 1997; Hall 1998; Pathé and Mullen 1997; Tjaden and Thoennes 1998). Specifically, international research has shown that the majority of those who are stalked experience traumatic stress symptoms (Briere and Runtz 1989; Pathé and Mullen 1997) and other forms of psychological, social and vocational damage (Blaauw et al. 2002; Brewster 1998).

In Ireland, Nwachukwu et al. (2012) looked at the experiences of 274 psychiatrists and found that 25.1% of their participants considered that they had been stalked, 5.5% were being stalked at the time of the survey, and 4% had been stalked more than once (Nwachukwu et al. 2012, 90). The participants reported suffering psychological distress and that the behaviour negatively impacted their work, social life and their partners/spouses. The Union of Students in Ireland conducted an online survey of students' experiences of harassment, stalking, violence and sexual assault with 2,752 respondents (1,811 women, 926 men and 15 other). While the report, *Say Something* (2013), focused primarily on physical and sexual violence some key findings are noteworthy. Over 30% of women or 'other' respondents reported harassment or intimidation while at their current institution (USI 2013, 7). Ten per cent of the women who completed the survey disclosed experiencing obsessive behaviour that made them afraid or concerned for their safety. Five per cent of men reported that they too had similar experiences. Three in ten of those who reported experiencing obsessive behaviour believed that the experience had negatively affected their mental health and well-being, while over 40% believed that their relationships had been impacted, with a similar number believing that their studies had been impaired (USI 2013, 8).

Our findings, which are set out in Tables 5.5 and 5.6, conform with this research. The emotional and psychological consequences reported by our 892 respondents were severe, ranging from anxiety and depression to suicidal thoughts, self-harming behaviours and suicide attempts. The two most common psychological consequences reported by our respondents indicate the sheer fear and terror that the perpetrator's actions can induce with 84% ($n = 750$) experiencing anxiety and 64% ($n = 584$) fear. Increased distrust ($n = 558$) was the next most frequently reported consequence, with depression mentioned 437 times and panic attacks identified 383 times. Most worryingly, suicidal thoughts and self-harming behaviours were mentioned 265 and 148 times respectively. Suicide attempts were reported 92 times. These indicate the serious psychological sequelae of the experiences respondents suffer which impact their mental health.

Effects on physical health such as fatigue are not uncommon with tiredness mentioned 433 times and sleep disturbances 511 times. Physical changes such as weight changes ($n = 319$) and appetite changes ($n = 301$) were mentioned. Nausea

Table 5.5 Physical and psychological consequences

	Count
Anxiety	750
Fear	584
Increased distrust	558
Sleep disturbances	511
Depression	437
Tiredness	433
Paranoia	386
Anger	385
Panic attacks	383
Agoraphobia	365
Irritation	330
Weight changes	319
Appetite changes	301
Confusion	284
Headaches	272
Suicidal thoughts	265
Nausea	218
Weakness	191
Aggression	164
Self-harming behaviours	148
Physical injuries (inflicted by the person engaging in the behaviour/actions)	99
Suicide attempts	92
Purging (the use of laxatives, forced vomiting)	48

(n = 218), weakness (n = 191) and purging (n = 48) were present. Physical injuries (inflicted by the person engaging in the behaviour/actions) were reported 99 times.

Our survey also unearthed a panoply of broader negative outcomes, including impaired interpersonal and vocational functioning and enforced changes to lifestyle, as a direct result of the perpetrator's behaviour (Table 5.6).

What is evident from the findings is that respondents attempt to cope with the perpetrator's behaviour by making changes to their own lives, habits and routines. This self-regulation of behaviour consists of various strategies respondents employ to avoid the perpetrator (e.g. changing jobs, n = 170; changing routes home, n = 385; moving house, n = 193). The data shows that self-regulation as a coping strategy has social and psychological consequences for respondents, leading to various degrees of social isolation and apprehension. At a low level, this is indicated by changing behaviours such as shopping outside of their locality (n = 159) or reducing or stopping altogether walking their dogs (n = 137). At a more severe

Table 5.6 Changing habits and behaviours

	Count
Suffered the expense of counselling, expense of therapies, expense of legal advice, or expense of installing security systems	401
Changed your route home from work or school	385
Gave up social activities	370
Stopped leaving the house alone	314
Had work performance adversely affected	308
Reduced contact with family and friends	290
Changed phone number	247
Lost contact with family and friends	209
Moved house	193
Changed jobs	170
Changed email address	165
Shopped outside of your local area	159
Stopped/reduced walking your dogs	137
Installed closed-circuit television (CCTV)	103
Reduced working hours	97
Repaired damaged property	97
Changed or sold your car	61
Changed school/college (if this happened while you were at school/college)	51
Changed identity	17

level, change behaviours included a reduction in their working hours ($n = 97$), a reduction in contact with family and friends ($n = 290$) and giving up social activities ($n = 370$). It is highlighted most starkly by the fact that 17 respondents went to the effort of changing their identity to avoid their perpetrator.

While these behavioural and significant life changes may have the desired effect of avoiding the perpetrator, they also have the immediate effect of social isolation and the longer-term effect of psychological distress. Poor mental health outcomes seem highly likely for respondents without appropriate intervention and care and therefore it is not surprising that almost half (45%, $n = 401$) of respondents suffered the expense of counselling, therapies, legal advice, or the costs of installing security systems.

Law in Ireland

The offence of stalking has been connected to Violence Against Women and Girls since its inception. As noted previously, the first anti-stalking legislation in the world was introduced in 1989 in California following the murder of Rebecca Schaeffer (Purcell et al. 2004). Research on the prevalence of PRS confirms this linkage as accurate. In Europe, EU member states have been required, subject to the issuing of a reservation, to criminalise stalking as part of a suite of measures to reduce gender-based Violence Against Women and Girls. This is set out in Article 34 of the Council of Europe Convention on Preventing and Combating Violence Against Women and Domestic Violence (Istanbul Convention), which was adopted in 2011 and entered into force in 2014.

As of May 2016, van der Aa (2018) found that 21 member states had passed anti-stalking or anti-harassment criminal legislation.[4] Since then five other EU member states have introduced new stalking offences. Latvia (Latvian Public Broadcasting and Mače 2018) and Greece (General Secretariat for Demography, Family Policy and Gender Equality of the Ministry of Labour and Social Affairs 2022) did so in 2018, Bulgaria in 2019 (Šimonović 2019), and Cyprus (Anon 2021) and Lithuania (Human Rights Monitoring Institute 2021) in 2021. Only 2 of the EU-27 do not have specific stalking or harassment offences. Denmark issued a reservation to Article 34, preferring to utilise non-criminal sanctions in response to stalking although increased punishment is permitted if offences are committed in a stalking context (van der Aa 2018). Estonia did not issue a reservation but stalking falls under its civil code (European Institute for Gender Equality 2019). It is of course possible for criminal prosecutions under other offences to proceed in both jurisdictions if the stalking behaviour fits within the definition of those offences; indeed the increased penalty possibility provided for in Denmark recognises this. Unfortunately relying on pre-existing offences does not necessarily offer those being stalked adequate protection or adequately deter those who stalk because it is not the individual behaviours themselves that are problematic, but the repetitive and unwanted nature that changes them from harmless to harmful.

There is not yet a specific stalking offence in Ireland, but it was thought that Ireland had already met its obligations under the Istanbul Convention through the criminalisation of harassment with section 10 of the *Non-Fatal Offences Against the Person Act 1997* (*1997 Act*) as amended by the *Harassment, Harmful Communications and Related Offences Act 2020*. The harassment offence was introduced into Irish law with little debate, but it is clear from the 1994 Law Reform Commission Report that informed the contents of the *1997 Act* that the harassment offence was intended to criminalise harassing and stalking behaviour: 'acts of harassment which interfere seriously with a person's right to a peaceful and private life should be captured by the criminal law and not simply those which give rise to a fear of violence. An offence of harassment would capture, for example, the acts of the infatuated psychotic who follows a woman in order to gain her affections' (LRC 1994, 257–258). This conflation of stalking and harassment was also evident in the then-Minister for Justice's introduction of the various provisions contained within the *Non-Fatal Offences Against the Person Bill 1997* which became the *1997 Act*:

> [s]ection 10 provides for the important new offence of harassment which is aimed at what is commonly called "stalking". We are all aware of high profile cases of stalking but such behaviour is not necessarily peculiar to people in the spotlight. Unfortunately, it can occur in everyday life when a person, usually a woman, becomes the object of the stalker's affection

— perhaps obsession is a better word — and that person is subjected to sustained harassment and intimidation in a perverted attempt by the stalker to gain the attention or affection of the unfortunate person concerned. This harassment can have a profoundly detrimental effect on the life of the victim. (Dáil Debates 1997)

Ireland was not unique in conflating harassment and stalking. All jurisdictions with a common-law tradition in Europe—England, Wales, Scotland (which is a hybrid common and civil law system), Northern Ireland, Ireland and Malta (also a mixed system)—originally enacted harassment offences that were intended to cover stalking. However, anti-stalking advocates argued that while harassment and stalking share similarities, stalking is a qualitatively worse experience. Ann Moulds, a prominent anti-stalking advocate and founder of Action Scotland Against Stalking, explained the distinction in the following way: '[s]omebody might harass another person because they are not happy with them or whatever, but that is slightly different from the intimate relationship that [a] stalker has with his victim. There is an emotional relationship between two people, and it is an unequal relationship' (LRC 2016, [2.56]). Researchers in the area have also argued that stalking is worse than harassment, suggesting that when harassing behaviour persists for more than two weeks it shifts into stalking (Purcell et al. 2004).

A preliminary analysis of the results of our survey would suggest some agreement from our respondents that stalking is worse than harassment. Participants were asked whether they would name or identify their experiences as stalking or harassment but also given the options of 'I don't know' and 'both'. The most popular selection was 'both' ($n = 426$), greater than the combined total of harassment ($n = 270$) and stalking ($n = 72$). One hundred and sixteen respondents selected 'I don't know'. While the majority of those who proceeded to explain their selection did not rank the behaviours, there were indications in some responses that stalking was perceived to be worse. Some of the participants who selected 'stalking' as the term that best described their experience used emotive language to explain their selection, describing feeling like prey, being hunted, controlled, persecuted and targeted. Similar implications were present in the responses of those who selected 'harassment'. It was not possible to judge from most of the 'both' responses whether stalking was perceived to be worse than harassment as a very limited number of respondents explicitly or implicitly made a comparison.

Arguments that stalking is worse than harassment convinced all the above-named jurisdictions, bar Ireland, to supplement their existing harassment offences with stalking offences (van der Aa 2018). In the United Kingdom, the first jurisdiction to do so was Scotland via section 39 of the *Criminal Justice and Licensing (Scotland) Act 2010*. This new stalking offence led to a dramatic increase in the number of prosecutions for harassment and stalking. In the 10-year period before the introduction of the offence, there were 70 harassment prosecutions. Within four months of the new offence being introduced, there were 150 prosecutions in the Strathclyde region alone (LRC 2016, [2.66]). England and Wales followed suit with the *Protection of Freedoms Act 2012* inserting sections 2A and 4A into the *Protection from Harassment Act 1997*. As in Scotland, the introduction of these new offences led to a dramatic upsurge in reports of harassment and stalking. Reports to the police trebled between 2014 and 2018 (BBC 2018). In 2019 the number of charges was double that of 2015 (Crown Prosecution Service 2020). These dramatic increases in reporting and prosecutions do not suggest a sudden upsurge in stalking and harassing behaviours. Instead, they suggest that those being stalked did not recognise that the harassment offences applied to the behaviour that they were being subjected to and did not report it. Finally, in 2022, section 1 of the *Protection from Stalking (Northern Ireland) Act 2022* introduced a new stalking offence in Northern Ireland.

Post Brexit, there are two common-law jurisdictions in the EU: Ireland and Malta. Malta introduced a stand-alone stalking offence into its Criminal Code in 2015 (van der Aa 2018). Ireland is currently in the process of introducing a new stalking offence but it has taken some time to get to this point. In 2013, the Law Reform Commission took the view that a stalking offence was not needed as the harassment offence was 'sufficiently broad in scope to encompass behaviour that is colloquially known as stalking' (LRC 2013, [2.90]). However, three years later it was convinced by arguments such as those advanced by Moulds and by the success of the offences introduced in Scotland, England and Wales to recommend that a new stalking offence be created as an aggravated form of harassment 'because it involves an intense obsession or fixation on the part of the perpetrator which creates an unwanted intimacy between the stalker and victim' (LRC 2016, [2.57]).

This recommendation did not attract government support but effective lobbying by Ring and McDowell prompted Lisa Chambers to seek to introduce a stand-alone stalking offence in July 2021.[5] As of September 2022, the Department of Justice's position in respect of this Private Member's Bill was that a new stalking offence was unnecessary (McGreevy and O'Halloran 2021). However, the killing of Ashling Murphy as she jogged along the Grand Canal in Tullamore on a January 2022 afternoon revived memories of the March 2021 killing of Sara Everard in the UK and re-ignited the conversation on gender-based violence. In June 2022, the Irish government published its third national strategy on domestic, sexual and gender-based violence (Department of Justice 2022). Included in this strategy was a commitment to introduce a new stalking offence. The *2022 Bill*, published September 2022 and promoted by Minster for Justice Helen McEntee, provides for this offence. It is expected that the *2022 Bill* will complete the legislative process in 2023.

Section 13 of the *2022 Bill* as initiated[6] proposes to substitute section 10 of the *1997 Act* with new text. The new section 10(1) will modify the existing offence of harassment by simplifying the language and extending it to cover situations where the victim retrospectively becomes aware of the harassing actions. The new section 10(2) will define a separate stalking offence while the new section 10(3) will give illustrative examples of what constitutes stalking and harassing behaviour. Together subsections 2 and 3 will capture most of the categories of behaviour that were canvassed in our survey and confirmed as being experienced in Ireland—unwanted behaviours, malicious communications, reputational damage and threats and abuse. Section 10(6) provides that the same maximum penalty will apply to both offences, but the language used in the definition of the offences makes it clear that stalking is the more serious offence. In addition to the possibility of a fine and/or imprisonment, section 10(4) will allow for the imposition of an order restraining the convicted person from communicating with or about or being within a specified distance of the person stalked/harassed at various venues. Separately, and importantly, section 16 of the *2022 Bill* as initiated[7] will allow a person experiencing harassment/stalking to apply for a similar order without the necessity of a criminal conviction. Although there are some ways in which the text of this offence can be improved (O'Sullivan and Staunton 2023), the government's intention to create a new stalking offence is welcome and will bring Ireland into line with the other common-law jurisdiction in the EU and with our common-law neighbours.

Conclusion

It is vital that the new legislation in Ireland does not just appease public opinion but also adequately supports and protects targets of stalking while simultaneously providing An Garda Síochána with sufficient powers to address the various behaviours before they escalate to acts of physical harm. It is also important that An Garda Síochána are informed about the core behaviours and patterns that are common to the stalking process so that they can implement the law effectively. The difficulty from a policing perspective is determining the point at which nuisance attention passes over into threatening behaviour. An integrated approach to education and training for An Garda Síochána and for police forces in other jurisdictions is needed to rectify this problem.

In the 1990s, Burgess et al. recognised that '[s]talking behaviour is yet another repetitive interpersonal intrusive act that can have lethal consequences' (1997, 398). The international research discussed in this chapter bears this out. The trick is for police personnel to be able to recognise and link patterns of nuisance behaviours to the potential real risk of violence that they can become. If this is achieved, it will go a long way in ameliorating the psychological impact of the acts of the person who engages in stalking and potentially reduce some of the physical, economic and social consequences suffered by those who are at the receiving end of such nuisance behaviours. Understanding the different behaviours and the associated features of stalking can also protect at-risk individuals by helping them to identify the warning signs and seek official intervention from those who recognise the risk before a more serious crime takes place.

Discussion Questions

- Why are stalking and harassment linked to Violence Against Women and Girls?
- What types of behaviour do those who stalk tend to engage in and why is it important to develop a profile?

- What are the benefits of having stand-alone stalking offences even when harassment offences exist?

Notes

1. For further details on the methodology used, see O'Sullivan and Staunton (2023). This Report forms the basis for the content of this chapter.
2. The Irish police force. When translated into English, An Garda Síochána means guardians of the peace.
3. This compared with 0.3% of women who are 60 years old or older.
4. At the time, this would have included the United Kingdom as Brexit had not yet occurred.
5. *Non-Fatal Offences Against the Person (Amendment) (Stalking) Bill 2021*. The first author was involved in the drafting of this legislation.
6. The numbering of this section has changed to section 23 as part of the legislative process.
7. The numbering of this section has changed to section 27 as part of the legislative process.

Bibliography

An Garda Síochána. 2022. Domestic, sexual and gender-based violence. https://www.garda.ie/en/about-us/our-departments/office-of-corporate-communications/news-media/an-garda-siochana-domestic-sexual-and-gender-based-violence-report-sept-22.pdf. Accessed 5 December 2022.

Anon. 2021. Stalking in Cyprus is now a criminal offence. *For the Women*. https://forthewomen.com.cy/en/stalking-in-cyprus-is-now-a-crime/. Accessed 5 December 2022.

BBC. 2018. Stalking reports treble as prosecution rates fall. https://www.bbc.com/news/uk-england-44887574. Accessed 5 December 2022.

Bjerregaard, Beth. 2000. An empirical study of stalking victimization. *Violence and Victims* 15(4): 389–406.

Blaauw, Eric, Frans W. Winkel, Ella Arensman, Lorraine Sheridan, and Adrienne Freeve. 2002. The toll of stalking: The relationship between features of stalking and psychopathology of victims. *Journal of Interpersonal Violence* 17(1): 50–63.

Breire, J., and M. Runtz. 1989. The trauma symptom checklist (TSC-33). *Journal of Interpersonal Violence* 4(2): 151–163.

Brewster, Mary P. 1997. *An exploration of the experiences and needs of former intimate stalking victims: Final report submitted to the National Institute of Justice*. West Chester, PA: West Chester University.

Brewster, Mary P. 1998. *An exploration of the experiences and needs of former intimate stalking victims* Washington, DC: National Institute of Justice.

Budd, Tracey, and Joanna Mattinson. 2000. *Stalking: Findings from the 1998 British Crime Survey (Research Findings No. 129)* London: Home Office.

Burgess, Ann W., Timothy Baker, Deborah Greening, Carol R. Hartman, Allen G. Burgess, John E. Douglas, and Richard Halloran. 1997. Stalking behaviors within domestic violence. *Journal of Family Violence* 12(4): 389–403.

Churcher, Frances P., and Marc Nesca. 2013. Risk factors for violence in stalking perpetration: A meta-analysis. *FWU Journal of Social Sciences* 7(2): 100.

Crown Prosecution Service. 2020. Stalking analysis reveals domestic abuse link. https://www.cps.gov.uk/cps/news/stalking-analysis-reveals-domestic-abuse-link. Accessed 5 December 2022.

Dáil Debates (15 April 1997) https://www.oireachtas.ie/en/debates/debate/dail/1997-04-15/speech/408/. Accessed 5 December 2022.

Department of Justice. 2022. Zero tolerance: Third national strategy on domestic, sexual and gender-based violence 2022–2026. https://www.gov.ie/en/publication/a43a9-third-national-strategy-on-domestic-sexual-and-gender-based-violence/. Accessed 5 December 2022.

Dietz, Noella A., and Patricia Yancey Martin. 2007. Women who are stalked: Questioning the fear standard. *Violence Against Women* 13(7): 750–776.

Douglas, Kevin S., and Donald G. Dutton. 2001. Assessing the link between stalking and domestic violence. *Aggression and Violent Behavior* 6(6): 519–546.

Englebrecht, Christine M., and Bradford W. Reyns. 2011. Gender differences in acknowledgment of stalking victimization: Results from the NCVS stalking supplement. *Violence and Victims* 26(5): 560–579.

European Institute for Gender Equality. 2019. Legal definitions in the EU Member States: Stalking and Estonia. https://eige.europa.eu/gender-based-violence/regulatory-and-legal-framework/legal-definitions-in-the-eu?ts=stalking&c[]=EE. Accessed 5 December 2022.

European Union Agency for Fundamental Rights. 2015. *Violence against women: An EU wide survey*. Luxembourg: Publications Office of the European Union.

Fitz-Gibbon, Kate, and Sandra Walklate. 2018. *Gender, crime and criminal justice* (3rd ed.). London: Routledge.

Fremouw, William J., Darah Westrup, and Jennifer Pennypacker. 1997. Stalking on campus: The prevalence and strategies for coping with stalking. *Journal of Forensic Science* 42(4): 666–669.

General Secretariat for Demography, Family Policy and Gender Equality of the Ministry of Labour and Social Affairs. 2022. Greece's report on the implementation of the Council of Europe convention on preventing and combating violence against women and domestic violence (Istanbul Convention). https://rm.coe.int/inf-2022-4-state-report-greece/1680a60a4e. Accessed 5 December 2022.

Hall, Doris M. 1998. The victims of stalking. In *The psychology of stalking*, ed. J. Reid Meloy, 113–137. San Diego: Academic Press.

Harmon, Ronnie B., Richard Rosner, and Howard Owens. 1995. Obsessional harassment and erotomania in a criminal court population. *Journal of Forensic Sciences* 40(2): 188–196.

Healy, Ann. 2020. 'Dangerous' student stalker sentenced to seven years in jail. *Irish Times*. https://www.irishtimes.com/news/crime-and-law/courts/circuit-court/dangerous-student-stalker-sentenced-to-seven-years-in-jail-1.4265164. Accessed 19 December 2022.

Heylin, Liam. 2021. Man jailed for attempting to break into woman's home to rape her. *The Irish Examiner*. https://www.irishexaminer.com/news/courtandcrime/arid-40220453.html. Accessed 5 December 2022.

Human Rights Monitoring Institute. 2021. Lithuania criminalizes stalking. https://www.liberties.eu/en/stories/lithuania-criminalizes-stalking/43788. Accessed 5 December 2022.

Jones, C. 1996. Criminal harassment (or stalking). *Juristat* 16(12)

Kienlen, Kristine K., Daniel L. Birmingham, Kenneth B. Solberg, and John T. O'Regan. 1997. A comparative study of psychotic and nonpsychotic stalking. *Journal of the American Academy of Psychiatry and the Law Online* 25(3): 317–334.

Langhinrichsen-Rohling, Jennifer. 2012. Gender and stalking: Current intersections and future directions. *Sex Roles* 66(5): 418–426.

Latvian Public Broadcasting and Z. Mače. 2018. 11 cases started since introduction of anti-stalking law. https://eng.lsm.lv/article/society/crime/11-cases-started-since-introduction-of-anti-stalking-law.a276100/. Accessed 5 December 2022.

Law Reform Commission. 1994. *Report on non-fatal offences against the person*. Dublin: Law Reform Commission.

Law Reform Commission. 2013. *Report on aspects of domestic violence.* Dublin: Law Reform Commission.

Law Reform Commission. 2016. *Report on harmful communications and digital safety.* Dublin: Law Reform Commission.

MacNeela, Pádraig, Kate Dawson, Theresa O'Rourke, Siobhán Healy-Cullen, Lorraine Burke, and W. Flack. 2022. *Report on the national survey of student experiences of sexual violence and harassment in Irish HEIs.* Dublin: HEA. https://www.gov.ie/en/publication/09bb5-report-on-surveys-of-experiences-of-sexual-violence-and-harassment-in-higher-education/. Accessed 5 December 2022.

McEwan, Troy, Paul E. Mullen, and Rosemary Purcell. 2007. Identifying risk factors in stalking: A review of current research. *International Journal of Law and Psychiatry* 30(1): 1–9.

McGreevy, Ronan, and Marie O'Halloran. 2021. Harassment law 'just not good enough' in dealing with stalking. *Irish Times.* https://www.irishtimes.com/news/ireland/irish-news/harassment-law-just-not-good-enough-in-dealing-with-stalking-1.4680950. Accessed 5 December 2022.

Meloy, J. Reid. 1996. Stalking (obsessional following): A review of some preliminary studies. *Aggression and Violent Behavior* 1(2): 147–162.

Meloy, J. Reid., ed. 1998. *The psychology of stalking: Clinical and forensic perspectives.* San Diego: Academic Press.

Meloy, J. Reid. 1999. Stalking: An old behaviour, A new crime. *Forensic Psychiatry* 22(1): 85–99.

Meloy, J. Reid, and S. Gothard. 1995. Demographic and clinical comparison of obsessional followers and offenders with mental disorders. *The American Journal of Psychiatry* 152(2): 258–263.

Mullen, Paul E., and Michele Pathé. 1994. Stalking and the pathologies of love. *Australian & New Zealand Journal of Psychiatry* 28(3): 469–477.

Mullen, Paul E., Michele Pathé, and Rosemary Purcell. 2009. *Stalkers and their victims*, 2nd ed. Cambridge: Cambridge University Press.

Nwachukwu, Izu, Vincent Agyapong, Leah Quinlivan, John Tobin, and Kevin Malone. 2012. Psychiatrists' experiences of stalking in Ireland: Prevalence and characteristics. *The Psychiatrist* 36(3): 89–93.

Ornstein, Petra, and Johanna Rickne. 2013. When does intimate partner violence continue after separation? *Violence Against Women* 19(5): 617–633.

O'Sullivan, Catherine, and Ciara Staunton. 2023. *Stalking and harassment: An investigation of experiences in Ireland.* https://www.ucc.ie/en/media/mandc/2023StalkingandHarassmentReport.pdf. Accessed 21 March 2023.

Owens, Jennifer Gatewood. 2016. Why definitions matter: Stalking victimization in the United States. *Journal of Interpersonal Violence* 31(12): 2196–2226.

Pathé, Michele and Mullen, Paul E. 1997. The impact of stalkers on their victims. *British Journal of Psychiatry*170(1): 12–17.

Purcell, Rosemary, Michele Pathé, and Paul E. Mullen. 2002. The prevalence and nature of stalking in the Australian community. *Australian & New Zealand Journal of Psychiatry* 36(1): 114–120.

Purcell, Rosemary, Michele Pathé, and Paul E. Mullen. 2004. Stalking: Defining and prosecuting a new category. *International Journal of Law and Psychiatry* 27(2): 157–169.

Schultz, Amy Sides, Julia Moore, and Brian H. Spitzberg. 2014. Once upon a midnight stalker: A content analysis of stalking in films. *Western Journal of Communication* 78(5): 612–635.

Scottish Government. 2020. *Domestic abuse and stalking charges in Scotland, 2019–20.*

Scottish Government. 2022. *Domestic abuse and stalking charges in Scotland, 2020–21.* https://www.copfs.gov.uk/media/xg1iwhm3/domestic-abuse-publication-2021-22-final.pdf . Accessed 5 December 2022.

Sheridan, Lorraine P., Eric Blaauw, and Graham M. Davies. 2003. Stalking: Knowns and unknowns. *Trauma, Violence, & Abuse* 4(2): 148–162.

Sheridan, Lorraine, and Graham M. Davies. 2001. Violence and the prior victim–stalker relationship. *Criminal Behaviour and Mental Health* 11(2): 102–116.

Sheridan, Lorraine, Graham Davies, and Julian Boon. 2001. The course and nature of stalking: A victim perspective. *The Howard Journal of Criminal Justice* 40(3): 215–234.

Šimonović, Dubravka. 2019. *Official visit to Bulgaria, 14–21 October 2019 by United Nations Special Rapporteur on violence against women, its causes and consequences*. https://www.ohchr.org/en/statements/2019/10/official-visit-bulgaria-14-21-october-2019-united-nations-special-rapporteur. Accessed 5 December 2022.

Spitzberg, Brian H., and William R. Cupach. 2007. The state of the art of stalking: Taking stock of the emerging literature. *Aggression and Violent Behavior* 12(1): 64–86.

Stark, Evan. 2007. *Coercive control: How men entrap women in personal life*. Oxford: Oxford University Press.

Taylor-Dunn, Holly, Erica Bowen, and Elizabeth A. Gilchrist. 2021. Reporting harassment and stalking to the police: A qualitative study of victims' experiences. *Journal of Interpersonal Violence* 36(11–12): NP5965-NP5992.

Thomas, Kurt, Devdatta Akhawe, Michael Bailey, Dan Boneh, Elie Bursztein, Sunny Consolvo, Nicola Dell et al. 2021. Sok: Hate, harassment, and the changing landscape of online abuse. In *2021 IEEE Symposium on Security and Privacy (SP)*, 247–267. IEEE.

Thomas, Stuart D.M., Rosemary Purcell, Michele Pathe, and Paul E. Mullen. 2008. Harm associated with stalking victimization. *Australian & New Zealand Journal of Psychiatry* 42(9): 800–806.

Tjaden, Patricia Godeke, and Nancy Thoennes. 1997. *Stalking in America: Findings from the National Violence Against Women Survey*. Denver: Center for Policy Research.

Tjaden, Patricia Godeke, and Nancy Thoennes. 1998. *Stalking in America: Findings from the National Violence Against Women Survey*. Washington, DC: US Department of Justice.

Townsend, Mark. 2020. New measures to beat stalking could put victims at risk. *The Guardian*. https://www.theguardian.com/uk-news/2020/jan/19/new-stalking-prevention-orders-victims-at-risk. Accessed 5 December 2022.

Union of Students of Ireland. 2013. *Say Something: A study of students' experiences of harassment, stalking, violence and sexual assault*. Dublin: Union of Students of Ireland.

van der Aa, Suzan. 2018. New trends in the criminalization of stalking in the EU member states. *European Journal on Criminal Policy and Research* 24(3): 315–333.

Walker, Lenore E., and J. Reid Meloy. 1998. Stalking and domestic violence. In *The psychology of stalking*, ed. J. Reid Meloy, 139–161. San Diego: Academic Press.

Women's Aid, *Femicide Watch*. ND. https://www.womensaid.ie/about/campaigns/femicide-in-ireland.html. Accessed 22 January 2023.

Zona, Michael A., Russell E. Palarea, and John C. Lane Jr. 1998. Psychiatric diagnosis and the offender-victim typology of stalking. In *The psychology of stalking*, ed. J. Reid Meloy, 69–84. San Diego: Academic Press, 1998.

Zona, Michael A., Kaushal K. Sharma, and John Lane. 1993. A comparative study of erotomanic and obsessional subjects in a forensic sample. *Journal of forensic sciences* 38(4): 894–903

Table of Legislation

Europe

Council of Europe Convention on Preventing and Combating Violence against Women and Domestic Violence (Istanbul Convention)

Ireland

Criminal Justice (Miscellaneous Provisions) Bill 2022.

Harassment, Harmful Communications and Related Offences Act 2020.

Non-Fatal Offences Against the Person Act 1997.

Non-Fatal Offences Against the Person Bill 1997.

Non-Fatal Offences Against the Person (Amendment) (Stalking) Bill 2021.

United Kingdom.

Criminal Justice and Licensing (Scotland) Act 2010.

Protection from Harassment Act 1997.

Protection from Stalking (Northern Ireland) Act 2022.
Protection of Freedoms Act 2012.

6 The Role of Technology in Stalking and Coercive Control Among Young People

James Banks and Catrin Andersson

> **Key Points**
>
> - Information communication technology is widely used by young people.
> - Technology facilitated coercive control and stalking behaviour can cause serious immediate and legacy harms to young people.
> - Legal, technological and educational responses involving state agencies, private organisations and citizenry are all required to prevent and mitigate the harm caused by technology facilitated coercive control and stalking.

Introduction

The UK represents one of the world's 'leading digital nations' (Department for Media, Culture and Sport 2022) with almost all (99%) children, young people and adults aged between 3 and 44 being recent internet users (Office of National Statistics 2021; Ofcom 2022a). Whilst households with internet access reached saturation a number of years ago (Livingstone and Smith 2014), individual ownership of multiple Internet enabled digital devices, such as mobiles phones, personal computers, security systems, lighting, heating and home assistants, continues to grow,

J. Banks (✉) · C. Andersson
Sheffield Hallam University, Sheffield, UK
e-mail: J.Banks@shu.ac.uk

C. Andersson
e-mail: C.Andersson@shu.ac.uk

M. Mellins et al. (eds.), *Young People, Stalking Awareness and Domestic Abuse*,
https://doi.org/10.1007/978-3-031-32379-9_6

further facilitating interconnectivity that transcends physical boundaries. Notably, the uptake and use of such technologies is particularly pronounced among young people.

Information and communication technology (ICT) has become an integral part of the daily life of a significant proportion of young people across the globe. According to the United Nations specialised agency for ICT, The International Telecommunication Union (ITU), 71% of young people aged between 15 and 24 were using the internet in 2020 (ITU 2022). By comparison 57% of other age groups across the world were using the internet, meaning that young people were 1.24 times more likely to go online than other age groups (Ibid.).

The pervasiveness of ICT and degree to which it is embedded in the day-to-day lives of many young people presents both opportunities and challenges. Undoubtedly, the importance of ICT for personal, educational and work-related purposes intensified during the Covid-19 pandemic. For example, internet and social media use doubled among 12–16 year olds in the UK throughout the pandemic, with young people not only using websites and applications, such as YouTube, Snapchat and TikTok, to view content but also increasingly to create, upload and share their own material (Brudvig and van der Wilk 2022; Ofcom 2022b). The ubiquity of ICT enables young people to eschew the limitations of space and time and has the potential to positively impact their lives in multiple ways (Livingstone and Helsper 2010). For example, through the internet, young people can connect with their peers, develop and maintain relationships, access communities of like-minded individuals and/or those with shared interests, reduce social isolation and loneliness, and increase access to knowledge and information, whilst breaking down barriers and traditional social divides. Thus, it is clear that the affordances of ICT mean that it will continue to have a significant role in the lives of young people.

Yet at the same time as offering a range of potential benefits, increased adoption of and engagement with ICT increases young people's exposure to a host of cyber risks. Such risks may relate to potentially harmful content, contacts, conducts or contracts (Livingstone and Stoilova 2021) that can negatively impact a young person's safety, health and wellbeing. Consequently, academics from across a range of disciplines have sought to explore the risks posed by ICT to young people, with a view to enhancing safeguards for those online. A particular focus of this work has been aggressive or sexual harms including hate speech, cyberbullying, sexual messaging and pornography (see, for example, Tynes 2006; Flood 2009; Crofts et al. 2015; Hamm et al. 2015). In addition, academics have begun to explore how ICT may be a conduit for a range of other abusive behaviours.

This chapter introduces readers to the role of technology in facilitating and enhancing stalking and coercive and controlling practices. We begin by exploring young people's engagement with ICT and how this enhances the capabilities of individuals to engage in, and be a victim of, stalking and coercive and controlling behaviours. The chapter illustrates how the unique characteristics of information communication technologies—namely storage, synchronicity, replicability and mobility (Baym 2015)—can be weaponised to control, intimidate, isolate, shame and surveille (Stark 2007). Drawing on studies centred on survivor and practitioner testimony, we illustrate how emerging technologies enhance the capability of individuals to engage in synchronous and asynchronous contact both during a relationship or after a relationship has ended. Emails, text messaging, phone calls and social media posts feature as means through which individuals may be harassed, intimidated and threatened by current or former partners, whilst geolocation technologies, such as the mapping of posts on Facebook, have been augmented by recent innovations, such as Apple's AirTags, to enable perpetrators to appear omnipresent regardless of their location. Discussion develops to critically consider the implications of technology facilitated stalking and coercive and controlling behaviour for policy and practice. Legal, technological and educational responses to prevent and mitigate harm are given consideration, as is the role of state agencies, private organisations and citizenry. In particular, we examine the responses of criminal justice agencies and domestic abuse advocates and assess the regulation and governance of online abuse by telecommunications businesses and social media organisations, making recommendations for the better governance of developing technologies in order to protect young people.

The Role and Function of ICT in Stalking and Coercive Control

Young people have been quick and prominent adopters of the use of technology as a communications tool. By 2020, 99.5% of men and women aged between 16 and 24 in the UK had used the Internet in the last three months (ONS 2021). This widespread use of ICT to communicate with friends, family and others whilst increasing interconnectivity also reduces the amount of control individuals have over personal data and presents a challenge to privacy. For example, disclosing personal information on social media platforms has become normalised. In addition, smartphones, by default, store Global Positioning System (GPS) locations and the coordinates of photos (Hamid and Maple 2013), whilst many people also voluntarily share their physical location through the 'check-in' function on social media sites such as Facebook.

These technological functions mean that surveillance is both 'enabled and encouraged', as public or semi-public messages and information can be recorded and archived (Tokunaga 2011) for a variety of purposes. ICT's ability to bridge physical distance and facilitate anonymity encourages more harmful behaviours compared to in-person communication (Stonard 2020). Youths as young as thirteen years old acknowledge that ICT enables them to easily monitor their partner's online activity (Stonard 2020) and check their 'online status' via social media (March et al. 2022), although this is often viewed as relatively harmless behaviour. However, young people's increased engagement with social media has been associated with cyberstalking perpetration (Marcum et al. 2017). Other serious and controlling behaviours linked to cyberstalking can include checking a partner's emails or logging into their accounts, communicating or creating a fake account and posing as their partner, monitoring their partner by location settings (March et al. 2022) or engaging in sexting (Mori et al. 2020; Reyns 2019). In short, as this section illustrates, ICT can play an important role in acts of stalking and coercive control, functioning in a number of ways.

It is difficult to dispute that the distinct characteristics of ICT—namely, storage, synchronicity, replicability and mobility (Baym 2015)—have significantly enhanced the scope for stalking and coercive control within relationships. Technology facilitated abuse often occurs in tandem and is interrelated with in-person abuse (Barter et al. 2017; Duerksen and Woodin 2019; Gilbar et al. 2022; Marganski and Melander 2018; Stonard 2020), although the behaviours are similar in both forms of offending (Fiolet et al. 2021). It has been argued that ICT has simply provided 'old abuse with new tools' (Cuomo and Dolci 2021) because of the ease with which partners and ex-partners can be contacted and monitored. This perspective is echoed in interviews with domestic abuse service providers where it is noted that: 'The technology abuse, it's really just another…form of control…' (Fiolet et al. 2021, 3).

A number of recent studies highlight how the use of ICT in acts of abuse among adults (Dragiewicz et al. 2021; Messing et al. 2020; Woodlock et al. 2020, 2022) and young people is commonplace (Barter et al. 2017; Burke et al. 2011; Marganski and Melander 2018). For example, Smith-Dardon et al. (2017) found that a third of an American sample of 727 middle and high school children engaged in electronic aggression (i.e., cyberstalking, harassment and coercive sexting) in a romantic relationship. Similarly, in an Australian sample of 527 women and men between 16 and 25 years old, over half of the participants had experienced one or more technology facilitated behaviours, including humiliation, monitoring and control, threats and sexual coercion, in the last 12 months (Brown et al. 2021). Collectively, such work illustrates how technology is a tool which extends the reach and repertoire of coercive and controlling behaviours in relationships (Harris and Vitis 2020; Stark 2007; Woodlock et al. 2022).

A large proportion of research on ICT facilitated IPV concerns female victims. Research has shown that women and girls consistently report higher cyberstalking victimisation rates than men or boys (Ahlgrim and Terrance 2021) and the impact on women and girls tends to be more serious. As such, coercive and controlling behaviour facilitated by technology exacerbates gendered violence (Harris and Vitis 2020).

Woodlock (2017) explored the nature of stalking involving mobile technology and its effect on IPV survivors. Utilising the SmartSafe study[1] conducted by the Domestic Violence Resource Centre Victoria (DVRCV) in Australia, data was drawn from two online surveys, focus groups and interviews with 152 domestic abuse workers and 46 victims/survivors. Woodlock (2017) applied the findings to Stark's (2007) framework of coercive control identifying three broad themes that reflect the cyberstalking perpetrators' goals: omnipresence, isolation, humiliation and punishment—within an overarching aim of control and intimidation—which we explore in detail below.

First, ICT amplifies the effects of stalking on IPV victims and survivors through the 'the omnipresent' perpetrator (Stark 2007). The very nature of ICT guarantees increased access to the victim, as a consequence of the lack of spatial and temporal barriers (Woodlock 2017; Yardley 2021). Perpetrators have the ability to contact or monitor victims at all hours of the day (Boethius et al. 2022; Cuomo and Dolci 2021; Dragiewicz et al. 2021; Stonard 2020). A victim of ICT facilitated domestic abuse verbalises the idea of perpetrator omnipresence as 'I'm always in your inbox...' (Melander 2010, 265). A compound effect of the technological nature of the abuse is that harassment can be multimodal because it can occur virtually anywhere simultaneously on multiple devices, applications and platforms (Cuomo and Dolci 2021).

Perpetrator omnipresence typically transpires in three consecutive stages: overt, covert and retributive (Yardley 2021). Overt omnipresence occurs when the use of monitoring and control are not hidden, but they appear to be 'normal' behaviours used by perpetrators. This can be achieved through numerous text messages or phone calls (Woodlock 2017). Covert omnipresence follows when the behaviours are more secretive, and the victim does not know or does not have proof that they are being monitored. The behaviours associated with this type of omnipresence can be difficult to prevent because of their covert nature (Cuomo and Dolci 2021; Dragiewicz et al. 2019).

Retributive omnipresence represents the stage in which a survivor leaves a relationship and the perpetrator switches strategy to remain in control. Coercive control, including stalking, through ICT usually escalates or begins at separation of a relationship (Dragiewicz et al. 2019,2021; Woodlock et al. 2022). Perpetrators thus extend the reach of coercive control after the relationship has ended (Dragiewicz et al. 2021). The perpetrator may draw on information that was accessed during the overt and covert phases of omnipresence. Some of this information may have been retrieved by unauthorised access to personal information or accounts (Dragiewicz et al. 2019; Stonard, 2020). Retributive omnipresence is strongly linked to isolation and humiliation as the perpetrator aims to tarnish the survivor's image (Yardley 2021).

Second, isolation is another key aim of perpetrators of coercive and controlling practices through ICT. In the context of stalking, this can be achieved through technology facilitated direct and indirect harassment of the victim's loved ones (Woodlock 2017). The purpose is to ostracise the victim, by distancing or removing them from their social network (Boethius et al. 2022; Cuomo and Dolci 2021; Douglas et al. 2019; Dragiewicz et al. 2019; Woodlock et al. 2020).

Third, humiliation and punishment can take a variety of forms, for example, exposing personal information (i.e., doxing) (Freed et al. 2018), through the non-consensual use of sexual content (Boethius et al. 2022; Cuomo and Dolci 2021) and sexting (Woodlock 2017). Threatening to use sexual images obtained through sexting is an increasingly frequent occurrence among young adults (Branch et al. 2017; Mori et al. 2020). The threats may materialise through the release of sexual images or videos on Facebook (Woodlock 2017) or through text messages (Branch et al. 2017) in order to publicly humiliate and punish the victims (Woodlock 2017).

As reflected in the perpetrator goals, coercive control and stalking both occur and thrive in a 'spacelessness' that is enabled by ICT (Harris and Vitis 2020;

Woodlock et al. 2022). Coercive and controlling behaviours often used to occur in physical 'private spaces' prior to technological advances (Harris and Woodlock 2019). As such, ICT has enhanced the efficacy of these behaviours in incomparable ways and become integral to many perpetrators' schemes (Dragiewicz et al. 2021). Technology enables these behaviours to be economical, convenient and efficient for perpetrators (Cuomo and Dolci 2021), as they can more easily undertake, hide and cover their activities using ICT devices (Stonard 2020).

Types of Technology Used for Coercive Control and Stalking Behaviours

As we detail below, a variety of technology is used for stalking depending on the purpose of the activity (e.g., harassment, communication, monitoring). This includes, but is not limited to, smartphones with applications, computers and, to a lesser extent, GPS devices and smart systems with video and/or audio (e.g., baby monitors, security systems) (Rogers et al. 2022). Stalking using ICT is generally unsophisticated in nature, relying heavily on readily available software and applications (Freed et al. 2018).

Mobile phones or smartphones are most frequently used in the perpetration of technology-based coercive and controlling behaviours (Boethius et al. 2022; Freed et al. 2018), primarily for text messaging (Woodlock 2017; Woodlock et al. 2020; Douglas et al. 2019) or sending emails (Boethius et al. 2022; Woodlock 2017; Woodlock et al. 2020). However, research has shown that social media facilitated stalking is becoming more commonplace (Woodlock 2017; Douglas et al. 2019; Boethius et al. 2022), particularly via Facebook (Woodlock et al. 2020). Social-nmedia platforms are attractive because they can offer the perpetrator anonymity (Kaur et al. 2021) and blur the lines between personal communication and public information (Dragiewicz et al. 2018).

Data suggests that the use of GPS in stalking and controlling behaviours is less common than assumed, but its use is likely to be underestimated because victims are often unaware that they are being/have been tracked and therefore unable to report it (Dragiewicz et al. 2018; Woodlock 2017; Woodlock et al. 2020). The GPS function in mobile/smartphones can extend to a number of applications that track individuals' movements (Hamid and Maple 2013). Dual use applications, such as Find My Friends or Find My App, are designed for legitimate use (Freed et al. 2018). However, many dual use applications are used for surveillance of intimate partners, an issue which is exacerbated by companies often condoning such nefarious activities (Chatterjee et al. 2018). An example of a dual use application which has emerged recently is Apple's AirTag. The AirTag is a small tracker device linked to an Apple product's 'Find My' application (i.e., iPhone, iPad and iPod) that helps the user locate any item to which the tracker is attached. In response to concerns of person tracking, further security settings have been added so that if an AirTag is placed on another person, this person will receive a notification that this has occurred (https://www.apple.com/uk/airtag/). Nevertheless, there is a time lag of several hours before the person gets a notification that a foreign AirTag is attached to them. In addition, many people have reported being unable to hear the notification that warns them that someone else's AirTag is on their person or vehicle (Fry 2022).

Spyware applications that gather information from a computer system without the user's permission is another tool of concern, as it has the capability to drastically enhance stalking and coercive behaviours. Intimate partners appear to be one of the key target groups for spyware products (Hamid and Maple 2013). The most popular products capture phone calls, SMS messages, internet browsing, GPS location, photos and videos, and content from applications, such as WhatsApp and Facebook. Premium versions of, for example, MSpy, can block calls and websites, gain keylogging capability to retrieve passwords or inputted text. Regardless of the intended purpose, this type of product reflects an invasive level of data-monitoring, namely surveillance (Harkin et al. 2020).

Freed et al. (2018) found in their study that the use of Spyware is actually quite rare. However, much like GPS tracking, it is difficult to prove its use due to the difficulties in detecting such software, even when victims suspected it is being used. Moreover, removal of such technologies can also be problematic as such actions would be known to the perpetrator and can lead to an escalation of abuse. Surveillance tools, including Spyware (Harkin et al. 2020), are generally easily and cheaply obtained due to commoditisation of these products (Freed et al. 2017). Disconcertingly, marketing information focuses on the user of the product (not the consequences of the receiver), and legal disclaimers put responsibility on the user rather than the company (Harkin et al. 2020).

What Is the Impact of ICT Facilitated Stalking and Coercive Control?

The impact of ICT facilitated coercive and controlling behaviours on victims is often overlooked in research. A scoping review[2] of 22 empirical qualitative and quantitative studies on technology facilitated abuse within intimate relationships, including participant samples of various ages, concluded that there are four principal ways in which the impact of offending on victims can be categorised; the often-overlapping categories are social, mental health, financial and omnipresence (Rogers et al. 2022), which are closely linked to the perpetrator goals (Woodlock 2017) discussed earlier in this chapter.

A high proportion of adult victims report detrimental effects of coercive control and stalking on their mental health and overall wellbeing (Woodlock 2017; Dragiewich et al. 2019; Fiolet et al. 2021; Truman 2011). As previously noted, technology facilitated domestic abuse can exacerbate a victim's experience, and for some, result in additional trauma (Dragiewicz et al. 2019). Some victims report symptoms of Post-Traumatic Stress Disorder (PTSD) following cyberstalking or abuse incidents (Mumford et al. 2022). Additionally, low moods and depressive symptoms that lead to a pessimistic world view are also common. Following these primary emotional responses are often secondary emotional responses, such as anger and aggression (Worsley et al. 2017).

The feeling that the perpetrator is omnipresent ensures that there is a constant impact on the victim's wellbeing and sense of safety (Fiolet et al. 2021; Woodlock et al. 2020; Woodlock 2017). In addition, the isolation that may result from the victim needing to move or change employment and/or social networks to evade the perpetrator can further impact their wellbeing (Woodlock 2017) whilst also having financial consequences (Dragiewicz et al. 2019). Even though victims may detach themselves from or leave the perpetrator, they often feel the need to monitor or 'check-in' on them through internet devices which adds to the victim's emotional burden (Dragiewicz et al. 2019).

In both young and old victims, invasion of privacy and the curtailment of technology can be seen as damaging and infringing on victims' basic dignity and freedom (Dragiewicz et al. 2019; Stonard 2020). Victims may also feel as though they are never free from the perpetrator's influence (Woodlock 2017) and that they lack control over their lives (Stonard 2020). These significant impacts are aggravated by concerns around the lasting effects of internet communications between victims and perpetrators because any such communication leaves a digital trace which is nearly permanent (Stonard 2020). As such, not only the perpetrator but also the digital traces of ICT facilitated abuse are omnipresent (Rogers et al. 2022).

Victims of all ages engage in a number of behaviours to cope with their experiences. Coping strategies include avoiding or ignoring the perpetrator by restricting social media activity (see Rogers et al. 2022), confronting the perpetrator (which can make stalking worse), acquiring social support or using cognitive reframing (e.g., changing their view of the experience or trying to understand the perpetrator) (Worsley et al. 2017). Victims may also distance themselves from technology to prevent contact, although abuse often escalates if the victim disengages with ICT (Cuomo and Dolci 2021; Dragiewicz et al. 2019, 2021). Young people find it especially helpful to block, change accounts or passwords to try to avoid the perpetrator (Stonard 2020).

When it comes to seeking help to cope with the experiences of ICT-related stalking and coercive control, many victims do not seek help (Mumford et al. 2022). Numerous studies have reported that most help-seeking is from informal sources, such as friends and family, rather than contacting formal services or support groups (Begotti et al. 2022; Fissel 2021; Woodlock 2017; Worsley et al. 2017). Recent quantitative research involving 1,215 young Americans shows that technological support is the most common type of help-seeking for this age group (Mumford et al. 2022). Teenagers have also reported using social media to 'vent' or communicate with friends as a more public way of coping. This provides a means to 'emotionally offload' which helps them cope with their experiences (Stonard 2020).

Victims can be both empowered (Douglas et al. 2019) and disempowered (Stonard 2020) by technology. Reflective of this dualism, ICT facilitated coercive control and stalking have been framed as a 'double-edged sword' (Boethius et al. 2022). Some victims have reported on the positive role of technology in helping them cope with their experiences (Douglas et al. 2019; Stonard 2020), whilst others highlight how they have harnessed it (Woodlock et al. 2022) to offer 'technology-facilitated resistance' to abusive behaviours (Rogers et al. 2022). Both young and old adults use ICT to 'defend' and protect themselves, including finding support, obtaining evidence against the perpetrator and to avenge the perpetrator (Boethius et al. 2022; Douglas et al. 2019; Stonard 2020).

Responding to Coercive Control and Stalking Behaviour

As discussion so far illustrates, ICT now plays a fundamental role in coercive control and stalking behaviour and can cause serious immediate and legacy harms to young people. Economic, convenient and efficient, technology facilitated coercive control and stalking has facilitated and accelerated incidents of abuse by extending the spatial and temporal control of offenders (Cuomo and Dolci 2021). As Vitis and Segrave (2017, 5) note, 'technology is altering, intensifying and facilitating gendered violence'. Consequently, technology facilitated coercive control and stalking, although not a new form of abuse, is a developing challenge for criminal justice professionals, domestic abuse workers and other groups and organisations. Furthering our understanding of technology facilitated coercive control and stalking experienced by young people is essential if effective legal, policy and practice responses to such abuse are to be instituted (McGlynn et al. 2021). Discussion now turns to critically consider responses to date and the potential avenues for further preventing and mitigating the harm experienced by young people through coercive control and stalking behaviours.

In the UK, acts of technology facilitated coercive control are prosecuted under the Domestic Abuse Act 2021 whilst technology facilitated stalking may incorporate a range of offences that fall under Protection from Harassment Act 1997, the Offences Against the Person Act 1861, the Sexual Offences Act 2003 and the Malicious Communications Act 1988. As discussed in earlier sections of this chapter and noted by DeKeseredy (2021), online victimisation is often intertwined with offline victimisation, as victims of domestic abuse can experience multiple forms of victimisation. This polyvictimisation (Mitchell et al. 2018), in which technology enables *both* online and offline coercive and stalking behaviours, presents new challenges for justice systems, as they seek to respond effectively to the various ways in which abuse and violence may be enacted.

Professional and academic understanding of the role of technology, the organisational dynamics of offending behaviour and how and where services need to adapt their approach to help and support young people experiencing technology facilitated coercive control and stalking behaviour is still in its infancy (Douglas et al. 2019; Havard 2020). Raising awareness and understanding of, and improving responses to, such incidents among criminal justice professionals through training is, however, clearly an important mechanism through which harm may be more effectively prevented and mitigated. This is essential, as evidence (Woodlock et al. 2020) indicates that criminal justice professionals neither have a full understanding of the impact of technology facilitated coercive and stalking behaviour nor are they always equipped with the technological knowledge and expertise to support victims and prevent or minimise future harm. For example, survivors of technology facilitated coercive control who participated in Dragiewicz et al.'s (2019) study into domestic violence and communication technology found that often when survivors reported incidents of technology facilitated coercive control (TFCC) police officers stated that there was nothing they could do to help. Problematically, both the police and courts may fail to recognise that an offence has taken place or appropriately identify and respond to potential risks and harms relating to TFCC and stalking behaviour (Woodlock et al. 2020). Moreover, police officers may not be equipped with the training and technical competencies to check and secure digital devices, such as laptops and mobile phones, provide guidance on how to collect evidence or see if an individual is being monitored (Dragiewicz et al. 2019). Similarly, it is reported that courts did not ask questions regarding TFCC as there appeared to be 'uncertainty about what evidence would be useful in court, how much evidence should be collected for use in court, and how to present it to the court in a way that would be useful' (Dragiewicz et al. 2019, 31).

The lack of appropriate criminal justice responses may well be because technology facilitated stalking and coercive behaviour is not yet seen as a serious part of IPV by (all) criminal justice practitioners (Woodlock 2013; Powell and Henry 2018; Dragiewicz et al. 2019). Woodlock et al. (2020, 375) note that digital behaviours may be interpreted by criminal justice professionals as a 'minor annoyance' and consequently 'using this as evidence of harassment or abuse was not necessarily a straightforward process because some community services, courts, and police failed to recognise the significant impacts and risks created by Digital Coercive Control'. Indeed, both police officers and courts are reported as prioritising physical forms of abuse over other types of harmful action, such as TFCC and stalking behaviour, which are not seen as being particularly 'dangerous' (Dragiewicz et al. 2019).

The failure of criminal justice agencies to recognise or respond to acts of technology facilitated coercive and stalking behaviour can compound the harm experienced by survivors of abuse. Drawing on Smith and Freyd's (2014) concept of 'institutional betrayal', wherein acts of courage are met with disbelief or downplayed, Woodlock et al. (2022) suggest that victims may experience further trauma from the criminal justice system's 'institutional response' when reporting incidents of domestic abuse. Previous studies of TFCC (Woodlock 2013) and cyberstalking and law enforcement (Millman et al. 2017) reported that police officers would minimise or dismiss the harm caused or blame victims for their victimisation. Officers would often focus on the online behaviour of victims and their perceived unwillingness to change their internet activities or close online accounts. Such acts of institutional betrayal not only relate to police officers but were also evident in the courtroom where judges and barristers focused their attention on physical forms of violence (Dragiewicz et al. 2019). Woodlock and colleague's (2022, 13) interviews with 20 female survivors highlight how 'institutional processes that minimized or dismissed the harms of TFCC as a nonphysical form of abuse' compounded 'the grief and loss associated with TFCC and leaving an abusive relationship'.

Thus, the training of criminal justice practitioners to understand the role and impact of technology facilitated abuse and how best to respond to such crimes experienced by young people is essential. This will better enable practitioners to intervene with measures that reduce the potential for harm to occur whilst also supporting evidence collection and ensuring that any harm and its impact is appropriately recognised and responded to at all stages of the criminal justice process. The desire for training is evident in Powell and Henry's (2018, 304) interviews with police officers and other practitioners who note that there is:

> [A] need to extend the training and resources for police to respond more effectively to victims of TFSV [technology-facilitated sexual violence]. In particular, some police stakeholders expressed the desirability of resourcing for intelligence practitioners, trained to conduct online research identifying and documenting malicious online behaviours that are domestic violence or stalking related. Our stakeholders also commonly identified a need for training local police to respond less dismissively when victims present with a report of technology-facilitated abuse, stalking or harassment.

In turn, if officers and other criminal justice professional adopt trauma informed responses, they may be better positioned to understand that technology facilitated stalking and coercive behaviour, which they perceive as innocuous, has serious implication for survivors and respond accordingly.

The need for raising awareness and training extends beyond the criminal justice system to other sectors, most significantly domestic abuse help and support workers, who may increasingly encounter technology facilitated coercive control and stalking behaviour among young people. As Cuomo and Dolci (2022, 3) note: 'While not universally reflective of all domestic violence agencies or individual advocates, scholars have noted that the domestic violence field is generally "behind the curve" when it comes to technology'. However, evidence indicates that practitioners have become acutely aware of the role of technology in coercive and controlling and stalking behaviours during the COVID pandemic, recognising the need for services to provide technological advice (Woodlock 2017) whilst also utilising online tools as part of their advocacy work (Hodes 2021; Wood 2021). Despite this, it appears that domestic abuse practitioners, like police officers, as generalists, are often not well equipped to help victims disengage with technology (Harris and Woodlock 2022a). Problematically, where technological knowledge and skills do exist they are unequally distributed across the support service. Consequently, staff who are recognised as being comfortable with technology may become overloaded with referrals from less confident and competent colleagues, whilst this expertise may not be retained if a staff member moves to a new role in different area or to a new job (Cuomo and Dolci 2022). Ensuring that a range of services are able to effectively support young people experiencing technology related coercive and stalking behaviours is therefore a priority.

Developing trauma informed and survivor centred community-based resources that utilise technical expertise has proven successful in empowering 'survivors with the skills and knowledge to more safely use and engage with technology in their everyday lives and relationships' (Cuomo and Dolci 2022, 3). Cuomo and Dolci (2022) report on a Seattle-based Technology-Enabled Coercive Control (TECC) Clinic wherein a volunteer technical specialist, who has received training in understanding coercive and controlling behaviour, is paired with a survivor experiencing TECC. The study's findings indicate that such an approach can assist in filling the knowledge gap of advocates and support the integration of technology considerations as a regular part of safety planning alongside trauma informed specialised consultation resources. By instituting technology related considerations, as part of standard safety planning, individuals are better equipped to prevent and respond to TECC and mitigate the harm that can result from digital security breaches and invasions of privacy.

However, as Woodlock et al. (2020, 368) note: 'A major dilemma faced by practitioners is how to promote and facilitate client safety from DCC while still enabling safe use of technology so clients can remain connected to family, friends, and community'. Studies have consistently demonstrated that technology related safety planning focuses on responsibilising individuals (Millman et al. 2017; Burke et al. 2011; Harris and Woodlock 2019). Advice from criminal justice practitioners or other non-governmental agencies is often focused on victims changing their online behaviours—the accounts, passwords and settings they use, the social media and other sites they frequent and the information they give out—or better still limiting/stopping their use of digital technology. In short, 'the focus is generally on the need for women to stop using technology' (Harris and Woodlock 2019, 539). In addition, police may place the burden on victims to collect evidence of coercive and stalking behaviour by saving text messages and emails and taking screenshots (Dragiewicz et al. 2019).

For young people experiencing coercive control and/or stalking behaviours, ICT can act as a key conduit for help and support from both formal organisations and informal networks, particularly when they may be geographically isolated from physical forms of help and support (Harris and Woodlock 2022b). Indeed, it has been noted by Woodlock and colleagues (2020) that safety may not always be increased by 'switching off' digital devices. Drawing on survey data from 546 Australian domestic abuse practitioners, they noted how victims would often be put under pressure by police, courts and other help and support services to disengage, replace or alter the settings of internet enabled devices, and close social media accounts and other platforms such as banks and utilities that may be accessed online. Disconcertingly, practitioners in this study highlighted that such measures do not always work to increase the safety of women instead leading to heightened feelings of fear and vulnerability, direct in-person contact from the perpetrator or an escalation in retaliation. In addition, these measures may create a 'sense of unpredictability' as they are no longer have information regarding the perpetrator's state of mind (Ibid., 375). This is significant given that evidence (Weisz et al. 2000) indicates that the most accurate prediction of the likelihood of perpetrator violence in the future will come from a victim's judgement. Thus, when supporting young people, it is important that criminal justice professionals and domestic abuse workers and advocates avoid simply telling young people to stop using technology as this is neither likely to increase their safety or present a reasonable course of action for individuals for whom computers, mobile phones and other forms of communication are an integral part of their lives.

Alongside improving the legal responses and protections for victims of technology facilitated coercive control and stalking, preventing and mitigating harm can be achieved through a more considered approach to the ways in which ICT is designed and operated. Indeed, it has been recognised that criminal law may not always be the 'first or best way to respond to the range of technology-facilitated harms that victims experience' (Powell and Henry 2018, 304). Telecommunications companies and social media platforms can also do much more to protect young people from coercive, stalking and other abusive behaviours. Quite rightly, platforms are under increasing social pressure to prevent harm and abuse experienced by young people (Dragiewicz et al. 2018).

As Dragiewicz et al. (2018) note, online communications are shaped by both the design of platforms and the ways in which they governed. Online communications and the potential for coercive, controlling and stalking behaviours are shaped by the platform architecture and algorithms. User features 'are oriented towards the maximisation of content sharing and user interaction, encouraging the publication of private details within a medium with instantaneous and international reach' (Salter 2016, 2725). Thus, it is essential that social media and other telecommunications companies think carefully about how they construct back-end frameworks and front-end user interfaces, how they may intentionally or unintentionally facilitate abuse or enable those experiencing coercive and stalking behaviour to prevent or mitigate harm by 'blocking users', reporting abuse or engaging in other creative means through which counter abuse (Dragiewicz et al. 2018).

By recognising that they are not merely 'passive facilitators of communications' (Dragiewicz et al. 2018, 615) social media companies and other telecommunications businesses can actively play a role in limiting and preventing coercive practices and stalking behaviours that are experienced by young people. This may be achieved through ensuring that users have access to user friendly options and technologies that prevent or limit unwanted intrusions, secure their profiles, accounts and other data, and block, filter and alert companies to unwanted intrusions, content and activities. Effective mechanisms through which users are able to report abuse and unwanted behaviour that are supported by trained and responsive support staff are also essential. At present, telecommunications businesses and social media companies wield 'disproportionate power' in how they review and respond to reported content and behaviour, whilst their rules and requirements are often enforced in an inconsistent and contradictory manner (Dragiewicz et al. 2018). In order to overcome such challenges and better serve the needs of those experiencing coercive control, stalking and other abusive behaviours through the platforms:

> Telecommunications firms will need to spend considerable time with their diverse stakeholders to understand the range of human rights issues and develop mechanisms to track

> this impact over time. This is not a straightforward or simple task, but it is a necessary precondition to developing effective responses to GBV and other abuses online. (Suzor et al. 2019, 94)

Allied to engaging young people in developing 'technological fixes' to mitigate and prevent abuse, ICT may be made safer by addressing the ways in which young people interact with and through technology. As Klein (2012, 127) notes, 'Ending abuse is not only about specialized services delivered by trained professionals. It is perhaps more importantly about 'humdrum' cultural change in which everyone does things a little differently every day'. Working with young people to help them consider their relationship with technology, expectations around privacy, and each other, and how this can result in coercive or stalking behaviours would be an important step in such change.

One would hope that businesses under pressure to better protect young people and others will prioritise the development of effective mechanisms that are responsive to the needs of those who may experience coercive control and stalking that is routed through information communication technology. However, given that such measures may run counter to the commercial imperatives of businesses, states must be willing to instigate the development of regulatory frameworks that compel telecommunications and social media organisations to reduce opportunities for information communication technologies to be used as a conduit for abuse and harm.

Gaps in the Empirical Literature

Some of the current gaps in the literature on ICT facilitated stalking and coercive control include the lack of research around gender and ethnic diversity of victims, characteristics and behaviours of perpetrators and witnesses, and the overall impact of technology facilitated stalking and coercive control behaviours (Rogers et al. 2022). Research on technology facilitated abuse tends to focus on women victims and in studies which included men and women victims the results have not distinguished between the two sexes (Henry et al. 2020). Research on LGBTQI+ individuals' victimisation is also needed, particularly with a focus on qualitative methods. Whilst there is no shortage of quantitative studies per se, especially on young people, there is a lack of quantitative research on the prevalence of technology facilitated abuse in the general population (Bailey et al. 2021).

Much of what we know about technology-based abuse comes from English speaking countries, notably the US, the UK, Australia and Canada (Afrouz and Robinson 2022; Rogers et al. 2022). Methodological gaps in the literature are clear in terms of research designs and sampling. The majority of studies use a cross-sectional research design, and to get a better understanding of how experiences of stalking and coercive control may change over time, longitudinal research designs are needed (Douglas et al. 2019; Henry et al. 2020). Moreover, participant samples for mixed methods and qualitative studies are generally quite small, especially those around domestic abuse (Woodlock 2017; Stonard et al. 2017). In order to better understand the full range of experiences of young people, we need to move away from the narrow confines of convenience sampling of university students (Douglas et al. 2019; Henry et al. 2020).

Conclusion

This chapter demonstrates the increased centrality of ICT in the lives of young people and how such technology may act as a conduit for stalking and coercive behaviours. Facilitating interconnectivity that transcends space and time, ICT has been heralded for its ability to overcome physical boundaries, expediate the sharing of knowledge and information and enable individuals to connect and build communities. However, alongside the many benefits afforded by ICT, it also poses challenges in terms of the ease with which personal data many be shared and personal privacy diminished, and the harms that may occur as a consequence. Coercive control and stalking have emerged among a range of abusive behaviours that may be facilitated by ICT. Conducted primarily through smartphones and computers, but also GPS and other smart systems, the anonymity afforded by the internet, alongside its ability to transcend physical boundaries, means that such technologies are economic, convenient and efficient conduits for such harms (Cuomo and Dolci 2021). Thriving in the 'spacelessness' that ICT facilitates, perpetrators are able to appear omnipresent and use technology to isolate, humiliate and punish. Evidence indicates that technology facilitated coercive control and stalking can have significant immediate and legacy impacts, causing social, mental, financial and omnipresent harms (Rogers et al. 2022).

Understanding the organisational dynamics of technology facilitated coercive control and stalking behaviour, the impact of such crimes, and how best to prevent and mitigate harm is an ongoing endeavour. Whilst legal frameworks are in place to prosecute perpetrators of technology facilitated abuse committed against young people, a lack understanding of the impact of technology facilitated coercive and stalking behaviour among criminal justice practitioners means they do not always effectively respond to such crimes nor are they well placed to prevent or minimise future harm. Evidence indicates that police officers and court officials may fail to recognise abuse and potential risks, and if they do recognise such behaviour they may trivialise it. This can lead to victims feeling that they have been betrayed by an institution whose professionals exhibit disbelief or downplay the seriousness of technology facilitated coercive control or stalking behaviour compounding the harm they experience as a consequence of such crimes. As such, ensuring that criminal justice practitioners are adequately trained to understand and respond to technology facilitated abuse experienced by young people is essential.

Elsewhere, domestic violence support services need to ensure that technology related support and safety planning forms part of their response to harms experienced by young people as this has proven to be an effective approach to mitigating future harm (Cuomo and Dolci 2022). In doing so, domestic violence practitioners, like their criminal justice counterparts, must ensure that they do not simply advocate that young people disengage with technology, but work with them to ensure that they optimise the technology related safeguards that are available to them. In turn, ensuring that user friendly options and technological safeguards, alongside transparent and responsive reporting are developed by telecommunication and social media business should be mandated and monitored by states. In order, to develop effective solutions to online abuse organisations must seek to engage with their users to better understand and respond to the challenges and harms that young people face. Finally exploring, understanding and, where necessary, addressing young people's expectations of and relationships with technology and each other can also serve to prevent abuse. Ultimately, it is only through a combination of law, technology and education and guidance, involving young people, the telecommunications industry, social media organisations and criminal justice and domestic violence professionals, can coercive control, stalking and other abusive behaviour be effectively responded to.

Discussion Questions

- How does technology facilitate coercive control and stalking among young people?
- How may we best prevent or mitigate technology facilitated coercive control or stalking among young people?
- What role should social media organisations and the telecommunications industry play in stopping coercive control and stalking among young people occurring through their platforms?

Notes

1. It is worth noting the major limitations of this study, namely the limited sampling strategy and small sample size.
2. The scoping review included research from countries with shared cultural values—the UK, Ireland, USA, Canada, New Zealand and Australia.

Bibliography

Afrouz, R., and Robinson, K. 2023. 'Domestic and family violence for culturally and linguistically diverse communities in Australia during COVID-19.' *Pandemic, Practice*, 35(3), pp. 235–254.

Ahlgrim, B. and Terrance, C. 2021. 'Perceptions of cyberstalking: Impact of perpetrator gender and cyberstalker/victim relationship', *Journal of Interpersonal Violence*, 36(7–8), NP4074–NP4093.

Apple Inc. 2022. https://www.apple.com/uk/airtag/

Barter, C., Stanley, N., Wood, M., Lanau, A., Aghtaie, N., Larkins, C., and Øverlien, C. 2017. 'Young people's online and face-to-face experiences of interpersonal violence and abuse and their subjective impact across five European countries', *Psychology of Violence*, 7(3), pp. 375–384.

Baym, N. K. 2015. *Personal connections in the digital age*, Malden, MA: Polity Press.

Begotti, T., Ghigo, M. A., and Acquadro Maran, D. 2022. 'Victims of known and unknown cyber-stalkers: A questionnaire survey in an Italian sample', *International Journal of Environmental Research and Public Health*, 19(8), p. 4883.

Boethius, S., Åkerstrom, M., and Hydén, M. 2022. 'The double-edged sword—abused womens experiences of digital technology', *European Journal of Social Work*.

Branch, K., Hilinski-Rosick, C., Johnson, E., and Solano, G. 2017. 'Revenge porn victimization of college students in the United States: An exploratory analysis', *International Journal of Cyber Criminology*, 11(1), pp. 128–142.

Brown, C., Sanci, L., and Hegarty, K. 2021. 'Technology-facilitated abuse in relationships: victimisation patterns and impact in young people', *Computers in Human Behavior*, 124, pp. 106897.

Brudvig, I. and van der Wilk, A. 2022. Covid-19 and increasing domestic violence against women: The pandemic of online gender-based violence [Online] http://webfoundation.org/docs/2020/07/WWWF-Submission-COVID-19-and-the-increase-of-domestic-violence-against-women-1.pdf (Accessed 15 October 2022).

Burke, S. C., Wallen, M., Vail-Smith, K., and Knox, D. 2011. 'Using technology to control intimate partners: An exploratory study of college undergraduates', *Computers in Human Behavior*, 27(3), pp. 1162–1167.

Chatterjee, R., Doerfler, P., Orgad, H., Havron, S., Palmer, J., Freed, D., Levy, K., Dell, N., McCoy, D., and Ristenpart, T. 2018. 'The spyware used in intimate partner violence', *2018 IEEE Symposium on Security and Privacy (SP)*, pp. 441–458.

Crofts, T., Lee, M., McGovern, A., and Milivojevic, S. 2015. *Sexting and young people*. Basingstoke: Palgrave Macmillan.

Cuomo, D., and Dolci, N. 2021. 'New tools, old abuse: Technology-enabled coercive control (TECC)', *Geoforum*, 126, pp. 224-232.

Cuomo, D., and Dolci, N. 2022. 'The TECC Clinic: An innovative resource for mitigating technology-enabled coercive control', *Women's Studies International Forum*, 92, pp. 1–10.

DeKeseredy, W. S. 2021. 'Image-based sexual abuse: Social and legal implications', *Current Addiction Reports*, 8, pp. 330–335.

Department for Media, Culture and Sport. 2022. *Mapping informal cyber security initiatives for young people aged 5–19* [Online] https://www.gov.uk/government/publications/mapping-informal-cyber-security-initiatives-for-young-people-aged-5-19/mapping-informal-cyber-security-initiatives-for-young-people-aged-5-19 (Accessed 15 October 2022).

Douglas, H., Harris, B. A., and Dragiewicz, M. 2019. 'Technology-facilitated domestic and family violence: women's experiences', *The British Journal of Criminology*, 59(3), pp. 551–570.

Dragiewicz, M., Burgess, J., Matamoros-Fernández, A., Salter, M., Suzor, N. P., Woodlock, D., and Harris, B. 2018. 'Technology facilitated coercive control: Domestic violence and the competing roles of digital media platforms', *Feminist Media Studies*, 18(4), pp. 609–625.

Dragiewicz, M., Harris, B., Woodlock, D., and Salter, M. 2021. 'Digital media and domestic violence in Australia: Essential contexts', *Journal of Gender-Based Violence*, 3, pp. 377–393.

Dragiewicz, M., Harris, B., Woodlock, D., Salter, M., Easton, H., Lynch, A., Campbell, H., Leach, J., and Milne, L. 2019. *Domestic violence and communication technology: Survivor experiences of intrusion, surveillance, and identity crime. Australian Communications Consumer Action Network* [Online]. https://eprints.qut.edu.au/131143/ (Accessed 15' October 2022).

Duerksen, K. N., and Woodin, E. M. 2019. 'Technological intimate partner violence: Exploring technology-related perpetration factors and overlap with in-person intimate partner violence', *Computers in Human Behavior*, (98), pp. 223–231.

Fiolet, R., Brown, C., Wellington, M., Bentley, K., and Hegarty, K. 2021. 'Exploring the impact of technology-facilitated abuse and its relationship with domestic violence: A qualitative study on experts' perceptions. *Global Qualitative Nursing Research*, 8, 23333936211028176.

Fissel, E. R. 2021. 'The reporting and help-seeking behaviors of cyberstalking victims', *Journal of Interpersonal Violence*, 36(11–12), pp. 5075–5100.

Flood, M. 2009. 'The harms of pornography exposure among children and young people', *Child Abuse Review*, 18(6), pp. 384–400.

Freed, D., Palmer, J., Minchala, D., Levy, K., Ristenpart, T., and Dell, N. 2017. 'Digital technologies and intimate partner violence: A qualitative analysis with multiple stakeholders', *Proceedings of the ACM on Human-Computer Interaction*, 1(CSCW), pp. 1–22.

Freed, D., Palmer, J., Minchala, D., Levy, K., Ristenpart, T., and Dell, N. 2018. '"A stalker's paradise": How intimate partner abusers exploit technology', *Proceedings of the 2018 CHI Conference on Human Factors in Computing Systems*, pp. 1–13.

Fry, E. 2022, April 29. Voices: Apple's smart trackers are being weaponised against women—Why are they still on sale? *The Independent.*

Gilbar, O., Charak, R., Trujillo, O., Cantu, J. I., Cavazos, V., and Lavi, I. 2022. 'Meta-analysis of cyber intimate partner violence perpetration and victimization: different types and their associations with face-to-tace IPV among men and women', *Trauma, Violence, & Abuse*, 15248380221082087.

Hamid, T., and Maple, C. 2013. 'Online harassment and digital stalking', *International Journal of Computer Applications*, 76(12), pp. 1–6.

Hamm, M., Newton, A., Chisholm, A., Shulman, J., Milne, A., Sundar, P., … Harling, L. 2015. 'Prevalence and effect of cyberbullying on children and young people: A scoping review of social media studies', *JAMA Pediatrics*, 169, pp. 770–777.

Harkin, D., Molnar, A., and Vowles, E. 2020. 'The commodification of mobile phone surveillance: An analysis of the consumer spyware industry', *Crime, Media, Culture*, 16(1), pp. 33–60.

Harris, B., and Vitis, L. 2020. 'Digital intrusions: Technology, spatiality and violence against women', *Journal of Gender-Based Violence*, 4(3), pp. 325–341.

Harris, B., and Woodlock, D. 2019. 'Digital coercive control: Insights from two landmark domestic violence studies', *The British Journal of Criminology*, 59(3), pp. 530–550.

Harris, B., and Woodlock, D. 2022a. "You can't actually escape it': Policing the use of technology in domestic violence in rural Australia', *International Journal for Crime, Justice and Social Democracy*, 11(1), pp. 135–148.

Harris, B., and Woodlock, D. 2022b. 'Spaceless violence: Women's experiences of technology-facilitated domestic violence in regional, rural and remote areas', *Trends and Issues in Crime and Criminal Justice*, 644, pp. 1–14.

Havard, T. E. 2020. 'Beyond the power and control wheel: How abusive men manipulate mobile phone technologies to facilitate coercive control', *Journal of Gender-Based Violence*, 4(2), pp. 223–239.

Henry, N., and Powell, A. 2018. 'Technology-facilitated sexual violence: A literature review of empirical research', *Trauma, Violence & Abuse*, 19(2), pp. 195–208.

Henry, N., Flynn, A., and Powell, A. 2020. 'Technology-facilitated domestic and sexual violence: A review', *Violence Against Women*, 26(15–16), 1828–1854. https://doi.org/10.1177/1077801219875821

Hodes, C. 2021. 'Safety planning with survivors of domestic violence: How COVID-19 shifts the focus', In Tosone, C. (ed), *Shared trauma, shared resilience during a pandemic. Essential clinical social work series*, Springer, pp. 61–67.

ITU. 2022. Youth Internet Use [Online]. https://www.itu.int/en/about/Pages/default.aspx (Accessed 15 October 2022).

Kaur, P., Dhir, A., Tandon, A., Alzeiby, E. A., and Abohassan, A. A. 2021. 'A systematic literature review on cyberstalking. An analysis of past achievements and future promises', *Technological Forecasting and Social Change*, 163, pp. 120426.

Klein, R. 2012. *Responding to intimate violence against women: The role of informal networks.* New York, NY: Cambridge University Press.

Livingstone, S., and Helsper, E. 2010. 'Balancing opportunities and risks in teenagers' use of the internet: The role of online skills and internet self-efficacy', *New Media & Society*, 12(2), pp. 309–329.

Livingstone, S., and Smith, P. K. 2014. 'Annual research review: Harms experienced by child users of online and mobile technologies: The nature, prevalence and management of sexual and aggressive risks in the digital age', *Journal of Child Psychology and Psychiatry*, 55(6), pp. 635–654.

Livingstone, S., and Stoilova, M. 2021. *The 4Cs: Classifying online risk to children* [Online]. https://doi.org/10.21241/ssoar.71817 (Accessed 15 October 2022).

March, E., Szymczak, P., Di Rago, M., and Jonason, P. K. 2022. 'Passive, invasive, and duplicitous: Three forms of intimate partner cyberstalking', *Personality and Individual Differences*, 189, 1.

Marcum, C. D., Higgins, G. E., and Nicholson, J. 2017. I'm watching you: Cyberstalking behaviors of university students in romantic relationships. *American Journal of Criminal Justice*, *42*(2), 373–388.

Marganski, A., and Melander, L. (2018) 'Intimate partner violence victimization in the cyber and real world: Examining the extent of cyber aggression experiences and its association with in-person dating violence', *Journal of Interpersonal Violence*, 33(7), pp. 1071–1095.

McGlynn, C., Johnson, K., Rackley, E., Henry, N., Gavey, N., Flynn, A., and Powell, A. 2021. "It's torture for the soul': The harms of image-based sexual abuse', *Social and Legal Studies*, 30(4), pp. 541–562.

Melander, L. A. 2010. 'College students', perceptions of intimate partner cyber harassment', *Cyberpsychology, Behavior, and Social Networking*, 13(3), pp. 263–268.

Messing, J., Bagwell-Gray, M., Brown, M. L., Kappas, A., and Durfee, A. 2020. 'Intersections of stalking and technology-based abuse: Emerging definitions, conceptualization, and measurement', *Journal of Family Violence*, 35(7), pp. 693–704.

Millman, C. M., Winder, B., and Griffiths, M. D. 2017. 'UK-based police officers' perceptim of, and role in investigating, cyber-harassment as a crime', *International Journal of Technoethics*, 8, pp. 87–102.

Mitchell, K.J., Segura, A., Jones, L.M. and Turner, H.A. 2018. 'Poly-victimization and peer harassment Involvement in a technological world', *Journal of Interpersonal Violence*, 33(5), pp. 762–788.

Mori, C., Cooke, J. E., Temple, J. R., Anh, L., Lu, Y., Anderson, N., Rash, C., and Madigan, S. 2020. 'The prevalence of sexting behaviors among emerging adults: A meta-analysis', *Archives of Sexual Behavior*, 49(4), 1103–1119.

Mumford, E. A., Rothman, E. F., Maitra, P., and Sheridan-Johnson, J. 2022. 'U.S. young adults' professional help-seeking in response to technology-facilitated abuse', *Journal of Interpersonal Violence*. https://doi.org/10.1177/08862605221140042

Ofcom. 2022a. *Children and parents: Media use and attitudes report 2022* [Online]. https://www.ofcom.org.uk/__data/assets/pdf_file/0024/234609/childrens-media-use-and-attitudes-report-2022.pdf (Accessed 15 October 2022).

OfCom. 2022b. *UK's internet use surges to record levels* [Online]. https://www.ofcom.org.uk/about-ofcom/latest/media/media-releases/2020/uk-internet-use-surges (Accessed 15 October 2022).

Office of National Statistics. 2021. *Internet users, UK: 2020* [Online]. https://www.ons.gov.uk/businessindustryandtrade/itandinternetindustry/bulletins/internetusers/2020 (Accessed 15 October 2022).

Reyns, B. W. 2019. Online pursuit in the twilight zone: Cyberstalking Perpetration by College students', *Victims and Offenders*, 14(2), pp. 183–198.

Rogers, M. M., Fisher, C., Ali, P., Allmark, P., and Fontes, L. 2022. 'Technology-facilitated abuse in intimate relationships: A scoping review', *Trauma, Violence, and Abuse*.

Salter, M. 2016. 'Privates in the online public: Sex(ting) and reputation on social media.' *New Media and Society*, 18(11), pp. 2723–2739.

Smith, C. P. and Freyd, J. J. 2014. 'Institutional betrayal', *American Psychologist*, 69, pp. 575–587.

Smith-Darden, J. P., Kernsmith, P. D., Victor, B. G., and Lathrop, R. A. 2017. 'Electronic displays of aggression in teen dating relationships: Does the social ecology matter?' *Computers in Human Behavior*, *67*, 33–40.

Stark, E. 2007. *Coercive Control*. Oxford: Oxford University Press.

Stonard, K. E., Bowen, E., Walker, K., and Price S. A. 2017. '"They'll always find a way to get to you": Technology use in adolescent romantic relationships and its role in dating violence and abuse', *Journal of Interpersonal Violence*, 32(14), pp. 2083–2117.

Stonard, K. E. 2020. '"Technology was designed for this": Adolescents' perceptions of the role and impact of the use of technology in cyber dating violence', *Computers in Human Behavior*, 105, 106211

Suzor, Nicolas, Dragiewicz, Molly, Harris, Bridget, Gillett, Rosalie, Burgess, Jean, and Van Geelen, Tess. 2019. 'Human rights by design: The responsibilities of social media platforms to address gender-based violence online', *Policy and Internet*, 11(1), pp. 84–103.

Tokunaga, R. S. 2011. 'Social networking site or social surveillance site? Understanding the use of interpersonal electronic surveillance in romantic relationships', *Computers in Human Behavior*, 27(2), pp. 705–713.

Truman, J. L. 2011. *Criminal victimization, 2010.* Washington, DC: Bureau of Justice Statistics.

Tynes, B. 2006. 'Children, adolescents, and the culture of hate online', In Dowd, N., Singer, D. and Wilson R. F. (eds), *Handbook of children, culture, and violence*, New York, NY: Sage, pp. 267-289.

Vitis, L., and Segrave, M. 2017. 'Introduction', In Vitis, L. and Segrave, M. (eds), *Gender, Technology and Violence*, Abingdon: Routledge.

Weisz, A., Tolman, R., and Saunders, D.G. 2000. 'Assessing the risk of severe domestic violence', *Journal of Interpersonal Violence*, 15(1), pp. 75–90.

Wood, C. 2021. 'Digital services aided domestic violence survivors during pandemic, New York officials say', State Scoop [Online]. October 7, 2021, https://statescoop.com/new-york-domestic-violence-digital-services/ (Accessed 15 October 2022).

Woodlock, D. 2013. 'Technology-facilitated stalking: Findings and recommendations from the SmartSafe Project', Domestic Violence Resource Centre Victoria [Online]. http://www.smartsafe.org.au/sites/default/files/SmartSafe-Findings-Booklet.pdf (Accessed 15 October 2022).

Woodlock, D. 2017. 'The abuse of technology in domestic violence and stalking', *Violence Against Women*, 23(5), 584–602.

Woodlock, D., McKenzie, M., Western, D., and Harris, B. 2020. 'Technology as a weapon in domestic violence: Responding to digital coercive control', *Australian Social Work*, 73(3), 368–380.

Woodlock, D., Salter, M., Dragiewicz, M. and Harris, B. 2022. '"Living in the darkness": Technology-facilitated coercive control, disenfranchised grief, and institutional betrayal', Violence Against Women.

Worsley, J. D., Wheatcroft, J. M., Short, E. and Corcoran, R. 2017. 'Victims' Voices: Understanding the emotional impact of cyberstalking and individuals', *Coping Responses*. SAGE Open, 7(2), 215824401771029.

Yardley, E. 2021. 'Technology-facilitated domestic abuse in political economy: A new theoretical framework', *Violence Against Women*, 27(10), pp. 1479–1498.

7 Stalking and Coercive Control: Commonly Used Strategies in Honour-Based Abuse Against Young People

Sadiq Bhanbhro

Key Points

- The definition and features of honour-based abuse (HBA).
- The prevalence of HBA globally and in the UK.
- Common strategies, i.e., coercive control and stalking, used in HBA against young people.
- Research, policy and practice recommendations to understand and prevent HBA against young people.

Introduction

Honour is a universal concept, but its meaning, value, and applications vary from time to time, culture to culture, region to region, and class to class. Generally, the term honour has positive meanings such as high respect, great esteem, and the quality of knowing and doing what is morally right. The term is also used for rewards and recognitions such as the Queen's honours. However, it becomes controversial when honour is combined with violence, abuse, and killings, creating a new category of violent crime mainly associated with certain cultures and communities.

It is noted that honour crimes exist across countries, cultures, and religions. Social, cultural, and political conditions which may lead to honour crimes (HBA and honour killings) are wide-ranging and not culturally specific nor religiously sanctioned. It is important to consider that, despite the wide use of the labels

S. Bhanbhro (✉)
Sheffield Hallam University, Collegiate Campus, Sheffield, UK
e-mail: s.bhanbhro@shu.ac.uk

M. Mellins et al. (eds.), *Young People, Stalking Awareness and Domestic Abuse*,
https://doi.org/10.1007/978-3-031-32379-9_7

(such as honour crimes, honour-based abuse, honour-based violence, and honour killings), there can be no honour in abuse, violence, and murders. Where religion, culture, or customs are used to exert and justify power or control over others, particularly women and girls, this can only be a misuse of that culture, religion, and tradition. Therefore, I have adopted the term honour crimes in this chapter to avoid unnecessary cultural specifications to demonstrate that whatever the excuse, honour or otherwise abuse, violence, and killings are a crime and are human rights violations.

Historical Practices Based on Honour

No community, culture, or class has the monopoly on defending one's honour through violence. It has been a historical and cross-cultural phenomenon; it was attributed as an underlying reason for horrible violent practices, including *duelling* in England, *foot binding* in China, *wife immolation* in India, and the honour-based system of retribution in the Southern States of the USA. Although these practices have been carried out in different geographical and historical contexts, the underlying reasons were similar and had significant parallels to honour-based abuse and violence.

Duelling was an ancient practice that involved a fight between two men using matched weapons, usually because one person dishonoured or insulted the other personally or his female family members. In many cultures, honour was and is considered bigger than life. Thus, it was fought not so much to kill the opponent as to gain satisfaction, that is, to restore one's honour by demonstrating a willingness to risk one's life for it (Britannica 2008a; Shoemaker 2002). *Chinese foot binding* was an ancient custom of breaking and tightly binding the feet of young girls to change their shape and size. Feet altered by footbinding were known as *lotus feet*, and the shoes made for these feet were known as *lotus shoes*. It aimed to change the female's feet to conform to family ideals of beauty and marriageability to protect its honour and reputation in the respective community or social group (Brown and Satterthwaite-Phillips 2018; Smith 2022). *Sati* was an ancient Hindu tradition that commonly existed in India. The practice required widows to jump into the funeral pyre of their deceased husbands. There were many reasons behind the practice, however, the common reason was that a husband is a protector of honour attached to his wife, and after his death, no one will protect his honour. Therefore, the widow should immolate herself with him (Doniger 2022; Menski 1998).

The honour-based retribution system in the Southern United States is a relatively recent practice. The traditional culture of the Southern United States is called a *culture of honour*, in which honour norms were highly valued. The insults on one's reputation were answered with violence as a retribution strategy to enforce one's rights and deter predation against one's family, home, and possessions (Nisbett and Cohen 1996). These honour-based practices were outlawed through political, social and legal measures, but still, several types of honour-based abuse and violence exist in many cultures and communities. The two common parallels between these practices and existing honour-based abuse, violence, and murders are the underlying notion of honour and the use of violence to protect or restore the honour of an individual or social group.

This chapter draws on primary and secondary research to discuss coercive control and stalking behaviours within Honour-Based Abuse (HBA) contexts perpetrated against young people in the UK. Coercive control is defined as behaviour involving a pattern of threats, humiliation, and intimidation, and stalking is a behaviour involving regular surveillance (physical and/or online) in a way that makes the targeted person feel scared, distressed, or threatened. Given the wide use of the term Honour-Based Abuse (HBA) by the UK government and domestic abuse sector organisations, this exact term has been adopted herein for its familiarity and consistency within the book. HBA is a form of domestic abuse, and research recognises that coercive control is central to the perpetration of HBA (Idriss 2017; Karma Nirvana 2008). Similarly, stalking has been commonly used as one of the key strategies to track the victims and their activities (Bhanbhro 2021). This chapter defines the notions of honour and Honour-Based Abuse (HBA). It discusses the commonly used strategies, such as stalking and coercive control in HBA against young people in the UK, and possible solutions to prevent it.

Definition of the Concepts: Honour, Dishonour, and Shame

The notions of honour, dishonour, and shame are universal. Still, their understanding, meaning, value, and applications vary from culture to culture, region to region, and class to class. Thus, there is not a single definition of these concepts. Nevertheless, the most widely used definition of honour in the literature is: "a person's value in his own and others' eyes" (Pitt-Rivers 1968, 503). The second part of the definition is significant in analysing and understanding HBA. Though some consider honour to be a personal quality and about the appraised value of a person in their own eyes, it ultimately depends upon recognition and validation from the group members. In the context of HBA, honour works in tightly knit social groups or communities in which most members not only know each other but are related to each other by blood or marriage. In such social groups or communities, honour is one of the major sources of a person or family's social position within its respective social group. In this social group, family honour is highly valued and aggressively protected. For example, in the UK, when a father from such a social group suspects his daughter has a boyfriend, it will harm his family's reputation in his social group. In this scenario, the family's social group is not its neighbours or people who know them but the people and families who are related to them. Also, their opinions will matter to them when they make choices and decisions (Bicchieri 2016) and impart validation to the social status based on honour (Pitt-Rivers 1968, 503). It is important to note that the physical distance among such group members is not that important, especially in this digital age, when everyone is connected through mobile technology. Therefore, honour plays a key role in maintaining and assessing the social position of an individual, family, or social group in the social structure that is subjected to damage through their social and moral behaviours, specifically, the sexual conduct of women and girls (Abou-Zeid 1965; Campbell 1964; Pitt-Rivers 1968).

Dishonour and shame are secondary concepts to honour and play a vital role in the implication of honour through abuse and violence. They are brought about by women's and girls' actions or alleged actions, which other group members would judge as dishonour or shameful for their family. As explained in the above example, having a boyfriend is considered a dishonoured act brought by the girl to her family, which brings shame to the family among other group members, who validate the family's honour-based social position. By contrast, a male family member's same action or type of action is not viewed as a source of dishonour for the family, although it may be considered his personal dishonour.

In so-called honour crimes (HBA and honour killings), the sources of dishonour refer to a woman's sexuality, which encompasses aspects of her body, behaviours, choice of clothing, communication, and virginity status. Various behaviours and actions of women and girls are interpreted as sources of dishonour and shame for an individual man or a social group. This can trigger the use of HBA as a means to control, limit damage, punish, or eradicate so-called dishonour. The so-called dishonourable actions largely relate to men exercising power and control over women and girls, restricting them from crossing three key borders between what is considered honourable and dishonourable. The three borders are neatly conceptualised in Table 7.1 and refer to (i) sexual, (ii) bodily, and (iii) social aspects and are fundamental for preserving an individual or social group's honour (Bhanbhro 2021).

Honour Based Abuse (HBA)

HBA involves violence and abuse (such as forced marriages, honour killing, and female genital mutilation), including murder, committed by people who want to defend or restore the real or perceived tarnished honour of an individual or a social group. The author views any type of honour crime as a social practice, a patterned and routinised set of behaviours of people in a social group rather than an isolated individual behaviour. This social practice operates within a tight social group. The social group can be a family (joint and extended family), clan, caste, community, or tribe (as described in Table 7.2). The joint and extended family systems are key features of the social group where honour crimes tend to occur more. Victims of HBA can be men, boys, lesbians, gays, bisexuals, and transgender people, but are more likely to be women and girls. In the UK context, HBA is more prevalent among young girls.

Honour crimes, or HBA, is an umbrella term which includes a range of harmful practices committed using the pretext of honour, such as domestic abuse (Reddy 2014); violence or death threats; economic abuse (Chowbey 2017); sexual and psychological abuse; acid attacks; forced marriage (Noack-Lundberg et al.

Table 7.1 Sexual, bodily, and social borders

Sexual • Pre-marital sex • Extra-marital sex • A woman or girl being raped • Getting pregnant from the sexual relationship • Having a boyfriend	**Bodily** • Wearing revealing/tight clothes • No proper purdah • Adopting a western lifestyle by migrant women and girls living in the Western countries
Social • Asking for a share in the inheritance • Disobedience to parents and/or family men • Working outside of the home • Moving away from their family house before marriage • Going out without the permission of parents or other male members of a family • Talking to an unrelated man • Using mobile phone • Using social media	**Social (predominantly related to marriage)** • Marriage: – without consent of family – outside one's social group (concerned norm circles) – by eloping with a man of her own or another social group – with a man from a lower caste – with a non-Muslim man • Asking for a divorce • Saying no to cousin's marriage • Complaint to relevant authorities against parents who tried to arrange a forced marriage

2021; Foreign and Commonwealth Office and Simmonds 2013); forced suicide (Gorar 2022); forced abortion; female genital mutilation (World Health Organisation 2022); assault; and being held against one's will (Aplin 2022; Gill and Gould 2020; Bhanbhro et al. 2016; Hester et al. 2015; Nesheiwat 2005). These harmful practices are described in Table 7.3. There are widely used alternative terms for HBA, including honour-based violence, honour-related violence, patriarchal violence, honour killing, and murder in the name of honour. Killing or attempted killing of a person (in most cases, it is a woman or a girl) in the name of saving or restoring the honour of a family, clan, or community (commonly known as honour killing) is an extreme form of HBA.

The ideology that triggers the harmful behaviour towards their family members is that women and girls are carriers of family honour, which is considered a precious social resource. Given the social, cultural, and economic value of family honour that lies with women and girls, the social groups have rules and practices to protect that value they have placed in honour. For example, if a young woman marries without her family or parents' consent, this act would be considered dishonourable for the family. This young woman's behaviour can trigger gossip about her family's reputation, showing that the family is exposed to dishonour and shame in its concerned social group. As a result, the family, particularly the male members, will attempt to restore the family honour. The action could involve a harsh warning to killing, and any harmful behaviour in between, which may be threatening language, stalking, harassing, forcing her to leave her husband, or killing her. The actions and behaviour to protect or restore family honour are context-specific

Table 7.2 Description of social groups

Term	Definition
Family	A group of two or more persons related by birth, marriage, or adoption who live together is called a family
Joint Family	A family in which two or more families live in one house. For example, if someone has two sons and both are married, have one or two children, and live in a single house. This type of family is called a joint family, where children live with their grandparents, parents, uncles, aunts, and children in the same house. Another important feature of a joint family is that the members of a joint family hold a common property. Generally, the head of the family is a man who manages the property on behalf of its members (Britannica 2017). This type of family is common in South Asia, i.e. India and Pakistan
Extended Family	This type of family comprises almost every blood relative, parents, grandparents, uncles, aunts, cousins, and possibly spouses. These people live in various locations and come together for holidays or special occasions (Britannica 2009). This type of social arrangement is also common in India and Pakistan
Clan or kin group	A group of families who trace their descent from a common ancestor and share the same surname is known as a clan (Britannica 2008b)
Tribe	A group of clans forms a tribe. Every tribe has a male tribal chief with the power to make significant decisions about his tribe. A tribe has a common descent, language, and culture (Britannica 2022)
Community	A group of people or families who follow a common culture, traditions, norms, and values is called a community. In the context of HBA, the community comprises families with the same ethnicity, language, and socio-cultural understanding and significance of family honour. It is also not necessary for families that make a community to live in the same geographical area. They can live in different places in the same country or region or different countries but adhere to a family honour system

and they could vary from slight (warning or threatening) to extreme (forced divorce or killing) (Fig. 7.1).

The top right box of the figure depicts the role of gossip in HBA. The available literature (such as Dogan 2013; Hasan 2002; Glazer and Ras 1994) and the author's own research demonstrates that gossip has a central role in HBA. It is viewed as a necessary and sufficient device to ensure appropriate female behaviour is maintained and which operates through public opinion (Glazer and Ras 1994). In the author's study within the UK Pakistani community, the significance of gossip was ubiquitously represented in the Urdu language phrase "*log kia kahein gey*" (what will people say). It is important to note that the opinion of random people or acquaintances is not important in family honour. Still, the judgement of one's social group members will trigger the family to take appropriate action to intact the family honour. The phrase was used as a mechanism for social control (Bhanbhro 2021), and the female participants from the UK viewed gossip and rumours as a critical catalyst to others enacting HBA. One such participant, a 24-year-old female participant 'Nargis', expressed her concerns about gossiping,

Table 7.3 Descriptions of harmful practices

Practice	Description
Domestic abuse	Domestic abuse comprises broad categories of behaviour, including physical or sexual abuse, violent or threatening behaviour, controlling or coercive behaviour, economic abuse and psychological, emotional, or other abuse (Domestic Abuse Act 2021). The perpetrator of domestic abuse is a close family member or current or former partner, which can happen anywhere and is a crime
Economic abuse	Economic abuse is any person's behaviour substantially affecting another person's ability to acquire, use, or maintain money or other property, or obtain goods or services (Domestic Abuse Act 2021)
Sexual violence and abuse	Sexual violence and abuse are any behaviour thought to be of a sexual nature which is unwanted and takes place without consent. Sexual violence and abuse can be physical, psychological, verbal, or online. Any behaviour of a sexual nature that causes you distress is considered sexual violence or abuse. Sexual abuse is a crime which occurs between strangers, friends, acquaintances, current or ex-partners, or family members
Psychological abuse	Psychological abuse involves the regular and deliberate use of various words and non-physical actions. They are used to manipulate, hurt, weaken, or frighten a person mentally and emotionally; and/or distort, confuse, or influence their thoughts and actions within their everyday lives, changing their sense of self and harming their well-being (Kaukinen 2004)
Acid attack	Acid attacks are a form of violence in which acid or another corrosive substance is thrown at a person—usually a woman or a girl—to maim, torture, or kill them
Forced marriage	A forced marriage is where one or both people do not (or, in cases of people with learning disabilities or reduced capacity, cannot) consent to the marriage as they are pressurised, or abuse is used to force them to do so. It is recognised in the UK as domestic or child abuse and serious human rights abuse (The Foreign, Commonwealth and Development Office 2022)
Forced suicide	Families may deploy a strategy of forcing women to kill themselves to remain technically innocent of murder. However, it may not be clear whether an individual woman has committed suicide due to direct coercion to spare her family men from going to prison. It could be an outright murder disguised as self-killing, or a woman killed herself due to the unbearable pressures of the restrictions upon her life (Honour-Based Violence Awareness Network 2021)

(continued)

This is a real problem in our community. When a girl is suspected of having a boyfriend, as rumours spread like fire, her family starts controlling her movements and stalking her to track her activities. Even though she doesn't have a boyfriend, community people make up gossip about her. As a result, the trapped girl's life is ruined.

Table 7.3 (continued)

Practice	Description
Forced abortion	A family could force a woman to have an abortion if the family alleged that the woman might have become pregnant without wedlock or from an extramarital affair
Female Genital Mutilation	Female genital mutilation (FGM) involves the partial or total removal of external female genitalia or other injuries to the female genital organs for non-medical reasons (World Health Organisation 2022). This mutilation is intended to maintain family honour by preserving the woman's virginity until marriage and controlling the woman's sexuality before and after marriage. The intended result is a reduction of her libido to ensure that she will not be tempted to engage in premarital or extramarital sexual behaviour

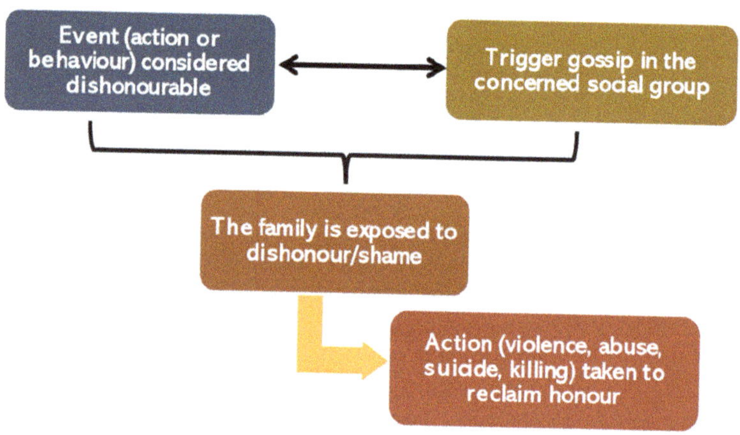

Fig. 7.1 A model showing how honour is implicated through abuse, violence, and killings

The above quote shows even if it is a mere rumour or suspicion, which is also not a crime (having a boyfriend), the emotional and psychological abuse through stalking, controlling, and policing the behaviour of the victims can have a disastrous impact on one's life. All these tools, including surveillance, stalking, and coercive control for inflicting physical and psychological harm to innocent persons, are about maintaining power and control. Therefore, I argue that HBA is one of the practices of the honour system, which is the system of power and control.

Theories Related to HBA

Two widely used explanations in the literature exist to understand honour crimes, including HBA and honour killings. First, it is condoned by a specific culture type known as 'honour culture', which authorises its members, mainly males, to resort to abuse, violence, and murders to save family honour (Khan et al. 2018; Kurkiala 2003; Lowe et al. 2018). According to the second theory, violence against women and girls is committed by men using any available excuse, honour is merely one such excuse that serves as a reason where the real cause is down to the socio-economic and political structures of society that are essentially patriarchal and universally oppressive for women (Begikhani 2005; Pimentel et al. 2005; Sev'er and Yurdakul 2001).

Both explanations are likely to have some truth within them. However, neither is supported by sufficient empirical data. In addition, the first explanation, which is probably the most prevalent, is reactionary in the sense that it appears to close the door on the potential for change. Culture is treated as being essential and beyond criticism. In the 'cultural explanation' of honour crimes, the culture, traditions, and religion of particular communities are taken as causes of violent crime for the sake of honour. Conversely, some scholars have criticised the cultural explanation. For example, Montoya and Agustin (2013) argue that the "culturalised forms of violence" largely ignore the gendered nature of violence, and the cultural framing of violence creates a dichotomy between non-violent Europeans and violent others. Similarly, Meetoo and Mirza (2007) argue that in domestic violence discourses, including honour killings, the victim women have been highly *ethnicised*. In turn, the cultural/racial classification not only stigmatises particular acts of violence but entire communities (Montoya and Agustin 2013; Abu-Lughod 2011; Bhanbhro et al. 2016).

Thus, when honour-based abuse is dismissed as a cultural issue, the communities in which it prevails are stigmatised. Those who suffer violence also face their suffering being brushed off as a cultural problem (Ewing 2008; Montoya and Agustin 2013). In addition, some scholars argue that cultural understating and representation of violence conceals more pressing and central structures of violence affecting women and political processes that shape it (in those parts of the world where culture is usually blamed for such violence). It is necessary to be mindful of this when analysing and understanding violence in cultural terms per se (Abu-Lughod 2011; Ewing 2008; Shah 2007).

The Prevalence of HBA Worldwide and in the UK

HBA occurs worldwide in various cultures, some regions being hotspots, such as South Asia and the Middle East (Fisk 2010; Mayell 2002). Some authors (see Abu-Rabia 2011; Cooney 2014; Idriss 2017; Khan et al. 2018) identify these regions' cultures as rigid, collectivist, patriarchal, place a high value on family honour, and are highly sensitive to the opinion of social group members. Also, men in these cultures are authoritarian, aggressive, and violent; in contrast, women are compliant, conforming, and passive victims.

The United Nations (UN) agencies and the European Committee on Equal Opportunities for Women and Men define so-called "honour crimes as a complex issue but may be defined as a crime that is, or has been, justified or explained (or mitigated) by the perpetrator of that crime on the grounds that it was committed as a consequence of the need to defend or protect the honour of the family". The UN has identified honour crimes in more than 30 countries, including Albania, Brazil, Denmark, Egypt, India, Iran, Iraq, Israel, Jordan, Lebanon, Morocco, the Netherlands, Palestine, Pakistan, Sweden, Syria, Turkey, Yemen, the UK and the USA. Estimating prevalence rates of HBA worldwide is problematic because there are no reliable statistics as it is not a recorded crime category in any country except the UK.

In 2000, the UN Population Fund estimated that at least 5000 women and girls worldwide are murdered yearly in the name of so-called honour—although these figures are contested. Some researchers and activists believe that the rates are much higher. Nonetheless, of the 5000 internationally reported honour killing cases, 2000 are from India and Pakistan, according to the international digital resource centre Honour Based Violence (HBV) Awareness Network (HBV Awareness Network 2021). Also, the annual reports published by the Human Rights Commission of Pakistan (HRCP) show that over 15,222 honour killings have been recorded in the country between 2004 and 2016. This figure excludes attempted honour killings and other forms of honour-related violence. This means an average of 1170 honour killings annually and 22 per week (HRCP 2019). More recent statistics show that the problem persists. In 2021, 128 women were killed in Sindh province of Pakistan in the name of honour (Soomro 2022), and in Punjab province, between July and December 2021, 90 women were killed, 2439 were raped, and 9529 women were kidnapped for honour (The News International 2022).

Since 2019 England and Wales police forces have started recording offences identified as related to so-called 'honour-based' abuse (HBA). The UK police and Crown Prosecution Service currently use the following definition of so-called HBA,

> an incident or crime involving violence, threats of violence, intimidation, coercion or abuse (including psychological, physical, sexual, financial or emotional abuse) which has or may have been committed to protect or defend the honour of an individual, family and/or community for alleged or perceived breaches of the family and/or community's code of behaviour. (Home Office 2022)

In the year ending March 2022, there were 2887 HBA-related offences recorded by the police in England and Wales. This was an increase of 6% compared with the year ending March 2021, when 2725 offences were recorded in England and Wales, excluding Greater Manchester Police (GMP), who could not provide data for the year ending March 2020 following the implementation of a new IT system in July 2019. The GMP covers 6 geographical command areas with population diversity; thus, its data on HBA would have shown a significant increase in HBA offences. In 2021, there was an increase of 18% compared with the previous year ending March 2020, with 2024 HBA-related offences (Home Office 2022).

The Home Office has collected the above figures from police forces on a mandatory basis since April 2019. The data before 2019 also presents a bleak picture.

For example, in 2015, the BBC reported more than 11,000 honour-related violence incidents, including 29 honour killings and attempted killings of women and girls, which were recorded by the UK police forces from 2010 to 2014 (Talwar and Ahmad 2015). The recent figures above show that the number of HBA offences recorded by police forces in England has soared over the past five years. The statistics show a persistent increase in HBA incidents yearly, which means the recorded incidents of HBA are just the tip of the iceberg, finding year after year, given its hidden and unreported tendencies.

Common Strategies Used Within HBA: Coercive Control and Stalking

The notions of 'honour' underlying abuse, violence, and killings within the HBA context do not operate in isolation but exist within an organised system of social and cultural structures called the 'honour system'. The system comprises structures of cultural (norms, values, beliefs, customs, and traditions) and social (gender, class, caste, kinship, and ethnicity) and operates through rules, social entities, and practices (Bhanbhro 2021). The constant surveillance of women and girls by their families is one of the honour system's major tools to protect the honour associated with them. The family members vigilantly supervise women and girls' behaviour, activities, and social mobility. Male and female children are trained from an early age to behave in a certain way consistent with the honour norms and conform to the system's rules. For example, Her Majesty's Inspectorate of Constabulary's (HMIC) HBA victim/survivor voices project report (2015) states that coercive control was the most common abuse involving HBA. It included monitoring social activity, removing phone and internet access, house arrest, removing passports, withholding visa documents, and attempts to shame the victim using the internet, email, and social media.

Policing women and girls' behaviour, activities, and social mobility through elaborated rules, restrictions, and practices to avoid alleged honour violations is an integral part of the honour system. For example, if a young person, in the HBA context, mainly a female, is found or allegedly perceived to be involved in any action given in Table 7.1, will imply that the person has violated the family's honour and brought dishonour and shame to the family. This is explained by 'Nuzhat', a respondent within recent research by Bhanbhro, who said,

> if women expose themselves by wearing revealing clothes or too tight clothes, it can become an issue of dishonour for their families. The [family] men .... would be mocked as '*beghairat insan*' (a person without honour) by their *biradri* or community.

Consequently, the family takes action against the person who brought or tried to bring dishonour to the family. That action can include controlling and coercive behaviour, assault, threats to kill, harassment, and stalking.

Coercive control and stalking are commonly used strategies in HBA. For example, the 2022 HBA figures (2887) show 17% of controlling and coercive behaviour and 6% of stalking offences involving HBA were recorded by tagging them with offence categories. Similarly, in 2021 figures (2725), 14% of controlling and coercive behaviour and 5% of stalking offences involving HBA were recorded by the police (Home Office 2022). The figures show often that the use of coercive control is HBA because the control is established without obvious violence against the victim. It is to remember that HBA affects people of all ages and genders but often begins early in the family home, mainly against girls and young women. Therefore, from an early age, coercive control is deeply embedded in socialisation, masked as obedience, discipline, and family duties according to family honour norms and values. It is built on expectations about behaviour made clear to them at a young age. Also, in the countries like the UK, where laws are strict, coercive control is a strategy that could be used secretly or wrapped as family customs and traditions.

Research by the author suggests that at an early age, coercive control is used by a family to stop young people from crossing the borders (sexual, bodily, and social) and ensure adherence to acceptable and unacceptable behaviours. Hence, the control masked as obedience to parents, grandparents, extended family members, or elder siblings is often established without overt violence against the victim. Likewise, surveillance through stalking is maintained to abide by the family norms of honour by not involving in activities and behaviours considered sources of dishonour for the family. Stalking is someone repeatedly behaving in a way that makes you feel scared, distressed, or threatened. It can include regularly following someone, watching or spying on someone and checking their social media activity and communication (i.e., internet use, email, or phone). See the below example of how surveillance is maintained through community gaze.

Case Study: Stalking Through Community Gaze

Nuzhat, 22, was a college student. One day it was her friend's birthday. She was invited to the cinema to celebrate her friend's birthday. Nuzhat was reluctant to go because of what her family would say, but as the college finished early and her other friends also decided to go, she joined them. She was standing in the ticket and booking area with her girlfriends, and some boys were standing nearby. Nuzhat's male cousin saw her standing there and told his parents that he saw Nuzhat with a boy in the cinema. Her cousin's father told Nuzhat's father that she had a boyfriend and his son saw them in the cinema together. A suspicion was created in her father's mind that she had stained the family's honour; therefore, she must be stopped from damaging it further. Consequently, Nuzhat's father instructed her brothers, male cousins, and some male neighbours, mainly taxi drivers, to keep an eye on her.

After this, wherever Nuzhat went, someone was stalking her. Nuzhat was always sacred and distressed, and her studies were disturbed. She said that she "was treated like a criminal at home". She explained to her family that she had no boyfriend and went to the cinema with her female classmates, but no one believed her; everyone believed her cousin's made-up story. Even neighbours who were part of their social group started rumours that Nuzhat may elope with the boy, and they made up many other stories. She described her "family as furious and that she was always taunted that she had made the family a laughing stock". Not only did people follow her and track her activities, but her family called everyone from her contact list to find out about the people she was talking to. They also spoke to her friends from the college to get information about Nuzhat's activities in the college. She was prevented from visiting her friends' homes. Nuzhat said, "I had nightmares, my mental health was deteriorating, but no one cared. Even my college teachers didn't take notice of my situation. At home, everyone was concerned about so-called family honour". Nuzhat was strictly instructed not to speak about this situation to anyone at college. So, she was scared to tell anyone. Meanwhile, the stalking continued, but they didn't find her with a boyfriend. After almost a year, things settled; however, Nuzhat said, "I was punished for the sin I didn't do, and I lived in hell for almost a year".

Nuzhat said stalking girls in her community is common and discreet because her community is a closely knit group of families. Most of Nuzhat's community members live on the same street and know each other. Also, many of her community's men are taxi drivers, and they go to all corners of the city every day, so while working, they can keep an eye on her community's young people, mainly girls. Nuzhat said, "if a taxi man sees something, he would report it to the concerned young person's father or elder brother, and in many cases, family restriction for young people starts from that point".

As explained above that HBA occurs in a closely knit social group or network (i.e., family, clan, community), and male members are the key actors. The network peoples' participation in any action or behaviour, such as stalking (as in the above example), to intact or restore their social group member's honour is voluntary and reciprocal. They involve in the activities through a collective commitment to enforcing honour norms in their social network. The social group members' expectations of participating in social practices are mediated through positive and negative sanctions. The one who conforms to the practice by involving in the activities receives praise, reward, and social and economic support.

In contrast, the one who does not participate in the practice gets punishment, disapproval, and, in some cases, socially shunned. It is a reciprocal arrangement; if a social group member supports another member in need (in the above example, protecting family honour), he will get back the same support when needed. The main purpose of this arrangement is to intact the patriarchal system of power and control over women and girls.

HBA Impact

Violence against women and girls, which is purportedly committed in the name of 'honour', is a form of gender-based violence (GBV). GBV refers to harmful acts and practices directed at individuals based on their gender and is rooted in gender inequality, power abuse, and harmful norms. GBV is a serious violation of human rights and a life-threatening health and protection issue.

HBA involves direct emotional/psychological harm, including distress, anxiety, low self-esteem, fear, fear, isolation, helplessness, and dependency on a family. It can negatively affect women and girls' emotional and mental well-being if they are directly victimised or witnessed. As they may live in constant fear for their safety within households, it can impact their day-to-day life, for example, their ability to access social and healthcare services. The Her Majesty's Inspectorate of Constabulary (HMIC) inspection study (2015) in the UK found that two of the 36 victims and survivors of HBA, including forced marriage, had attempted self-harm, including suicide, and 11 reported taking medication for anxiety or depression (Hester et al. 2015). Similarly, the negative impact of HBA, including anxiety, depression, desperation, hopelessness, mental abuse, reduced self-esteem, and suicide, was highlighted in research studies (Sedem and Ferrer-Wreder 2015; Dickson 2014; Sabbe et al. 2013). Living under a controlled honour system has a massive impact on young people. It ranges from living in constant fear and difficulties to making life choices such as choosing a life partner or living in a student accommodation instead of home to enjoy a less restricted life.

Implications for Policy, Practice, and Research

This chapter lays the groundwork for future empirical research into the subject by demonstrating that honour crimes (HBA and honour killings) are not timeless and essential to the social groups and communities in which it occurs. The essentialist view has confused and limited empirical research. More primary research on the subject is feasible, reducing the reliance on secondary and tertiary data sources. Further studies are required to develop an evidence-based and sensitive method that better encapsulates the communities' perspectives and relevant social structures and is utilised in honour crimes prevention strategy and policymaking.

Honour crimes, including abuse, violence, and killings, are not isolated individual incidents but the collective social practices of the honour system. The system is patriarchal as it predominantly works to the advantage of men by providing them power and control over women and girls. The powers do not lie within individual men but within the system's social structure; thus, the system ascribes the power to its agents (men) to enforce family honour through harmful practices.

Common approaches have been suggested to address violence against women and girls in the name of honour and otherwise: introducing strict laws, training police, cultural competency building of prosecutors, more shelter homes for victims, etc. These efforts are necessary but not sufficient to prevent HBA. Therefore, there is a need to bring change from within to alter the social structures and narratives that create a viable environment for perpetrators of HBA.

Public and policy discourses on HBA often arise from journalism and mainstream media rather than empirical research, scholarship, and theory. Moreover, the perspectives of communities where HBA is prevalent have been afforded less attention. Therefore, further empirical research is needed to investigate and understand the underlying narratives and assumptions behind HBA. Future research needs to investigate and understand the common characteristics of the social groups in which family honour is highly valued and fiercely protected. The collected research evidence on those social groups will provide avenues for targeted social interventions to prevent HBA.

There is a need to improve the official recording of HBA nationally. In the UK, cultural and religious sensitivity to HBA may be reduced by focusing on specific social groups with specific social forces that support honour crime instead of certain cultures and communities. This could be achieved by encouraging conscious efforts, including:

- By engaging targeted social groups to bring change from within;
- Ensuring a change in attitudes, perceptions, and behaviours of community members, particularly young people, about the notions of honour and its implications through harmful practices.
- Bringing a clear understanding of young people concerning family honour and their communication skills developed to discuss these sensitive issues in a family.
- Uplifting young people's skills to report incidents like stalking and their consequences to concerned people and organisations.
- Developing clear pathways for young people to access support.

Discussion Questions

- How is the notion of 'honour'-based abuse/violence understood historically and culturally?
- How might we involve social groups and communities, particularly young people, to bring about change in order to prevent HBA?
- How do we develop the capability and empower young people to communicate with parents, family members, guardians, and peers about harmful practices like HBA and to understand and spot early signs of them?

Bibliography

Abou-Zeid, Ahmed. 1965. Honour and shame among the Bedouins of Egypt. In John Peristiany (Ed.), *Honour and shame: The values of Mediterranean society*. London: Weidenfeld and Nicolson.

Abu-Rabia, Aref. 2011. Family honour killings: Between custom and state law. *The Open Psychology Journal*, 4: 34–44.

Aplin, Rachael. 2022. Evaluating the value of the police Independent Advisory Group (IAG): Honour Based Abuse Crime (HBA), Forced Marriage (FM) and Female Genital Mutilation (FGM). *Women's Studies International Forum*, 90: 102556.

Abu-Lughod, Lila. 2011. Seductions of the "honour crime". *Differences*, 22: 17–63. https://doi.org/10.1215/10407391-1218238.

Begikhani, Nazand. 2005. Honour-based violence among the Kurds: The case of Iraqi Kurdistan. In Welchman, L., and Hossain, S. (Eds.), *'Honour': Crimes, paradigms, and violence against women* (pp. 209–30). London: Zed Books.

Bicchieri, Cristina. 2016. *Norms in the wild: How to diagnose, measure, and change social norms*. New York: Oxford University Press.

Britannica, T. Editors of Encyclopaedia. 2008a. *Duel*. Encyclopedia Britannica. https://www.britannica.com/topic/duel.

Britannica, T. Editors of Encyclopaedia. 2008b. *Clan*. Encyclopedia Britannica. https://www.britannica.com/topic/clan.

Britannica, T. Editors of Encyclopaedia. 2017. *Joint family*. Encyclopedia Britannica. https://www.britannica.com/topic/joint-family.

Britannica, T. Editors of Encyclopaedia 2009. *Extended family*. Encyclopedia Britannica. https://www.britannica.com/topic/extended-family.

Britannica, T. Editors of Encyclopaedia. 2022. *Tribe*. Encyclopedia Britannica. https://www.britannica.com/topic/tribe-anthropology.

Bhanbhro, Sadiq. 2021. *Uncovering community notions of honour and their relation to honour killings* (PhD Dissertation). Sheffield Hallam University.

Bhanbhro, Sadiq, Anna Cronin de Chavez, and Adelaide Lusambili. 2016. Honour-based violence as a global public health problem: A critical review of the literature. *International Journal of Human Rights in Healthcare*. https://doi.org/10.1108/IJHRH-10-2015-0032.

Brown, M. J., and Satterthwaite-Phillips. D. 2018. Economic correlates of footbinding: Implications for the importance of Chinese daughters' labour. *PloS One*. https://doi.org/10.1371/journal.pone.0201337.

Campbell, John, Kennedy. 1964. *Honour, family, and patronage: A study of institutions and moral values in a Greek mountain community*. Oxford: Oxford University Press.

Chowbey, Punita. 2017. Women's narratives of economic abuse and financial strategies in Britain and South Asia. *Psychology of Violence*, 7: 459–468. https://doi.org/10.1037/vio0000110.

Cooney, Mark. 2014. Death by family: Honour violence as punishment. *Punishment and Society*, 16: 406–427. https://doi.org/10.1177/1462474514539537

Dickson, Pat. 2014. Understanding victims of honour-based violence. *Community Practitioner*, 87: 30–33.

Dogan, Recep. 2013. Honour killings in the UK communities: Adherence to tradition and resistance to change. *Journal of Muslim Minority Affairs*, 33: 1–17. https://doi.org/10.1080/13602004.2013.853978.

Doniger, W. 2022. *Sttee*. Encyclopedia Britannica. https://www.britannica.com/topic/suttee.

Domestic Abuse Act 2021. UK Public General Act, 2021, C17. https://www.legislation.gov.uk/ukpga/2021/17/contents/enacted.

Ewing, Katherine, Pratt. 2008. *Stolen honour: stigmatising Muslim men in Berlin*. Stanford: Stanford University Press.

Fisk, Robert. 2010. The crime wave that shames the world. *The Independent*, September 7. http://www.independent.co.uk/voices/commentators/fisk/robert-fisk-the-crimewave-that-shames-the-world-2072201.html.

Foreign and Commonwealth Office and Simmonds, M. 2013. What is a forced marriage? London: Foreign and Commonwealth Office. Available from: https://www.gov.uk/government/publications/what-is-a-forced-marriage. Accessed January 1, 2023.

Gill, Aisha K., and Gould, Deborah. 2020. The role of family coercion, culture, expert witnesses and best practice in securing forced marriage convictions. *Journal of Gender-Based Violence*, 4: 89–105.

Glazer, Ilsa, and Ras, Wahiba, Abu. 1994. On aggression, human rights, and hegemonic discourse: The case of a murder for family honour in Israel. *Sex Roles*, 30: 269–288. https://doi.org/10.1007/BF01420994.

Gorar, Mukaddes. 2022. Honour suicide and forced suicide in the UK. *The Journal of Criminal Law*, 86: 308–326.

Hasan, Manar. 2002. The politics of honour: Patriarchy, the state and the murder of women in the name of family honour. *Journal of Israeli History*, 21: 1–37. https://doi.org/10.1080/13531040212331295842.

Hester, Marianne, Gangoli, Geetanjali, Gill, Aisha, Mulvihill, Natasha, Bates, Lis, Matolcsi, Andrea, Walker, Sarah-Jane, Yar, Kurda. 2015. *Victim/survivor voices—A participatory research project. A Report for Her Majesty's Inspectorate of Constabulary' Honour'—Based Violence Inspection.* London: HMIC. https://www.justiceinspectorates.gov.uk/hmicfrs/wp-content/uploads/university-of-bristol-hbv-study.pdf. Accessed November 26, 2022.

Home Office. 2022. *Statistics on so-called 'honour-based' abuse offences, England and Wales, 2021 to 2022.* https://www.gov.uk/government/statistics/statistics-on-so-called-honour-based-abuse-offences-england-and-wales-2021-to-2022/statistics-on-so-called-honour-based-abuse-offences-england-and-wales-2021-to-2022. Accessed December 1, 2022.

Honour-Based Violence Awareness Network. 2021. http://hbv-awareness.com/forms-of-hbv. Accessed January 10, 2023.

Human Rights Commission Pakistan. 2019. Data and archives from 01/01/2014 to 31/12/2014. *HRCP*. http://hrcp-web.org/hrcpweb/data-main/

Idriss, Mazher, Mohammad. 2017. Not domestic violence or cultural tradition: Is honour-based violence distinct from domestic violence? *Journal of Social Welfare and Family Law*, 39(1): 3–21. https://doi.org/10.1080/09649069.2016.1272755

Karma Nirvana. 2008. *Survivors of honour-based violence and forced marriage in the UK: Sample Study compiled by Karma Nirvana.*

Kaukinen, Catherine. 2004. Status compatibility, physical violence, and emotional abuse in intimate relationships. *Journal of Marriage and Family*, 66(2): 452–471. https://doi.org/10.1111/j.1741-3737.2004.00031.x.

Khan, Roxanne, Saleem, Shamam, and Lowe, Michelle. 2018. "Honour"-based violence in a British South Asian community. *Safer Communities*, 17(1): 11–21. https://doi.org/10.1108/SC-02-2017-0007.

Kurkiala M, 2003. Interpreting honour killings: The story of Fadime Sahindal (1975–2002) in the Swedish press. *Antrhopology Today*, 19(1): 2.

Lowe, Michelle, Khan, Roxanne, Thanzami, Vanlal, Barzy, Mahsa, and Karmaliani, Rozina. 2018. Attitudes toward intimate partner "honour"-based violence in India, Iran, Malaysia, and Pakistan. *Journal of Aggression, Conflict and Peace Research*, 10(4): 283–292. https://doi.org/10.1108/JACPR-09-2017-0324.

Mayell, Helen. 2002. Thousands of women killed for family "honour". *National Geographic News*, February 12.

Menski, Werner. 1998. Sati: A Review Article. *Bulletin of the School of Oriental and African Studies*, 61: 74–81. http://www.jstor.org/stable/3107292.

Meetoo, Veena, and Heidi Safia Mirza. 2007. There is nothing "honourable about honour killings": Gender, violence and the limits of multiculturalism. *Women's Studies International Forum*, 30: 187–200

Montoya, Celeste, and Agustín, Lise, Rolandsen. 2013. The othering of domestic violence: The EU and cultural framings of violence against women. *Social Politics*, 20(4): 534–557. https://doi.org/10.1093/sp/jxt020.

Nesheiwat, Ferris. 2005. Honour crimes in Jordan: Their treatment under Islamic and Jordanian Criminal Laws. *Penn State International Law Review*, 23: 251–281.

Nisbett, Richard. E., and Cohen, Dov.1996. *Culture of honour: The psychology of violence in the South.* Westview Press.

Noack-Lundberg, Kyja, Aisha K. Gill, and Sundari Anitha. 2021. Understanding forced marriage protection orders in the UK. *Journal of Social Welfare and Family Law*, 43: 371–392.

Pimentel, Silvia, Pandjiarjian, Valéria and Belloque, Juliana. 2005. The "legitimate defence of honour," or murder with impunity? A critical study of legislation and case law in Latin America. In Welchman, L., Hossain, S. (Eds.), *'Honour': Crimes, paradigms, and violence against women* (pp. 245–262). London: Zed Books.

Pitt-Rivers, Julian.1968. Honour. *The International Encyclopaedia of the Social Sciences*, 6: 503–511. http://honorhonorhonor.blogspot.com/2013/01/honor-by-julian-pitt-rivers.html. Accessed November 26 2022.

Reddy, Rupa. 2014. Domestic violence or cultural tradition? Approaches to 'Honour Killing' as species and subspecies in English Legal Practice. In A. K. Gill, C. Strange, K. Roberts (Eds.), *'Honour' killing and violence.* London: Palgrave Macmillan. https://doi.org/10.1057/9781137289568_2

Sedem, Mina, Ferrer-Wreder, Laura, Anne. 2015. Fear of the loss of honour: implications of honour-based violence for the development of youth and their families. *Child and Youth Care Forum*, 44: 225–237. https://doi.org/10.1007/s10566-014-9279-5.

Sabbe, Alexia, Oulami Halima, Zekraouni, Wahiba, Hikmat, Halima, Temmerman, Marleen, Leye, Els. 2013. Determinants of child and forced marriage in Morocco: stakeholder perspectives on health, policies and human rights. *BMC Int Health Hum Rights*, 13. https://doi.org/10.1186/1472-698X-13-43

Sev'er, Aysan., and Yurdakul, Gökçeçiçek. 2001. Culture of honour, culture of change: A feminist analysis of honour killings in rural Turkey. *Violence Against Women*, 7(9): 964–998. https://doi.org/10.1177/10778010122182866.

Shah, Nafisa. 2007. Making of crime, customs and culture: The case of karo kari killings of upper Sindh. In J. Bennet (Ed.), *Scratching the surface: Democracy, traditions, gender* (pp. 135–155). Lahore: Heinrich Boll Foundation.

Shoemaker, R. B. 2002. The taming of the duel: masculinity, honour and ritual violence in London, 1660–1800. *The Historical Journal*, 45: 525–545. https://doi.org/10.1017/S0018246X02002534.

Smith, T. Marie. 2022. *Footbinding*. Encyclopedia Britannica. https://www.britannica.com/science/footbinding. Accessed January 16, 2023.

Soomro, Imdad. 2022. Karo-Kari claimed 176 lives in Sindh in 2021: Study. *The News International*, February 4. https://www.thenews.com.pk/print/930710-karo-kari-claimed-176-lives-in-Sindh-in-2021-study. Accessed January 16, 2023.

Talwar, Divya, Ahmad, Athar. 2015. *Honour crime: 11,000 UK cases recorded in five years.* British Broadcasting Corporation. http://www.bbc.co.uk/news/uk-33424644. Accessed December 4 2022.

The European Committee on Equal Opportunities for Women and Men. 2003. *So-called "honour crimes"*. https://assembly.coe.int/nw/xml/XRef/X2H-Xref-ViewHTML.asp?FileID=10068andlang=EN.

The Foreign, Commonwealth and Development Office. 2022. *Forced marriage.* https://www.gov.uk/guidance/forced-marriage.

The News International. 2022. In the name of honour in six months: '2,439 women raped, 9,529 kidnapped, 90 killed in Punjab'. *The News International*, February 7. https://www.thenews.com.pk/print/931530-in-the-name-of-honour-in-six-months-2439-women-raped-9-529-kidnapped-90-killed-in-Punjab. Accessed January 15, 2023.

United Nations Population Fund. 2000. *The state of the world's population* (Research Report). UNFPA. http://web.unfpa.org/swp/2000.

World Health Organisation. 2022. *Female genital mutilation.* https://www.who.int/en/news-room/fact-sheets/detail/female-genital-mutilation. Accessed January 16, 2023.

'Honour'-Based Stalking

8

Mohammad Mazher Idriss and Rahmanara Chowdhury

Key Points

- Definitions of stalking and its relationship to 'honour'-based abuse.
- Consideration of case studies where stalking was a feature, including stranger-stalking.
- Nuanced levels of consideration in relation to honour-based stalking including role of intersectionality and additional stakeholders.
- Use of the web model of domestic violence and abuse for greater understanding of victim experiences.

Introduction

This chapter brings together some pivotal case studies relating to honour-based abuse (hereafter, 'HBA') and explores them in relation to the web model of domestic violence and abuse (hereafter, 'DVA') (Chowdhury 2021; Chowdhury and Winder 2022). HBA concerns male violence against women, including so-called 'honour' killings, where women are harmed or killed for allegedly violating cultural norms relating to sexuality and who are perceived to have 'tarnished' their family's good name and reputation. However, it is increasingly recognised that men

M. M. Idriss (✉)
Manchester Law School, Manchester Metropolitan University, Manchester, UK
e-mail: m.idriss@mmu.ac.uk

R. Chowdhury
Department of Social Sciences, Nottingham Trent University, Nottingham, UK
e-mail: rahmanara.chowdhury@ntu.ac.uk

M. Mellins et al. (eds.), *Young People, Stalking Awareness and Domestic Abuse*,
https://doi.org/10.1007/978-3-031-32379-9_8

may be victims too (Idriss 2020, 2021). The case studies presented herein (including both female and male victims) are crucial to developing a nuanced, and often deeply hidden, understanding of the phenomena of HBA. Given that no two cases are the same, there is an acute need to further enhance the understanding of HBA to develop better informed preventative and supportive interventions, and to assess risk to victims. The web model of DVA was developed specifically with research conducted within UK Muslim communities. It aimed to increase the understanding of domestic abuse within Muslim communities at an academic and practitioner level, in direct response to the lack of representation within the field at present. It visually demonstrates how domestic abuse occurs within UK Muslim communities at four levels. These are the individual psycho-social-spiritual level, the stakeholder level, at the level of intersectionality and finally, the macro level. Within an HBA stalking context, the significance of these four levels becomes paramount. The victim (that is, the person currently affected by HBA and stalking) is placed centrally to ensure the reality of their lived experience is given precedence. The role of active stakeholders within stalking, whether positive or negative, demonstrates the need to look beyond the victim. How intersectionality manifests and directly impacts on the lived experience adds further layers of barriers or potential avenues for drawing on resources. Finally, an appreciation of narratives and structures at the macro level highlights comprehensive contextual factors requiring attention. The interconnected network of relationships, further to the interaction between the four levels, results in a broader range of considerations for both the victim of HBA and practitioners supporting them. The web model of DVA is applied to the case studies within this chapter, exploring how it can enable increased understanding of the nuances within HBA, all within the context of stalking, not only by individuals, but family groups and communities at large, who *collectively* stalk by proxy. Central to this is the individuality of cases and how the web model can facilitate increased recognition of nuances, thereby directly informing resulting interventions and risk assessments. It is argued that within the context of HBA and stalking, considerations at each of these levels are imperative to the safety of HBA victims. Moving away from the one size fits all approach and umbrella terms for lived experiences that are very individual in nature, the web model seeks to empower both practitioners and the clients they work with. By understanding individual dynamics, the intended outcome is to work towards tailored and meaningful support in cases that involve stalking by a variety of different actors.

This chapter first begins with providing definitions of key terms for behaviours or collection of behaviours, before providing a comprehensive illustration of 'honour'-based stalking, and then introducing the web model of DVA.

Stalking

Stalking concerns repeated and unwanted conduct, such as unwanted communication, harassment and intrusive behaviours (Bracewell et al. 2022). Definitions of stalking relate to an intentional pattern of fixated, unwanted and intimidating behaviours that create a sense of fear and anxiety in a victim (Logan and Walker 2019; Bracewell et al. 2022). Individuals that stalk may send unwanted messages; make unwanted calls; follow victims; carry out surveillance; use offensive or sexual language in communications; issue threats and carry out sexual harassment, kidnap and physical assaults (this list is not exhaustive: Bracewell et al. 2022). Social media can also provide a convenient way for people to carry out stalking behaviours—text messages, phone calls and hurling abuse on social media can all create a pattern of control which is harmful, infiltrating every aspect of a victim's life, affecting their mental and emotional health, employment and other social relationships. Critically, stalking behaviours demonstrate a perpetrator's ever-presence, making victims feel they have no escape (Short et al. 2015; Woodlock 2017; Bracewell et al. 2022). Government agencies, the public and victims still hold inaccurate perceptions and understandings of stalking behaviour (Boehnlein et al. 2020; Bracewell et al. 2022). This is particularly true in relation to 'honour'-based stalking where the 'honour' of the family is at stake—whilst public perceptions of stalking behaviour by strangers are not entirely accurate because those doing the stalking are often known to victims, in some HBA scenarios, stranger-stalking can also be a feature. Whilst known family members may stalk HBA victims to control their behaviours, as will be discussed below, strangers unbeknown to the victim may take part in stalking activity against the victim as part of organised community networks.

'Honour'-Based Abuse

So-called HBA involves acts in response to be behaviour that brings 'shame' upon the family (Idriss 2015). HBA usually concerns the infliction of violence upon women and young girls for reasons usually (and allegedly) involving their sexual behaviour (Gill et al. 2014; Idriss and Abbas 2010; Julios 2015; Welchman and Hossein 2005). Families often impose control mechanisms to limit the 'shame' brought upon them, ranging from minor criticism to serious physical abuse and violence, to extreme acts of so-called 'honour' killings. Acts of HBA may occur because families wish to control the sexuality of women, to prevent undesirable relationships, whether sexual or not, or to prevent women from behaving too 'westernised' or in a manner that is deemed inappropriate and at odds with the cultural customs and norms expected within different families and communities. As a phenomenon, there has been increased recognition of HBA in the UK in the last two decades following some very high-profile criminal prosecutions and convictions of so-called 'honour' killings. Tulay Goren; Heshu Yones; Banaz Mahmod and Shafilea Ahmed are all examples of young females aged twenty or below (and Muslim), all victims of so-called 'honour' killings and who were murdered by male relatives for supposedly acting too 'westernised' and for engaging in sexual relationships outside marriage (Idriss 2017).

There is no single definition of the concept of 'honour' and from a historical perspective, its meaning from Latin is derived from the terms 'honos' or 'honoris' which is understood to mean being 'brave' and 'courageous' (Metlo 2012). The word 'honour' itself is a word that varies from culture, region and language and so an exact definition is difficult to ascertain (Idriss 2018). It has several meanings relating to pride, reputation and virtue where young women are brought up within controlling and traditional environments (Akinpar 2003; Ortner 1978; Sen 2005). The Urdu word 'izzat' may also be used, which is understood to mean 'respect' and good character as defined by 'honour' cultures. Izzat embodies the reputation of the individual and the family, with an expectation that when izzat has been violated, the family will exact punishment. The notion of 'honour' is also gendered in the sense that generally men possess the core elements of 'honour', whilst women and young girls can only possess 'shame' (Idriss 2018). Inequalities between men and women are thus reproduced by the concept of 'honour', where women are the bearers of 'honour', whilst men control and regulate women's behaviour, as women pose a threat to male 'honour' (Gill 2010, 2014). 'Honour' is therefore connected to a person's position within a constructed social order—the more 'honourable' they perceive themselves to be, the higher their position within that constructed social order (Idriss 2018). Where a woman has acted 'irresponsibly' and broken the 'honour' code of the family, families perceive that they have no choice but to remove that stain on their reputation (Welchman and Hossein 2005). This can lead to corrective action, including condemnation, coercive control, stalking, violent acts and abuse, ostracization by others in the family or community, and in extreme cases, so-called 'honour' killings (Idriss 2018). A major characteristic of HBA and so-called 'honour' killings in comparison to other types of abuse is the involvement of extended family and community members—multiple perpetrators are often involved in these cases and not just a single perpetrator (Idriss 2018).

The Web Model of DVA

The web model of DVA (Chowdhury 2021; Chowdhury and Winder 2022) was developed as a result of empirical research conducted with UK Muslim communities. The research was funded by the Economic and Social Research Council (ESRC). Qualitative research carried out with DVA survivors and professionals working in a supportive capacity with survivors, their families and perpetrators was utilised through a multi-perspective interpretative phenomenological analysis (MP-IPA) lens. This facilitated an in-depth idiographic understanding of DVA experiences. Whilst the model was developed in specific to relation to DVA behaviours, its versatile nature enables applicability to HBA and stalking (see Fig. 8.1).

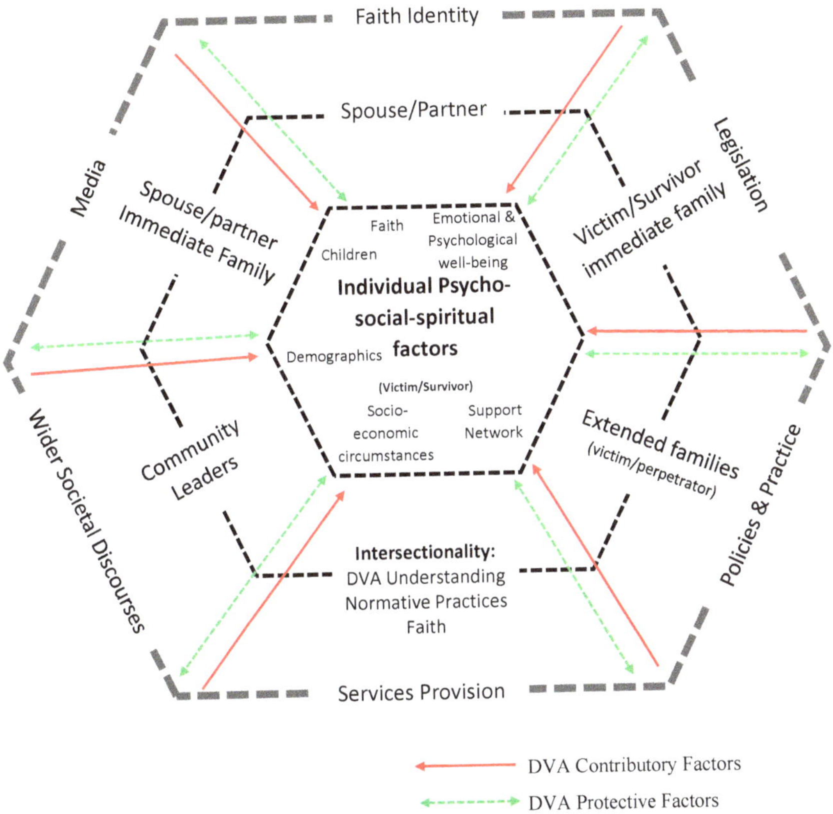

Fig. 8.1 Web model of DVA (Chowdhury 2021; Chowdhury and Winder 2022)

The web model of DVA takes a holistic approach and presents four levels of consideration to be taken into account when working with victims of HBA and stalking. The four levels are:

1. Individual psycho-social-spiritual level—focussed on understanding who the person at the core of the HBA experience is and what their individual circumstances are.
2. Stakeholder level—ascertaining who else may be involved and in what capacity. Such stakeholders may be those identified in the model or additional others.
3. Intersectionality—accommodating intersectionality and how such factors impact on the HBA experience. Extends to all protected characteristics as required.

4. Macro level—the structures within wider society, whether directly or indirectly related, and how these impact HBA victims and specific communities.

Placing victim voices within the context of interconnected close-knit communities is at the heart of the model. Only by understanding the network of relationships and interconnections between the four levels presented within the web model, and as experienced by victims, can a more accurate understanding of HBA and stalking behaviours be ascertained. The individualised contextualisation of the web model enables and facilitates individually tailored support regardless of who the victim may be. Therefore, statutory bodies are encouraged to work in collaboration *with* victims through application of the web model.

This next section aims to illuminate the complexities and risks regarding the nature of 'honour'-based stalking through presenting real issues from recent case examples. This can make difficult reading but offers essential learning to be able to improve policing and other agency responses, and general societal awareness.

'Honour'-Based Stalking

Within this section key insights about 'honour'-based stalking are presented from real case examples, and the nuances of the improvements required to keep people safe are illustrated.

Banaz Mahmod

The murder of Banaz Mahmod, a 20-year-old divorcee of Iraqi Kurdish origin, is perhaps the leading example of so-called 'honour'-based stalking of those under the age of 25. Banaz was ultimately murdered on the instruction of her uncle, Ari Mahmod, and father, Mahmod Mahmod, because she had a romantic relationship with an Iranian Kurdish man who the family did not approve, and which was deemed to have 'dishonoured' the family. Banaz was not allowed to make any decisions about her life, and decisions about marriage had to be ratified by male relatives. Banaz had previously been forced into marriage at a young age to a man she did not love or have a loving relationship with. Marriages in 'honour' cultures are regulated because it is believed that a woman's actions will have a reflection on the family and will affect their ability to marry off others as part of the process of marital transactions. However, the guardianship over women in these types of cases amounts to a level of surveillance akin to stalking. Why? The purpose is to protect a woman's market value and to maintain the reputation of the family's name, much like commercial businesses would do to protect their brand name.

Banaz had an elder sister named Bekhal, who had already left the family home to escape domestic abuse and forced marriage. Bekhal was considered to have already tarnished the family's brand name because she had been seen by Ari Mahmod talking to an unrelated man. In another incident, Bekhal had also been threatened with immolation because she had been seen by a cousin talking to another unrelated man. Bekhal had been under surveillance by her family and uncle, watched closely, to see whether she was behaving appropriately and in line with the family's expectations. But the surveillance was not committed by, or limited to, just family members. The community itself acted as the 'eyes and ears' for the family when it concerned regulating women's behaviour. Mahmod, the father, had been harassed by the local community because of Bekhal's departure, and community members had sent faxes and made calls ridiculing him for failing to control his daughter; to them he had failed in his masculine duty to exert control over his daughter (Payton 2010). The desire to protect the family brand name can create a very extreme level of surveillance and guardianship over women as it relates to 'social capital' (Bond 2012, 2014). The family council meeting that decided Banaz had to be murdered was itself based on a cousin's visual report that Banaz had kissed her boyfriend outside Mitcham Underground Tube Station (Payton 2010).

During the time that Banaz was married, she had been referred to a psychiatrist because she claimed that she was afraid to leave the house because she was being followed by community members known to her husband. The psychiatrist concluded that this was not paranoia or delusional observation by Banaz—this was the extreme reality of her lived experience and her daily life (Payton 2010). Yet the police officers investigating her complaints described her as melodramatic and delusional, that she was telling lies. Banaz had been threatened by at least four men who had been stalking her, yet the police did not believe her accounts and considered them to be exaggerated (Payton 2010). Risk assessments and safeguarding procedures are therefore necessary in HBA cases because the hidden and insidious risks can be easily missed and yet they can be an extremely serious collective form of violence and abuse akin to organised crime, as the authors have explained elsewhere (Idriss 2017). Banaz went to the police on multiple occasions, who failed to properly appreciate the 'death zone' or the 'one chance rule' that some HBA cases may present because of the number of perpetrators involved and the relevance of stalking.

HBA is often viewed as a form of domestic abuse (Idriss 2017) and the term 'honour'-based domestic abuse is often used to explain cases of domestic abuse that involve 'honour'-based rationales and motivations (Hitchens and Daly 2021). This is technically correct, as it reflects many cases that fall under this umbrella term. The advantage of subsuming 'honour'-based domestic abuse is that it helps to avoid creating a distinct category of violence against women and girls that appears to be committed by South Asian Muslims and minority groups. Of course, creating social divisions and hostility between communities is counterproductive and very harmful to community relations. It is clearly dangerous to automatically categorise acts of abuse within minority and Muslim households as being related to 'honour' or minority culture. However, the suggestion that domestic abuse and HBA are one and the same, and therefore require similar forms of intervention, ignores the unique characteristics of individual HBA cases (Idriss 2017). Whilst racial stereotyping is a serious issue, it is also naïve to ignore the differences between domestic abuse and HBA when a 'one size fits all' approach masks the specific needs of HBA victims.

The involvement of multiple perpetrators, as well as stalking by family and community members, known and unknown to the victim, is a serious feature in HBA scenarios, very much like the Banaz case. Banaz did not always know who was 'watching' her. There was a large conspiracy and community support for her murder, with DCI Caroline Goode commenting that over fifty people were aware of what was going to happen to Banaz and yet the police were met with a complete wall of silence during their investigations (Idriss 2017). Some of those involved, undoubtedly, would have been stalking Banaz up to the point when she was murdered by hired killers (Payton 2010). The Crown Prosecution Service in its literature has expressly stated that those not directly related to a victim may become involved in enforcing 'honour' codes of behaviour and that it is important to visualise risks and threats beyond immediate family members, such as fathers, brothers and uncles (Crown Prosecution Service 2008). The CPS has made express references to organised contract killings in one out of nine cases of death, where a primary inciter of acts of violence contracts another to carry out the so-called 'honour' killing of a woman (Crown Prosecution Service 2008; Johal 2003). Such is the level of organisation—multiple perpetrators; multiple victims; premeditation; planning; preparation and clinical organisation, all with the intention to get rid of a woman who has 'stained' the family (Idriss 2017). Banaz wanted to be believed, have her feelings validated and not have her experiences minimised or trivialised by the police who did not understand the nature of her victimisation; a common experience amongst victims of stalking generally (Taylor-Dunn et al. 2021). Sadly, like many, Banaz was let down. She was controlled and stalked by her family and the community, which eventually led to her murder.

Bounty Hunters

Responses to potential cases of HBA need to be tailored to the individualities of cases. Whilst it can be convenient to think that there is only a single perpetrator involved, this approach can be extremely short-sighted and risky, since any intervention must be based on the level and nature of risk posed to the victim. Intervention policies and processes must therefore consider that the victim may not just be subjected to abuse or violent acts by a single perpetrator, but the community at large, an organised conspiracy with varying levels of support from the extended family and community members (Payton 2010, 2014). Such close-knit communities can form actual networks of spies who will actively stalk and track down victims who have escaped the family home. It is well known for photographs to be circulated to shopkeepers, and taxi drivers to act as bounty hunters and used to find women who have been deemed to have stained 'family honour' (Payton 2010). This creates serious challenges not just for those agencies and authorities which seek to protect and shelter women, but also for the police during their criminal investigations, when they are met with walls of silence from the community and who may be possible perpetrators themselves. In another example, it was reported in *The Guardian* in 2010 that a taxi driver doubled up as a bounty hunter for £5,000 per hunt. He would track down young women in the Bradford, Leeds, Huddersfield and Sheffield areas, often because they were fleeing a forced marriage and brought them back to their families (Badshah 2010). This is a clear example of stalking by proxy because whilst the local community thought he was dropping off and picking up passengers, his taxi driver work had provided him with the perfect disguise to exploit his contacts with fellow taxi drivers and shopkeepers to track down girls who had fled. In these instances, it was not the father, or brother, or uncle tracking down a daughter, sister or niece, but it was a third party (often completely unknown to the victim) tracking down a girl. Some of these bounty hunters can also make friends with local government officials, such as those in housing departments and in the Department for Work and Pensions, to obtain National Insurance numbers as a means of tracking down girls. They may also turn up to police stations to report a missing girl to track down a woman who has escaped and to take advantage of an innocent police officer offering to help. It is for this reason why public protection units within police forces do not include the whereabouts of girls who have fled the family home on police databases—some police forces are savvy to the tactics used by perpetrators.

Although his role was never to physically harm girls, the bounty hunter did return girls to their families so that they could be forced into marriage of their parents' choosing. In essence, his role in stalking and tracking down girls only perpetuated the abuse that those parents were inflicting on girls. Why are families so willing to go as far as hiring bounty hunters? Again, it is because they have a shared value system where 'honour' takes precedence over everything else. It takes priority as it relates to 'social capital' and the 'value' and reputation of the family brand name (Bond 2012, 2014). Together with patriarchal structures and religious value systems, the 'honour' code must be protected at all costs—if tracking down a girl helps to bring her back to the family, save face and control her sexuality, families will continue to use bounty hunters to achieve their aims. The local community grapevine is also a very useful tool so word can quickly spread about the whereabouts or location of a missing girl. Community members act as the 'eyes and ears' for the rest of the community, which on the face of it, positively fosters a sense of close community relationships, but in the instance of HBA it is used as a tool of control to track down missing girls and bring them back to their families. Other tactics are equally concerning. The news article further explains that some families hire female bounty hunters to pose as domestic abuse victims to enter women's refuges and shelters to locate missing girls (Badshah, 2010). Such is the determination of families that the authorities must provide victims with new passports and National Insurance numbers so that they cannot be tracked down (Badshah 2010).

Male Victims of 'Honour'-Based Stalking

'Honour'-based stalking is not only confined to female victims. Male victims may be stalked too, or their associates. In the authors' recent publication on male victims of HBA and forced marriages, undertaken through case file analysis of data obtained from a gender-informed domestic abuse organisation, a 19-year-old British-Pakistani male sought refuge because his family had been 'dishonoured' by his relationship with a white British woman (Idriss 2021). The male victim's family had felt that he had brought 'shame' upon the family because he was having a sexual relationship with a white woman whilst studying at university. The male victim was besotted with his girlfriend and wanted his relationship to continue, although his family wanted him to end the relationship. Stalking was a method used to intimidate both the male victim and his girlfriend—indeed, his girlfriend was stalked and kidnapped by relatives, dragged into a car, and told to stop seeing the male victim. Although she was released shortly after without any harm, the fact remains that this was yet another example of a woman who had been stalked because her behaviour was deemed to have encouraged the male victim, thereby bringing 'shame' on his family. The threat of harm against the woman was used to intimidate the male victim and to stop him from seeing his girlfriend. This example is interesting in how it relates to stalking—the male was a victim, but his girlfriend was the one who was stalked—it involved stalking by exposing the third party (i.e., the girlfriend) to intimidation to apply pressure on the son to conform to his family's wishes not to have a white girlfriend (Idriss 2021). However, the male victim loved his girlfriend and continued with his relationship with her, entering a male refuge to escape further abuse and threats and enrolling at another university away from his family. The male victim's natal family members were the main abusers, but just like the other accounts mentioned above, other parties and a range of actors became involved when it came to the stalking and kidnap of the girlfriend.

Breaches of Court Orders

Other instances of stalking in HBA cases can also relate to breaches of court orders, such as Non-Molestation Orders (NMOs) and Forced Marriage Protection Orders (FMPOs). NMOs are injunctions that aim to prevent an existing or former partner from harming a victim and/or children, including physical violence, harassment, intimidation and psychological abuse. Breaches of NMOs are treated very seriously by the courts and become an arrestable offence. Similarly, an FMPO is an injunction that prevents perpetrators from forcibly taking a victim out of the country for a forced and unwanted marriage. The Order can impose restrictions against forcing a person into a marriage and can include the surrender of passports of victims to the authorities to prevent them from being taken out of the country. Again, a breach of an FMPO can lead to criminal sanctions, including a prison sentence or a fine (Idriss 2015). Yet breaches of these types of Orders are rarely considered as examples of stalking. Despite being subjected to FMPOs, far too often victims of HBA and forced marriages are stalked for long periods of time, yet these crimes can be viewed in silo, in isolation, and connections by the authorities investigating these crimes may fail to recognise patterns of persistence. It is not uncommon for potential victims of forced marriages to be harassed and intimidated by other family members in the home who may not be subjected to FMPOs. Whilst technically FMPOs can apply to others not named in the Order (i.e., they must have knowledge of the FMPOs existence at least to be subjected to it: Idriss 2015), this may be difficult to prove and it is rare for breaches to apply to those not named in the Order, such as other family or community members who do not live in the family home. Therefore, FMPOs may lack effectiveness and those outside the family home may exploit opportunities to harass, intimidate and threaten victims into a forced marriage whilst avoiding liability. Furthermore, the Covid-19 pandemic has only helped to facilitate stalking behaviours by allowing family members to control, humiliate, threaten, monitor and isolate their victims (Bracewell et al. 2022; Safety4Sisters 2020). In 2019, the Centre for Women's Justice spearheaded a super-complaint stating that the police fail to use protective measures in cases involving violence against women and girls and put forward excuses for not pursuing breaches of these court Orders (CWJ 2019). This includes 'minor breaches', yet a breach is a breach no matter how 'minor' they may appear to be. The police often treat each report as isolated incidents, but in a stalking context, this misses the context of the obsession and fixation of perpetrators undertaking the stalking, and the alarm and distress caused to victims in HBA and forced marriage cases. In November 2022, a super-complaint on the police response to stalking was submitted by the Suzy Lamplugh Trust on behalf of the National Stalking Consortium (Super-complaint on the police response to stalking, 2022). It reported that only 5% of reported stalking to the police in the year ending March 2022 resulted in a charge by the Crown Prosecution Service, and that criminal sanctions are rarely pursued by the police. If the mindset of the authorities is to treat each incident separately, then the context of 'honour'-based stalking will be missed, and behaviours viewed in isolation may look routine and harmless. This, indeed, was the case with Raneem Oudah (aged 22), when her husband murdered both her and her mother. Despite being the subject of an NMO which had not yet been formally processed, the perpetrator continued to harass, stalk and intimidate Raneem, who wanted to leave the relationship because of his violence and abuse. She was murdered in a so-called 'honour' killing because she failed to conform to his wishes. Raneem even called the police asking for help on the day of her murder, only to be dismissed by one call handler, at which point, she was then attacked by her perpetrator (her dying screams being heard by the police officer). West Midlands Police were later criticised for failing to protect Raneem (Bindel 2022).

The next section explains how existing approaches are inadequate in relation to HBA and stalking, and the authors propose a more nuanced approach to assessing risk through the web model of DVA.

The Need for New Approaches to Understanding and Addressing HBA and Stalking

Whilst there is no one given theory towards understanding honour-based abuse (HBA), there are numerous approaches to discerning the various facets that form HBA. The need for understanding HBA through a multidisciplinary intersectional lens has been outlined by Gill (2014). It has further been argued that HBA-related offences must be understood as distinct to domestic violence and abuse (DVA) in order to accurately understand, assess and mitigate risk (Idriss 2017). The case studies discussed herein highlight how addressing HBA under the banner of DVA has resulted in missed safeguarding opportunities which could have potentially saved lives. This calls for a new methodological approach which centres the victim. Existing research, whilst useful for providing insight into the aetiology of abuse, does so predominantly from the lens of perpetrator behaviours, thereby overlooking victim expertise. Much of existing DVA research such as the Duluth power and control wheel (Pence and Paymar 1993), the cycle of violence (Walker 1979) and the assertion of male dominance and control (Dobash and Dobash 1979), emanate from a western feminist lens based on US and UK predominantly Caucasian samples. Whilst research has since been carried out with additional population groups, legislation and service provision has been primarily informed upon these foundations. Evidence demonstrating the UK as being at the forefront of DVA legislation is apparent (Candela 2016). However, the lack of representation and the incorporation of HBA under DVA raises questions pertaining to the validity and suitability of current approaches to HBA. The nested ecological model (Heise, 1998) extends some way to account for wider factors to be considered, but its generic nature remains lacking in individuality and alternative sociocultural and intersectional perspectives.

The PATRIARCH model (Belfrage et al. 2012) was developed in Sweden and consists of both risk factors (e.g., those related to the violence involved) and victim vulnerability factors (see Table 8.1).

Table 8.1 PATRIARCH Model (Belfrage et al. 2012)

Risk factors	Vulnerability factors
1. Serious violent threats or thoughts 2. Violent acts 3. Honour-based violent acts 4. Violent criminality 5. Escalation 6. Attitudes that support honour violence 7. High degree of insult 8. Origin from an area with known sub-cultural values 9. Lack of cultural integration 10. Personal problems	11. Inconsistent attitude and/or behaviour 12. Extreme fear 13. Inadequate access to resources 14. Unsafe living situation 15. Personal problems

Whilst this risk assessment tool has demonstrated positive results in identifying levels of risk for HBA victims, it fails to take into account the full lived experiences of some HBA victims. Given that this is a tool used by law enforcement, this is understandable. However, the centrality of the victim voice remains absent. The PATRIARCH model further identifies that usually entire families, not just male members, would be involved in HBA perpetration and therefore highlights considerations around close-knit communities. Yet, these crucial elements remain absent from the PATRIARCH tool itself. Additionally, is the consideration of victim experiences within the process of interacting with and reaching out for support from statutory agencies, as outlined above. Without the wider contextual knowledge, it is argued that a complete and accurate understanding of the dynamics being navigated by victims and survivors cannot be ascertained. Thereby resulting in risks potentially being underestimated and victim needs remaining unmet with tragic consequences, as demonstrated in the case studies above.

The web model of DVA endeavours to fill this void as a means of empowering both victims/survivors and practitioners supporting them. The model is organised according to four levels: individual psycho-social-spiritual level; stakeholder level; intersectionality level and macro level. It should be noted that whilst the model has stipulated areas for consideration under each of the levels, it is not necessary that these remain static. Rather, they are encouraged to be individualised to each case as per the adaptable nature of the model. The web model of DVA (see Fig. 8.1) will be applied to the aforementioned cases details to provide a new holistic approach to understanding and addressing the nuances of HBA, whilst centralising victims. Although the web model of DVA was developed in relation to female DVA experiences within UK Muslim communities, this does not imply that HBA, stalking and forced marriage are necessarily seen as DVA offences, nor that it is exclusive to Muslim communities. Rather, the model offers a level of versatility which accommodates the multifarious manifestations of HBA and stalking behaviours as will be demonstrated below.

Application of the Web Model to HBA Case Studies of Young People

Level One—Individual Psycho-Social-Spiritual Factors

At this level, the individual circumstances of the person at the heart of the abuse are emphasised. In the case of Banaz Mahmod, missed opportunities for identifying risk presented itself within her previous forced marriage and the case of her sister leaving home due to the same risks. Had practitioners and statutory organisations sought to understand the specific psycho-social-spiritual factors specific to Banaz, these warning signs would likely have emerged. The level of risk may potentially have remained underestimated due to a lack of general awareness at the time in relation to understanding HBA dynamics. Indeed, the evidence suggests it was brushed off as domestic issues, yet the similar historic patterns should have raised immediate safeguarding concerns. Questions surround the potential role of conscious and unconscious bias within this. This further raises questions regarding why patterns need to be proven when risk of harm is self-evident. Statutory bodies would have further been able to identify Banaz's (lack of) ability to access safety and support in addition to the exact nature of her victimisation. Prominent within this was the absence of social support and complete isolation. This would have been exacerbated by Banaz's young age and the HBA emanating from the guardians within the family. Even the authorities let Banaz down where they were mandated to provide support. Whilst she did disclose her fear of imminent threat to her life, the level of risk was underestimated by police. Despite risk to life being a prominent feature of risk assessment tools used by police and other agencies, reliability and effectiveness of such tools have been questioned since their adoption (Turner et al. 2019). This raises the question of how reflective such tools are of individual circumstances, and differences in how HBA may manifest. The need to move away from a 'one size fits all' risk assessment towards a better understanding of the nuances of each situation is therefore advocated (Turner et al. 2019). The sheer panic and alarm that was brushed away by the police as over-dramatisation, with the use of the web model of DVA would have facilitated the way for identifying Banaz's emotional and psychological desperation. Amalgamating this together and a very clear picture emerges of a seriously isolated young woman, desperately fighting for her life. The only viable sources of support closed their doors and thereby heightened the risk of the eventual tragic outcome.

Understanding the nuanced psycho-social-spiritual factors for each individual thereby becomes critical in any case of HBA. Central to this is understanding the victim and their circumstances through a more holistic victim-centred lens.

Level One Key Issues

- Individual psychological, social and spiritual factors pertaining to each victim.
- Whether such factors are indicators of risk or whether additional sources of support can also be identified within such factors.
- Levels of social support and isolation including ability to access safety and support.
- Victim reports of fear of harm or risk to life,
- Historical patterns of HBA, stalking and FM-related behaviours within immediate and wider victim family.
- Statutory agencies understanding of exact nature of victimisation—over reliance on risk assessment tools and their potential role in the young person not being seen or heard.
- Potential role of preconceived ideas and cultural misconceptions surrounding young people and minorities from the authorities.

Level Two—Stakeholders

The level of the stakeholders within the web model of DVA represents firstly that there is not always one perpetrator, and secondly, that there potentially may be more than one victim. As demonstrated within HBA cases, often there are numerous perpetrators though perhaps one ringleader (Idriss 2017). Such individuals are deemed to be more than just bystanders. They play an active role within the abuse, whether that may be in a positive or harmful capacity. Understanding who these additional stakeholders are, and the exact nature of their role, would have alerted the authorities to the extensive danger Banaz was facing. Coupled with her isolation, this should at minimum have raised the perceived risk of potential harm. In mapping out stakeholders according to the expertise of the person at the centre of the abuse, a detailed insight into the dynamics of the situation and who else authorities need to be aware of would have surfaced. This is a consideration that is excluded within current risk assessments (Turner et al. 2019). Whilst greater understanding of the need to consider additional stakeholders has been ascertained and advocated (Payton 2010, 2014), this would be detected much earlier with the use of the model. Extending beyond this, precise names and relationships could be mapped out, allowing for the authorities to conduct a more holistic and realistic assessment of risk. The vulnerability of the young person, however, must also be considered within this. Victims may not be fully cognisant of who may be a source of support and who may ultimately increase the risk they face. Elders and extended family members, in particular, may be thought of as 'safe' when they may be the very opposite. Despite this, working in collaboration *with* victims is anticipated to lead to more accurate safety planning. The alternative, as seen in the case study of the bounty hunter, is that any member of the public could easily persuade the authorities that they are the 'good Samaritan'. Equally, where there are secondary victims, such as in the case of the male victim, this would also be identified through application of the web model. In cases where victims may not be fully aware of who the additional stakeholders may be, statutory services would be able to utilise the model to determine a worst-case scenario and conduct safety planning accordingly. Centring the victim's expertise within this is crucial and holds potential to increase understanding of nuances by authorities supporting young people facing HBA, stalking and forced marriage.

Level Two Key Issues

- Identification of who else is involved—often there is more than one person perpetrating HBA related behaviours.
- Identifying whether there is more than one victim.
- Ascertaining additional stakeholders who may be a resource and provide safety for the victim(s).
- Victim vulnerability in misplacing trust with potential harmful stakeholders.

- Statutory agencies working collaboratively with victims hold potential for increased understanding of nuances and more accurate safety planning.

Level Three—Intersectionality

Incorporating intersectionality in addressing HBA enables the protected characteristics of the victim to be considered. This results in providing insight into any additional barriers and corresponding risks (Anthias 2014; Anitha and Gill 2011). Within the web model of DVA, intersectionality includes understanding of abusive behaviours within communities, cultural normative practices, and approaches to faith. Whilst the focus herein will be on these three, it should be noted that these could extend to include all protected characteristics as required.

Understanding of Abusive Behaviours

Within a DVA context, there is little understanding of what constitutes abusive behaviours, with many forms of abuse often overlooked or accepted as the norm (Chowdhury and Winder 2022). The only exception is physical violence. Within HBA, it therefore becomes important to ascertain what the understanding of abuse is for both the victim and those surrounding the victim and/or perpetrating the abuse. This will then provide increased insight into the contexts statutory bodies may be working within and the responses they may receive.

Cultural Normative Practices

In cases of HBA, cultural normative practices become significant regardless of what culture that may be. It is important to note that cultural normative practices can apply to any community. As discussed, the very notion of HBA being steeped in cultural notions of 'honour' and 'integrity' imply an increased sense of risk (Gill 2010, 2014; Idriss 2018). Cultural normative practices here usually relate to specific expected behaviour norms within that community. Therefore, for some communities notions of honour and integrity indicate risk; however, risk may manifest in alternative ways for different communities. It is therefore important to speak to the victim to understand the significance of any cultural normative behaviours and whether they pose any risk. Within a DVA context, research demonstrates that whilst culturally informed behavioural dynamics do not always instigate DVA, they can sustain structures which allow the upholding of abuse (Chowdhury and Winder 2022). This is further evident across various population groups, for example, the notion of resocialisation of DVA perpetrators whereby they are welcomed back into communities, often at the expense of the victim, within orthodox Jewish communities (Zakheim 2011). Further, within Gypsy, Roma and Traveller (GRT) communities, hypermasculine male gender roles are normalised, resulting in abuse and violence being accepted as the norm, making it more difficult to challenge (Allen 2012; Lau and Ridge 2011).

Approaches to Faith

Parallel to this, holistic approaches to faith were found to be a protective resource that victims could draw upon within Muslim DVA cases. Reductionist (limiting faith to a set of rules and regulations) and androcentric (male focussed) approaches to faith, however, were found to result in the enabling of abuse and were usually externally imposed upon victims (Chowdhury and Winder 2022). In identifying this, it facilitates recognition of where resources can be drawn upon but equally where additional forms and sources of potential harm exist. It also allows for non-faith communities to be factored in through the inclusion of additional social categories in place of faith as an intersectional consideration (Anthias 2014).

Knowledge of intersectionality coupled with the other levels of the web model of DVA holds potential to enhance the foundations upon which better informed risk assessments, and a more accurate understanding of each case can be ascertained. Therefore, whilst the example of Muslim communities has been discussed here, this extends beyond faith communities. In HBA cases where certain norms become incorrectly associated with specific population groups (Gill 2014), risks may not only be underestimated, but actively diluted as with Banaz. For example, HBA pre-cursor behaviours such as male coercive control being assumed to be common to certain communities and therefore being ignored and brushed aside by being labelled as over-dramatisation. Knowledge of intersectionality and how it shapes the HBA experiences would therefore be deemed as integral to increased understanding by statutory services.

Level Three Key Issues

- Levels of awareness and understanding of HBA related behaviours by victims and those perpetrating abuse.
- Cultural normative practices specific to individual communities and whether they feed into HBA behaviours.
- Approaches to faith (holistic versus reductionist and androcentric) and how these impact HBA experiences.
- Impact of all other protected characteristics on HBA experiences.

Level Four—Macro Level Factors

Structures and dynamics at the macro level consistently present as key considerations in victims reporting abuse and seeking protection. Such structures include, but are not limited to, legislation, institutional policies and practices, the provision of services, media and wider societal narratives.

In the case of the bounty hunter case study, macro level structures eventually identified the risk presented from apparent wider community well-wishers. In changing their procedures in this regard, statutory services directly protected victims from increased harm. Macro level factors may not always necessarily reflect the direct issue at hand, in this case HBA. Rather, macro level factors can potentially relate to societal structures which facilitate the misunderstanding of specific communities and assumed associations around certain behaviours. For example, the notion of macro structures viewing Muslim communities as hybridised threats was put forward by Abbas (2007) and Abbas and Awan (2015). Such depictions naturally influence individuals working within macro level structures. The labelling of some behaviours as inherent to certain population groups by macro level structures thereby risks underestimating the danger victims may be facing. If victims feel they will only be judged within statutory services and not heard, then this too results in increasing the level of risks faced and leaves victims with nowhere safe to access support. Where structures at the macro level do not understand or accommodate the needs of the lived reality of victims, then those needs remain unheard (Chowdhury and Winder 2022). This is exemplified in the case of NMO breaches being looked at on an individual basis rather than as historical patterns of behaviours, despite that any such breach should be treated as serious. In gaining a better understanding of the dynamics present at the macro level, statutory services will benefit from greater insight into what victims are required to navigate to access support and have their voices heard. This is referred to as interactional justice by Mulvihill et al. (2019) in specific relation to victim experiences with police in England and Wales.

The web model extends beyond this and considers all statutory services, political spectrums and media platforms. For example, within Muslim DVA cases, it was found that victims were being prevented by their communities from reaching out for help whilst simultaneously feeling like they could not reach out to services. Negative media and political narratives asserting Muslims as a homogenous entity to be feared (Chowdhury and Winder 2022) were expressed as underlining this. Such findings confirmed research by Kunst et al. (2012) denoting Muslim communities being viewed under suspect lens by macro structures, further exacerbated by counter terrorism measures on the political spectrum (Hickman et al. 2011). This was felt to contribute to the shape of services in that victims had to first explain their identities to services before any safeguarding concerns could be raised. In this manner, macro level structures became directly connected to the risk victims face (Chowdhury and Winder 2022).

In the case of Banaz, not only was she in daily fear of who was monitoring her movements, she further faced the impossible task of convincing the police that she was not exaggerating and that the threats to her life were both real and substantial. Had her circumstances been explored holistically and across all four levels presented in the web model, devoid of presumptions and of preconceived ideas, her voice may have been heard and taken more seriously. She may even still have been alive today.

Level Four Key Issues

- Structures and dynamics present at the macro level and how these impact on victims reaching out for help.
- Such structures may not necessarily be directly related to HBA but have consequential impacts for HBA victims.
- Structures include but are not limited to legislation, institutional policies and practices, the provision of services, media and wider societal narratives.

Conclusion

This chapter provides an original contribution to the understanding of HBA and 'honour'-based stalking, through providing case details of young people, in particular, young women, and a more holistic lens currently lacking within academia and practice. The web model of DVA focusses on placing the victim at the heart of interventions. Yet, its unique feature is its ability to support practitioners in developing a more holistic understanding of the circumstances specific to each victim, without losing the centrality of the victim voice, regardless of which community is being discussed. This is currently lacking from both an academic and practice perspective.

Within an HBA and stalking context, such a holistic approach, which further facilitates the understanding of cultural nuances, is all the more significant in order to avoid underestimating risk to life and safety. Application of each level of the model facilitates increased understanding of potential harm at that level, as well as any potential protective factors which could be utilised. Combined consideration of all four levels would provide a deeper and more accurate holistic picture of the victim experience. It further facilitates the detection of patterns of abusive behaviours from a variety of sources; a central consideration within HBA. Such a holistic approach is transformative to the understanding and practice of working with HBA. It is recognised that training and education would need to be incorporated for victims to fully benefit from statutory services adopting the web model of DVA within their everyday processes.

The web model therefore encourages a more comprehensive manner of working *with* clients rather than being limited by the confines of a risk assessment tool. By placing the lived expertise of victims as central, this holds potential to further empower victims with greater self-understanding of the nuances of their circumstances, within a safe space. Simultaneously, statutory bodies would be educated through working in collaboration *with* victims, whereas current interventions focus on services provided *to* victims.

Existing discussions surrounding HBA, stalking and forced marriage, contextualise these offences under the banner of DVA. This chapter is an important contribution towards considering these offences in their own right. In line with previous research (Idriss 2017), it is evident within the case studies presented that HBA, stalking and forced marriage hold their own distinct patterns and considerations. When labelled under the banner of DVA, such nuances become obscured and thereby risks to life are underestimated or misunderstood. Given the lives that have been tragically lost, it is critical to ensure the differences in these offences can be better ascertained to prevent further harm or loss of life. The web model facilitates this very process and application to the aforementioned case studies demonstrates the need for a nuanced understanding of HBA cases which extend beyond the DVA parameters, in a structured, proactive and holistic manner.

Discussion Questions

- What are the current concerns in relation to understanding and addressing HBA related offences?
- What are the underlying nuances within HBA related offences?
- How can the web model of DVA support in victim-centred improved care by statutory organisations?

Bibliography

Abbas, T. 2007. Muslim minorities in Britain: Integration, multiculturalism and radicalism in the post-7/7 period. *Journal of Intercultural Studies*, *28*(3), 287–300.

Abbas, T., & Awan, I., 2015. Limits of UK counterterrorism policy and its implications for Islamophobia and far right extremism. *International Journal for Crime, Justice and Social Democracy*, *4*(3), 16–29.

Akinpar, A. 2003. The honour/shame complex revisited: Violence against women in the migration context. *Women's Studies International Forum*, *26*(5), 425–442. https://doi.org/10.1016/j.wsif.2003.08.001

Allen, M. 2012. Domestic violence within the Irish travelling community: The challenge for social work. *British Journal of Social Work*, *42*(5), 870–886.

Anitha, S. and Gill, A.K., 2011. Reconceptualising consent and coercion within an intersectional understanding of forced marriage. *Forced Marriage. Introducing a social justice and human rights perspective*, pp. 46–66.

Anthias, F. 2014. The intersections of class, gender, sexuality and 'race': The political economy of gendered violence. *International Journal of Politics, Culture, and Society*, *27*(2), 153–171.

Badshah, N. 2010, August 29. The taxi driver who doubled as a bounty hunter. *The Guardian*.

Belfrage, H., Strand, S., Ekman, L. and Hasselborg, A.K. 2012. Assessing risk of patriarchal violence with honour as a motive: Six years experience using the PATRIARCH checklist. *International Journal of Police Science & Management*, *14*(1), 20–29.

Bindel, J. 2022. 'Auntie, he will kill me': The woman murdered while the police asked her for paperwork. *The Telegraph*, 31 October 2022.
Boehnlein, T., Kretschmar, J., Regoeczi, W., & Smialek, J. 2020. Responding to stalking victims: Perceptions, barriers, and directions for future research. *Journal of Family Violence*, 35, 755–768.
Bond, J. 2012. 'Honour as property', Columbia. *Journal of Gender and Law*, *23*(2), 202.
Bond, J. 2014. Honour as familial value. In A. K. Gill, C. Strange & K. Roberts (Eds.), *Honour killing and violence: Theory, policy and practice*. Hampshire: Palgrave MacMillan, pp. 89–107.
Bracewell, K., Hargreaves, P., & Stanley, N. 2022. The consequences of the Covid-19 lockdown on stalking victimization. *Journal of Family Violence*, *37*, 951.
Candela, K. 2016. Protecting the invisible victim: Incorporating coercive control in domestic violence statutes. *Family Court Review*, *54*(1), 112–125.
Chowdhury, R. 2021. Web model of domestic violence and abuse. *figshare*. Brunel University London. Figure. https://doi.org/10.6084/m9.figshare.19416452.v2
Chowdhury, R., & Winder, B. 2022. A web model of domestic violence and abuse in Muslim communities—A multi perspective IPA approach. *Social Sciences*, *11*(8), 354.
Crown Prosecution Service. 2008 December. *CPS pilot on forced marriage and so-called honour crime—Findings*. London: Crown Prosecution Service Inspectorate (HMCPSI).
Centre for Women's Justice (CWJ). 2019. *Police failure to use protective measures in cases involving violence against women and girls*. https://www.centreforwomensjustice.org.uk/news/2019/3/20/cwj-launch-super-complaint-police-failure-to-use-protective-measures-in-cases-involving-violence-against-women-and-girls (last accessed 9 November 2022).
Dobash, R. E., & Dobash, R. 1979. *Violence against wives: A case against the patriarchy*. New York: Free Press, pp. 179–206.
Gill, A. 2010. Reconfiguring 'Honour-based violence as a form of gendered violence'. In M. M. Idriss & T. Abbas (Eds.), *Honour, violence, women and Islam* (pp. 218–231). London: Routledge-Cavendish.
Gill, A. K. 2014. Introduction: 'Honour' and 'honour'-based violence: Challenging common assumptions. In A. K. Gill, C. Strange, & K. Roberts (Eds.), *Honour killing and violence: Theory, policy and practice* (pp. 1–26). Hampshire: Palgrave MacMillan.
Gill, A. K., Strange, C., & Roberts, K. Eds. (2014). *Honour killing and violence: Theory, policy and practice*. Hampshire: Palgrave MacMillan.
Heise, L. L. 1998. Violence against women: An integrated, ecological framework. *Violence Against Women*, *4*(3), 262–290.
Hickman, M. J., Thomas, L., Silvestri, S., & Nickels, H. 2011. *Suspect communities?: Counter-terrorism policy, the press, and the impact on Irish and Muslim communities in Britain*.
Hitchens, J., & Daly, N. 2021. *Forced marriage law and practice*. Bloomsbury Professional.
Idriss M. M., & Abbas T. (Eds.). 2010. *Honour, violence, women and Islam*. Routledge-Cavendish.
Idriss M. M. 2015. Forced marriages—The need for criminalisation? *Criminal Law Review, 687*.
Idriss M. M. 2017. Not domestic violence or cultural tradition: Is honour-based violence distinct from domestic violence? *Journal of Social Welfare and Family Law, 39*(1), 3.
Idriss M. M. 2018. Key agent and survivor recommendations for intervention in honour-based violence in the UK. *International Journal of Comparative and Applied Criminal Justice*, *42*(4), 321.
Idriss M. M. (ed). 2020. *Men, Masculinities and Honour-Based Abuse*. Routledge.
Idriss M. M. 2021. Abused by the patriarchy: Male victims, Masculinity, "Honor"-Based Abuse and Forced Marriages. *Journal of Interpersonal Violence*, *37*(13–14), NP11905–NP11932.
Johal, A. 2003. Struggle not submission: Domestic violence in the 1990s. In R. Gupta (Ed.), *From homebreakers to jailbreakers: Southall black sisters* (pp. 28–50). London: Zed Books.
Julios, C. 2015. *Forced marriage and 'honour' killings in Britain—Private lives, community crimes and public policy perspectives*. Surrey: Ashgate.
Kunst, J. R., Tajamal, H., Sam, D. L., & Ulleberg, P. 2012. Coping with Islamophobia: The effects of religious stigma on Muslim minorities' identity formation. *International Journal of Intercultural Relations*, *36*(4), 518–532.

Larkin, M., Shaw, R., & Flowers, P. 2019. Multiperspectival designs and processes in interpretative phenomenological analysis research. *Qualitative Research in Psychology, 16*(2), 182–198.
Lau, A. Y. H., & Ridge, M. 2011. Addressing the impact of social exclusion on mental health in Gypsy, Roma, and Traveller communities. *Mental Health and Social Inclusion.*
Logan, T. K., & Walker, R. 2019. The impact of stalking-related fear and gender on personal safety outcomes. *Journal of Interpersonal Violence, 36*(13–14), NP7465-NP7487.
McInally, W. and Gray-Brunton, C. 2021. Research made simple: Using multiperspective interpretative phenomenological analysis to explore healthcare phenomena. *Evidence-Based Nursing, 24*(3), 71–73.
Metlo, Z. 2012 April. *The perception of honour among the British-Pakistani community in Watford, United Kingdom.* PhD Thesis: University of Leeds.
Mulvihill, N., Gangoli, G., Gill, A.K. and Hester, M. 2019. The experience of interactional justice for victims of 'honour'-based violence and abuse reporting to the police in England and Wales. *Policing and Society, 29*(6), 640–656.
Ortner, S. 1978. The virgin and the state. *Feminist Studies, 4*, 19–35.
Payton, J. 2010. Collective crimes, collective victims: A case study of the murder of Banaz Mahmod. In M. M. Idriss & T. Abbas (Eds.), *Honour, violence, women and Islam* (pp. 67–79). London: Routledge-Cavendish.
Payton, J. 2014. Honor, collectivity and agnation: Emerging risk factors in honor-based violence. *Journal of Interpersonal Violence, 29*, 2863–2883.
Pence, E. and Paymar, M. 1993. *Education groups for men who batter: The Duluth model.* New York: Springer Publishing Company.
Safety4Sisters. 2020. *Locked in abuse, locked out of safety—The pandemic experiences of migrant women.* https://www.safety4sisters.org/blog/2020/10/19/locked-in-abuse-locked-out-of-safety-the-pandemic-experiences-of-migrant-women (last accessed 9 November 2022).
Sen, P. 2005. "Crimes of honour", value and meaning'. In L. Welchman & S. Hossein (Eds.), *'Honour'—Crimes, paradigms, and violence against women* (pp. 42–63). London: Zed Books.
Short, E., Guppy, A., Hart, J. A., & Barnes, J. 2015. The impact of cyberstalking. *Studies in Media and Communication, 3*(2), 23–37.
Smith, J. A. 2004. Reflecting on the development of interpretative phenomenological analysis and its contribution to qualitative research in psychology. *Qualitative Research in Psychology, 1*(1), 39–54.
Smith, J. A. 2011. Evaluating the contribution of interpretative phenomenological analysis. *Health Psychology Review, 5*(1), 9–27.
Super-complaint on police responses to stalking. November, 2022. https://www.suzylamplugh.org/super-complaint-submitted-on-police-response-to-stalking (last accessed 9 November 2022).
Taylor-Dunn, H., Bowen, E. and Gilchrist, E.A., 2021. Reporting harassment and stalking to the police: A qualitative study of victims' experiences. *Journal of Interpersonal Violence, 36*(11–12).
Turner, E., Medina, J. and Brown, G. 2019. Dashing hopes? The predictive accuracy of domestic abuse risk assessment by police. *The British Journal of Criminology, 59*(5), 1013–1034.
Walker, L.E. 1979. *The battered woman syndrome.* New York: Harper and Row.
Welchman, L., & Hossein, S. (Eds.). 2005. *'Honour': Crimes, paradigms and violence against women.* London: Zed Books.
White, J. W., Yuan, N. P., Cook, S. L., & Abbey, A. 2013. Ethnic minority women's experiences with intimate partner violence: Using community-based participatory research to ask the right questions. *Sex Roles, 69*(3), 226–236.
Woodlock, D. 2017. The abuse of technology in domestic violence and stalking. *Violence Against Women, 23*(5), 584–602.
Zakheim, S.F. 2011. Healing circles as an alternative to batterer intervention programs for addressing domestic violence among Orthodox Jews. *Partner Abuse, 2*(4), 484–496.

Part III

Stalking Support Services and Healthy Relationship Education

9 Paladin National Stalking Advocacy Service: Supporting and Engaging Young People

Saeeda Mayat and Louise Neville

Key Points

- The need for specialist young people's services and how supporting young victims of stalking differs to supporting adult victims of stalking.
- The impact of stalking on young people and how young people may present.
- Additional barriers that young victims of stalking face.
- The nature of social media usage. Generations have grown up with technology being an integral part of their life with tracking apps used paradoxically to instil a sense of safety. What does this mean, what are these differences and how can having a better understanding illicit a better response.
- Risks and how they differ for young people and how they perceive risk.
- The importance of young people's voices being central to service development and delivery. The need to effectively engage with young people in the service from inception to closure.

S. Mayat · L. Neville (✉)
Paladin National Stalking Advocacy Service, Harlow, UK
e-mail: louise@paladinservice.co.uk

M. Mellins et al. (eds.), *Young People, Stalking Awareness and Domestic Abuse*,
https://doi.org/10.1007/978-3-031-32379-9_9

Introduction

Paladin National Stalking Advocacy Service (NSAS), with support from the Tudor Trust, developed the first young peoples (YP) specific stalking support service in 2018. In this chapter we explore why Paladin felt there was a need for specialist YP support, what we have learned about the young person's experience and how we can use this to improve our response to young people.

About this chapter: This chapter is very much about our experience in developing and delivering a young person's stalking advocacy service. It is based on primary observations and evaluations. Although we have considerable experience as a team working with young people, we are not psychologists, academics or educational specialists, nor do we work with perpetrators. This chapter is based on the 300 cases we have advocated for and supported over the last four years within a multiagency context.

Paladin NSAS

First, a bit about Paladin. Paladin was established in 2013 following successful campaigning by the parents of victims of stalking, Paladin founders, and partner agencies for law reform. Their pioneering work saw the introduction of stalking legislation in 2012 within the Protection of Freedoms Act, 2012. Victims of stalking started coming forward and it quickly materialised that there was a need for a specialist stalking advocacy support, particularly for those that were at a higher risk of harm. The law was new and it was going to take many years of raising awareness for it to be an integral part of law enforcement, indeed this challenge continues.

The well-established network of domestic abuse services was able to offer support to those that fell under the definition of domestic abuse, however, although well intentioned, this support often failed to recognise the heightened risk of post-separation stalking within the context of obsessively controlling relationships. Victims who were no longer in a relationship were being turned away with safety advice, or worse, cases were closed and this issue was exacerbated if people moved out of the area. Victims of stalking who were not ex-intimates were further isolated from support, their only option being generic services who lacked the knowledge or the skills to understand what support they needed.

> The [DV service] were quite good. They were, you know, as supportive as they could be with the situation, but on the stalking side of things, they didn't really have a clue. (Paladin service user)

The initial principle aims of the charity were to:

- Provide victim advocacy to individuals at high risk of harm from stalking through trained ISACs (Independent Stalking Advocacy Caseworkers).

- Provide training to a range of professionals including the Police, Probation Service, Social Services and the third sector.
- Scrutinise the stalking laws to ensure consistency of application.
- Continue to lobby Parliament for further changes to Law and Practice.
- Raise awareness of the dangers of stalking.

Legislations have now been in place for 10 years. New reforms have been introduced such as Stalking Protection Orders; stalking point of contact (SPOC) lead for each Police Service that is overseen by the National Police Chiefs Council (NPCC); networks of stalking support services; specialist multiagency stalking threat assessment units and a National Stalking Consortia. Stalking is better recognised and agencies are working hard to close the gaps.

The work of the Paladin Trauma Informed ISAC team has evolved in response to progress to reflect service user's needs. ISAC's advocate for those assessed at a 'high risk of harm' within a multiagency setting so that they may achieve the best possible outcomes, to increase safety and disrupt perpetrator behaviour. They carry out detailed risk assessments using specialist tools, which then inform the safety, support and risk management plan. Unfortunately, experience tells us that despite the many positive changes within the Criminal Justice System, many victims of stalking continue to not receive the response they should when they call the Police. Whilst the number of stalking reports to police increase each year (there were 118,411 reports in the year ending March 2022, a 20% increase on the previous year according to the Police Recorded Crime Open Data Tables, 2022) the charge and convictions rate remain woefully low at only 5% (Crime Outcomes in England and Wales, 2022). A gap Paladin and partner agencies work tirelessly to reduce by giving victims a voice and making sure they are heard within this complex system.

Emergence of Young People's Service

Despite a year on year increase in referrals, concerningly, we found that referrals from young people between 16 and 25 made up less than 4% of our referrals. We knew from our past experience of working in the Violence Against Women and Girls (VAWG) sector and delivering young people specific services, that often young people were the most marginalised and at-risk group. According to 'Define the Line', a 2017 study by Refuge and Avon, more than half of young adults aged 16–21 reported experiencing controlling behaviour from a partner. Many well known stalking cases within the media were of young women. For instance: Alice Ruggles was 24 when she was stalked and murdered in 2016; Shana Grice was 19 when she was stalked and murdered in 2016; Jayden Parkinson was aged just 17 when she was stalked and murdered in 2013; Kirsty Treloar was 20 when she was stalked and murdered in 2012; Arsema Darwit was 15 years old when she was stalked and murdered in 2008; Clare Bernal was 22 when she was stalked and murdered in Harvey Nichols in 2005.

In 2018 VICE in partnership with Paladin conducted a poll of 12,000 'Vice Snapchat' users aged 13 to 24. It found 35% had personally experienced stalking and 56% knew someone who had been stalked. A further 85% stated that they would support police action of informing people if a partner had previous convictions of stalking or domestic abuse. Although this survey method of data collection is not rigorous, based on the large number of young people that participated, it was evident that stalking was far more prevalent in young people, despite the low numbers that were accessing services for support. Furthermore, young people expressed a desire to do something about it, yet they were not accessing services.

The harsh realisation was that the traditional setup of support services meant we were not approachable to young people. If young people weren't accessing support, their voice, the risks they faced, the nuances of their experience, the challenges and barriers they incurred and the opportunity to make a difference to their safety were all missing. We recognised there was a need to engage with young people in a different way. Therefore, focus groups were held with organisations that young people frequented to establish their experiences and what gaps existed within the provision. Some of the young people expressed that they would be very reluctant to attend an office or call an unknown professional and speak openly about abuse. Trust, language, openness to listen, a non-judgemental approach and time were all factors that emerged. Young people needed space to develop trust and rapport with professionals that were willing and able to work in a less stringent, more creative way.

Funding was subsequently secured, and a specialist young person's worker was employed. As a result, extensive awareness raising work took place with colleges; universities; domestic abuse charities; various young people specific services and national conferences. We also enhanced our online presence, redesigned and reviewed our content to appeal to a younger audience in response to these young people focus groups.

Based on the feedback and our research, we re-structured the way we worked to reflect the needs of young people. The service user journey for the young person was mapped out, separate to that of the adult cases. The referral process was adapted, the method of contact and how we engaged changed, the language we used was adapted, and we reviewed professional bias and judgement we may have, which was impacting on our work with young people. We realised there were a lot of unhealthy demands placed on victims within the sector and this invariably blamed young people for 'not engaging'. Incidentally 'not engaging' is a term we try to avoid at Paladin, as we feel it absolves agencies of responsibility, with the blame firmly placed on the victim for not wanting to access support. This is symbolic of 'defensive practice' that we have seen permeating throughout services over the last 15 years. An aspect we will touch on periodically throughout this chapter.

Slowly referrals started coming through, with professionals requesting training to learn how they could improve their response to young people reporting stalking. We realised it was imperative that we continued to consult with young people within our service provision and that they remained an integral part of raising awareness. Thus, the 'Paladin Youth Ambassador Scheme' emerged. Young people from across England and Wales were invited to apply for the role to be part of service development, to inform our practice, and raise awareness in their local areas. This proved a great success and we will talk more about this project later in the chapter.

Learning Points

- An absence of referrals from a marginalised group does not mean the issue does not exist for them, it may mean your service is not accessible. It is incumbent on us to consider those reasons so that we can work to address them and ensure a more inclusive service.
- Having a specialist young person's service that is run the same as adult services will not illicit a meaningful difference on its own. The young person's voice has to be interwoven through the whole service user's journey, which will mean an overhaul of how you work from pre-inception to post case closure.

The Impact of Stalking on Young People

Vignette

The best way to appreciate the young person's experience is through the lens of a young person vignette. Azma's case is one example, and although each YP's experience can vary vastly, it does illustrate the type of stalking a young person may be subjected to. It also highlights some of the barriers they encountered, their own response to the stalking, as well as the response they received from people around them including professionals. Finally, this vignette also underlines the difference that can be made by expert support from a trained YP ISAC's.

Azma was referred into Paladin, when she was 19. Azma had moved away from home to start University and was enjoying independent living and student life having made some new friends. Azma got herself a part time job in a café near the university campus. Everything was going well.

One day whilst she was working a customer came into café and chatted to her as the café was quiet. This is the first and only time she conversed with this person. Azma got the impression he liked her, but didn't think anything of it. The only information she knew about him was that he too was a student at the university.

Azma then started to receive messages via her Instagram. The context to the messages was 'I want to be with you', 'can we meet for a drink' and similar questions. Azma recognised his profile photo and replied once to say she had a boyfriend.

He then started coming to her work a few times a week, he would buy a drink and then sit at a table and stare at her for long periods of time. Her colleagues thought he was a bit creepy, but mostly laughed it off. Eventually, her manager asked him to leave and he was told he would not be allowed back in. He then started to loiter outside the café instead. Friends told her to ignore him and he would eventually get the message, lose interest and stop. Next, she spotted him outside her lectures.

The messages on Instagram continued, Azma tried to block him. The situation escalated. He set up multiple accounts in an attempt to contact Azma, the content of the messages changed, they were increasingly sexual and threatening in nature.

Azma was receiving more than 70 messages a day from the stalker. He also found out who her friends were and started to follow them on Instagram. Some of her friends had open profiles, something she could not tell them to stop having, he was able to obtain information about Azma and any nights out she was having with her friends and would turn up where they were. As a consequence, she stopped going out with her friends.

Azma started to become concerned but was unsure of what to do, she decided to speak to the welfare team at the university. She realised she was quite frightened to leave her house and had started to isolate herself from her friends. They were supportive and encouraged her to contact the police. Azma called the police, it took a long whilst to get through and often she felt like giving up. A new officer was sent out on each occasion and each time she had to repeat the story again. She felt they didn't take her seriously, concluding it was just someone who was interested in her and that it was harmless. They focused on the incident she was reporting and not the full context of what was happening. Azma was advised to 'block him', 'change your number' and on one occasion an officer remarked 'must be nice to be getting all this attention'.

Azma felt dismissed, and that there was a lack of understanding about how scared she was and how much this had disrupted her life at university. She contemplated leaving university and going back home. Azma was still not calling this stalking.

The university welfare team referred the case to Paladin and the YP ISAC. The ISAC confirmed to Azma that what she was going through was stalking. A full chronology of incidents was made with Azma; a risk assessment was conducted and they together explored measures to increase her safety. The YP ISAC contacted the police to gain some clarity. An officer was appointed to the case. However, the university welfare team contacted the YP ISAC as the police had called them to advise that an officer was going to go out and give the stalker 'words of advice'.

The YP ISAC contacted the officer as a matter of urgency highlighting the risks associated with this course of action. College of Policing Guidance for police on responding to Stalking (2020) advises against doing this for stalking cases due to the increased risk this might pose as there is no way of knowing how the stalker will react (knowing the Police had been called). It would also give him the opportunity to dispose of any evidence and offer no protection for Azma by way of bail conditions. This was a pattern of behaviour that demonstrated the stalker was obsessed and fixated, investing excessive amounts of time pursuing Azma. The police officer explained it had been an instruction from his sergeant and that the YP ISAC would need to speak to the Sergeant to explain the concerns.

The YP ISAC spoke to the sergeant and had a detailed conversation about the nature of incidents, the frequency, the escalation and severity of the case and the impact it was having on Azma. They discussed the changes she had been forced to make to her daily life. The Sergeant agreed there was enough evidence to arrest for stalking. The stalker was arrested and bailed under investigation, as soon as he was released, he escalated his behaviour breaching his police bail conditions by attempting to make contact with Azma. This continued until he was charged under Section 4a of the Protection from Harassment Act 1997 for Stalking involving fear of violence or serious alarm or distress. He was remanded into custody until his trial.

The YP ISAC worked tirelessly and sensitively to gain Azma's trust, liaising with the Police as Azma found it difficult to speak to them directly. Azma felt dismissed by them previously. Azma continued to access support through Paladin and she gained the confidence to continue supporting the prosecution. Azma had been considering leaving university but stayed on, continuing her studies. The stalker received a custodial sentence with a lifetime restraining order. The impact for Azma is still ongoing, below is an extract from her impact statement:

> It is so exhausting to have to stay completely aware of my surroundings whenever I am in the library, on my way to and from university, or coming out of lectures. Some days I would be so exhausted I would be unable to hold up a conversation with my housemate, I found it tiring to cook, to go to the shops, tidy my room or keep up an everyday routine. Simple things that I should be enjoying, like going for a drink, meeting a friend, or even checking my social media, fill me with fear. My friends would pass comment that "I wasn't smiling as much" or "I wasn't as chatty as normal". This just made me feel sadder and I became more isolated as I felt like a burden. Going to sleep frightens me as sometimes I wake up from a nightmare and I can't move.

Azma further details the difference the YP ISAC support made to her.

> The ISAC provided me with advice and support that I wouldn't have been able to go so far in the case without. I also think that it helped me realise the seriousness of what was happening. After talking to the police at first, I could leave feeling very powerless, upset and angry but with Paladin's support I started to feel less powerless. I am so grateful for the support Paladin gave me.

Azma's case demonstrates the significance of the young person's voice and the importance of listening to her experience and calling the behaviours stalking. Azma knew what she was experiencing was not right, she was feeling increasingly worried and had already taken steps to try and keep herself safe. Azma even approached professionals for help, trusting them to know what to do.

There is an expectation that when young people turn 18, they are immediately ready to comprehend and navigate the complexities of life, even though many of these experiences they may have not come across before. Indeed, these systems are complex and difficult for most people to navigate and young people need even more support and guidance through this. We find young people will often allude to knowing more than they do in an effort to reassure themselves and adults around them, internalising their concerns, reluctant to ask for help until they are extremely worried. This is particularly evident when working with those young people that have not experienced accessing services growing up, which we will discuss later in the chapter.

Azma's case also demonstrated the role specialist trauma informed YP ISACs can play in ensuring agencies provide the response needed and that the victim's voice is heard. This cannot be stressed enough. We've extracted a sample of comments from our YP feedback forms that further demonstrate the need for specialist services.

> Having you…on my side is so good, I didn't know how much support was out there. (YP age 19)

> Without your intervention, my ex would not have been arrested for stalking, and I would still be living in limbo, waiting for a knock on the door or a car following too closely. (YP age 23)

> You helped me with understanding the stalking law better, you also helped me deal with the police when they wasn't doing their job properly. You made me feel at ease with everything going on and that it wasn't my fault, I was scared to ask for help, I thought it was my fault. (YP age 18)

> Thank you so so much for all your help…. it's so reassuring having you there! (YP age 18)

> If I didn't access Paladin, I more than likely would either be in the same situation with my ex or even worse, it wasn't until speaking to you I realised just how serious things were and how they could end up if I didn't do something. (YP age 19)

> You helped me get information, gaining access to services and options which I didn't even know were available. This was unquantifiable help during a very distressful time.'(anonymous YP)'This is one of the best phone calls I've ever had, I feel like finally someone understands. (YP age 22)

> I feel a million times safer. We go for walks [with child], we play in the park, we go out to meet friends. All these things were impossible before because I deemed them too dangerous. (YP age 24, client has a young child)

> You're always there with fresh ideas and tonnes of support when things go pear shaped, and have been just as important to me as my IDVA. More so, in that you send all those letters on my behalf. (YP age 20)

Learning Points

- There may be a lot more to a situation than is initially disclosed by the young person. They may not use language that meets the criteria for 'red flags'. Exploration in a non-judgemental, supportive manner can be the difference between correct identification and implementation of effective safe interventions and a young person feeling dismissed or worse, incorrectly reassured that there is nothing to worry about.
- Every safety measure put in place has a potential consequential impact that needs to be explored, considered and mitigated for. A stalking perpetrator is unlikely to stop their behaviour and is more likely to find another way.

Additional Barriers that Young People Face When Accessing Support

We have looked at why we started the service, explored a case study and considered the potential impact of stalking, we now move on to discuss what we have specifically observed when supporting young victims of stalking—what stands out as different? To do this we need to explore the barriers that young people face.

The Paladin team have over thirty years' combined experience of working with young people in a variety of services and settings. When delivering training to professionals specifically in relation to young people, we try to address some of the judgements we may hold by starting with the following exercise. Before reading on, do this exercise yourself.

Think of five words to describe young people?

How did you do? On the whole what we receive are largely negative terms:

> 'Challenging;' 'Difficult;' 'Hormonal;' 'Chaotic;' 'Fun;' 'Risk-takers' and 'Irrational'.

Do your terms differ from our most popular suggested words? If yours are mostly positive well done, you have overcome the first hurdle. The negative judgements we hold can create the first additional barrier that young people face when accessing support. Professionals and services may not verbalise their views on young people, however, it becomes evident in their approach to support, with an underlying current of judgement and blame that results in young people not accessing support. The judgements we hold need to be tackled head on with open dialogue so they can be demystified.

Language can be another barrier that prevents young people accessing support. As professionals, certain terminology can become the norm that holds different meanings outside the sector. We are told by our young people's focus groups that the terms 'domestic violence' or 'stalking' 'feel like a serious 'adult issue' that happens to older couples that are married or living together' or to 'celebrities'. Young people therefore don't associate what they are experiencing with these terms. Therefore when they are asked, young people may play down the situation, believing they can handle it. If you recall in Azma's case she had experienced numerous incidents of increasingly concerning nature, however, despite her taking personal steps to keep safe, Azma was not calling it stalking.

Paladin's School Development Worker (SDW) had to revisit the training package she had created whilst delivering a focus group for young people. It was evident that the words used in the commonly suggested acronym FOUR (Fixated, Obsessive, Unwanted, Repeated) meant something different to the group. This became apparent when examples of the behaviours were discussed, they knew the words but the wider understanding within the context of stalking needed to be explored.

> We broke each word down and put it into language that they would understand and associate with, talking about examples of the types of things a stalker might do that they could relate to. (Paladin SDW).

Professionals in the Criminal justice system often use language that is not youth friendly and can misinform as well as be overwhelming.

> I had one case where a young person had been told by an officer that her case had been filed. What this young person took from this conversation is that her case had a file and was ongoing. When in actual fact we had to clarify with her that the case had been closed and there would be no further police investigation/action. (YP ISAC)

Some examples of language and jargon that is commonly used can also result in victim blaming. On a peer support group carried out with young people at Paladin, we asked young people what safety advice they had initially received from professionals.

Here are some of the examples;

> Change your phone number… You can't expect anything from us if you don't change your phone number.

> An officer told me not to answer calls from No Caller ID. But I knew he was back on shift and would be ringing me. My phone rang on No Caller ID and when I answered it, It was the officer on my case. He said: "I told you not to answer No Caller ID calls."

> Delete social media.

If we are not accessible as professionals we are missing the moment to ascertain and measure the true risks that young people encounter and thus the opportunities for effective intervention. It should not be acceptable for reports to have phrases such as 'appropriate action was taken based on the information we were told', or 'we could not have for-seen what happened', and 'we were not aware of the full extent of the situation as the victim withheld this information'. Whilst we accept not all cases can be thwarted, often there are opportunities for further exploration. We need to be honest about when these opportunities are not realised so that we can implement change to ensure we are hearing the young person's voice and preventing harm.

Another barrier that young people face is concerned with social media use. Social media pays a huge part of young people's lives, it is interwoven within the fabric of their existence. Yet many professionals lack understanding of both the specific social media platforms and the manner in which young people use them. We need to include these vital online aspects as part of our assessments to fully understand the risks and behaviours young people are experiencing. Paladin's Youth Ambassadors recently discussed the online education they received at school. There was a consensus that they thought online education was written by adults with vastly different life experiences and with little understanding of the significance of social media to their overall lives. The group agreed that there was a lot of worst-case scenario teaching rather than addressing more likely scenarios. The reality that the people they know may pose the greatest risk of harm to them was not explored.

> I felt so scared that I was going to meet a paedophile online that I came off all my accounts. Then I slowly went back on them, and this has never happened. I just didn't listen to any of the advice again. (Youth Ambassador age 16)

Another concerning message that was also communicated to young people was the advice to block people and come off social media as a means of keeping safe. Wider guidance on the implications of this and what to do if the person is someone you know was often not discussed.

The College of Policing Guidance for Police on Responding to Stalking (2020, 5) states that Officers should be mindful not to advise victims to block stalkers or come off social media, this can increase risk as the perpetrator may source other means, including physical approaches. It can also mean that vital evidence is potentially lost should the person decide to report to the police. Coming off social media is unrealistic and extremely isolating for a young person. It encourages young people to withhold information and blame themselves when they don't follow the advice. Guidance on privacy settings is also important to note. 'Social media is designed to connect and not to protect', a key point to remember. Generic safety advice that is often given to young people is to 'keep yourself private', however, this is not straight forward and can actually be unhelpful. Default settings on social platforms are public for lots of different reasons and it is important to understand each platform then has its own list of further settings that would need reviewing. Many young people use social apps to earn money (for instance selling art work, dog walking, connecting with friends, blogging and social influencing). They may not be able to make these profiles private. It is more helpful to have an honest conversation about their specific social media use.

There needs to be an aligning of the information that is provided to young people to avoid mixed messages and judgements from professionals, which would lead to a more realistic safety plan. Online education that encourages critical thinking, developed *with* young people as opposed to *for* them would lead to better outcomes. Our fear and perceived inability, particular within statutory and victim services, of being unable to keep up with current online trends is stopping us from safeguarding our young people. There is a deep chasm developing between that of the young person's online experience and well informed adults who have a deep and thorough understanding of young people's experience. We need to identify our tech champions internally and know where to go for further guidance. *Professional curiosity* is key here and being open to understanding new trends so we can effectively work with young people and keep them safe.

Learning Points

- Paladin was the first stalking service to have a specific young people advocate (YP ISAC). We identified the specialist skills needed to work with young people and employed advocates who had this expertise. Encouragingly, Paladin has been approached by services looking to appoint young people's advocates, but this remains a postcode lottery. Whilst we have seen an increase in funding for adults impacted by stalking through the Ministry of Justice and the Home Office, no specialist funding has been made available for stalking involving young people between the ages of 16 and 25.
- An interesting lesson for Paladin has been the realisation that not all young people know everything about technology, nor do they all have the same capability. This presumption can actually mask their vulnerability and does not allow for effective safety advice.

Risks—Young People and How They See Risk

When discussing stalking and risks it is vital to acknowledge factors that are specific to young people. Young people are more visible. They may still live at home with family members, in house shares or small student lodging. This often means they spend a lot of time outside of the home with friends as well as socialising online. Young people are also more likely to attend bigger institutions such as college or university and access public transport more regularly. Often, to support studies they will be in customer facing jobs, such as catering and retail where they will meet a variety of people. They are more visible and are in situations that mean they interact more with people. This may be one of the contributing factors to why Paladin sees more stalking referrals from non ex-intimates in younger age groups—this could be an acquaintance, an old friend, a colleague or a stranger. From analysing the data from our over 25s referrals, it is notable that 32% of these victims are being stalked by non ex-intimates, in comparison to 49% within our young people cases.

For young people the life transition from childhood to adulthood is an extremely formative period, a crucially important factor that needs to be remembered. The impact and trauma they experience through the stalking experience can therefore have longer term effects on them due to the developments and learning they are going through. It helps to have some basic understanding of brain development if we are to work with young people in a meaningful manner. We now know that young people's brains are still developing until their mid-twenties. The latest part to develop is the pre-frontal cortex—the part that manages how we understand risk. This is extremely relevant when it comes to stalking and managing risks and safety. Whilst this is not an in-depth tutorial on brain development, and other chapters of this book authored by Forensic Psychologists may indeed cover such points in greater depth, it is important to highlight some of our perspectives in this area so that we can work with young people more effectively.

In Nicola Morgan's book, *Blame My Brain* (2005), Morgan discusses how the brain changes in adolescence in a practical sense and how this will impact young people in different ways. Neurons start to change and reduce, the ones which are used become more fixed, and new neural pathways are formed, in order to enable young people to cope with adult life. This means that the experiences we have as teenagers shape the adults we become, so having good experiences as adolescents is important. Young people don't appreciate risk and often make decisions that appear illogical and dangerous, because ultimately the pre-frontal cortex is still in development stage. This part of the brain is involved in understanding risks and consequences in particular. In this way young people 'can't think ahead to look at consequences', (Morgan 2005, 91).

To appreciate consequences of risky behaviour, one must have the ability to think through potential outcomes and understand the permanence of consequences. Due to an immature pre-frontal cortex, young people are not skilled at doing this. If you recall your young adult self, you can probably think of activities or behaviours that now, on reflection, you would not consider to be safe. As professionals working with young people, we need to understand the developmental process and adapt our approach, so that we are more supportive and less judgemental.

An important factor of our work at Paladin is about the victim's perception of risk and fear and to ensure that this is an integral part of our assessments. We find when working with young people we have to explore this far more, as often we find the young person's perception of fear does not match what they are experiencing. They may be taking extensive measures to keep themselves safe, but will not verbalise that they are fearful for their life, as they do not recognise this within their experience.

> I had one case and she said she wasn't scared of the Perpetrator, this was a Perp who had infiltrated every part of her life. When we talked about it more, it turns out she was moving round the house by crawling on the floor and sitting on the floor with the lights off. He used to drive past the house and watch her and she didn't want him to know she was in, if she

> closed the curtains, he'd know she was home. 'Are you scared?' is not that simple, especially for young people. (YP ISAC)

We have also observed a difference in the manner in which young people present dependent on their life experiences, each presenting with its own challenges. Young people who have experienced trauma and difficulties in life—and as a result have already received statutory or agency involvement—have often had to identify their own risk and learn how to manage it. They have started to build muscle memory, but this doesn't necessarily mean they are using safe methods of handling risky situations, as these are based on their interpretation and reaction to the risk. The challenges with working with this young person may be mistrust of agencies, reluctance to call the police, they may appear obstructive, argumentative and have complex needs. There is a risk that this person, despite having numerous people involved, may slip through the net, as they may be 'difficult to work with', their experience may be normalised or the specific stalking risk will not be recognised amidst the catalogue of other pressing issues. However, conversely one of the potential benefits of people being exposed to multiple agencies is that they are more likely to be offered specialist services.

> If my son was not on a child protection plan, I would have had no idea your service and the IDVA (Independent Domestic Violence Advisor) service existed, or even that what was happening to me was stalking. (YP Age 21)

In cases with multiple agency involvement, identifying one key professional who co-ordinates the support for the young person is key. Ideally, this specialist will bring skills to prioritise the needs and risks of the case and can be vital to ensuring the young person feels heard. In some instances, Paladin's YP ISAC will work with the young person via this professional (that already has a trusting relationship with the young person) rather than working with the YP directly.

On the other hand, a young person who has not encountered trauma or abuse within their lives and has grown up with safe people around them that they can trust, will not have been exposed to situations where they need to develop any risk management skills. Often, these young people can be overly trusting of professionals, accepting that they know what is best, and are less likely to use language to say they are scared or fearful, believing 'it wouldn't happen to them'. They can play down the situation and seek validation from the professional around them. Again, there is a reluctance to call the Police, a theme common with many young people we work with. The reasons for this are widespread and are outside the scope of this chapter, but one of the common reasons discussed by young people is concerned with believing the situation does not warrant police intervention or feeling that they are less likely to be taken seriously by the criminal justice system. These young people who have not had exposure to wider services will rely more on schools, colleges and their care-givers to provide the information to help them to recognise risk. The need for professional curiosity is therefore vital in this field of work. On average there are 100 incidents before a victim of stalking will call the police (Sheridan, 2005), for a young person this is even higher. If a young person has resorted to calling the police or expressing concern about a situation, it is highly likely there is far more to the situation than has initially been disclosed. How these young people are spoken to, the questions they are asked and the advice they are given could determine whether we, as professionals, are afforded the opportunity to put in place safe interventions, or if the young person is left feeling dismissed and at risk.

Final Thoughts: The Importance of Young People's Voices

At the beginning of the chapter we spoke about the Youth Ambassador scheme. This scheme was launched to ensure we had the voice of young people in our service.

The initial idea was that the role would be developed by young people, and they would be involved in awareness raising, consulting on the issues faced by young people, research, publicity and shaping policy. We had a staggering response to this scheme and we rolled out training in three different locations to accommodate the numbers. After one year of the young people's ISAC being in post, Paladin saw a dramatic increase in referrals from young people 16–25 years. The referrals for under 25s now account for 22% of all referrals that are received by Paladin. The demand for the service has become such that the one Young Person's ISAC is now a Young People's team. The very essence of youth work is about empowering young people and ensuring they have a voice. It is important to note that Article 12 of The UN Convention on the Rights of the Child states that young people should be consulted with regard to matters that concern them.

Each young person presents with their own challenges and individual barriers that need to be overcome, however, it is important to appreciate that they are also vulnerable, still learning, and when exposed to danger may not acknowledge it or know how to deal it. We have to understand the intersectional nature of the barriers that they present with, and as professionals we need to do better. It is evident that at present we are letting our young people down. It is important that we are positive and open to change so that we don't develop our own bias when working with young people. Youth work is about relationships as Young (1999) articulates in 'The Art of Youth Work', this includes 'The ability to make and sustain meaningful relationships within which young people engage in the process'.

A service for young people should never be designed without young people. As you can see through this chapter, we have tried to ensure the voice of young victims of stalking is always at the centre of our work. We have learned a lot at Paladin about stalking amongst young people, but the biggest lesson has been that doing things with and not for young people will not only empower, but build resilience moving forward.

Discussion Questions

- How many young people currently access your service, explore the reasons for this?
- How much of what you are doing is 'tick boxing' and is this contributing to effective interventions or value adding work for young people?
- What is the organisational culture on professional curiosity?

Bibliography

College of Policing Guidance for Police on Responding to Stalking. 2020. https://library.college.police.uk/docs/college-of-policing/Stalking-and-Harassment-2020.pdf. Accessed 15th December 2022.

Crime outcomes in England and Wales 2021 to 2022. GOV.UK. https://www.gov.uk

Morgan, Nicola. 2005. *Blame my brain: The amazing teenage brain revealed*. London: Walker Books.

Police Recorded Crime Open Data Tables. March 2022. https://www.gov.uk/government/statistics/police-recorded-crime-open-data-tables 26. Accessed 20th December 2022.

Refuge and Avon. 2017. *Define the line*. https://www.youtube.com/watch?v=iIMZytBAhc0. Accessed 12th January 2023.

Sheridan, L. 2005. *Network for surviving stalking 2005 survey report key findings*. http://www.le.ac.uk/press/stalkingsurvey.html. Accessed 20 December 2022.

Young, K. 1999. *The art of youth work*. Dorset: Russell House Publishing.

10 'They Didn't Want to Upset the Client': Stalking in Hands-on Occupations

Laura Scarr and Morag Claire Kennedy

Key Points

- This chapter will consider the literature on stalking covering the scale, scope, nature and impact by using theoretical perspectives, statistics, and academic research to build a picture of stalking within hands-on occupations such as the beauty aesthetic industry (including tattoo/piercing artists, spa therapists, beauty therapists and nail technicians).
- The responses to stalking experiences from both a legislative and workplace point of view will be explored, accompanied by analysis of areas for requiring change.
- The above points will be compared and contrasted with our conducted research in order to establish relevant patterns and areas requiring further research.

Introduction

There is a distinct lack of literature surrounding stalking, which is far more limited when it comes to stalking within hands-on occupations. Few studies provide empirical research on the nature, impact, and support available to those within hands-on occupations, with much of the focus being on stalking healthcare professionals. This chapter seeks to address this gap by highlighting employee and employer experiences of stalking within this context, with the inclusion of participants from

L. Scarr · M. C. Kennedy (✉)
Nottingham Trent University, Nottingham, UK
e-mail: morag.kennedy@ntu.ac.uk

M. Mellins et al. (eds.), *Young People, Stalking Awareness and Domestic Abuse*,
https://doi.org/10.1007/978-3-031-32379-9_10

the United Kingdom who were all aged 18–30. The experiences investigated fall into the categories of harassing/stalking incidents which have occurred, employers' approaches and the support victims received. These areas, in particular, were studied to help clarify the confidence in recognising/reporting stalking experiences, the frequency/type of incidents, and any gaps in responses that required addressing.

Whilst all genders can both perpetrate and be on the receiving end of stalking, this study worked within the parameters of feminism in terms of its creation, theoretical stance, and delivery to ensure the research was conducted *with* participants rather than *on* them. Equally, we recognised that research of this kind cannot be value-free (Harding 1991). Given the gender differences in terms of stalking experiences, we were interested in recognising any distinctions between genders surrounding victim experiences, the motivations of stalkers, and the effects of stalking. Lastly, this chapter will draw on literature to explain the different types of stalkers, the theoretical perspectives behind stalking behaviour, and the current legal approaches. It will do so with the acknowledgement that this scoping study begins a discussion on stalking within hands-on occupations, which is a nearly non-existent field of research.

Prevalence of Stalking

As of March 2021, there were 215,173 incidents recorded by police that were domestic abuse-related harassment and stalking which accounts for 25% of all domestic abuse crimes (Office for National Statistics 2021). In March 2020, 11,617 men and 13,642 women were subjected to stalking with 70.5% of perpetrators being male (Napo 2011; Office for National Statistics 2020). Also, since July 2021 the East Midlands Police have documented a 99% increase in stalking and harassment offences (Forte 2021). However, it is impossible to quantify the true picture of stalking and harassment. The Suzy Lamplugh Trust (2021, 1) has described the number of recorded crimes in relation to stalking as a 'drop in the ocean'. This may be due to misreporting of this crime type with many reports classifying stalking as either harassment, a violation of a protection order or domestic abuse (Brady and Nobles 2017). Similarly, some victims may not want to report the crime. For example, male victims have voiced feeling ridiculed or not taken seriously when reporting their experiences of stalking to police (Harmes and Forde 2018). On average an individual will have experienced 100 stalking incidents before contacting police (Office for the Police and Crime Commissioner for Norfolk 2020). Therefore, the dark figure of crime may be partly attributed to a combination of misconceptions of victim status and negative experiences with police. It must also be noted that prior research suggests that offenders are rarely charged with stalking (Jordan et al. 2003; Tjaden et al. 2000). Many are charged with either domestic abuse related crimes or lesser offences such as harassment, property crimes, or trespassing (Jordan et al. 2003; Logan 2010; Woodruff 2010).

Nature of Stalking

In terms of anti-stalking legislation, differences lie in what constitutes stalking. This includes the minimum number of occurrences for an individual's conduct to be considered stalking as well as physical harm being prioritised over psychological harm (Blaauw et al 2002; Finch 2001). These responses will be further discussed later in the chapter. To make matters worse, researchers' and clinicians' definitions also differ. For example, Meloy (1996) and McCann (1998) use the term *obsessional following*, Rosenfeld (2000) terms stalking *obsessional harassment*, Cupach and Spitzberg (1998) refer to stalking as *obsessive relational intrusion*. With that being said, it is clear that researchers and clinicians are referring to the same experience. The Suzy Lamplugh Trust offers a more cohesive definition describing stalking as 'a pattern of fixated and obsessive behaviours which is repeated, persistent, intrusive and causes fear of violence or engenders alarm and distress in the victim' (Suzy Lamplugh Trust 2019, 1).

Currently, the Domestic Abuse Act (2021) does not highlight any links to stalking despite the wide range of evidence supporting its relationship to stalking offences. However, on the 31 January 2022, a policy paper regarding plans to publish a comprehensive strategy focusing on tackling domestic abuse perpetrators was announced to be released. So far, the strategy details one of its pledges as the assessment and management of risks of perpetrators who commit both domestic abuse and stalking offences (Home Office 2022). One proposed method is to use electronic tagging for a further 3,500 offenders on release from prison who are still deemed a threat and to form a new domestic abuser register. This register will require known offenders of domestic abuse, to inform police when opening a joint bank account with a new partner, or if they change address (Home Office 2022). Unfortunately, whilst this strategy accounts for the gendered nature of domestic abuse, it does not acknowledge women with multiple protected characteristics and their increased risk of abuse and further difficulties in accessing support. A wide community of deaf, disabled, migrant, Black and minority, and LGBTQ+ women and girls may have additional needs/risks that have not been addressed (EVAW 2022).

Stalking can be displayed in a manner of ways/settings, with the recent COVID-19 pandemic restrictions and widely popular use of social media making stalking offences easier to commit (Bracewell et al. 2020). The National Stalking Helpline found that 100% of reports received included forms of online stalking, with this pattern of behaviour escalating over lockdown periods. In fact, victims have referred to themselves as 'sitting ducks' as they were aware of the perpetrators having easier access and more time to victimise (CPS 2020: 1). It must be noted that a discussion of specific online stalking behaviours will be kept to a minimum in this chapter given our focus on stalking within hands-on occupations.

As mentioned above, for stalking to be considered a crime there needs to be a pattern of acts/behaviours which intend to cause the victim(s) harm (Fox et al. 2011). Without this repeated behaviour, the acts can be considered legal if they are standalone (Brady and Nobles 2017). To illustrate, victims may experience being spied on, followed, repeated unwanted contact (through social media, text, email, gifts, mutual friends), threats to cause harm, suicide or engage in image-based abuse, property damage, spreading rumours through social/professional environments (Bracewell et al. 2020; Brady and Nobles 2017). Otherwise harmless behaviours (i.e. sending a card) could be considered legal when both the context and intent are not contemplated (Brady and Nobles 2017). In fact, Sheridan and Lyndon (2012) found in their study of 1,214 self-identified victims of stalking that those who experienced heightened social, emotional, and physical impacts are victims who had prior relationships with their stalkers. Furthermore, Spitzberg and Cupach (2014) categorised the 5 coping strategies used by victims to allow them to manage these impacts. First is *moving toward*, where some victims may try a 'reasoning' route, in attempts to negotiate a different form of relationship such as friends instead of romantic partners. Another strategy is *moving away*, which is avoiding the stalkers altogether in order to reduce the stalker's access to them as much as possible. The third strategy is *moving against* which refers to the victim harming/threatening the stalkers as a method of deterrent. The fourth strategy is known as *moving inward* which involves the act of victims empowering themselves to effectively manage the stalking behaviour, for example self-defence classes. Lastly, *moving outward* is the involvement of asking for help/support such as confiding in friends or relatives (Acquadro Maran and Varetto 2018). It must be noted that within Spitzberg and Cupach's research male victims of stalking were less likely to *move outward* than female victims (Acquadro Maran et al. 2020; Spitzberg et al. 1998). Furthermore, many victims used a number of strategies in an attempt to stop stalking behaviour, a single strategy was not successful on its own (Acquadro Maran et al. 2014).

Theoretical Perspectives of Stalking

To further understand the phenomenon of stalking, theoretical perspectives need to be considered to partly explain why stalking behaviour occurs. It is believed that parental bonding and attachment impact stalking behaviour (Cassidy et al. 2013). In brief, it is believed that early child–parental relationships determine relationship perceptions through adulthood. For example, Mackenzie et al. (2008) found in their sample of 129 stalkers that they were more likely to have insecure attachment styles than the general population. In addition, Bartholomew and Horowitz (1991) explain how the insecure attachment style may sometimes manifest in individuals feeling anger and needing 'justice' when they feel they have been rejected in addition to their preexisting negative view of self/others.

These offences may have involved a particular 'stalker type' with research showing that there are 5 distinct classifications: the rejected stalker, the intimacy-seeking stalker, the resentful stalker, the incompetent suitor, and the predatory stalker (Mullen et al. 2000; Mullen and Pathé 2001). Briefly, the *rejected stalker* is usually triggered by the breakdown of the relationship causing them to feel 'rejected' and so seek revenge. The *intimacy seeker* may feel an emotional connection to their target, who is often a stranger, as they yearn for a relationship out of feelings of loneliness. Next, is the *resentful stalker*, who again usually targets strangers/acquaintances and resorts to inducing fear to gain control due to their own delusional beliefs of being wronged. Following this, is the *incompetent suitor* whose motivations arise from lust/loneliness and so seeks a short-term scenario such as a date/sexual relationship. Finally, is the *predatory stalker* who seeks sexual gratification or attaining the knowledge to assist them in committing sexual assault. This type of stalking behaviour is carried out to fulfil the power stalkers crave and usually involves males stalking female strangers (Mullen et al. 2000; Mullen and Pathé 2001). For a fuller understanding of these typologies please see Fig. 10.1. However, further clarification is needed regarding the typology in terms of whether the duration and diversity are constant across all stalkers and their victims or whether stalking behaviour itself evolves consistently over time (Sheridan et al. 2003). Furthermore, whilst this typology is useful, it is important to keep in mind that it is based on forensic and clinical samples (Cheyne and Guggisberg 2018).

A further theoretical perspective to consider is the involvement of 'safety work', as coined by Liz Kelly (2012) and Vera-Gray (2018). This term is used to 'describe

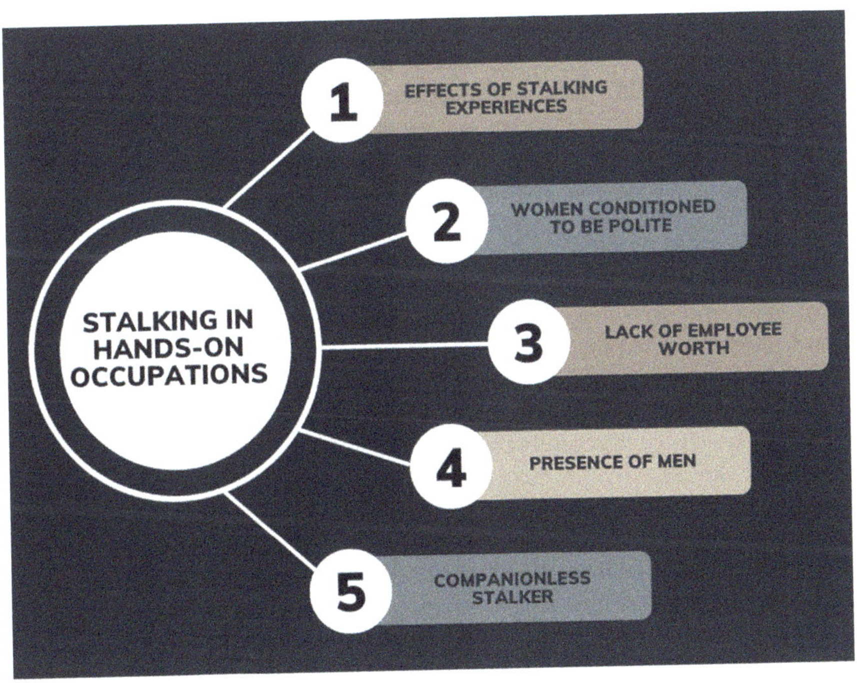

Fig. 10.1 Emergent themes relating to stalking in hands-on occupations. This provides a visual representation of the five themes which emerged as part of this scoping study on stalking within hands-on occupations

the strategising and planning that women and girls undertake in responding to, avoiding and/or coping with men's violence' (Vera-Gray 2016, 134). In brief, 'safety work' is heavily linked to the notion of 'unsafety of femininity' as individuals (many women in particular) exhibit avoidant behaviour to protect themselves from harm such as changing routes to homes, areas they frequent, and relying on bodily adaptations (Vera-Gray and Kelly 2020, 217). To illustrate, physical characteristics in line with femininity like makeup, long hair, and jewellery also tend to be avoided for this same reason (Vera-Gray and Kelly 2020). Moreover, this avoidant behaviour can be equally evident in crossing of the street, avoiding eye contact, using your phone, putting keys between your fingers, the conditioned response of politeness if approached, and taking headphones out. These behaviours can be avoided entirely or can be avoided in particular contexts such as being out alone during the evening. As Vera-Gray explains, gendered expectations have altered thoughts/behaviours so much so that safety work is frequently subconscious and hidden. The 'safety work' behaviours women have been exhibiting since childhood are something women simply *are* rather than what women *do* (Vera-Gray 2018).

Effects of Stalking

Another area requiring acknowledgement is the evidential impacts of stalking on victims, which range from the direct mental/physical impacts to the extended side effects that can hold negative outcomes on the victim's everyday life. A primary example is the NVAW study which reported that as a result of being stalked, 7% of participants left work permanently and a further 26% lost time at work. Consequently, this led to both professional and friend relationships suffering as victims isolated themselves through fear (Tjaden et al. 2000). In addition, the follow-up study performed by Dreßing et al. (2020) on their 2003 epidemiological study reported that 27.7% of participants were placed on sick leave due to health impacts as 39.7% had developed a sleep disorder (Gass et al. 2020). Furthermore, out of 159 participants that completed the Davidson Trauma Scale, Turmanis and Brown (2006) reported that 21% achieved a trauma rating of over 40, which has links to post-traumatic stress disorder (Turmanis and Brown 2006).

Additionally, during the active stage of being stalked, it is common for victims to experience self-doubt regarding whether they are overreacting as many signs of stalking are not illegal when there is no malicious intent involved. For example, sending messages over social media or showing up in areas the victim frequents. All the previous impacts may manifest in feelings of insecurity/inability to trust others, struggling to be intimate within relationships, changing appearance, moving home/job, and avoiding aspects of daily routines such as going to the gym or walking a certain route home (Korkodeilou 2017). Overall, stalking can incur major effects on physical health, mental health, and professional and social life. These impacts combined with being victimised can also have serious financial consequences such as leaving employment, loss of wage from sick leave, costs to repair property damage or increase home security, legal fees, and breaking tenancy agreements for relocation purposes (Korkodeilou 2017; Logan et al 2006).

Legal Remedies Related to Stalking

The 25 November 2012 saw stalking become legally recognised as an offence under the Protection of Freedoms Act 2012 although presently there is no statutory definition that encompasses stalking (Badcock 2002; Kamphuis and Emmelkamp 2000). In fact, stalking was the term given to a number of acts that abusers used to force their partners to remain in a relationship (Walker and Meloy 1998). However, section 2a of the Protection from Harassment Act 1997 offers examples of associated acts of stalking such as spying, forcing contact, and following. In addition to this, section 4a states how stalking can relate to incurring fears of violence or serious distress/alarm. However, these examples/definitions can be quite vague and subjective, as the reality of stalking can range from the deliberate ruin of professional reputations to threats to reveal sexuality. Both the elements and process of stalking can differ significantly (Sheridan et al. 2003). Despite the Protection from Harassment Act 1997 being useful to some extent, stalking is not defined within the act. Instead, it simply states that an individual should not engage in activities which amount to harassment of another person (Sheridan et al. 2003). However, the nature of stalking means it occurs on a broad spectrum accompanied by technology and social media which is consistently evolving. As such, even if a more concrete definition existed for stalking, it would run the risk of becoming quickly outdated.

Moreover, one current response to stalking behaviour is the 2 year-long stalking protection orders (SPO) that places a legal ban on perpetrators contacting the individuals they have stalked. Nevertheless, there are significant flaws within SPOs (Townsend 2020). To illustrate, receiving the order does not reflect upon criminal records, the orders are favoured over prosecution, and occasionally police can lack urgency in responding to SPO breaches (Suzy Lamplugh Trust 2021; Townsend 2020). Additionally, only 356 SPO applications were made across 31 forces over the 18 months of the introduction of the orders (Lowe 2022). A further problem identified with attending police officers is the failure in recognising persistent incidents from a stalker and instead treating each offence as an isolated case. This similar issue can be observed in cases of domestic abuse and coercive control (Myhill and Hohl 2016; Wiener 2017). Due to the incoherent approach, this does not provide the full picture for other police staff and prosecutors who may underestimate the magnitude of the impact on the victim.

Additionally, the DASH (Domestic Abuse, Stalking, Harassment, and Honour Based Violence Assessment) risk assessment tool (DASH-RIC) is often used to provide safeguarding professionals clarity on the risks involved in cases of domestic abuse. This allows for the appropriate agencies to provide services from police, health, education, housing, social care, Independent Domestic Violence Advisor (IDVA), and specialist support services (Norfolk County Council 2022). Unfortunately, it has been identified that professionals require proper training in the real risks of domestic abuse, which can aid in implementing more appropriate charges such as stalking or coercive control instead of harassment (Turner, Medina and

Brown 2019). Given the DASH-RIC follows the same assumptions of the violence model, thereby prioritising physical violence, it does not take into account the other impacts of stalking behaviour (i.e. emotional, financial etc.) and tends to disregard victims' subjective experiences (Myhill and Hohl 2016; Robinson 2010). However, a specialist risk identification checklist for harassment and stalking cases does exist in the form of S-Dash although one of its downfalls is its employment can depend on the individual police officer attending the scene (Robinson et al 2016). It must be noted that studies have shown that this objective measure has poor accuracy in identifying future harm (Medina et al 2015). For example, the data available to predict future harm is messy and difficult to acquire. The specialist police data is biased from both a recording and reporting perspective, the systems in place to gather this data do not adequately measure repeat victimisation, especially when it concerns the same victim, and often victims and perpetrators are unreachable (Ariza et al. 2016). There are also cases where the victim or perpetrator is unwilling to acknowledge the abuse, minimise it, or fail to disclose it. Similarly, some forms of abuse are not well documented by police data such as psychological harm (Ariza et al. 2016). To make matters worse, the use of police data to predict future harm can also amplify institutional biases already present within the criminal justice system (Starr 2014). In addition, it must be noted that there is little consensus on what constitutes future harm, with any data on future harm being far from simple to analyse (Ariza et al. 2016). This coupled with inconsistent or a complete lack of police training and guidance in relation to DASH-RIC is a cause for concern (Ariza et al. 2016; Robinson 2010).

Stalking in the Workplace

Furthermore, whilst the Health and Safety at Work etc. 1974 Act places a legal duty upon employers to ensure the health, safety, and welfare at work for their employees, there remains questions on how best to approach this. To illustrate, the Suzy Lamplugh Trust has reported an abundance of phone calls regarding employers wanting advice on dealing with employees accused of stalking or how best to protect their staff (Suzy Lamplugh Trust 2019). In addition, many companies often perceive the lines to be blurred between criminal law and employment law as signs of stalking can change when within professional settings (Horman 2016). This is understandably concerning as 90% of corporate security professionals have intervened in cases of men stalking women, and 75% of those who domestically abuse their partners will stalk them at their workplace (Paladin 2021). Additionally, stalkers will adapt their methods to incorporate individuals' place of work such as repeatedly making formal complaints to employers to sabotage the individual's work reputation (Sheridan et al. 2019; Swanberg et al. 2005). Furthermore, in cases where the individual has a public profile, any complaints/threats are usually readily dismissed as being expected due to the accessibility of their reputation (Horman 2016).

Whilst the Health and Safety at Work Act (HASWA) 1974 has been heavily influential in the period of 1974–2015, with a decrease in fatal injuries (84%) and non-fatal injuries (70%), there remains gaps in the HASWA that require acknowledgement (Augustin and Brooks 2015). However, Humphreys (2007) found that the HASWA itself was mainly compiled of 'safety' aspects with employee health and welfare as a secondary thought. The terms 'health' and 'welfare' are not defined within the HASWA, which can provide insight as to why employers may have a poor understanding of their role in the health and welfare of employees (Humphreys 2007).

Stalking in Healthcare Settings

Moreover, this research aims to study stalking and harassment of individuals working specifically within hands-on occupations thus it proves vital to acknowledge any previous studies with a similar objective to identify patterns. Firstly, Sandberg et al (2002) reportedly found that 50% of 82 clinical staff participants within an American inpatient psychiatric facility experienced stalking, harassment, and threatening behaviour. Also, Paraschakis and Konstantinidou (2012) found that 20% of psychiatrists had experienced stalking, this parallels with the findings from Mastronardi et al. (2012) Italian study. This study was conducted with 500 participants of equal male to female ratio, within mental health centres in Rome which suggests that the targeting of staff within hands-on occupations is shared across various countries and cultures. However, this also highlights the lack of support, guidance, and training for those in the hands-on occupation industry which is clearly necessary.

Additionally, Acquadro Maran and Varetto (2018) studied stalking amongst health professionals in relation to gender and found clear distinctions surrounding the effects of stalking between males and females. To illustrate, males were more likely to suffer from feelings of anger at being victimised, whilst females felt anxiety and depression. On the other hand, it was also found that both males and females utilised the *moving away* strategy mentioned previously by Spitzberg and Cupach (2014) in an attempt to create distance between themselves and their stalkers. However, the use of these coping strategies decreased once there was a detected increase in stalking behaviour, which may signify the fatigue caused to the victim by the relentless and stressful harassment (Acquadro Maran and Varetto 2018).

Currently, the Health and Safety at Work etc. 1974 Act places the employees' health, safety, and welfare as a legal duty of employers to ensure (The National Archives 2021). Moreover, it was reported that 90% of corporate security employees have intervened in three or more incidents of a man stalking a woman, with 75% of domestic abuse stalkers often frequenting the victim's workplace (Paladin 2021). Interestingly, the Suzy Lamplugh Trust helpline recorded heightened numbers of calls regarding employers seeking guidance on how to approach stalking within their workplace or employees that have had stalking accusations made against them (Suzy Lamplugh Trust 2019). There is a clear absence of guidance or procedure within workplace management of stalking incidents as organisations often lack clarity on the differences between criminal law and employment law. It remains vital to provide detailed assistance to employers as stalking incidents within work may often differ from the patterned stalking behaviour experienced outside of work. A prime example of this may be the stalker submitting numerous damaging complaints about the victim, in a bid to purposely damage their professional reputation. Often, in cases when the individual being stalked has a public profile, the reports of stalking or harassment are frequently dismissed as being expected within their line of work (Horman 2016).

As highlighted above, there is a substantial lack of research into hands-on occupations, with much of the general stalking literature being outdated. To our knowledge, no research has been conducted on stalking within the beauty aesthetic industry. Whilst some research exists in terms of stalking within healthcare settings, this is sparse at best. No research appears to consider stalking from both an employee and employer perspective, which sets this research apart from others within the field. Again, there appears to be limited statutory guidance on how both employees and employers deal with stalking incidents at work and the support available to those involved. This reiterates the need for more research to be conducted in this area.

Our Study

This research was undertaken using qualitative methods of enquiry as a response to concerns voiced by the Hollie Gazzard Trust regarding the lack of research into hands-on occupations and stalking. This was a scoping study given the dearth of research on this topic in the United Kingdom. The study utilised a qualitative approach, which included open-ended semi-structured interviews conducted over both Microsoft Teams and phone calls, with five participants between April and July 2021. The sample included four female participants and one male participant. In terms of the employee/employer split, four participants identified as employees and one identified as an employer. All participants were over the age of 18 years. Interviews were restricted to online or telecommunication environments as this research was conducted during the COVID-19 pandemic and, as such, could not be conducted in person. Each interview lasted between 60 and 90 minutes, and was audio-recorded and transcribed verbatim.

Employment ranged from a tattoo/piercing artist, spa therapist, psychiatric nurse, beauty therapist, and nail technician. Participants were asked to share their experiences of stalking as an employee or employer depending on their position within their workplace. Within the interviews, the questions were broad, such as 'Tell me about a time where you have felt uncomfortable by something a client has said, especially after any treatment or physical contact made'. 'What were your concerns over your safety after these incidents?' 'Did you inform your manager and what action did they take?' 'In your opinion, what else could have been done to support you and ensure your safety at work?' 'How have your experiences changed the way you view working?' This allowed participants to provide as much detail as they felt comfortable during interviews.

Purposive and snowballing sampling was used to recruit participants, with the study being advertised on social media sites such as Twitter, Instagram, and Facebook (Bryman 2012; Silverman 2005). Other recruitment methods included emailing the recruitment poster to health and wellbeing companies which specialised in treatments involving hands-on occupations (i.e. beauty salons, hairdressers) as well as using 'word of mouth' (Etikan et al. 2015). Ethics was approved by the School of Social Sciences Research Ethics Committee at Nottingham Trent University. Thematic analysis was used to analyse the data and produce themes (Braun and Clark 2006).

Whilst this scoping study has weaknesses in line with both the sample size, gender, and employee–employer ratio, there are some significant strengths to this study. For example, this scoping study involves in-depth case study work which enables a multi-faceted understanding of stalking within hands-on occupations in its real-life context, thereby providing an insight into the experiences of those within this industry. It is not a representative sample, but still provides meaningful insights into this area. The drawbacks include four out of five participants being female so there is still a lack of focus on male victims/survivors. This also extended to the employee–employer ratio, with four of the participants identifying themselves as employees and one identifying as an employer. Whilst it is relatively common for qualitative research to have a smaller participant sample than quantitative research due to its quality rich data, the sample size of this study remains small (Bryman 2012). This therefore impacted the overall internal and external validity of the research (Queiros et al. 2017). However, when studying an under-researched area recruitment is one of the main challenges and this rang true for this study. Although every effort was made to recruit participants through a number of means, recruitment proved difficult with the ongoing COVID-19 pandemic. In addition, the participant sample was primarily white British thus it may not be accurate to generalise results due to the possible differences ranging across cultures, races, and ethnicities (Redwood and Gill 2013). The researchers also acknowledge that sexuality was not taken into account in this study so this also may alter the types of stalking and how it manifests within the workplace.

Findings

This scoping study aimed to explore both employee and employer perspectives of the nature, impact, and support available to those experiencing stalking within hands-on occupations. This section of the chapter is structured around five themes which emerged from the data: (i) Effects of Stalking Experiences; (ii) Women Conditioned to be Polite; (iii) Lack of Employee Worth; (iv) Presence of Men; and (v) Companionless Stalker.

Effects of Stalking Experiences

> ...It was kind of sad in a way but like you say we did kind of make a joke of it to probably try make us feel a bit better... (Kate: lines 377–378)

One prominent impact of stalking discovered in the study was the participant's conscious/subconscious adaptation of various coping methods in order to prepare themselves for situations perceived to be threatening. The above illustration highlights how one participant and their colleague would utilise humour to manage the situation with one client showing harassing behaviour, who was permitted to continue treatment at their salon by their employer. This particular method of coping was encompassed in Carol Brooks Gardner (1995) *Passing By: Gender and Public Harassment* seven strategies of women's responses with ignoring, staged compliance, and repressing being some examples of this. Additionally, Gardner coins the strategy of 'redefining the situation' as altering the incident from inappropriate to comedic using humour (Brooks Gardner 1995). In this case, humour may have been present in attempts to subdue feelings of dread and anxiety.

> ...I actually stopped parking down that street and like I now park like a few streets over... (Hannah: lines 152–153)

> ...if I just need to nip through the reception area when he's in there to do something or call somebody then he's going to be there, and I would have to think of different ways of doing things to stay away from him... (Kate: lines 324–326)

Moreover, the above evidence from research interviews further conveys a certain avoidant form of behaviour amongst participants, by avoiding areas where their known stalker resides which can impact day-to-day life such as work commutes. This idea is supported by Elizabeth Stanko in *Everyday Violence: How Women and Men Experience Sexual and Physical Danger* who states that '*images of danger become subtly woven into our perceptions about a place*' which is certainly true of the two examples above (Tyner 2012, 12). This is the idea that by individuals avoiding areas which bring on feelings of uneasiness, they have accepted the likelihood of violence within those particular contexts. Additionally, this notion can be similarly applied to people in the same manner as places/spaces whereby certain people can be avoided to lessen feelings of anxiety (Tyner 2012).

> ...I shove my hair up and I don't put any makeup on, I really don't ever want to make an effort when I go to work just because I don't want to entice anything. (Hannah: lines 417–421)

Comparably, one participant details their efforts in discouraging specific undesired attention which draws symmetry to Elizabeth Stanko's theories stated in the previous section. The evidence displayed from this research highlights how the acknowledgement of a dangerous situation has led participants to stray away from daily routine which signifies a specific adapted avoidant behaviour. This behaviour is often exhibited by women and is referred to as 'safety work' by Vera-Gray (2018). Often, in professional environments such as work, space, and movement can be restricted thus preventative attempts may rely on bodily adaptations. To illustrate, Vera-Gray and Kelly (2020, 217) hold the belief that women's safety work is cultivated by the 'unsafety of femininity', which supports the above evidence of the participant's lack of hairstyling and makeup. Therefore, these conscious displays of safety work by participants are evidently fueled by their recognition of how unsafe being 'feminine' can be.

Women Conditioned to Be Polite

Furthermore, another central theme identified through thematic analysis was *Women Conditioned to be Polite*. At first glance, there is an array of causes which can ingrain the difficulty some women may find in saying 'no', from gender differences, patriarchal standards, and toxic work culture. The quotes below show participants' concerns about potentially being unprofessional despite being subjected to unacceptable behaviour from a client which Hochschild (1983) terms as 'emotional labour'. Also, Hochschild states employees may have the importance of sales engrained into them. The presence of emotional labour is often management requiring employees to upkeep a certain 'professional' emotional front whilst simultaneously suppressing other emotions in order to maintain a client's happiness (Bishop and Hoel 2008).

> Yeah, I never felt comfortable to stand there in the salon, whether I was on my own or another member of staff was there, and say no because I kind of felt like it was expected of me to just put up with it. (Kate: lines 168–170)

> …we were all under the same impression of oh you know we need to put up with this otherwise X will be angry with us… (Kate: lines 242–243)

> …no checking on the other girls to see how they felt about it, no conversation to say are you happy to him if he comes in? Like it was just expected… (Hannah: lines 400–401)

> …but she was made to go back into the room and carry on with the treatment because they didn't want to upset the client. (Sam: lines 98–99)

Furthermore, given the inability to say 'no' was found amongst female participants, but not the male participant signifies possible external causes, for example, societal expectations of women being compliant and submissive in comparison to men. As this research only included one male participant, it is not exhaustive by any means, but still provides supportive insight for other studies in this area. One illustration of this is shown by Heilman and Okimoto (2007), who state that women may avoid saying 'no' out of fear of being deemed unfriendly and the potential consequences of rebelling behavioural expectations (Heilman and Okimoto 2007). In addition, Heilman and Chen (2005) found in their study of performance evaluations of both men and women that although the genders may exhibit similar behaviour that the response to similar behaviour differed. To illustrate, whilst women were critiqued when they declined help, men who did the same faced no consequences (Heilman and Chen 2005). To some extent, this provides supporting evidence and explanation as to why it proves more difficult for women to be 'disobedient' over men. There also remains the aspect of guilt to consider as Jones and Kugler (1993) state that after women recognise that their behaviour is failing to align with moral/societal expectations, that they may experience guilt as a response to this (Jones and Kugler 1993).

Finally, during this research this theme notably occurred frequently, which may point to the influencing factor of personality traits. These personality traits can be explained by the Big Five Traits of Conscientiousness and Agreeableness (Balliet 2010). To illustrate, individuals with heightened conscientious traits will find increased difficulty in saying 'no' as conscientiousness relates to compliance levels when committing citizenship behaviours. In addition, Schmitt et al. (2009) discovered in their study that the conscientious trait that influences saying 'no' was higher amongst women rather than men. Also, those who found difficulty in saying 'no' also have higher rates of agreeableness and the need to put others before themselves, which for the majority was found to be women. Therefore, there proves to be a wider explanation from gender expectations and toxic work culture behind women feeling obligated to be 'polite' (Schmitt et al. 2008).

Lack of Employee Worth

> [Employers are]...just concerned about money they're not really concerned about you, you're just a number at the end of the day erm, they're just more concerned about the clients paying. (Sam: lines 221–222)

> ...it's almost like moneys more important than your staff or their safety I think is how it made me feel. (Kate: lines 60–61).

> ...my boss just wanted the money more than my happiness. (Kate: lines 143)

The following theme, as represented by the data displayed above, showcases the importance of money over staff wellbeing. This research highlighted the failure of adequate support from management despite complaints from employees of sexual harassment, feelings of being uncomfortable in their own place of work and inappropriate behaviour/comments. Notably, on multiple occasions management's favoured approach of dealing with the harassment was passing the client onto a different staff member. Evidently, there is a correlation with the current study despite the decades between when both studies were conducted. Money is reinforced as a priority every time management uses threats or continues to allow the individual displaying unwanted behaviour to receive a service, which showcases the influence of greed over psychological/physical turmoil of employees.

Presence of Men

The data above displays the varying attitudes and perspectives towards the influence of men within the workplace, with the first quote relating to issues of the approach from male management towards reported incidents.

> ...usually, women would feel more comfortable with a female doctor so I feel like I would be more comfortable talking to a female member of staff. (Sam: lines 362–364)

Conversely, the two following pieces of data relay how the presence of male employees/management can act as a deterrent to individuals displaying inappropriate actions/behaviour. Although the gathered data provides contradicting points of view, there remains space for questioning especially regarding the societal norms in relation to patriarchy. To illustrate further, the Man Box survey (2017) found that many young men still viewed the responsibility of a male to be physically protective yet unemotional, despite voicing that they viewed women as equals. This suggests the extent of how far these patriarchal expectations have been engrained and deemed as second nature (Heilman et al. 2017). Although this was a male-based sample, the main findings of males being seen as the protector from stalking/harassment evidently correlate with the findings from the current study. This suggests that women also hold similar beliefs or may even adhere to this perspective for matters of protection (Burrell 2019).

> Yeah, a lot of the time if X was there, erm, if they were working in the room together or if they just knew he was in the room next door it wouldn't happen it was it was usually if it was like his day off.... (Stella: lines 84–87)

> ...we would have sent somebody up there obviously a male presence to obviously make it known that to make sure that she was okay. (Stella: lines 96–97)

Furthermore, both Casey et al (2016) and Ricardo (2014) found a significant relationship between violence against women and girls and the effects of gender norms. Additionally, Jewkes et al. (2015) express how there is an acknowledged social expectation of manhood which holds having control and dominance over women as important. The support of these hegemonic ideologies of masculinity is enforced by violence in situations where feelings of undermined masculinity occur. A further viewpoint to acknowledge is that of 'cultural scaffolding' of rape as theorised by Gavey (2018). Briefly, this entails how the battle for dominance over vulnerability, that has derived from gender norms, can cause a catalyst effect of psychological impacts that lead to sexual violence. The contemporary outlook on manhood makes space for a violently misogynistic manner of pertaining dominance and this occurs more frequently amongst men who have strong desires of upholding the fantasy of manhood. On the occasion where men perceive vulnerability, feelings of entitlement can occur regarding women's bodies, sex, and affections (Burrell 2019).

Companionless Stalker

As shown in the quotes below, participants frequently referred to isolation or the recent experience of losing a partner in relation to the individual subjecting them to harassing behaviour. The previously mentioned typology of stalkers suggests in these circumstances that the individuals could be classed as intimacy seekers as they have a desire to fulfil a relationship with a stranger or acquaintance and escalation to this typology is usually derived from social isolation (NYSCP 2019; Mullen et al. 2009; Ogloff et al 2020). Moreover, the only male participant involved in the current study experienced nonsexual harassment/stalking from fellow employees, with the four female participants experiencing sexually derived harassment/stalking from clients. These experiences differed in frequency: the male participant's experience was continuous whilst the female participants were more sporadic.

> …he'd just lost his wife, so I don't know if he was just completely not thinking about what he was saying…. (Sam: lines 313–314).

> …erm and I think to a degree she felt sorry for him because he'd lost his wife and he probably wanted a bit of company. (Kate: lines 152–153)

> …the impression that I got from him was that he was very lonely he didn't really have anybody else. (Hannah: lines 99–100)

The participants working in tactile occupations may be taken as insight into perhaps why individuals turn to services from hands-on occupations to receive physical contact. Moreover, another form of stalker typology remains a possibility in the current research, as Mullen et al. (2000) explain the similar motivations of incompetent suitors is to target strangers/acquaintances out of loneliness.

A final notable occurrence to explore is bereavement, which has been found to be present in a large volume of young people and adults in custody. In turn, this could suggest the possibility that grief is a contributing factor to offending behaviour (Vaswani 2014, 2018). Delving into this topic further, Vaswani (2014) reports differing manners of avoidant and non-avoidant approaches to grief that were observed within her study. The avoidant techniques found were reportedly correlated to stoicism and the distraction from feelings that is often perceived as being a 'typical' male approach to self-medication. On the other hand, this approach proved dysfunctional for long-term results as it often led to detachment. This was observed when participants found difficulty in perceiving consequences of their actions, which was accompanied by uncertainty in terms of their future (Vaswani 2014). Although this study's sample mainly included young males, this literature aids in adding the necessary explanation as to why bereavement and loneliness is such a notable theme within the current research.

Concluding Remarks

Due to stalking in hands-on occupations being an area which is currently under-researched, there are evidently numerous gaps to acknowledge. As already realised, there is a lack of general stalking literature due to stalking being recently declared a crime with remaining obscurity surrounding it (HMIC and HMCPSI 2017). However, the research base on stalking within the workplace/hands-on occupations is even smaller. Whilst the data presented above details the increased links between stalking, domestic abuse, and death, there is a dearth of research into this area. Filling this gap would prove imminent to the protection of victims through the early detection of risks such as workplace stalking.

Furthermore, whilst there are research studies conducted in various countries as mentioned prior, the participation of the LGBTQ+community and BAME population have been neglected (Langenderfer-Magruder et al 2020). This current absence of literature will assist in failing stalking survivors as there is no supporting evidence to use in the formation of tailoring approaches/interventions. This is especially concerning when considering how identified risks/needs differ amongst various protected characteristics, with examples of this being the consistent threat of revealing the sexual identity of minority ethnic transgender individuals due to religious beliefs of 'honour' (Harvey et al. 2014). However, specific demographics such as male survivors and survivors who are LGBTQ+from strong religious backgrounds may prove challenging to study due to the stigma, past inappropriate responses from police, and feelings of fear if others know of their experience/circumstance (Owen et al. 2018). Thus, not only does this highlight large gaps within the overall literature of stalking, but this also raises questions as to how well stalking survivors are supported and protected by local authorities.

A Note from Our Collaborator

Hollie was murdered in the salon where she worked, doing the job she loved. My background in risk management has always given me some cause for concern in the situations that Hollie would be faced with when she shared with me what kind of day she had. Hands-on occupations in the main are dominated by young women trying to forge a career in something that they love, without having much thought for their own safety through vulnerable situations they often find themselves in or being subjected to such behaviour because of the 'job'.

Since the loss of Hollie my own knowledge and interest in the protection of violence against women and girls and, particularly from stalking, has increased immeasurably. The vulnerability of particularly young girls in hands-on occupations is of particular concern of mine and therefore I wanted this piece of research carried out. Whilst the qualitative sample size was small, the findings match my own thoughts around the dangerous situations that young girls in these hands-on service occupations are found in or, put in by their employers. Furthermore, it is particularly concerning that employers put 'money' before safety.

It is quite clear to me that many of these young women are not sufficiently prepared for situations they may encounter and are insufficiently equipped with the tools to be able to say 'No'. They are conditioned to be polite, often use avoidance behaviour, and consciously or subconsciously use various coping methods. I find this totally unacceptable.

From my own experience and from the limited research here, it is evident that employers are ill equipped to provide training, advice, and guidance to employees and often put 'money' before employee 'safety'. Many of these industries have national associations and they should ensure that training is available and mandatory for businesses to undertake and include within apprenticeship education.

Whilst this piece of research is limited it provides sufficient information to suggest that more research needs to be undertaken to fully identify the impact of stalking in hands-on occupations, and what can be done to fill the gaps in education and training of both employers and employees and protect victims and potential victims by early identification of associated risks.

Putting 'money' before 'safety' is never acceptable.

Nick Gazzard—Founder and CEO of Hollie Gazzard Trust.

Discussion Questions

- Are the experiences of heterosexual individuals comparable to those from the LGBTQ+ community when it comes to stalking in hands-on occupations?
- What cultural differences exist between white and BAME individuals in terms of help seeking for stalking within hands-on occupations?
- How can we change this notion that money is more important than staff wellbeing?

Bibliography

Acquadro Maran, Daniella, Antonella Varetto, and Massimo Zedda. 2014. Italian nurses' experience of stalking: A questionnaire survey. *Violence and Victims* 29(1): 109–121.

Acquadro Maran, Daniella, and Antonella Varetto. 2018. Psychological impact of stalking on male and female health care professional victims of stalking and domestic violence. *Frontiers in Psychology [Online]*..

Acquadro Maran, Daniella, Antonella Varetto, Ilenia Corona, and Maurizio Tirassa. 2020. Characteristics of the stalking campaign: Consequences and coping strategies for men and women that report their victimization to police. *PLoS ONE* 15(2): 1–14.

Ariza, Juan. Josa. Medina, Amanda Robinson, and Andy Myhill. 2016. Cheaper, faster, better: Expectations and achievements in police risk assessment of domestic abuse. *Policing* 10(4): 341–350.

Augustin, Kizzy and Oliver Brooks. 2015. The effectiveness of the Health and Safety at Work Act. Safety and Health Practitioner. https://www.shponline.co.uk/legislation-and-guidance/an-analysis-of-the-effectiveness-of-the-health-and-safety-at-work-act/ Accessed 26 August 2022.

Badcock, Richard. 2002. Psychopathology and treatment of stalking. In *Stalking and psychosexual obsession: Psychological perspectives for prevention, policing and treatment*, eds. J. C. W. Boon and L. Sheridan, 125–139. Chichester, UK: Wiley.

Balliet, Daniel. 2010. Conscientiousness and forgivingness: A meta-analysis. *Personality and Individual Differences* 48: 259–263.

Bartholomew, K., and L. Horowitz. 1991. Attachment styles among young adults: A test of a four-category model. *Journal of Personality and Social Psychology* 61(2): 226–244.

BBC News. 2017. Stalking victims being failed, say watchdogs. *BBC*, June 16, 2022.

Bishop, V., and H. Hoel. 2008. The customer is always right?: Exploring the concept of customer bullying in the British employment service. *Journal of Consumer Culture 8*(3): 341-367.

Blaauw, E., F. W. Winkel, E. Arensman, L. Sheridan, and A. Freeve. 2002. The toll of stalking: The relationship between features of stalking and psychopathology of victims. *Journal of Interpersonal Violence* 17: 50–63.

Bracewell, K., P. Hargreaves and N. Stanley. 2020. The consequences of the COVID-19 lockdown on stalking victimisation. *Journal of Family Violence*. https://doi.org/10.1007/s10896-020-00201-0.

Brady, P. Q., and M. R. Nobles. 2017. The dark figure of stalking: Examining law enforcement response. *Journal of Interpersonal Violence* 32(20): 3149–3173.

Braun, V., and V. Clark. 2006. Using thematic analysis in psychology. *Qualitative Research in Psychology*, 3(2): 77–101.

Brooks Gardener, Carole. 1995. *Passing by: Gender & public harassment*. California: University of California Press.

Bryman, Alan. 2012. *Social research methods*. Oxford: Oxford University Press.

Burrell, Stephen. Robert. 2019. *Engaging men and boys in the prevention of men's violence against women in England*. Ph.D. Thesis, Durham University. http://etheses.dur.ac.uk/13074/1/SRBurrell_PhDThesis.pdf. Accessed 22 June 2022.

Casey, E., N. T. Masters, B. Beadnell, E. A. Wells, D. M. Morrison, and M. J. Hoppe. 2016. A latent class analysis of heterosexual young men's masculinities. *Archives of Sexual Behavior* 45(5): 1039–1050.

Cassidy, J., J. Jones, and P. Shaver. 2013. Contributions of attachment theory and research: A framework for future research, translation, and policy. *Development and psychopathology* 25(4): 1415–1434.

Cheyne, N., and M. Guggisberg. 2018. Stalking: An age old problem with new expressions in the digital age. In *Violence against women in the 21st century: Challenges and future directions*, eds. M. Guggisberg and J. Henricksen, 161–190. Hauppauge, New York: Nova Science Publishers.

CPS. 2020. *Stalking Analysis reveals domestic violence*. https://www.cps.gov.uk/cps/news/stalking-analysis-reveals-domestic-abuse-link. Accessed 20 June 2022.

Cupach, W. R., and B. H. Spitzberg. 1998. Obsessional relational intrusion and stalking. In *The dark side of close relationships*, eds. B.H. Spitzberg and W.R. Cupach, 233–263. Mahwah, NJ: Lawrence Erlbaum.

Domestic Abuse Act. 2021. Domestic abuse act. *Home Office*. https://www.legislation.gov.uk/ukpga/2021/17/contents/enacted.

Dreßing H., P. Gass, K. Schultz, and C. Kuehner. 2020. The prevalence and effects of stalking deutsches ärzteblatt international. https://doi.org/10.3238/arztebl.2020.0347.

End Violence Against Women (EVAW). 2022. *Government releases plan to tackle domestic abuse as part of its wider VAWG strategy*. EVAW. https://www.endviolenceagainstwomen.org.uk/government-releases-plan-to-tackle-domestic-abuse-as-part-of-its-wider-vawg-strategy/. Accessed 16 August 2022.

Etikan, I., R. Alkassim, and S. Abubakar. 2015. Comparison of snowball sampling and sequential sampling technique. *Biometrics and Biostatics International Journal* 3(1): 1–2.

Finch, Emily. 2001. Is stalking a violent crime? *Police Review* 25–26.

Forte, Joe. 2021. Calls to bring stalkers to justice as cases spiral in the West Midlands. *Birmingham World*, 16 June 2022.

Fox, K. A., M. R. Nobles, and B. S. Fisher. 2011. Method behind the madness: An examination of stalking measurements. *Aggression and Violent Behavior* 16: 74–84.

Gavey, Nicola. 2018. *Just sex? The cultural scaffolding of rape*. London: Routledge.

Harding, Sandra. 1991. *Whose science? Whose knowledge?: Thinking from women's lives*. Ithaca, New York: Cornell University Press.

Harmes, L., and E. Forde. 2018. Male stalking victim: 'People don't take you seriously'. *BBC*, 16 June 2022.

Harvey, S., M. Mitchell, and J. Keeble. 2014. *Barriers faced by lesbian, gay, bisexual and transgender people in accessing domestic abuse, stalking, harassment and sexual violence services*. s.l.: Government Social Research.

Heilman, M. E., and J. J. Chen. 2005. Same behavior, different consequences: reactions to men's and women's altruistic citizenship behavior. *Journal of Applied Psychology 90*(3): 431–441.

Heilman, M. E., and T. G. Okimoto. 2007. Why are women penalized for success at male tasks?: The implied communality deficit. *Journal of Applied Psychology 92*(1): 81–92.

Heilman, B., G. Barker, and A. Harrison. 2017. *The "man box": A study on being a man in the US, UK, and Mexico*. Washington, DC and London: Promundo-US and Unilever.

Her Majesty's Inspectorate of Constabulary (HMIC) & Her Majesty's Crown Prosecution Service Inspectorate (HMCPSI). 2017. *Living in fear—The police and CPS response to harassment and stalking*. London: HMIC & HMCPSI. https://www.justiceinspectorates.gov.uk/hmicfrs/wp-content/uploads/living-in-fear-the-police-and-cps-response-to-harassment-and-stalking.pdf. Accessed 26 August 2022.

Hochschild, A. R. 1983. *The managed heart: Commercialization of human feeling*. Berkeley, CA: University of California Press.

Home Office. 2022. *Policy paper: Tackling perpetrators*. Home Office: Crown Copyright. https://www.gov.uk/government/publications/domestic-abuse-bill-2020-factsheets/tackling-perpetrators. Accessed 16 June 2022.

Horman, Rachel. 2016. When stalking comes to work. *BACP Workplace*: 91.

Humphreys, S. 2007. Health and Safety at Work Act 1974: Is it too late to teach an old dog new tricks? *Policy and Practice in Healthy and Safety* 5(1): 19–35.

Irvine, S., H. Clark, M. Ward, and B. Francis-Devine. 2022. *Research briefing: Women and the UK economy*. London: House of Commons Library. https://researchbriefings.files.parliament.uk/documents/SN06838/SN06838.pdf. Accessed 2 June 2022.

Jewkes, R. K, M. Flood, and J. Lang. 2015. From work with men and boys to changes of social norms and reduction of inequities in gender relations: A conceptual shift in prevention of violence against women and girls. *The Lancet* 385(9977): 1580–1589.

Jones, W. H. and K. Kugler. 1993. Interpersonal correlates of the guilt inventory. *Journal of Personality Assessment* 61(2): 246–258.

Jordan, T. K., R. Logan, and R. A. Walker. 2003. Stalking: An examination of the criminal justice response. *Journal of Interpersonal Violence* 18: 148–165.

Kamphuis, J. H., and P. M. G. Emmelkamp. 2000. Stalking: A contemporary challenge for forensic and clinical psychiatry. *British Journal of Psychiatry* 176: 206–209.

Kelly, Liz. 2012. Standing the test of time? Reflections on the concept of the continuum of sexual violence. In *Handbook on sexual violence*, eds. J. Brown and S. Walklate, xvii–xxvi. London: Routledge.

Korkodeilou, J. 2017. 'No place to hide': Stalking victimisation and its psycho-social effects. *International Review of Victimology* 23(1):17–32.

Langenderfer-Magruder, L., and N. E. Walls, D. L. Whitfield, S. K. Kattari, and D. Ramos D. 2020. Stalking victimization in LGBTQ adults: A brief report. *Journal of Interpersonal Violence* 35(5–6): 1442–1453.

Logan, T. K. 2010. *Research on partner stalking: Putting the pieces together*. Lexington: Department of Behavioral Science & Center on Drug and Alcohol Research, University of Kentucky.

Logan, T., J. Cole, L. Shannon, and R. Walker. 2006. *Partner stalking: How women respond, cope and survive*. New York: Springer Publishing Company.

Lowe, Y. 2022. *'Disaster' warning as ITV News exposes police failing to use new stalking powers.* ITV, 16 June 2022.
Mackenzie, R., P. E. Mullen, J. R. P. Ogloff, T. E. McEwan, and D. V. James. 2008. Parental bonding and adult attachment styles in different types of stalkers. *Journal of Forensic Sciences* 53(6): 1443–1449.
Mastronardi, V., A. Pomilla, and S. Ricci. 2012. Stalking of psychiatrists: Psychopathological characteristics and gender differences. *International Journal of Offender Therapy and Comparative Criminology* 57(5): 526–543.
May, T., A. Haracopos and M. Hough. 2000. *For love or money: Pimps and the management of sex work.* London: Home Office—Research, Development and Statistics Directorate.
Medina, J., D. Peralta, G. Brown, and K. Nixon. 2015. Using machine learning methods to improve domestic abuse risk Assessment. In *Society for evidence base policing annual meeting.* Manchester, 14–15 April.
Meloy, J. R. 1996. Stalking (obsessional following): A review of some preliminary studies. *Aggression and Violent Behavior* 1: 147–162.
McCann, J. T. 1998. Subtypes of stalking (obsessional following) in adolescents. *Journal of Adolescence* 21: 667- 675.
Mullen, P. E., M. Pathé, and R. Purcell. 2000. *Stalkers and their victims.* Cambridge, MA: Cambridge University Press.
Mullen, P. E., and M. Pathé. 2001. Stalkers and Their Victims. *Psychiatric Times*, 1 April.
Mullen, P. E., M. Pathé and R. Purcell. 2009. *Stalkers and their victims.* Cambridge, UK: Cambridge University Press.
Myhill, Andy. 2016. *Risk identification in cases of domestic abuse.* Ryton-on-Dunsmore: College of policing.
Myhill, A., and K. Hohl. 2016. The "golden thread": Coercive control and risk assessment for domestic violence. *Journal of Interpersonal Violence* 34(21–22): 4477–4497. https://doi.org/10.1177/0886260516675464.
Napo, 2011. *Stalking and harassment: A study of perpetrators.* Paladin. https://paladinservice.co.uk/wp-content/uploads/2013/06/Study-of-perpetrators.pdf. Accessed 20 July 2022.
Norfolk County Council. 2022. *The Multi Agency Risk Assessment Co-ordination (MARAC).* https://www.norfolk.gov.uk/safety/domestic-abuse/information-for-professionals/multi-agency-risk-assessment-coordination-marac. Accessed 22 July 2022.
North Yorkshire Safeguarding Children Partnership (NYSCP). 2019. *Domestic abuse practical guidance.* https://www.safeguardingchildren.co.uk/wp-content/uploads/2019/09/NYSCP-DA-Practice-Guidance-Nov-19-v1.1.pdf. Accessed 22 June 2022.
Office for the Police and Crime Commissioner for Norfolk. 2020. *Victims of stalking and harassment advised support is available.* https://www.norfolk-pcc.gov.uk/news/victims-of-stalking-and-harassment-advised-support-is-available/. Accessed 16 June 2022.
Office for National Statistics. 2020. *Stalking: Findings from the crime survey for England and Wales.* https://www.ons.gov.uk/peoplepopulationandcommunity/crimeandjustice/datasets/stalkingfindingsfromthecrimesurveyforenglandandwales. Accessed 7 August 2022.
Office for National Statistics. 2021.*Domestic abuse prevalence and trends, England and Wales: year ending March 2021.* https://www.ons.gov.uk/peoplepopulationandcommunity/crimeandjustice/articles/domesticabuseprevalenceandtrendsenglandandwales/yearendingmarch2021#:~:text=The%20police%20recorded%20215%2C173%20domestic,all%20domestic%20abuse-related%20crimes. Accessed 16 June 2022.
Ogloff, J. R. P., R. G. Veal, D. E. Shea, and T. McEwan. 2020. The role of psychopathy in stalking. In *Wiley international handbook of psychopathic disorders and the law*, eds. A. Felthous and H. Saβ, H, 731–728. London: Wiley.
Owen, S. S., T. W. Burke, and A. L. Few-Demo, and J. Natwick. 2018. Perceptions of the police by LGBT communities. *American Journal of Criminal Justice* 43: 668–693.
Paladin. 2021. *Key facts and figures.* https://paladinservice.co.uk/key-facts-and-figures/ Accessed 3 June 2022.

Paraschakis, A., and D. Konstantinidou. 2012. Stalking of psychiatrists by their patients: An unsettling reality. *European Psychiatry* 27(1): 1–1.

Queiros, A., D. Faria, and F. Almeida. 2017. Strengths and limitations of qualitative and quantitative research methods. *European Journal of Education Studies* 3(9).

Redwood, S., and P. Gill. 2013. Under-representation of minority ethnic groups in research—Call for action. *The British Journal of General Practice: The Journal of the Royal College of General Practitioners* 63(612): 342–343.

Ricardo, C. 2014. *Men, masculinities, and changing power: A discussion paper on engaging men in gender equality from Beijing 1995 to 2015*. Washington, DC: MenEngage.

Robinson, A. L. 2010. Risk and Intimate Partner Violence. In *Good Practice in Risk Assessment and Risk Management*, eds. H. Kemshall and B. Wilkinson, 119-138. London: Jessica Kingsley Publishers.

Robinson, A. L., A. Myhill, J. Wire, J. Roberts, and N. Tilly. 2016. Risk-led policing of domestic abuse and the DASH risk model. The College of Policing. https://library.college.police.uk/docs/college-of-policing/Risk-led-policing-2-2016.pdf. Accessed 31 October 2022.

Rosenfeld, B. 2000. Assessment and treatment of obsessional harassment. *Aggression and Violent Behavior* 5: 529–549.

Ruiz-Cantero, M., C. Vives-Cases, and L. Artazcoz. 2007. A framework to analyse gender bias in epidemiological research. *Journal of Epidemiology & Community Health* 61: 46–53.

Sandberg, D. A., D. E. McNiel, and R. L. Binder. 2002. Stalking, threatening, and harassing behaviour by psychiatric patients toward clinicians. *Journal of the Journal of the American Academy of Psychiatry and Law American Academy of Psychiatry and Law* 30: 221–229.

Schmitt, D. P., A. Realo, M. Voracek, and J. Allik. 2009. "Why can't a man be more like a woman? Sex differences in big five personality traits across 55 cultures": Correction to Schmitt et al (2008). *Journal of Personality and Social Psychology* 96(1): 118.

Silverman, David. 2005. *Doing qualitative research*. London: Sage.

Sheridan, L., and A. E. Lyndon. 2012. The influence of prior relationship gender and fear on the consequences of stalking victimization. *Sex Roles* 66(5–6): 340–350. https://doi.org/10.1007/s11199-010-9889-9.

Sheridan, L. P., E. Blaauw and G. M. Davies. 2003. Stalking knowns and unknowns. *Trauma, Violence, & Abuse* 4(2): 148–162.

Sheridan, L., A. C. North, and A. J. Scott. 2019. Stalking in the workplace. *Journal of Threat Assessment and Management* 6(2): 61–75.

Spitzberg, B. H., and W. R. Cupach. 2014. *The dark side of relationship pursuit: From attraction to obsession and stalking* (2nd ed.). Routledge. https://doi.org/10.4324/9780203805916.

Spitzberg, B. H., A. M. Nicastro, and A. V. Cousins. 1998. Exploring the interactional phenomenon of stalking and obsessive relational intrusion. *Communication Reports* 11(1): 33–47.

Starr, S. 2014. Evidence-based sentencing and the scientific rationalization of discrimination. *Stanford Law Review* 66(4): 803–872.

Suzy Lamplugh Trust. 2019. *Stalking in the workplace: What is the responsibility of the employer?* https://www.suzylamplugh.org/blog/stalking-in-the-workplace-what-is-the-responsibility-of-an-employer. Accessed 3 July 2022.

Suzy Lamplugh Trust. 2021. *Press Release* (Suzy Lamplugh: 35 Years). https://www.suzylamplugh.org/news/press-release-suzy-lamplugh-35-years. Accessed 3 July 2022.

Swanberg, J. E., T. Logan, and C. Macke, C. 2005. Intimate partner violence, employment, and the workplace: Consequences and future directions. *Trauma, Violence, & Abuse* 6: 286–312.

Tjaden, P., N. Thoennes, and C.J. Allison. 2000. Comparing stalking victimization from legal and victim perspectives. *Violence and Victims* 15: 7-22.

The National Archives. 2021. The National Archives. *Health and Safety at Work, etc Act, c. 37*. https://discovery.nationalarchives.gov.uk/details/r/9752222b-4019-4816-8ed8-2f098e4c8529.

Townsend, M. 2020. New measures to beat stalking could put victims at risk. *The Guardian*, 19 January.

Turmanis, S. A., and R. I. Brown. 2006. The stalking and harassment behaviour scale: Measuring the incidence nature and severity of stalking and relational harassment and their psychological

effects. *Psychology and Psychotherapy: Theory Research and Practice* 79(2): 183–198. https://doi.org/10.1348/147608305X53161.
Turner, E., J. Medina, and G. Brown. 2019. Dashing hopes? The predictive accuracy of domestic abuse risk assessment by police. *The British Journal of Criminology* 59(5): 1013–1034.
Tyner, J. A. 2012. *Space, place, and violence: Violence and the embodied geographies of race, sex and gender*. New York: Routledge.
Vaswani, N. 2014. The ripples of death: Exploring the bereavement experiences and mental health of young men in custody. *The Howard Journal of Criminal Justice* 53(4): 341-359.
Vaswani, N. 2018. *Adverse childhood experiences in children at high risk of harm to others: A gendered perspective*. University of Strathclyde. https://core.ac.uk/download/pdf/146504497.pdf. Accessed 26 August 2022.
Vera-Gray, Fiona. 2016. *Men's intrusion, women's embodiment: A critical analysis of street harassment*. Oxon: Routledge.
Vera-Gray, Fiona. 2018. *The Right Amount of Panic: How Women Trade Freedom for Safety*. Bristol: Policy Press.
Vera-Gray, Fiona, and Liz Kelly. 2020. Contested gendered space: public sexual harassment and women's safety work. *International Journal of Comparative and Applied Criminal Justice* 44(4): 265–275.
Walker, L. M., and J. R. Meloy. 1998. Stalking and domestic violence. In *The psychology of stalking: Clinical and forensic perspectives*, ed. R.J. Meloy, 140-159. San Diego, CA: Academic Press.
Wiener, C. 2017. Seeing what is 'Invisible in Plain Sight': Policing coercive control. *The Howard Journal of Crime and Justice* 56(4): 500–515.
Woodruff, K. 2010. An analysis of the police response to intimate partner stalking (Paper 783). http://diginole.lib.fsu.edu/. Accessed 27 June 2022.

The *EmilyTest*: The Education Sector in Crisis

11

Fiona Drouet and Poppy Gerrard-Abbott

Key Points

- Gender-Based Violence (GBV) in the education sector presents the most severe picture for issues of prevention, intervention, and support among UK young people.
- The unique characteristics of GBV in universities creates a particularly enabling environment for GBV and makes the context especially difficult to intervene in.
- GBV in universities has distinct features and challenges warranting a specialist focus.

Emily's Story

Fiona Drouet MBE, CEO of EmilyTest

My weekly treat to myself has always been fresh flowers, 'pale pink sweet avalanche roses' to be precise. My love of fresh flowers is something I inherited from my grandmother and it was a love Emily shared too. So suddenly having every room in our house filled with fresh flowers for an unimaginable reason became a presence my heart, body, and soul couldn't take. Every inch of me

F. Drouet (✉)
EmilyTest, Glasgow, UK
e-mail: fionadrouet@emilytest.co.uk

P. Gerrard-Abbott
University of Edinburgh, Edinburgh, UK
e-mail: pgerrard@ed.ac.uk

M. Mellins et al. (eds.), *Young People, Stalking Awareness and Domestic Abuse*,
https://doi.org/10.1007/978-3-031-32379-9_11

hurts unimaginably. A constant visual and sensory overload that screamed Emily was gone on every surface, in every room of our house—our beautiful, bubbly, intelligent, and kind little girl, was gone.

Emily achieving well at school had become something we grew to take for granted. She was incredibly bright, committed to her studies, and very focused on her dream of studying Law and French. Her ultimate dream is to practice Law in Paris, where the paternal side of our family is from. Growing up, we holidayed in France and had a strong affinity with Paris in particular. So much so that she had even selected the 'rue' she wanted to live on. High aspirations that we admired, embraced, and encouraged as her eyes lit up when she pictured her future. She'd grown up with the motto 'Semper Paratus', always ready to discover. And as a family, we have always encouraged our children to follow their dreams, that they could do anything they set their minds to.

So when Emily received her offer to study Law and French at university, that was one of her dreams on its way to becoming reality. We were a little concerned as the university was a few hours' drive away from home but as loving parents, we supported Emily and helped her prepare for this next adventure in her life. Before she had even arrived at university, she had made friends and chatted with her flatmates over Facebook. Her excitement was infectious and we were over the moon watching our little girl follow her dreams and embrace new opportunities.

She settled in well although found it a little challenging as, being only 17, she was unable to participate in Freshers' events with her friends. She quickly found other 17-year-olds who were also in pursuit of someone 18+ that looked like them so they could borrow their ID. Something Emily did with great success at first, but then learned a harsh lesson when an astute security person stopped her at the door of a club, spotting Emily bore no resemblance to the document picture, and promptly called the police. She was subsequently ushered back to the halls by some very friendly police officers who found it quite amusing when they asked what she was studying. She sheepishly told me of this 'adventure' on the phone as she prepared me to receive a call from the police. Finding it amusing (and feeling sorry for her as I could sense her worry as she believed she would have a police record) we had a chat about putting it down to a good lesson learned and perhaps wait until her 18th birthday which was, after all, only a few months away.

Life as a young university student was as it should be, making new friends, eating nonsense food, and partying, I'm sure probably more than we knew, but she was loving her new-found independence and the friendships she was making.

The side of university that we were seeing, however, the side that made us excited for our little girl, wasn't the full story. In October a friend of Emily's introduced her to this 'great guy', a Psychology student at the university who, although in the halls of residence, was a few years older than everyone else. They started a relationship that quickly grew intense in the absence of nagging parents. They spent every day together, increasingly missing lectures and tutorials to be with each other. To anyone on the outside, this looked like a blossoming romance, a very intense and passionate relationship but that couldn't be further from the truth.

During the six months they knew each other, he repeatedly physically, psychologically, and sexually abused Emily. It started as a loving and affectionate romance and progressively turned darker and darker with violent and coercive behaviours intensifying. Although she was concerned and spoke to her friends, they wrote it off as 'this must just be how it is', he's older, popular, and more experienced, whereas they were young and inexperienced, still finding their way. Emily shared some concerns about his behaviours, particularly sexually, but none of them wanted to stand out as the 'virgins on campus', especially not in front of the rugby boys who most found intimidating anyway. During one particularly violent assault during which Emily feared for her life, he repeatedly slapped her across her face, slammed her head down on her desk, and strangled her until she came to passing out. She later said to her friends she saw stars; she thought she was going to die. Soon after the assault, Emily approached a resident assistant staff for help. Seeing she was visibly injured they asked: 'Has he hit you Emily?', Emily replied, 'No, I don't want to get him into trouble'. They then walked outside with Emily and wrote their report as follows:

> 'Emily came to us concerned about her angry and aggressive boyfriend'
>
> 'Emily feels she's hitting the self-destruct button'
>
> 'Emily knows she needs to change her behaviour'
>
> 'No follow-up required'
>
> She was sent back to her room alone.

The perpetrator remained in his room which looked directly on to hers. In the following week Emily was assaulted a further three times, each time he turned up unannounced. Shortly after his last visit, scared, broken, and all alone, our little girl took her own life. Our little girl, with the world at her feet, full of dreams, aspirations, and hopes, was gone.

How could we not have known? Why weren't we told what was happening? Why couldn't Emily tell us?

Plunged into what can only be described as utter agony, we slowly uncovered the extent of multiple preventable failures to help our little girl. Knowing that she reached out for help but that help failed her in so many ways, breaks our hearts over and over again. Not getting the chance to save your child when they are so lost and losing hope is unbearable torture. Gaining the knowledge that it could and should have been different added another dimension to our pain. We couldn't let anyone else be plunged into this hell; there cannot be another young girl like Emily, left to suffer alone and in silence.

But what could we do? We had no idea where to start but we knew it could never happen again. We had to do something.

We approached the Scottish Government and formed our charity, EmilyTest. Over the years since we lost Emily, we have developed support cards, support stickers, risk assessments, and a GBV charter, all to ensure institutions are as safe as they can be for all students to live, work, and study. Everyone deserves to be free from the harms of gender-based violence but, if the worst should happen, they must receive informed and professional support. Poppy Gerard-Abbott, Principal Research and Policy officer at EmilyTest will detail that work in the second half of this chapter but suffice it to say, I believe the research-based framework we have developed, if implemented fully, would have saved Emily's life.

When we were preparing Emily for university life, we didn't prepare her for meeting someone who would slowly but determinedly destroy her. And while embarrassed to admit our naivety, it's important to be honest for the sake of others. We naively thought that she would be safe among like-minded students there to further their education and make lifelong friends. We assumed wrong, you always think it could never happen to you.

The sad reality is that data is beginning to reveal that GBV in student populations is higher than in the general population. 8% of women students have been raped, compared to ONS (2018) estimations of 4% of women in England and Wales. It concludes a clear indication that rape is higher among students than among the wider population. Yet progress across the sector has been slow and inconsistent. Students are ill-prepared for the risks and challenges they have a high chance of encountering.

Domestic abuse doesn't discriminate against age or background, it can happen to any one of us. But for a young person, who is experiencing independence for the first time and still trying to establish their identity, it can be utterly devastating. The long-term physical and psychological impacts are clearly evidenced. Earlier I mentioned one of the forms of violence perpetrated against Emily, strangulation. Evidence shows us someone subjected to strangulation in this context is at a significantly higher risk of further abuse and/or being murdered, yet how many of us know how that risk increases? How many of us know it is a red flag that should never be ignored? A victim will often suffer from internal injuries that do not appear on the outside. Immediately after an assault, the person may experience intense pain, vision changes, ringing in the ears, a swollen tongue, cuts in the mouth, swelling of the neck, difficulty swallowing, trouble breathing, or voice and throat changes. They may also have neurological damage caused by the restriction of oxygen flow to their brain. Symptoms often experienced include dizziness, headaches, vomiting, and extreme weakness. Behavioural changes are common too, the victim/survivor may become more combative, suffer PTSD, depression, nightmares, sleeplessness, psychosis, and last but not least, experience suicidal ideation. Sadly as a society, we do little to prevent such harm given a justice system that doesn't recognise these harms with the gravity it should. The perpetrator in Emily's case was sentenced to 180 hours of community service and a supervision order, Emily's sentence, we believe, was death.

Increasingly we see the lines between a healthy relationship and a controlling one become blurred. What constitutes healthy sex and relationships and what is abuse? Immersed in a world with films promoting rape, strangulation, and torture as a relationship to aspire to, and with an absence of adequate sexual education in our schools, we see a nation, if not a world, sleepwalking into an abuse-accepting society. While pornography may be viewed by many as a harmless form of entertainment, by some, it can have harmful effects on individuals and society, especially when children and young people are exposed to it. It can contribute to the objectification and devaluation of women, distort people's views of sexuality and relationships, and be addictive and harmful. It often involves exploitation and coercion of the performers. These potential harms should be taken into consideration when evaluating the role of pornography in society. There is no singular solution, it takes a multi-faceted approach to address a complex problem. The normalisation of such harms in society was evidenced in Emily's case as it emerged how many people knew of the abuse but didn't see it as wrong. Not necessarily because they are all bad people, but simply because such abuse is normalised and condoned daily. People continue to support her abuser, comforting themselves that there was 'another side of the story'. Their often unwitting complicity adds to the problem.

If you know a young person who is in an unhealthy relationship, it's important to remind them they are not alone. Physical, psychological, and sexual abuse are never the fault of the victim/survivor, they deserve to be in a relationship that is based on mutual respect and trust. By seeking help and support, you can take the first steps towards breaking free from an abusive situation and building a healthy and fulfilling life for yourself.

We must not normalise abuse, we cannot stand by and let it continue. That must be Emily's legacy—that no other family must endure this pain. There is no quick fix but determination coupled with a firm moral compass will result in much-needed change. We will continue to lobby and campaign in partnership with other organisations who understand the true cost of these harms. We must ensure that our young people are kept safe and are able to fulfil the future they deserve and that their dreams become a reality. It's the very least they deserve.

The Education Sector in Crisis

Poppy Gerrard-Abbott, Ph.D. Sociology and Social Policy

Background

Student populations are reported to have higher rates of GBV perpetration and lower rates of reporting than the general population (Revolt Sexual Assault and Student Room 2018; Office for National Statistics 2018), with international consensus building that, 'female students in general [are] at [...] increased risk' of GBV (List 2017) and a consistent picture that full-time students experience the highest GBV rates in comparison to other occupation groups (Office for National Statistics 2020). UK students prove three times more likely to be sexually assaulted than national averages (Lewis 2022), with rape statistics in particular underlined for being significantly higher than the general population, with 'as many as one in four undergraduate women experiencing rape' (Phipps and Smith 2012, 2). This picture of evidence began emerging following the release of the first UK study on

GBV in universities, authored by the National Union of Students (NUS) *Hidden Marks* (2010), making higher education (HE) a context of urgent interest for GBV researchers and campaigners, as well as instigating a 'turning point in responses' (Lewis 2018, 56) from university management bodies. Over a decade of sustained policy and practice changes unfolded from the higher education (HE) sector, most notably the publishing of Universities UK's (UUK) (2018) recommendations, in addition to the rollout of specialist GBV policies and practices in nearly every university in the UK.

The Present Sector Picture

Despite over a decade of reform since *Hidden Marks*, where 'some progress' (Humphreys and Towl 2020, 3) in GBV policy and practice improvement has taken place, the pace and depth of material change have been widely regarded by campaigners, government, and researchers as inadequate. Universities' handling of GBV is being frequently 'named and shamed' by supranational and domestic policymakers to constitute serious ongoing human rights issues, 'blighting' (Women and Equalities Committee 2018) equal participation in contemporary education in Britain. Activist complaints remain the same towards universities since campaigning began; that institutions are 'not doing enough' to deal with GBV prevalence rates, and GBV reports are subsequently, continuously 'failing' (Murray 2021) student victims/survivors.

Today's figures continue to reveal a bleak picture for GBV in education, with claims that prevalence levels and the handling of cases are at 'crisis' point (Tidman 2022). The most recent UK data, which appears to show GBV 'is increasing in universities' (Long and Hubble 2020, 3) has led to claims of sector policy and practice being ineffective, failing to establish 'minimum safeguarding standards' (Humphreys and Towl 2021). Media headlines such as 'Sexual assault claims "mishandled" by universities' (Lawthon 2021) remain a staple news feature and multiple, serious cases have occurred years into policy and practice reform, notably the 2016 death of Emily Drouet at the University of Aberdeen, who took her own life after experiencing a campaign of GBV from a fellow student, and the 2022 murder of Sabita Thanwani in her City University of London halls. Feminist students are still 'fighting some of the same battles as 25-even 40-years ago [with] the #MeToo…movement [being a] key indicator of this' (Fileborn and Loney-Howes 2019, viii).

Despite over a decade of change since *Hidden Marks*, rates of GBV perpetration remain persistently high and reporting rates remain persistently low, with both at similar or worse rates now than when the first research reports were released (Brook 2019; Culture Shift 2020, 2022; Our Streets Now 2022; Anyadike-Danes et al. 2022), meaning that 'instead of decreasing, the incidence thereof is *rising*' (Makhene 2022) and resulting in calls from sector leadership for GBV to be a policy priority 'more than ever before' (NUS 2022a). The UK data landscape is mirrored globally, where many countries are 'experiencing an increase in the prevalence of GBV committed' (Mutinta 2022). The US and UK present a 'consistent' picture data-wise that GBV is just as 'pressing' among their student demographics, with both contexts reporting aligned rates of perpetration and victimisation (Jones et al. 2020, 25). The author of the 'landmark' (Perkins and Warner 2017, 237) American study on GBV in education too concludes that across longitudinal intervention of 'neither containment nor reduction of rape was demonstrated' (Koss et al. 2022), much in line with the present picture of UK higher education. Despite the US, as the most developed context, being sixty years into reform 'the prevalence [...] has not changed' (Wiersma-Mosley and Jozkowski 2019, 1).

Emily's Story as a Case Study to Understand the 'GBV' Concept

The Scottish Government commissioned the creation of the world's first GBV 'Charter' for universities and colleges (EmilyTest 2021a), which my Ph.D. project co-authored. This is a multi-sector project to introduce minimum standards and best practices in GBV prevention, intervention, and support in further education (FE) and higher education (HE). Rolled out nationally across Scotland and soon to expand across the UK, the framework is colloquially known as 'Emily's Charter' created in memory of Emily, who took her own life in 2016 after being subjected to a campaign of domestic violence from a fellow student.

Emily's story entailed a non-linear hybrid of physical, digital, verbal, psychological, and sexual violence occurring prior to, during, and after the points of coupledom and separation with her partner, revealing GBV's ensemble across different 'subject positions, and never totally fixed [...] always contingent and precarious' (Mouffe 2013, 372). The abuse she was subjected to including repeated slapping, chokings, coercive control, public humiliation, stalking, home invasion, sexist verbal abuse, and social media-based harassment through threatening text messages and the dissemination of private and malicious communications about her.

The GBV in the education field has theorised violence and abuse in education spaces as needing an understanding of the 'overlapping categories [of] explicit [and] implicit' forms (Dunne et al. 2006, 2), as per Emily's case. Multiple spaces, actors, and events led to her death including numerous perpetrators, bullying from female peers, community enablement, porous staff training, lacking safeguarding prioritisation in strategy and governance, and harassment blurring online, offline, classroom, domestic and interpersonal life (EmilyTest 2021b). As literature on the education context is a new area, it has theorised GBV in a modern context. Providing one of the most recent developments in the study of GBV, the GBV in education field has produced understandings of how sexism and sexual violence have adapted to modern society, particularly in a digitised and globalised world. The innovations created by the birth of the field had a domino effect on UK policy and practice, causing rapid scope expansion to contemporary types of GBV, such as online forms. Understanding the more complex manifestations that come with modernisation trends, the field has led the way in confronting GBV as more complex than ever before; as morphing, multipronged, and crossing boundaries of multiple social worlds. In particular, the field kick-started focus on *institutional* contexts, shedding light on under-represented sites of endemic GBV 'galvanised [...] international exposes' (Lewis 2018, 53) globally in workplaces and social media settings, calling in experiences from all sectors and industries including the media, the police, and sports arenas. So-called 'upskirting', for instance, legislated against in the UK in 2019 under the Sexual Offences Act (2003) characteristically occurs in enclosed social environments such as 'public transport, in schools and colleges, workplaces', demonstrating the myriad nature of modern GBV with 'a key element of the abusiveness' *being* its multitudinous nature 'thus a double abuse' (Hall et al. 2022, 533). As upskirting involves media being captured *as well as* shared non-consensually, the abuse spans manifold violent 'craftsmanship' (2022, 532), including stalking, recording, and dissemination. Close inspection of the education field as a given institutional context offers, in microscopic detail, GBV's multilevel and complex characteristics, revealing its often non-binate nature '*not only* either a form of partner violence or stranger violence [which is] the [...] most common understanding of the victims/perpetrators relation' (Strid 2021). GBV's embeddedness into community networks, and its subsequent mirroring in social media networks, reveals its spanning across the boundaries of acquaintance, colleague, and bystander violence, with students' experiences tending to include hybrids of known and unknown parties, and both online and offline life. GBV has modernised to 'abuse [involving] photos and videos taken and/or uploaded without consent to porn sites and shared on messaging apps [...] deepfakes [...] cyberflashing [...] trolling, catfishing, and doxing, partially defined by their manifestation outside of conventional victim-perpetrator interactions: with no prior relationship or knowledge about the victim needed and without direct and/or physical interaction necessary, instead victimisation occurring by association with spaces of learning, working, socialising, being part of a community' (Glitch 2022). As endemic violence and abuse adapt to an ever-advancing technologised era, GBV's multitudinous nature becomes known: as a maze-like, transforming, webbed ecosystem. Studying GBV against the backdrop of modern life has revealed how present times have given rise to new forms, as well as coming to understand that modernity allows for a more in-depth understanding of how GBV has always been.

The GBV in education field has innovated understandings of GBV as multifarious: often pervasive, pluralistic, and periodic. Recognition of its continuous and boundless attributes supports a much more contemporary conceptual construction, namely an all-encompassing understanding of GBV's effects and events. The integration of all psycho-social dimensions to GBV's impacts become seen as fundamentally *part of* victimisation, such as victim *anticipation of* GBV and of stigmatising responses to disclosures. Such fear tactics and coercive-controlling effects on victim behaviour and health has led to scholarship naming GBV, particularly online GBV (Crelinsten 2022), as a form of 'terrorism', interchangeably used with terms 'intimate terrorism' or 'patriarchal terrorism' (Patra et al. 2018, 494), labelling which has seen take-up in the UK context following a lineage of prolific gendered murders during the COVID-19 pandemic which gave rise to a government directive 'elevat[ing] GBV to the same status [...] a terrorist attack [...] a major crimefighting priority' (Hamilton 2021).

The (personal) 'unpredictability' of severity and the constant probability of GBV evoke heightened alertness, locked hypervigilance, and emotional terror, propelling risk-mitigation behaviours. Thus, GBV operates through systems of power and control, being a constant potential without repeated events or even direct experience at all. Furthermore, coining terms such as so-called 'microaggressions' and 'everyday sexism', the GBV in education arena has also led understandings of how contemporary misogyny has evolved to adapt around modern *policy* frameworks, operating consciously around where socially acceptable 'lines' of behaviours sit and around what policy constitutes as clear-cut violent behaviours. Shifting sexism to enact behaviours sitting across or between policy categories of banned behaviours, modern institutional sexisms have morphed to behaviours less (easily) regulated and which are socio-culturally considered less clear-cut as defined violence, bringing into question whether sexism has indeed decreased as gender equality improves in society, or whether it has simply evolved in manifestation to escape intervention and punitive outcomes. Much more recent practice developments have consequently been dedicated to the targeting of 'policy-adapted' forms of GBV (characterised as being in the 'grey zone' of right and wrong) such as the now UK-wide *Erase the Grey* campaign authored by Glasgow Caledonian University (GCU) (2019).

Emily's case evidences the realities of GBV as umbrella, spectrum-based, and pluralistic manifestations (EmilyTest 2021a, b) and perpetrated by numerous people across boundaries of time and cultural sites (United Nations 1993) experienced in 'all levels' (Public Health Scotland 2021) of social life combining macro factors, such as patriarchal belief systems, meso factors such as institutional dismissal, and micro factors such as interpersonal relations. Its 'multidirectional[ity]' (Mahlori et al. 2018, 1) across social stratum means that a more accurate schematic of GBV is one mirroring its complex profusion, inclusive of multiple events coalescing to form a victim's experience of abuse. Beyond the 'primary' perpetrator, Emily experienced peer pressure from the university community, including attempted forced sexual acts with the perpetrator's friends, as well as secondary forms of victimisation like 'slut-shaming', pejorative street harassment, and peer abandonment. The charity set up in Emily's memory, *EmilyTest*, presented Emily's story to the Scottish Government (EmilyTest 2021a, 11) as one where a culture of enabling, as well as multiple missed opportunities for the community to come forward, accumulatively formed the GBV she experienced.

Contrary to mythical 'stranger danger' constructions, GBV is rarely confined to one type, to one place, and to one-time point (in a relationship). Literature is expanding on how abuse can begin pre-intimacy and often continues, or even heightens to its worst, and a most prolonged 'wilful pattern of intimidation' post-separation (Spearman et al. 2022). GBV operates fluidly across spatial, time, and relational boundaries, contravening mainstream constructions of GBV occurring within concrete and static statuses, conceptually and linguistically mirrored in policy and practice design around 'domestic' violence (DV), 'intimate partner violence' (IPV), and 'relationship abuse' (RA). Evidence reveals (abusive) relationships to often be non-linear (Scheffer Lindgren and Renck 2008) and in flux; entered, departed from, and re-entered relating to factors such as finances, housing, maternity, marital expectations, caring responsibilities, and the episodic nature of abuse (Rakovec-Felser 2014; Sani and Pereira 2020). Risk also changes *throughout* university years, with the freshers' period and first undergraduate year proving 'critical' (Frederick et al. 2020, 652) and factors such as income, educational development, and social networks contracting and expanding throughout study programmes, revealing the synergistic relationship between 'external' and 'internal' predicators, and moving variables such as domestic, economic, and occupational factors. Both a victims' experiences *of* GBV and their experiences of *responding* to it shift and morph according to the course of a person's life (Russo and Pirlott 2006, 181), particularly in the case of students concerning their morphing and precarious social trajectories, including fluctuating socioeconomic status, evolving relationships, and locational transience.

Multiple events amounting to months of violence took place before Emily made a disclosure, and she never submitted a formal complaint to the university, demonstrating the realities of GBV as pluralistic across timelines rather than black swan 'sledgehammer' events (Anitha and Lewis 2018, 61) that are unpredictable, unpreventable, isolated, stand-out acts of brutality. Her case evidences GBV as diversely manifesting, as an enablement jigsaw of 'complicit' masculinities and femininities (Jordan et al 2022), and as accumulative building blocks of discrimination. One of the most recent reports on GBV in education finds that 70% of victims/survivors' experiences of sexual violence in their place of study or work are situated in 'an ongoing pattern [...] rather than one-off incident' (Addington et al. 2021, 3) with GBV rarely confined to one type. Theoretically, politically, and empirically, applying a continuum-based approach facilitates the understanding that abuse manifests outside of singular, restrictive categories like 'physical violence' and 'sexual violence' and instead leans to fusion behaviours. As complex and 'multi-directional' (Beyene et al. 2019, 2) phenomena, GBV is often experienced multiple times, in multiple forms, and in multiple settings, such as the workplace, the street, and the home (Kelly 1987; Korkodeilou 2016) whereby a distinguishing feature of GBV is its embedded and mundane nature in society; interwoven in everyday gender relations. GBV perpetration characteristically affects multiple victims simultaneously, across time trajectories, experienced multiple times. Reporting figures and statistics of GBV should be 'approached with caution' (Dey 2020, 5) as merely indicative pictures of GBV's scale, reach, and impacts because 'it happens to girls [women students] all the time'. In contrast to the 'incidentialism' (Anitha and Lewis 2018, 1) outlook and 'case-ification' approaches mainstreamed in policy and practice, the realities of GBV are that it occurs in institutional life at prevalence rates spanning beyond the parameters of capability of research and of (university) GBV provisions. The mundane 'everydayness' and repetitive features of GBV in themselves are major obstacles to student victims/survivors' accessing of help services (Holland and Cortina 2017).

Thus far, UK research on GBV in education has been disproportionately quantitative. This has served an important role in creating succinct understandings about the problem of prevalent violence and abuse in universities. Creating 'headline' data communications, quantitative information has stimulated strong political and institutional responses, including awareness campaigns and policy change at nearly every UK university and across other education sites including colleges and specialist training institutions. Akin to the likes of the United Nations (UN) and World Health Organisation (WHO) and following suit of their most widely cited '1 in 3'[1] (women globally experience GBV) statistic, the most prominent authors in the field, the NUS, have promoted percentage-based representations of the problems and questions the field contends with, meaning that statistical data has characteristically constituted mainstream understandings of GBV in education in the UK. This trend aligns with wider gravitations in the global and domestic policy arenas where numerical data strategically provides policymakers with efficient evidence 'snapshots' of the problem(s) at hand; and offers the public and media with rapidly transmissible 'bitesize' information on complex social issues. The utility and impact of statistical data should be understood within specific parameters as awareness-raising in purpose and as having a change-making function. As my Ph.D. employed mixed methods and qualitative-leaning strategies of inquiry, the limitations concerning the dominance of quantitative methods were revealed—here, the most striking finding has been that GBV is endemic in educational institutions. Interwoven and normalised into everyday educational life—nightlife, the classroom, social life, student societies, domestic life, teacher–student relationships—GBV assumes a status as mundane and being of a scale methodologically near-impossible to capture numerically. Participants nearly always state its occurrence rate to be '100%' and existent everywhere, with one mature postgraduate interviewee (I) describing occurrence rates as: 'not hav[ing] one female friend [at university] who has not been involved in some kind of incident'. GBV is well-evidenced as ubiquitous in 'magnitude' (Strid 2021) within educational institutions, acute to the extent it is 'a feature of life' (Lewis 2018, 56) for students.

The past decade of quantitative-leaning evidence has provided relevant, but limited, understandings of GBV in education that warrant more detailed interrogation of the iterated statistical picture from the UK body of research. Unsurprisingly, the research finds that GBV is rife on university campuses, reinforcing existing data that it is a day-to-day part of campus life. Perpetrators are therefore, *embedded* across the student body. Every university department, course, halls of residence, social media page, and student community reportedly has a known 'Weinstein' character, with one participant from my Ph.D.'s LGBTQIA* Focus Group (FG) sharing: 'we had a person in our social circle in halls who [...] sexually harass[ed] quite a few of us and then ended up raping one of my close friends'. This further offers meaning to GBV as 'endemic' and 'omnipresent' for student populations. The research also uncovered how victimisation spans the institutional borders of universities. With student statuses being non-static—made up of multiple social spaces and identities, increasingly global and transient, and developing over a lifetime of study geared towards going to university it is common for 'a lot [of students and staff to] come to university already [having] ended up in situations where they were abused' (LGBTQIA* FG) experiencing GBV at multiple points across the education pipeline, at home, in the local community, in spaces such as work, sports, and social life, and even *shaping* decisions of whether to go to university and where.

GBV in Education as a Specialist Focus

GBV among students is often theorised as a problem of 'youth violence'. However, social scientific inquiry is revealing how age as a factor fails to provide singular explanatory capability to answer the question of why GBV is so high, and remains so severe, in universities. GBV research that contrasts university and non-university populations of the same age group, evidences the necessity of student populations to be treated as having distinct attributes 'not representative of other groups in the general population' (Barn and Powers 2021, 3530). The American literature body, which leads global scholarship on GBV in education, 'makes clear' that students are at 'substantial […] greater risk for certain forms of assault' than the general population *and* non-students in the same age group (Jordan et al. 2014, 191). Age remains a variable of consideration, with evidence suggesting that the youngest populations of student bodies may experience the greatest degrees of violence (Sivertsen et al. 2019). However, understanding why rates are the highest among students and why interventions are failing to change this requires a specialist focus on universities as a stand-out context and recognition of the potential of *social* factors to have the greatest explanatory capabilities.

Contemporary third and fourth wave feminism theorises GBV as having 'geographies' (Bowes and Fileborn 2022), as being contextually manifesting across cultural, political, and digital borders. HE unfolds 'its own versions' (Jeffries 2020, 3) of violence and abuse and thus presents a 'unique set of risks' (UN Women 2018, 5). The likes of Emily's story must be understood as existing along social lines with new typologies of violence arising from the environmental blueprints of education spaces. Understanding the particular institutional schema to universities, particularly pertaining to their community dynamics, the evolving body of UK literature aligns with global literature (Fedina et al. 2016; Weis 2015) in ascertaining HE as a 'unique social […] setting' (Garcia et al. 2012, 61) unravelling specific challenges. As newer waves of feminism address 'the deep intersections of gender […] and place' (Tsioulcas 2021) evidence on the distinct dimensions of university spaces is becoming pronounced, with the reasons for why rates are so high and why this particular context remains so hard to change being (sociologically) overlapping.

Violence to Maintain Power Norms

The distinct levels of institutionalised power circulating, and wielded by, universities (Bull and Rye 2018; NUS and 1752 Group 2018) shape GBV's pervasiveness as a symptom and outcome of institutional inequalities, cyclically arising from and producing 'entrenched cultures of sexual misconduct' (Page et al. 2019, 2).

Patterns of power are centrally defined to university cultures (Ahmed 2016), reflected in prestige values—such as academic staff 'professorial' identities, the university 'scholar', and the college sports player (Dempster 2009). Sharp power differentials exist within interactions between victims and the institution, expert-learner and supervisor-researcher relations, Ph.D.-undergraduate teaching dynamics, and demographical majorities and minorities. Differential power dynamics are observed in the 'distinct organisational structures, with specific implications for GBV: a senior layer of permanent positions, dominated by men' in leadership roles with marginalised community members found lower down in pay and authority structures, in casualised contracts and in administrative roles (Strid 2021). HE diversity and inclusion provisions are accused of 'window dressing' (Mathew 2021) on the basis that equalities projects take place against a backdrop of static institutional socioeconomic stratification, with seniority lines unmoved by such projects and remaining highly gender and class segregated.

Violence as a tool to maintain social orders and to police social hierarchies is a long-established viewpoint in feminism. When this theory is mapped onto the education space, GBV is seen as a mechanism to preserve the continuation of historical exclusion and privilege in the academy (Phipps 2020, 2018, 2015, 2017; Phipps et al. 2018; Phipps and Young 2015) and acting in backlash 'outrage masculinity' (Dhaliwal and Kelly 2020, 5) to equalities advancements in educational spaces 'women's encroachment on traditionally male environments'. GBV in universities can thus be understood as *psycho-social* phenomena, with violent behaviours manifesting around loci of (perceived) power loss, disrupted social orders, fear of change and the unknown, and concern about decreased cultural-political relevance and social ranking.

Student Economic Segregation

Economic struggle is well-evidenced as a serious problem in universities, with student campaigning groups applying the term 'cost of survival' to infer students' more pronounced struggle in the broader 'cost of living' crisis in the UK, otherwise coined by activists as the 'cost of survival' (NUS-USI 2022) in terms of students remaining in their study programmes. At present, one-third of students overall have £50 or less at the end of the month, 68% claim they can not meet the costs of their course, and 92% state finances damage their mental health, propelling the concept of a specific 'cost of learning' crisis (NUS 2022b).

Acutely impacted by austerity, inflation, and housing crises, students are characteristically positioned in needs-and-provider dynamics, with my Ph.D. observing GBV within *resource exchange*. Examining close links between localised economies, students' socioeconomic class positions, and gender orders in HE, expanding practices of sex work among students (Roberts et al. 2010, 2013; NUS 2016, 2018; Sagar et al. 2015, 2016; UCU 2019; Trueman et al 2020), in particularly precarious forms such as 'sugar baby' work and sex-for-rent/transport, are commonly undertaken to fulfil critical university life functions like food, educational materials, and meeting the economic pressures of social life. It is not unusual for students to be in gendered work with risks of violence in order to enter, and remain, in education (Turner and Phillips 2011), with most work existing secretly and/or within 'grey zone' forms of sex work, thus inhibiting data-collection and help-seeking. 'Sexual bribery' (Guschke et al. 2019, 12) recognised in the most recent UK Government VAWG strategy as a problem of serious scale in contemporary Home Office (2021, 18), widely exists between students and more powerful parties in their lives: managers, accommodation providers, local public service workers, and (wealthy) escorting clients in areas surrounding campuses, who access exchange-based, commodified intimacy from students. This 'supply and demand' opportunities are clear-cut in a market sense, with those lacking intimacy in their lives driven to student populations as the 'obvious' place to go, on the basis of their extreme economic need.

Student employment reveals a hidden, casualised but skilled economy, where an educated population seeks out flexible, high-paying work to meet the needs of their study environments, selling 'erotic capital' (Hakim 2010). Class and socioeconomics prove highly pertinent variables in multiple areas of GBV lived experience, with students in 'precarious working conditions, for example exchange students, PhD students, postdoctoral researchers, women on temporary contracts' (Strid 2021) being subject to heightened risk (of violence) and less organisational leverage to complain due to occupational secrecy and economic co-dependency, as well as higher levels of time poorness and lower degrees of community embeddedness for isolated, working students also impacting access to support networks and services.

Violence Enforcing the Gender Order

Education bears 'gender regime[s]' (Dunne et al. 2006, 3) routinely mediated in everyday life both explicitly and implicitly, representing some of the earliest and most pivotal learning of stereotypical gender roles and (hetero)sexuality performance (Butler 1990). Reaching learners at an influential point in their lives as they undertake adulthood transition, gender socialisation is pedalled across a pipeline of cultural messaging throughout the education trajectory, teaching lifelong lessons 'in gender' and expose young people to gendered trauma. Gender scripts are observed, ritualised, and transmitted in education spaces, such as sex-segregation and behavioural routines pertaining to youth market product consumption: accessory fashion, the tailoring of uniforms, manicuring pit-stops on the way to class, and collective and individual beauty grooming (Dane and Yoon 2013).

Practices considered 'rites of passage' such as courtship, virginity 'loss', and the formation of friendship groups, reveal the fundamentally *social* nature of gender and sexuality in education spaces, engaged with to outwardly communicate identity. Performing ally-ship iterates social bonds and reaffirms social connections, and is fundamentally part of repeated, affirmative expressions of gender and sexuality identities where social groups practice behaviours of 'power and intimacy…to build closed teams, and defend their privileges and positions […] strengthening power […] and defend hegemony' (Hammarén and Johansson 2014, 1) in institutional contexts. Theorised as distinct post-millennial masculinities in education spaces, this offers explanatory insight into lad cultures as 'expressions of masculine heterosexism' (O'Callaghan 2017, 1), performing misogyny towards as a method of affirmative communication towards each other and the wider community.

Both literature on school and university spaces highlight intra-gender sexisms and the cross-gender regulation of femininity and masculinity in their communities, with both males and females punishing 'transgressions across the boundaries of accepted gender behaviour' (Dunne et al. 2006, 3) to maintain or reassemble a shared 'public imagination' (Cohen 1987, 801) of social order and to punish behaviours considered 'destabilising' (Longstaff 2019, 224) to social orders. Contemporary analyses posit how power is multidirectional and forms the foundations upholding structural hegemonies, whereby marginalised groups both are subject to, and participate in, oppressed and oppressor realities. Women are 'key' in 'spreading [...] violent masculinity'. To 'justice to the full picture' in education, it must be recognised there are 'many women who have initiated, supported and incited' (ODIHR 2014, 49) GBV.

The sharp power differentials and social privilege hierarchies mean universities are 'defined by inclusion and exclusion' (Phipps and Smith 2012, 10) whereby community members employ reward and penalising tactics towards students' convergence and divergence to social stratification orders (Brickell 2010, 597) including gender norms. Practicing behaviours of inclusion/ostracisation, safety/bullying, embellishing/verbal abuse, agency/peer pressure, and access/deprivation (to the likes of tools, resources, play, and space), gender, class, and sexuality presentations are routinely regulated by peers and staff alike. Exposing learners to commentary and policies pertaining to the likes of physical contact between students and skirt length 'social pressures and surveillance of bodies, clothing and appearance' (Phipps and Smith 2012, 7), GBV in education literature has been leading in uncovering the centrality of inter-gendered violence in schools. This includes the 'telling off' of girls by female teachers and peers to promote obedient femininity and the use of humiliation by male peers and teachers to 'toughen' (Dunne et al. 2006, 8) boys into adulthood initiation and as a dominance performance over younger and lower-class males.

Universities as 'Island' Living

Bolstering the case for a specialist focus, this Ph.D. research found there are specific characteristics to GBV in the education context, offering innovations to the field relating to how GBV in universities presents unique manifestations and subsequently, unique challenges to combat (Humphreys and Towl 2021). However, the existing body of GBV in education research arguably has gaps in fully grasping how GBV manifests in universities, most pertinently how the community structures are uniquely enabling. Student participants' likening of universities to a 'container' or 'bubble' and describing it as 'a world of its own' and 'out in the sticks' revealed crossovers between GBV in rural, remote, and island residential life in the UK with GBV in the education sector, provoking similar kinds of environmental risks and anxieties for victims/survivors. The social networks of education contexts are distinct in that they are tight-knit and multiplex, hosting students' academic, economic, occupational, social, and political life together, giving rise to unique challenges shaping how GBV socially functions in university communities and how university social structures affect disclosures. Educational institutions are structurally interconnected and secluded, making surveillance, targeting, and bullying behaviours particularly possible.

Particular forms of GBV are prevalent on university campuses, with stalking being particularly flagged by participants, facilitated by the tight-knit nature of campus life. In one interview, 'stalking-by-proxy' was described as characteristic of university(-style) environments. This refers to a continuum of behaviours where community members branching out from the original perpetrator(s) can be avertedly and inadvertently involved with offending, such as stalking on someone's behalf to extend the 'eyes and ears' of the abuser(s). With community news-sharing being an important feature of student bonding through the (re)affirmation of mutual interests, information-divulging about community members in daily 'chit-chat' exchanges in university buildings can also work in favour of perpetrators: 'Say you go to the cinema here […] someone who knows of you or who knows your perpetrator may see you and innocuously says to others "oh, I saw Jane, she was wearing x" […] then Jane gets a text message saying "you have got a nice outfit on"[…] it's that really close community that is very difficult for a survivor' (Rural and Remote Scotland I). Stalking behaviours are furthermore, facilitated by the transience, hypermobility, and immersion of campus activity where the traffic and transit of everyday university life can shield and envelope patterns of individual, illegal behaviour such as obsessive and voyeristic watching and following. Students describe a bustling, rushed marketplace-like social life with a constant 'revolving door' effect of attendees: exchange students, visiting students and staff, staff on flexible working hours, international populations, mixed offline and online study programmes, variant gradients of part-time study, different programme start and end dates, drop-outs, and clearing programmes. Perpetrators can 'dip-in' to a student population without further accountability. Collecting evidence can be unusually time-sensitive and inaccessible in an environment of high turnover, reported by students as a having 'needle in a haystack' effect, compounded by the multidirectional nature of university life splitting students' attention and hampering knowledge-acquisition of GBV in the community: 'People can miss these things at the start of term […] or they arrive late. Students might be coming just for a semester and if they're coming from abroad, and it needs to be reiterated that there is a zero-tolerance policy towards sexual assault during the year' (Fife and NE Scotland FG).

The impacts of GBV on the emotional wellbeing and social life of victims/survivors are significant, creating long-term changes to their relationship with university-associated spaces, and positioning them in states of psychological hypervigilance affecting study concentration and mental health, as well as causing deliberate social isolation from campus life. The tight-knit environment of university campuses makes GBV, in particular stalking, a more inescapable experience as the victim/survivor is tied to the location in order to complete their studies, or even can be contractually obliged if they are a visa-holding and/or scholarship-funded student: 'Many voluntarily go in to house arrest, if they go out they will see their perpetrator and their friends and it's really difficult for them to predict and to avoid. You could change the pub you go in to but there's not that much of a choice' (Rural and Remote I).

The tangled structures of university environments furthermore, make *disclosure* often a high-risk, low-reward calculation, where confidentiality management is demanding and victims/survivors are forced to make multipronged considerations relating to housing, finances, studies, friendship circles, and employment when deciding to report and/or seek out advice and safety measures. Coming forward is often risky for victims/survivors because of the physically and socially tight-knit nature of student living and working. Access to the protections of confidentiality policies are important equality issues in universities, as data protection is often implicated by the structures of its community: 'for a survivor to come forward for support or because they have decided they are going to the police […] that can't be kept confidential in the same way that it can be in a larger population because as soon as the police starts investigating that, as soon as the social worker knocks on the door, the whole community knows […] This really impacts disclosures and the ramifications of disclosure […] it's nearly impossible to keep that secret in island [-like] life' (Rural and Remote I). Information transmission can have a wildfire effect, impacting a sense of much-needed dignity and control when victimisation has occurred: 'that's a big concern in rural communities, that if you tell one person, then everyone is going to know. You have to be aware of that all the time' (Rural and Remote Interview). Pertaining to the unique social dynamics of universities, participants describe experiences of 'trial by community' where staff and students exchange opinions about the events, and their perceptions of, local GBV cases. Creating true/false and guilty/innocent 'verdicts' is common before internal procedures have even reached their conclusions, and regardless of whether an official report of GBV is submitted by the victim. A double-bind is often experienced by victims/survivors, where community judgement reverberates and heightens in response to the submission of a formal complaint, the news of which quickly dissipates in the close-knit environment. Furthermore, attrition of civil cases in universities is poor, meaning the accused party is more likely to continue being and/or return to the university environment post-completion. However, universities often do not undertake interventions until the process is committed to: 'I know people who have experienced racist incidences in their flats [halls of residence], but they weren't able to move away from their flat'. Students shared that a case is not framed as having 'truth to it' and investigative potential until it has gone through formal reporting. Victims often have to lodge an official breach of student conduct complaint in order to access university responses, instigate interventions: 'if it is really true, why does she not complain?' (BAME I), and increase their case legitimacy within the community but paradoxically, reporting is widely experienced to increase their victims' vulnerability to secondary forms of violence, including accusations of lying from peers.

Interviews focused on the rural and remote parts of Scotland presented a picture that accurately illustrated GBV on campus, with many intriguing similarities emerged between GBV in educational environments and GBV in other circular communities. Disclosures can 'split' entire communities, 'If someone makes an accusation, whole communities can split according to family lines and allegiances with people. So there are the cultural issues on top of the practical [...] There's all sorts of implications for coming forward [...] that make people really visible as a survivor' (Rural and Remote Interview) and confidentiality and safety prove difficult to manage due to the fast transmission of information occurring in an environment where the community intimately inhabit the same spaces. Subsequently, deracination is a common victimisation response such as dropping out, moving house, switching course, changing friendship circles, changing appearance, and changing schedule and movements. Similar to the protective measures students often take to try and prevent GBV, student victims/survivors undertake burdens of 'safety work' (Kelly 1987; Vera-Gray 2018; Vera-Grey and Kelly 2020) to protect themselves from secondary backlash following on from GBV, taking numerous parties into consideration including the perpetrator, their friends, and community members with knowledge of the assault(s). The 'mental load' of secondary forms of violence, inclusive of the work of 'preventing' GBV and controlling narratives about incidences, involves victims/survivors making delicate calculations about who to turn to in order to maximise confidentiality and enhance safety: 'there is a lot of fear when it comes to speaking to other students about something that has happened and to you on campus and often people don't want to do that because what if it's a student that you know' (Glasgow FG), compounded by the realities that GBV is most likely to be perpetrated by people known to the victim/survivor, therefore arising from within their own social networks: 'the nature of sexual violence is that it is often someone you know [...] in a small community [...] can sometimes make it harder to find someone to talk to' (Rural and Remote IB).

Formal and informal disclosure proves overlapping in compacted social environments, and disclosure can be avoided by victims/survivors to deliberately avoid further personal trauma following on from the original incident(s): 'if someone has come forward with an allegation on somebody, if they continue to see that person on a daily basis on campus while their complaint is being dealt with, how retraumatising is that? [...] I know for myself and for other women who have been to university and have had that experience having to see their abuser every day, being in lectures with them and stuff like that. You can't escape them which adds to the trauma and the turmoil' (Disability FG). Confidentiality is a core issue in universities because of the close friendships staff can form with one another *and* across student boundaries through working in a village-like environment in academic departments and Students' Unions (SUs) where students are known as 'regulars' and are employed in university functions: '[staff have] got to be really careful about how people access the service, that they are comfortable [...] my identity is out there [...] As a worker, you have to be OK that you are visible. I am not going to go to Tesco at 10 pm at night like some social workers or doctors do [...] to really reiterate to service users that I will absolutely not share anything'. The tight-knit campus environment can squash disclosures, with many students describing university life as socially bustling with limited space and time to privately reach out for help. This has been exacerbated by students returning to family houses being in COVID-19 lockdown conditions in student housing and increasing work from home practices during the pandemic: 'Social workers and multi-agency partners are very worried about what is going to be revealed once lockdown lifts [...] saying that stuff out loud in your bedroom makes it part of home life [...] When we are speaking to people under lockdown, they are not wanting to go in-depth [...] The lockdown has also caused older triggers to re-emerge' (Rural and Remote I).

Due to the heavy focus on the social aspects of university life, many victims/survivors do not come forward because of the possibility of colleagues and friends becoming divided over practicing belief towards accounts. Cultural and peer pressures to have the 'student experience' often manifests as pressure for community members to maintain tight-knit community groups throughout their study period. The breakdown of friendship groups following GBV cases can be seen as nuisance interpersonal 'disputes' by peers, with community conflict being reported by participants to be often blamed on disclosing parties. Furthermore, victims/survivors openly sharing can increase unwanted attention and scrutiny at a time where victims/survivors are often compelled to do a 'disappearing act' to recover. When students experience GBV, it is common for them to significantly alter their lives to avoid the perpetrator(s) and the perpetrators' networks. One female Ph.D. participant shared that they are presently researching how and when to move from their city and university and permanently delete their social media profiles to escape their abusive ex-partner in the department. Similarly, a male student disclosed that he chose to 'start anew' as a response to his abusive relationship, where he: 'ended up leaving Dundee to come to Edinburgh to feel safer' (Male IF). Numerous participants reported that they fled their homes: 'That led to me contacting my RA and getting moved out of the halls' (Disability FG). Self-displacement is a common trauma response to GBV to regain (a sense of) control and safety and can include switching accommodation, changing tutorial classes, taking an interruption of studies, switching degree programmes, or leaving an institution altogether: 'Every young person – say, under 25 – who had been assaulted on the island were just so relieved to leave the island [...] to be free of the community scrutiny[...] They feel like their every move was being watched and their trauma response was that they just felt they couldn't stay in this community[...] sometimes, it's the case that someone escapes [...] it's been a kind of, run away' (Rural and Remote I).

The secondary effects of GBV among student populations are wide-reaching and touch every facet of their life, including exam preparation, finances, housing, and physical health. Participants discussed how university policies often do not recognise this breadth of impact, seeing such areas as falling within the private lives of students. Financial strain and the close physical proximity of (abusive) partners are common burdens for students, especially at the start and end of study programmes: 'I think it [policy and practice] also needs to speak about people's financial situations because I think at times, women are unable to leave because they can not sustain themselves financially [...] because someone could be a student but they rely on their boyfriend "if I leave him, I don't have anywhere to stay"' (BAME I).

Conclusion: Expanding Understandings of Victimisation

The socio-structures of localised contexts shape not only how GBV manifests but, just as importantly, how disclosures are received. Linking to prior discussion on island-like features, universities possess overlapping, multi-compartment social environments which indeed enable the advancement of the study of GBV in general but in particular, how secondary victimisation (SV) works.

One of the key contributions of the GBV concept is its broadening out of 'victimisation parameters' to be inclusive of primary and secondary forms, as well as theorising timelines of victimisation in their entirety—where SV has been traditionally theorised as a latter after-event to GBV and consequence of reporting, SV also operates in an *anticipatory* manner whereby victims do not disclose for *fear of* SV. The expansion of 'victimisation parameters' allows for experiences orbiting or 'before, during and after' primary perpetration to be theoretically integrated.

The UK has a rich body of criminological and socio-legal literature on the ways that legal systems in particular handle GBV complaints and replicate feelings of victimisation and trauma following on from the original incident(s). The most prominent term is 'secondary victimisation' (SV) (Williams 1984), referring to the processes and attitudes in legal systems that stereotype, degrade and alienate victims/survivors, known as 'retraumatisation' (1984, 67) although used interchangeably with terms like 'judicial rape' (Lees 1997), being 'raped again' (Temkin 2002), the 'second assault' or 'second rape' (Williams and Holmes 1981). Outside of criminology and law, HE research is addressing institutional and community responses to GBV *as* forms of SV, bridging analyses of the criminal justice system (CJS) to contexts outside of the legal arena. Transferring the concept of SV to the education context with terms like 'institutional betrayal' (Smith and Freyd 2014) GBV is being increasingly researched as being 'on trial' (Smith 2021) across both criminal settings and civic life.

The re-victimisation of survivors is thus multipronged, stemming from *community* (including collegial, peer, interpersonal, and familial) and *authority* responses, revealing lived experience overlaps pertaining to victim-blaming, shaming behaviours, stigmatising comments, isolation and ostracisation, judgement, dismissal, stigma, disbelief, and bullying, in addition to negative impacts on the critical functions of victims' lives such as job retention, housing insecurity, and mental health, conceptualising these as fundamental *to* the violence itself.

'Institutional betrayal' refers to the connection between increased post-traumatic symptoms and the trauma experienced from agents of (community and institutional) authority in victims/survivors' lives and within disclosure pipelines. The term is specifically 'applied to HEIs [higher education institutions]' and arises from, and within, the dependence relationship student victims/survivors possess with their universities in areas 'tied to their survival and/or upward mobility, such as education […] financial (e.g., graduate worker income, scholarship, financial aid) or preventing sexual violence from continuing' (Lorenz et al. 2022). 'Betrayal trauma' occurs when victims/survivors are unable to detach from the sites of abuses due to dependencies for survival. Victims therefore engage in intensive emotional and social self-regulation (Freyd and Birrell 2013) to manage such entanglements, causing 'inwards' destruction of repressing personal needs and emotions, and prolongs exposure to harm in ways multiplying risk. The recent integration of SV theorisation into the GBV in education field has exposed how 'individuals, rather than organisations' have been the 'focus in discussions of violence [...] regarding rape at [...] university'. Yet, feminist re-readings of organisation studies argue for problematisation to view institutions as active agents 'as a participant' in the trauma of GBV, and even can constitute a 'violent agency' in cases (Harris 2013, 568).

Feminist institutional analyses find that the distinct structures of universities make GBV inherently 'difficult to report' (Phipps and Smith 2012: 2), with their operational constituent parts deeply interlocking. The imbricated 'circular' or 'closed circuit' structure of universities means that perpetrators, their influence, and their allies are *embedded* into victims' lives, with abusers and/or their supporters existing even within equality and diversity functions themselves, causing GBV reports to be delayed, shelved, or retracted.

Lived experience of SV is described as having a suffocating or choking effect, where victims experience 'entrapment' webs (Peled et al. 2000) in their communities. Compounding the coercive elements of GBV, (student) victims/survivors are psychologically and literally stuck in an 'enclosure' of their own (re)victimisation. Reducing disclosure confidence, complicating confidentiality management, and increasing retaliation possibilities, the panoptical community effects make challenging GBV 'low-reward' in universities, with community intrusion and scrutiny having a paralysing effect on victim empowerment.

Discussion Questions

- Why should the field use the concept of GBV over others, such as a narrowed focus on domestic violence or sexual violence?
- What are the barriers or 'inhibitors' to effective intervention?
- What are the imperatives for effectively tackling GBV in universities: ethical, human rights, economic—what else?
- How is GBV among students an issue of equal education access?
- How can we understand this content with an intersectional lens?
- What factors mean that certain GBV forms disproportionately affect students?

Note

1. Nearly all domestic and global organisations who work on GBV promote this statistical reference. It has since formed the most commonly pushed, well-known data about GBV. Consequently this data 'one-liner' has played a significant cultural role in shaping public perceptions about GBV rates.

Bibliography

Addington, C., Sundari, A., Baars, V., Day, K., Domoney-Lyttle, Z., Downes, J., Gillies, J., Mabrouk, M., Marlow, E., McGookin, N. and McMillan, L. 2021. *Eradicating sexual violence in tertiary education: A report from UCU's sexual violence task group.* Universities & Colleges Union (UCU). https://www.ucu.org.uk/media/12269/UCU-sexual-violence-task-group-report-20211220/pdf/UCU_sexual_violence_task_group_report_20211220.pdf.

Ahmed, S. 2016. *Living a feminist life.* Duke University Press.

Anitha, S. and Lewis, R. 2018. *Gender based violence in university communities: Policy, prevention and educational initiatives.* Bristol University Press.

Anyadike-Danes, N., Reynolds, M., Armour, C. and Lagdon, S. 2022. *Unwanted and non-consensual sexual experiences reported by university students in Northern Ireland.* Ulster University. https://pure.ulster.ac.uk/en/publications/unwanted-and-non-consensual-sexual-experiences-reported-by-univer.

Barn, R. and Powers, R. A. 2021. Rape myth acceptance in contemporary times: A comparative study of university students in India and the United Kingdom. *Journal of Interpersonal Violence, 36*(7–8), pp. 3514–3535.

Beech, D. 2018, 8 March. *#TimesUp on sexual harassment in higher education: #PressforProgress on #IWD2018.* Higher Education Policy Institute. https://www.hepi.ac.uk/2018/03/08/timesup-sexual-harassment-higher-education-pressforprogress-iwd2018/.

Beyene, A. S., Chojenta, C., Roba, H. S., Melka, A. S. and Loxton, D. 2019. Gender-based violence among female youths in educational institutions of sub-Saharan Africa: A systematic review and meta-analysis. *Systematic Reviews, 8*(1), pp. 1–14.

Bowes, H. and Fileborn, B. 2022. Geographies of Gender-Based Violence: A Multi-Disciplinary Perspective. Bristol: Bristol University Press.

Brickell, C. 2010. Sex, space and scripts: Negotiating homoeroticism in history. *Social & Cultural Geography, 11*(6), pp. 597–613.

Brook, 2019. *Press Release: Our new research on sexual harassment and violence at UK universities.* Brook Charity. https://www.brook.org.uk/press-releases/sexual-violence-and-harassment-remains-rife-in-universities-according-to-ne.

Buchbinder, E. and Eisikovits, Z. 2003. Battered women's entrapment in shame: A phenomenological study. *American Journal of Orthopsychiatry, 73*(4), pp. 355–366.

Bull, A. and Rye, R. 2018. *Silencing students: Institutional responses to staff sexual misconduct in higher education.* Portsmouth Research Portal.

Butler, J. 1990. *Gender trouble: Feminism and the subversion of identity.* Routledge.

Cohen, S. 1987. *Folk devils and moral panics.* Routledge.

Copenhaver, S. and Grauerholz, E., 1991. Sexual victimization among sorority women: Exploring the link between sexual violence and institutional practices. *Sex Roles, 24*, pp. 31–41.

Crelinsten, R. 2022, 28 February. Online gender-based violence is endemic: It should be considered a form of terrorism. *Centre for International Governance Innovation.* https://www.cigionline.org/articles/online-gender-based-violence-is-endemic-it-should-be-considered-a-form-of-terrorism/.

Culture Shift. 2020. *Exceeding expectations.* Culture Shift. https://f.hubspotusercontent00.net/hubfs/2138509/CS%20White%20Paper%20Final.pdf.

Culture Shift. 2022. *Exceeding expectations 2.0.* Culture Shift. https://insight.culture-shift.co.uk/higher-education/exceeding-expectations-to-tackle-harassment-and-sexual-misconduct-in-he_

Dane, J. and Yoon, H. 2013. Lynx: The challenges of lad culture. In *The advertising handbook* (pp. 103–110). Routledge.

Dempster, S. 2009. Having the balls, having it all? Sport and constructions of undergraduate laddishness. *Gender and Education, 21*(5), pp. 481–500.

Dey, A. 2020. *North-South feminist dialogue: Sexual and gender based violence in higher education-report.* 1752 Group. https://1752group.files.wordpress.com/2021/09/8583a-nsfd-handbook-final-23july-2.pdf.

Dhaliwal, D. S. and Kelly, L. 2020. *The links between radicalisation and violence against women and girls*. London Metropolitan University.

Dunne, M., Humphreys, S. and Leach, F. 2006. Gender violence in schools in the developing world. *Gender and Education, 18*(1), pp. 75–98.

EmilyTest. 2021a. *Gender-Based Violence (GBV) charter for universities and colleges*. EmilyTest. http://emilytest.co.uk/gbvcharter/.

EmilyTest. 2021b. *Research report*. EmilyTest. http://emilytest.co.uk/gbvcharter/

Fedina, L., Holmes, J. L. and Backes, B. 2016. How prevalent is campus sexual assault in the United States. *National Institute of Justice, 277*, pp. 26–30.

Fileborn, B. and Loney-Howes, R. eds. 2019. *# MeToo and the politics of social change*. Springer Nature.

Frederick, A., Daniels, H. A., Grineski, S. E. and Collins, T. W. 2020. 'I've never felt like that inhibits anything': The gendered frameworks of Hispanic women college students in a STEM program. *Gender and Education, 32*(5), pp. 646–663.

Freyd, J. J. & Birrell, P. J. 2013. *Blind to betrayal*. Wiley.

Garcia, C. M., Lechner, K. E., Frerich, E. A., Lust, K. A. and Eisenberg, M. E. 2012. Preventing sexual violence instead of just responding to it: Students' perceptions of sexual violence resources on campus. *Journal of Forensic Nursing, 8*(2), pp. 61–71.

Glasgow Caledonian University. 2019. *Erase the Grey*. GCU. https://www.gcu.ac.uk/aboutgcu/commongood/erasethegrey.

Glitch, 2022. *The UK's new online safety law must protect women and girls from online abuse*. Change.Org. https://www.change.org/p/nadinedorries-the-uk-s-new-online-safety-law-must-protect-women-girls-from-online-abuse.

Guschke, B. L., Busse, K., Khalid, F., Muhr, S. L., and Just, S. N. 2019. Sexual harassment in higher education—Experiences and perceptions among students at a Danish University. *Kvinder, Køn & Forskning, 28*(1–2), pp. 11–30.

Hakim, C., 2010. Erotic capital. *European Sociological Review, 26*(5), pp. 499–518.

Hall, M., Hearn, J. and Lewis, R. 2022. "Upskirting," homosociality, and craft man ship: A thematic analysis of perpetrator and viewer interactions. *Violence Against Women, 28*(2), pp. 532–550.

Hamilton, M. 2021, 22 November. Violent crimes against women gets the same status as terrorist attacks. *The Times*. https://www.thetimes.co.uk/article/violent-crime-against-women-gets-the-same-status-as-terrorist-attacks-5tp2fn3pv.

Hammarén, N. and Johansson, T., 2014. Homosociality: In between power and intimacy. *Sage Open, 4*(1), p. 2158244013518057.

Harris, K. L. 2013. Show them a good time: Organizing the intersections of sexual violence. *Management Communication Quarterly, 27*(4), pp. 568–595.

Home Office (2021) Violence Against Women and Girls (VAWG) strategy 2021 to 2024: call for evidence. Available at: https://www.gov.uk/government/consultations/violence-against-women-and-girls-vawg-call-for-evidence/violence-against-women-and-girls-vawg-strategy-2021-2024-call-for-evidence.

HM Government. 2021. *The end-to-end rape review report*. House of Commons.

Holland, K. J. and Cortina, L. M. 2017. "It happens to girls all the time": Examining sexual assault survivors' reasons for not using campus supports. *American Journal of Community Psychology, 59*(1–2), pp. 50–64.

Humphreys, C. J. and Towl, G. J. 2020. *Addressing student sexual violence in higher education: A good practice guide*. Emerald Group Publishing.

Humphreys, C. J. and Towl, G. J. 2021. *How to do more than the bare minimum on sexual harassment and sexual misconduct*. Available at: https://wonkhe.com/blogs/how-to-do-more-than-the-bare-minimum-on-harassment-and-sexual-misconuct/.

Humprheys, C. & Towl, G., 2022. *Stopping gender based violence in higher education: Policy, practice and partnerships*. Routledge.

Jeffries, M. 2020. 'Is it okay to go out on the pull without it being nasty?': Lads' performance of lad culture. *Gender and Education, 32*(7), pp. 908–925. ISSN 0954-0253.

Jones, C., Smith, O., Skinner, T., Gangoli, G. and Rachel, F., 2020. *Overview and analysis of research studies on gender-based violence among UK University students and staff*. Durham University.

Jordan, A., Anitha, S., Jameson, J. and Davy, Z. 2022. Hierarchies of masculinity and lad culture on campus: Bad guys, good guys and complicit men. *Men and Masculinities*, p. 1097184X211064321.

Jordan, C. E., Combs, J. L. and Smith, G. T. 2014. An exploration of sexual victimization and academic performance among college women. *Trauma, Violence, & Abuse*, *15*(3), pp. 191–200.

Kelly, L. 1987. The continuum of sexual violence. *Women, Violence and Social Control*, pp. 46–60.

Korkodeilou, J., 2016. Stalking victims, victims of sexual violence and criminal justice system responses: Is there a difference or just 'business as usual'? *British Journal of Criminology*, *56*(2), pp. 256–273.

Koss, M. P., Swartout, K. M., Lopez, E. C., Lamade, R. V., Anderson, E. J., Brennan, C. L. and Prentky, R. A. 2022. The scope of rape victimization and perpetration among national samples of college students across 30 years. *Journal of Interpersonal Violence*, *37*(1–2), pp. NP25–NP47.

Lawthon, J. 2021 20 May. Sexual assault claims 'mishandled' by universities. *BBC News*. https://www.bbc.co.uk/news/uk-wales-57174251.

Lees. 1997. Ruling passions. sexual violence, reputation and the law. Buckingham: Open University Press.

Lewis, R. 2018. Approaches to tackling gender based violence in universities. *Actes du colloque international*, pp. 53–65.

Lewis, J. 2022. *House of Commons library briefing paper no. 9438: Sexual harassment and violence in further and higher education*. House of Commons.

Lewis, R., Marine, S. and Kenney, K. 2018. 'I get together with my friends and try to change it'. Young feminist students resist 'laddism','rape culture'and 'everyday sexism. *Journal of Gender Studies*, *27*(1), pp. 56–72.

List, K. 2017. *Gender-based violence against female students in European university settings*. Cambridge University Press.

Long, R. and Hubble, S. 2020. *Sexual harassment in education*. HM Government.

Long, R., Hubble, S. and Lewis, J. 2012. *Sexual harrassment in Education: Briefing paper*. House of Commons.

Longstaff, G. 2019. Masculinity and homoeroticism. In *Routledge international handbook of masculinity studies* (pp. 223–232). Routledge.

Lorenz, K., Hayes, R. and Jacobsen, C. 2022. "Title IX Isn't for You, It's for the University": Sexual violence survivors' experiences of institutional betrayal in Title IX investigations. CrimRxiv.

Mahlori, X. F., Byrne, D. C. and Mabude, L. A. 2018. Perceptions of gender-based violence among university staff: Interim results. *Sage Open*, *8*(3), p. 2158244018800163.

Makhene, A., 2022. Gender-based violence in higher education: An integrative review. *Open Journal of Social Sciences*, *10*(3), pp. 234–247.

Mathew, R. C. 2021. *The impact of Athena Swan accreditation on the lived experiences of early- and mid-career researchers: A qualitative study of an Athena Swan gold award-holding department*. University of York.

Mouffe, C. 2013. Feminism, citizenship, and radical democratic politics. In *Feminists theorize the political* (pp. 387–402). Routledge.

Murray, J. 2021, 17 May. Universities are failing to tackle rape culture on campus, students say. *The Guardian*. https://www.theguardian.com/world/2021/may/16/universities-rape-culture-on-campus-students-protest.

Mutinta, G. 2022. Gender-based violence among female students and implicatons for health intervention programmes in public universities in Eastern Cape, South Africa. *Cogent Social Sciences, 8*(1), p. 2079212.

National Union of Students. 2010. *Hidden Marks: A study of women students' experiences of harassment, stalking, violence and sexual assault*. It Stops Now. https://itstopsnow.org/sites/default/files/2018-02/Hidden%20Marks-A%20study%20of%20women%20students%27%20experiences%20of%20harassment%2C%20stalking%2C%20violence%20%26%20sexual%20assault%20%28NUS%29.pdf.

National Union of Students. 2016. *Student sex workers' survey*. NUS Connect. https://www.nusconnect.org.uk/articles/student-sex-worker-s-survey-09b3.

National Union of Students. 2018, 1 February. *Student sex worker briefing*. NUS Connect. https://www.nusconnect.org.uk/resources/student-sex-worker-briefing-2018.

National Union of Students. 2022a, 26 January. *Build trust not silence*. NUS. https://www.nus.org.uk/articles/build-trust-not-silence-let-s-end-the-use-of-ndas-for-sexual-violence.

National Union of Students. 2022b, 5 September. NUS Scotland. https://www.nus-scotland.org.uk/nus_scotland_sets_out_cost_of_living_demands.

National Union of Students & 1752 Group. 2018. *Power in the academy: Staff sexual misconduct in UK higher education*. NUS Connect. https://www.nusconnect.org.uk/articles/our-report-into-staff-student-sexual-misconduct.

National Union of Students Northern Ireland. 2022. *NUS-USI launches cost of survival campaign*. NUS-USI. https://www.nus-usi.org/nus_usi_launches_cost_of_survival_campaign.

O'Callaghan, C. 2017. A Wilde Scoundrel: Villainy and 'Lad Culture' in the filmic afterlives of Dorian Gray. In *Neo-Victorian Villains* (pp. 252–268). Brill.

Office for Democratic Institutions and Human Rights. 2014. *Preventing terrorism and countering violent extremism and radicalization that lead to terrorism: A community-policing approach*. ODIHR.

Office for National Statistics. 2018. *Women most at risk of experiencing partner abuse in England and Wales: Years ending March 2015 to March 2017*. ONS. https://www.ons.gov.uk/peoplepopulationandcommunity/crimeandjustice/articles/womenmostatriskofexperiencingpartnerabuseinenglandandwales/yearsendingmarch2015to2017.

Office for National Statistics. 2020. *Domestic abuse victim characteristics, England and Wales: Year ending March 2020*. ONS. https://www.ons.gov.uk/peoplepopulationandcommunity/crimeandjustice/articles/domesticabusevictimcharacteristicsenglandandwales/yearendingmarch2020.

Our Streets Now. 2022. *Student Safety Report*. OSN. https://ca21b2f8-c257-46b8-9565-f7ce019da093.usrfiles.com/ugd/ca21b2_d3b87691d6b44a30a592a9579b76f501.pdf.

Page, T., Bull, A. and Chapman, E. 2019. Making power visible: "Slow activism" to address staff sexual misconduct in higher education. *Violence Against Women, 25*(11), pp. 1309–1330.

Patra, P., Prakash, J., Patra, B. and Khanna, P. 2018. Intimate partner violence: Wounds are deeper. *Indian Journal of Psychiatry, 60*(4), p. 494.

Peled, E., Eisikovits, Z., Enosh, G. and Winstok, Z., 2000. Choice and empowerment for battered women who stay: Toward a constructivist model. *Social work, 45*(1), pp. 9–25.

Perkins, W. and Warner, J. 2017. *Sexual violence response and prevention: Studies of campus policies and practices*. Taylor Francis.

Phipps, A. 2015. *Sexism and violence in the neoliberal university*. Phipps Space. https://phipps.space/2015/12/02/sexism-and-violence/.

Phipps, A., Ringrose, J., Renold, E. and Jackson, C. 2018. Rape culture, lad culture and everyday sexism: Researching, conceptualizing and politicizing new mediations of gender and sexual violence. *Journal of Gender Studies, 27*(1), 1–8.

Phipps, A. 2017. (Re) theorising laddish masculinities in higher education. *Gender and Education, 29*(7), pp. 815–830.

Phipps, A. 2018. 'Lad culture' and sexual violence against students. In *The Routledge handbook of gender and violence* (pp. 171–182). Routledge.

Phipps, A. 2020. *Me, not you: The trouble with mainstream feminism*. Manchester University Press.

Phipps, A. and Smith, G. 2012. Violence against women students in the UK: Time to take action. *Gender and Education*, *24*(4), (pp. 357–373).

Phipps, A. and Young, I. 2015. Neoliberalisation and 'lad cultures' in higher education. *Sociology*, 49(2), pp. 305–322.

Public Health Scotland. 2021, 1 January. *Gender based violence.* Health Topics—Public Health Scotland. http://www.healthscotland.scot/health-topics/gender-based-violence.

Rakovec-Felser, Z. 2014. Domestic violence and abuse in intimate relationship from public health perspective. *Health Psychology Research*, *2*(3).

Revolt Sexual Assault & The Student Room. 2018. *National consultation into the sexual assault and harassment experienced or witnessed by students and graduates from universities across the UK*. Revolt Sexual Assualt. https://revoltsexualassault.com/research/.

Roberts, R., Jones, A. and Sanders, T. 2013. Students and sex work in the UK: Providers and purchasers. *Sex Education*, *13*(3), pp. 349–363.

Roberts, R., Sanders, T., Myers, E. and Smith, D. 2010. Participation in sex work: Students' views. *Sex Education*, *10*(2), pp. 145–156.

Russo, N.F. and Pirlott, A. 2006. Gender-based violence: Concepts, methods, and findings. *Annals of the New York Academy of Sciences*, *1087*(1), pp. 178–205.

Sagar, T., Jones, D., Symons, K., Bowring, J. and Roberts, R. 2015. Student participation in the sex industry: Higher education responses and staff experiences and perceptions. *Journal of Higher Education Policy and Management*, *37*(4), pp. 400–412.

Sagar, T., Jones, D., Symons, K., Tyrie, J. and Roberts, R. 2016. Student involvement in the UK sex industry: Motivations and experiences. *The British Journal of Sociology*, *67*(4), pp. 697–718.

Sani, A. I. and Pereira, D. 2020. Mothers as victims of intimate partner violence: The decision to leave or stay and resilience-oriented intervention. *Social Sciences*, *9*(10), p. 174.

Scheffer Lindgren, M. and Renck, B. 2008. Intimate partner violence and the leaving process: Interviews with abused women. *International Journal of Qualitative Studies on Health and Well-Being*, *3*(2), pp. 113–124.

Sivertsen, B., Nielsen, M. B., Madsen, I. E., Knapstad, M., Lønning, K. J. and Hysing, M. 2019. Sexual harassment and assault among university students in Norway: A cross-sectional prevalence study. *BMJ Open*, *9*(6), p. e026993.

Smith, C. P. and Freyd, J. J. 2014. Institutional betrayal. *American Psychologist*, *69*(6), p. 575.

Smith, O. 2021. Cultural scaffolding and the long view of rape trials. In *Sexual violence on trial* (pp. 241–253). Routledge.

Spearman, K.J., Hardesty, J.L. and Campbell, J. 2022. Post-separation abuse: A concept analysis. *Journal of advanced nursing*.

Spratt, V. 2021. *Toxic environments*. Refinery 29. https://www.refinery29.com/en-gb/2021/10/10709360/sexual-assault-at-universities-uk.

Strid, S. 2021, 21 May. *On the importance of addressing gender-based violence in universities and research organisations*. UniSafe. https://unisafe-gbv.eu/blog/on-the-importance-of-addressing-gender-based-violence-in-universities-and-research-organisations/.

Temkin, J. 2002. *Rape and the legal process*. Sweet & Maxwell.

Tidman, Z. 2022, 9 May. Students 'failed' over 'crisis' of sexual assaults at universities amid calls for tougher action. *The Independent*. https://www.independent.co.uk/news/education/education-news/sexual-assault-domestic-abuse-universities-b1971254.html

Trueman, G., Hagelberg, S. and Sanders, T. 2020. *Student sex work toolkit for staff in higher education*. University of Leicester.

Tsioulcas, A. 2021. *Trailblazing author, critic and activist bell hooks has died at age 69.* The NRP Group. https://www.npr.org/2021/12/15/1064509418/bell-hooks-feminist-author-critic-activist-died?t=1660042887744.

Turner, K. and Phillips, O. 2011, 14 December. *Students turning to prostitution to fund studies.* BBC News. https://www.bbc.co.uk/news/education-16157522.

United Nations. 1993. *Declaration on the elimination of violence against women*. UN General Assembly.

UN Women. 2018. *Guidance note on campus violence prevention and response.* United Nations. https://www.unwomen.org/en/digital-library/publications/2019/02/guidance-note-on-campus-violence-prevention-and-response.

Universities & Colleges Union. 2019, 7 June. *Sex workers and education briefing.* UCU. https://www.ucu.org.uk/media/10080/Sex-workers-and-education-briefing-Feb-19/pdf/Sex_workers_and_education_briefing.pdf.

Universities UK. 2018. *Changing the culture: One year on—An assessment of strategies to tackle sexual misconduct, hate crime and harassment affecting university students.* UUK. https://www.universitiesuk.ac.uk/policy-and-analysis/reports/Pages/changing-the-culture-one-year-on.aspx.

Vera-Gray, F. 2018. *The right amount of panic: How women trade safety for freedom.* Policy Press.

Vera-Gray, F. and Kelly, L. 2020. Contested gendered space: Public sexual harassment and women's safety work. In *Crime and fear in public places* (pp. 217–231). Routledge.

Weis, J. R. 2015. Title IX and the state of campus sexual violence in the United States: Power, policy, and local bodies. *Human Organization*, 74, pp. 276–286.

Wiersma-Mosley, J.D. and Jozkowski, K.N. 2019. A brief report of sexual violence among universities with NCAA Division I athletic programs. *Behavioral Sciences*, 9(2), p. 17.

Williams, J. E. 1984. Secondary victimization: Confronting public attitudes about rape. *Victimology*, 9(1), pp. 66–68.

Williams, J. E. and Holmes, K. A. 1981. *The second assault: Rape and public attitudes.* Greenwood Press.

Women and Equalities Committee. 2018. *Sexual harassment of women and girls in public places.* House of Commons.

12 Exploring Perceptions of Stalking-Like Behaviour for Autistic Young People Within a Neurodivergent and Strengths-Based Framework: Critiquing Relationships, Sex and Health Education Provision

Helen Bovill, Sarah Chicken, Eloise Bovill, Julie Buckland, and Kieran McCartan

Key Points

- There is little research or understanding of stalking-like behaviour for the general youth population and in particular for autistic young people.
- Like the general youth population, autistic young people will experience puberty and the physical and emotional changes this brings, and develop relationships and sexual feelings and desires.
- Autistic young people may be potentially more vulnerable to perpetration and victimisation in terms of stalking-like behaviour.

H. Bovill (✉) · S. Chicken · J. Buckland · K. McCartan
University of the West of England, Bristol, UK
e-mail: Helen2.Bovill@uwe.ac.uk

S. Chicken
e-mail: Sarah.Chicken@uwe.ac.uk

J. Buckland
e-mail: Julie2.Buckland@uwe.ac.uk

K. McCartan
e-mail: Kieran.Mccartan@uwe.ac.uk

E. Bovill
Graduate of Queen Mary University of London, London, UK
e-mail: Eloise-B@outlook.com

M. Mellins et al. (eds.), *Young People, Stalking Awareness and Domestic Abuse*,
https://doi.org/10.1007/978-3-031-32379-9_12

- Understanding the needs of autistic young people in terms of Relationships, Sex and Health Education provision is limited.

Introduction

Many young people do not have a strong understanding of stalking-like[1] behaviour as demonstrated by VICE UK who conducted a survey of 12,000 young people aged 13–24 years old and found that: '1 in 4 did not know stalking was a crime… an even greater number did not think that attempting to contact someone repeatedly by any means possible counts as stalking' (Allen and Kay 2020, slide 6). There are significant challenges facing all young people regarding stalking-like behaviour, for example:

- Prevalence of stalking-like behaviour on and offline.
- Insufficient knowledge to recognise stalking-like behaviour as either perpetrator or victim.
- A lack of awareness of the consequences and risks of stalking-like behaviour.

This chapter will consider these challenges with reference to autistic young people or young people who identify as on the autistic spectrum.[2] We will do this by exploring the validity of arguments suggesting autistic young people may be at greater risk to perpetrate stalking-like behaviours (Allely and Creaby-Attwood 2016; Mercer and Allely 2020; Nichols and Blakeley-Smith 2009). We will also examine whether autistic young people are more likely to be subject to a perception of autistic behaviours as stalking-like behaviours (Haskins and Silva 2006; Nichols and Blakeley-Smith 2009). We will present various arguments within this chapter which demonstrate:

1. Little is known about stalking-like behaviour and young people, either generally or specifically in relation to autism. What is known tends to be inconclusive, and demonstrates some engagement in stalking-like behaviours across the young population (Roberts et al. 2016; Ybarra et al. 2016).
2. Autistic young people, particularly female and gender-diverse, are more likely to be recipients of stalking-like behaviour (Green et al. 2019; Pearson et al. 2022; Weiss and Fardella 2018).

We will make the case that Relationships, Sex and Health Education (RSHE) is lacking for autistic young people and does not equip them with skills to form healthy intimate relationships.

Before we begin, we will briefly outline the theoretical framework that the chapter follows; the neurodivergent theoretical framework. This theoretical framework aligns with the 'form of life' theory which postulates autism should not be viewed as a deficit of mind, but rather a different way of experiencing the world

(Milton 2012). A theory known as the 'double-empathy problem' (Milton 2012) demonstrates that 'empathy is a two-way street' (Milton 2018) noting that whilst autistic people may find challenges in relating to non-autistic people; non-autistic people are similarly challenged in relating to autistic people.

The neurodivergent framework rejects the medical model (Oliver 2013) a school of thought which has dominated the field of autism (Autism Advocacy Network 2022). The medical model seeks biological causes and remedies for autism, where individuals are seen as passive recipients of medical care for a problematic disability which needs fixing and treatment. The medical model of autism recognises only deficiencies in autism and empowers others such as parents, doctors and teachers to diagnose and treat perceived deficiencies (Kapp 2019). Adopting a medicalised view can dehumanise, pathologise and reduce individuals to their autistic characteristics presenting them as a burden to society (Haque and Waytz 2012) which ignores intercultural and socio-economic factors (Lord and Jones 2012; Oishi, Kesebir and Snyder 2009). A social model (Oliver 2013) of autism seeks to give power back to the autistic young person and instead considers the social construct of autism where societal structures are disabling to the autistic young person. Proponents of the neurodivergent paradigm 'believe that society should work to eliminate stigma, create accommodations', and celebrate the contributions autistic people make to society (Psychology Today 2022, 3) aligning with the social model.

Singer (2017), an autistic sociologist, is said to have coined the term neurodiversity and recognises it as an intersectional umbrella term for enhancing the civil rights of neurological minorities. Opponents of neurodiversity believe the term undermines autism and the challenges faced by autistic individuals particularly when these have a major impact on life, and for people who need lots of persistent support (McGee 2021; Robison 2017).

Arguments related to whether autism is viewed as a disability or a different form of life, rarely consider how autistic individuals view themselves. Whilst some autistic young people acknowledge their disabled status, expressing a feeling of being 'different' to their peers, and a desire to be accepted by society, others view their status as 'neutral' and not central to how they perceive themselves at all (Nguyen et al. 2020). We use the neurodivergent paradigm as a lens to shift power back to the autistic young person. However, we recognise some language in the chapter continues to reflect the language of the medical model.

For transparency purposes, and to demonstrate the chapter is attempting to bring autistic young people into research about them as advocated by Kapp (2019) Nicolaidis et al (2019) and Pellicano et al. (2021) one member of the author team is an autistic young person, another is a parent of an autistic young person, another is an autistic academic; remaining authors have experience working with autism. We do not aim this chapter at mainstream or special education; our aim is to generally discuss this area to open a conversation which is thus far very limited.

Definitions and Characteristics of Autism

This section of the chapter will consider how characteristics of autism present, before beginning to consider how these presentations might interact with perpetration or victimisation of stalking-like behaviour.

The formal diagnostic name for autism is autism spectrum disorder (ASD), referring to a range of conditions, characterised by challenges with social skills, and restricted, repetitive behaviours or (RRBs) within speech and non-verbal communication (American Psychiatric Association 2013). Previously, Asperger's Syndrome, characterised by stronger verbal skills and sometimes high intellectual ability, was a separate definition to autism. By 2011 the Diagnostic and Statistical Manual of Mental Disorders (DSM-5) did not recognise this separate category and individuals who might have been diagnosed with Asperger's Syndrome are now diagnosed under the umbrella term of ASD (Autism Research Institute 2021, 1). To further complicate, high-functioning autism, which is not a medical or a diagnostic term is often used by educators, doctors and researchers to situate autistic individuals without intellectual impairment (Alvares et al. 2020). However, the term high-functioning is largely rejected within the autistic community as many individuals who may present as high-functioning find social interaction, communication and reading social cues challenging, they often need routine and order, and are subject to anxiety (Alvares et al. 2020).

The National Autistic Society (2022a) (n.d.) notes autistic young people may have difficulties in interpreting verbal and non-verbal cues and, whilst many autistic young people have very good language skills, others have limited or no speech. Challenges for autistic people include, but are not limited to, taking things literally, repeating what others say to them (known as echolalia), difficulty understanding social interactions which may make it difficult to understand others' perspectives, feelings or reactions; which may make it difficult to form friendships. This may contribute to fewer interactions with peers for autistic young people which means there are fewer opportunities to practice the boundaries of social interaction and to learn about societal rules which govern behaviour (Nichols and Blakeley-Smith 2009; Post et al 2014) and may be a contributing factor to perpetration or victimisation of stalking-like behaviour. For autistic young people, the subtle 'unwritten rules' of society can be even more hard to understand, making it challenging to navigate the unpredictability of the social world, such that routine and rules may be preferred. Autistic young people may be over or under-sensitive to external stimuli such as light, noise, touch, smell, taste, or sound meaning that they may under or over-react in social situations which can be hard for others to understand. Autistic young people may also be prone to extreme anxiety and meltdowns or shutdowns and be highly focused or fixate upon interests or hobbies. Fixation can mean that in pursuing these interests or hobbies autistic young people can lack understanding of the impact of fixated behaviour upon others, or misread an appropriate level of pursuance within a romantic relationship for example (Stokes et al. 2007).

Some autistic people may be particularly adept at social masking (or camouflaging) which is when an autistic person copies behaviour to fit in and 'pretend to be normal' (Hull et al. 2020; Lai et al. 2017). Recent studies show 70% of all autistic people masks (Cage and Troxell-Whitman 2019). This means that they may be vulnerable to exploitation by others to conduct behaviour with a view to being able to fit in. This may have particular relevance to gender, as an emerging body of research (Adams and May 2021; Hull, Petrides and Mandy 2020) has identified key differences in the presentation of autism between genders, and gender-diverse people (Warrier et al. 2020). These differences are thought to contribute to the gender disparity found in diagnosis rates, especially in autistic girls and women; where no or late diagnosis means that services and adjustments are not provided and may contribute to a propensity to perpetration or victimisation of stalking-like behaviour. Autistic girls and women are found to be more likely on the receiving end of stalking-like behaviour because they may struggle to read and understand cues of stalking-like behaviour of others, can be targeted because they are seen as vulnerable, or seek to fit in and please others; allowing stalking-like behaviour to go unchallenged (Green et al. 2019; Pearson et al. 2022; Weiss and Fardella 2018). Differences found in traits for autistic girls are that they are more likely to engage in imaginative and pretend play; their vocabulary often develops to contain more words related to emotions; they tend to have a greater awareness of and desire for social interaction and they develop more efficient masking techniques such as social mimicry and coping techniques (Eaton 2021). Some camouflaging behaviours include actively making eye contact despite discomfort, using rehearsed speech or jokes, altering speech volume and mimicking facial expressions. Autistic women describe camouflaging behaviours as 'pretending to be normal' (Holliday Willey 2015). This can lead to vulnerability to acceptance of stalking-like behaviours motivated by a strong desire to fit in, which can reduce the likelihood of either questioning or calling out behaviour which is inappropriate in nature.

Parents of autistic young people also have concerns for their children with regard to characteristics of autism and the potential impact of these upon relationships development. Nichols and Blakeley-Smith (2009) in a study of 21 parents of autistic young people found 'parents reported that their children struggle with understanding privacy, boundaries, personal space, and not being able to read social cues' (78). Parents in this study worried that their sons' and daughters' behaviours might be misinterpreted by others and perceived as stalking-like when often the young people are lonely and seeking friendship or that when trying to express affection or enact their curiosity it will be mistaken by others as sexual.

Through the use of focus groups, the research of Ballan (2012) explored the perspectives of parents of autistic young people in relation to sex education finding that the topics covered were viewed as limited and that there were misconceptions about what was interpreted as sexual behaviour. With a similar focus, Mackin et al (2016) utilised focus groups and telephone interviews with parents of autistic young people, findings revealed a parental perception of a lack of appropriate resources related to sex education for their children. Nichols and Blakeley-Smith (2009) note that parents of autistic young people have specific concerns for their daughters and sons around safety and others' perceptions of them, for example one parent noted 'I worry that my son might rape someone without even knowing it—he would focus on his own needs and not know what is appropriate' (79). Another parent noted issues with privacy, saying that they had discussed privacy with their daughter but was unsure whether she had understood it. Nichols and Blakeley-Smith (2009) have conducted clinical work with autistic young people and:

> [H]ave seen youth whose sensory interests lead them to touch women's legs and nylons, to smell or stroke someone's hair, to want to play with skin that wrinkles (e.g., elbows, knees), or to lick people's arms or faces. We have also worked with teens who start to unzip their pants on the way to the public bathroom, or stand immediately next to someone at the urinals. When these behaviors occur in young children, they are frequently tolerated or dismissed; however, when an adolescent or young adult engages in sensory seeking or socially inappropriate behavior, their actions are often interpreted as deviant, offensive, and intentional. (85)

In their paper, Nichols and Blakeley-Smith (2009) discuss the theory of 'counterfeit deviance' developed by (Hingsburger et al. 1991) which are 'behaviours that are a result of lack of sexual knowledge or social skills, or social naiveté' (Nichols and Blakeley-Smith 2009, 85). They also state that the unwritten rules in society are much harder for autistic young people to navigate, and these nuances need to be built into education programmes. Their paper concludes by recommending that professionals need a much stronger understanding of the particular needs of autistic young people, and much stronger education programmes need to be developed which deal with relationships and sex in their context. For example, they state that autistic young people might need to be specifically taught that it is okay to be naked in some contexts but not others. The studies of Ballan (2012) Mackin et al. (2016) and Nichols and Blakeley-Smith (2009) demonstrate the dissatisfaction of parents of autistic young people in relation to relationships, sex and health education (RSHE). We support this view and feel that the current education provision for autistic young people may not be good enough since it does not recognise their particular needs.

Autistic Young People and the Criminal Justice System

This section of the chapter will highlight that there is a lack of research regarding autistic people and the criminal justice system (CJS), and that the evidence that is available suggests autism and criminal offending may be linked; only in that there are cases of people with autism in the criminal justice system but that autism is not a predictive factor for offending behaviour (Chaplin and McCarthy 2022). In fact, because autistic people tend to behave within rigid rules, they are likely to abide by laws more than the overall population and they are also more likely to be a victim of crime (Autism Awareness Centre Inc. 2022, 1). In understanding the range and variety of autistic people in the CJS, exploring the challenges of collating and analysing this data is useful. In their recent meta-analysis, Collins et al. (2022) highlight inconsistent recording patterns, and a lack of breadth and depth of research needed to clearly identify accurate numbers of autistic people in the CJS. This lack of accurate, detailed knowledge means that there is likely a number of undiagnosed, and/or unrecorded autistic people in the CJS, who are not being supported effectively, and therefore are less likely to be successfully rehabilitated or desist. Additionally, Collins et al. (2022) note the causal factors for autistic people who offend are important to consider. In terms of rehabilitation, as well as prevention, multiple issues need to be addressed in diverse ways. A challenge here is making sure that frontline staff, are trained to deliver relevant prevention and rehabilitation content to autistic people, in sympathetic and appropriate ways. Blackmore et al. (2022) and Collins et al. (2022) consider that to improve services for autistic people in the CJS there needs to be better working with mental health services, and staff upskilling.

A more in-depth focus upon autistic young people and the CJS emerges from a recent report by the National Autistic Society (2022b) which has highlighted that autistic young people are at a greater risk of entering the CJS. Reasons for this may be misunderstanding of autistic characteristics and vulnerabilities by professional staff, which may lead to a higher risk of prosecution. This may be the case for stalking-like behaviour (Allely and Creaby-Attwood 2016; Haskins and Silva 2006; Stokes and Newton 2004). Mercer and Allely (2020) explore how autistic vulnerabilities associated with restrictive and repetitive behaviours (RRBs) may increase the risk of autistic young people being charged with stalking-like offences or encountering the CJS. This may be due to social naivety, through a desire to have friends, or by becoming unwitting accomplices of crime in the pursuit of trying to fit in and following others' instructions. Autistic young people may encounter the CJS because of offences stemming from aggression due to a reaction to an unexpected change in routine or environment, or agitation due to others not adhering to rules which they view as highly important. Additionally, police methods might exacerbate a situation, for example police viewing poor eye contact as a sign of guilt, or using restraint methods or handcuffs which might be very difficult for an autistic person and cause them to become agitated. Sirens and other noises may lead to sensory overload and simply being in contact with police may cause extreme anxiety to an autistic person who follows rules rigidly and/or may not have awareness of the crime they may have committed (National Autistic Society 2022b).

The report by the National Autistic Society (2022b) highlighted that school exclusions for autistic young people, and a lack of or late diagnosis of' autism, contributed to autistic young people's increased risk of entering the CJS, with autistic young people often not receiving the early support they need. The report notes there is an urgent need for greater understanding and support structures within schools for autistic young people, and associated services, to ameliorate the risk of autistic young people entering the CJS. Once in the CJS, the report highlights that action is needed regarding the support and reasonable adjustments that autistic young people should receive within the CJS.

Research on Stalking-Like Behaviour, Autism and Strengths-Based Approaches

Consideration will now be given to specific research regarding stalking-like behaviour in both the general youth population and the autistic youth population. This demonstrates the opening points of this chapter which state that stalking-like behaviour is little understood, under-researched and inconclusive, but demonstrates the young population generally can be vulnerable to stalking-like behaviour as either perpetrator or victim. The authors will introduce the concept of strengths-based approaches to support autistic young people, alongside their non-autistic peers.

Mercer and Allely (2020) conducted a scoping review of autism and stalking finding only five relevant sources. Limited research suggests characteristics associated with autism can lead to a higher risk of engaging in stalking-like behaviours or of being perceived as engaging in them (Allely and Creaby-Attwood 2016; Haskins and Silva 2006). Mercer and Allely (2020, 202) refer to these characteristics as 'innate vulnerabilities' such as 'repetitive' behaviours and 'persistent preoccupation' or Repetitive and restricted behaviours (RRBs). Research has found education for non-autistic young people is insufficient, so that some common social interaction behaviours of autistic young people are misinterpreted as stalking-like behaviour (Mercer and Allely 2020; Post et al 2014 and Stokes et al. 2007). For example, autistic young people might not understand the social 'norms and rules' around how long to pursue a potential romantic relationship, they may not understand when someone does not want to talk to them, or they may not know when a relationship finishes and how to leave it or how to end it appropriately. This can result in behaviour that can be viewed as inappropriate such as attempting to carry out conversations or relationships with a person who no longer wishes to do so.

Limited studies of the general youth population and stalking demonstrate that stalking-like behaviours can be found across the youth population. (Roberts et al. 2016; Ybarra et al. 2016). Ybarra et al. (2016, 4) study of 1586 United States households found stalking-like behaviours to be fairly common in young people generally, 'thirty-six percent (n = 396) of youth respondents reported engaging in at least one type of behaviour consistent with the definition of stalking'. Ybarra et al. (2016) study considered digital stalking, text messaging and internet use as a common modality in which stalking-like behaviour occurred. A further layer of detachment from people is introduced in technology-mediated communication which can lead to disinhibition in the general youth population. Artesani-Blanks (2017) notes that using social media makes it difficult to understand when you have crossed a social boundary and, for autistic people, social boundaries can be particularly blurred. For example, over liking a post or replying to a post or email an inappropriate amount may not be fully understood.

Roberts et al. (2016) conducted a systematic literature review of existing peer-reviewed literature on young people and stalking-like behaviour. The review suggested a range of adolescent stalker typologies amongst which was the 'socially awkward' type of adolescent stalker 'who simply desires a relationship but lacks the social skills to achieve this' (Roberts et al. 2016, 6). The 'socially awkward' typology is similarly found in the scant research of autistic young people (Mercer and Allely 2020). These similarities in behaviour across young people recognises this is a problem which is useful to be considered for all young people in education provision. Stokes and Newton (2004) note that the prevalence of stalking from autistic young people 'may result from frequent, eager and sometimes socially inappropriate attempts to contact others' (6). Stokes et al. (2007, 2–3) also note the desire for intimate relationships from autistic young people who may lack skills and knowledge to engage in these relationships.

Conversely, an emerging body of research posits that autistic adults may be more likely to be on the receiving end of stalking and intimate partner or familial abuse. Though this emerging research is with autistic adults, the studies explore the adults' experiences of victimisation throughout the life course from childhood. Pearson et al. (2022) conducted a qualitative study examining experiences of interpersonal victimisation from an autistic adult experience, finding autistic people frequently experience victimisation throughout their lifespan, including childhood and young adulthood, and from multiple sources (polyvictimisation). Pearson et al. (2022) noted that intimate partner abuse was the most common experience and their findings offered multiple reasons as to why autistic people may be particularly prone to experiencing polyvictimisation. Firstly, autistic people may struggle to identify when someone is acting in an inappropriate or abusive manner. Many autistic people struggle to understand subtext or manipulation techniques employed by abusers such as gaslighting,[3] and it may not occur to them that a person is being disingenuous. Secondly, many autistic people exhibit heightened compliance behaviour when exposed to stressful situations. This means that they may attempt to either pacify the abuser or try to ignore or trivialise behaviour which is inappropriate. Reasons given for this vary, from a need to please others or 'go along' with the manipulation in order to retain friendships, to confrontation avoidance for self-preservation. Finally, the study found that many autistic adults had experienced victimisation from authority figures as children and young people, either from familial abuse or from teachers failing to understand their disability. This can lead to a mistrust of authority figures and destruction of support networks, preventing autistic young people and adults from seeking help when experiencing victimisation.

These findings are similarly supported by an earlier paper by Weiss and Fardella (2018), which analysed self-reported instances of victimisation in autistic people compared to non-autistic people. This study found that autistic people experienced polyvictimisation more often than non-autistic people and that as with Pearson et al. (2022), this occurred from childhood through to adulthood, though the difference between the rates of victimisation becomes more dramatic in later life. Equally, autistic young people and autistic adults frequently experienced interpersonal abuse in more than one environment, whether that be in the home, school, workplace or within the community. Weiss and Fardella (2018) found in relation to childhood victimisation that autistic children were '7.3 times more likely to endorse sexual assault by a peer' (4). This study also found that autistic adults were more likely to report than non-autistic adults 'that as a child, they experienced physical abuse, psychological/emotional abuse from an adult, peer/sibling victimisation, various forms of bullying from peers, robbery, and sexual assault by a peer' (4). Experiencing polyvictimisation from childhood can make it difficult for an autistic young person to ascertain what 'normal' behaviour and boundaries are. Without a trusted support network to reach out to, and positive relationships to use as an example, it can be even more difficult for autistic young people to recognise the subtle signs of abuse or inappropriate behaviour.

Some research suggests that a strengths-based approach[4] may be beneficial when working with autistic young people (Lai and Szatmari 2019; Varjas et al. 2009; Weiss and Fardella 2018). Strengths-based approaches focus on adapting teaching strategy to the autistic young person, rather than expecting the autistic young person to adapt to the teaching. Additionally, strengths-based approaches aim to build self-efficacy by supporting autistic young people to see what they can do through awareness of their personal strengths and how to develop these (Lai and Szatmari 2019; Varjas et al. 2009; Weiss and Fardella 2018). Weiss and Fardella (2018) state that victimisation needs to be tackled in various contexts and they cite strengths-based school programming as an area for further investigation. They state that 'proactive and accessible programming that promotes inclusion and healthy relationships within relevant contexts (including the home, school, workplace, and community levels) are needed' (Weiss and Fardella 2018, 7). We will further investigate strengths-based approaches, or the adaptation of provision towards strengths-based approaches, in the following sections.

Autism and the Right to RSHE

This section of the chapter considers how autistic young people are constructed in terms of Relationships, Sex and Health Education (RSHE)[5] (Department for Education (DFE) 2019) and in turn how education programmes relate to their rights for provision. Social constructions of autistic young people tend towards depicting them as infantile, asexual and in need of protection. This can contribute to a societal belief that autistic young people should not be involved with RSHE as this is neither necessary nor appropriate (Dabner and Newman-Clarke 2021). Research frequently demonstrates young people with disabilities, including autism, have similar needs regarding RSHE to the non-disabled population (Hannah and Stagg 2016). Like the general youth population, studies indicate RSHE is beneficial in supporting the understanding of intimate relationship development for autistic young people (McCann et al. 2019). It is further proposed that young people with disabilities may have an extra vulnerability to potential negative consequences of sexual activity including unplanned pregnancies and sexually transmitted infections (McDaniels and Fleming 2016) indicating RSHE should be prioritised.

Hannah and Stagg (2016) argue autistic young people are not given adequate information to enable them to have safe and fulfilling sex lives since taught content is not reflective of their needs and suggest that education needed to be more bespoke for autistic young people in terms of both content and pedagogy. Frawley and Bigby (2014, p. 167) also note:

> There has been little progress in developing programs that recognise the rights of people with an intellectual disability to make choices and determine for themselves how they will have relationships and be sexual.

Michielsen and Brockshmidt (2021) identify a range of barriers to teaching RSHE to young people with disabilities. These barriers include misplaced perceptions of disabled people as lacking in sexual desire and a consequential view they need protection; and a lack of support for educators in how to approach the subject area with respectful sensitivity leading to a reluctance to take on this responsibility at all. Curriculum content based on non-disabled experiences is problematic and these issues are reflected in the scant literature which focuses upon autism.

We propose autistic young people should be at the centre of developing relevant information in a manner that recognises their needs and strengths and prioritises their rights and enhances opportunities to access RSHE. Provision should enable autistic young people to explore and rehearse social situations that are likely to arise within the context of developing healthy intimate relationships that all young people are likely to be exposed to. For example, the right for autistic young people to have relevant information and the opportunity to practice various consent scenarios; or what the hallmarks of a healthy relationship are; or what the red flags of a toxic or abusive relationship are; how to express emotions and talk about relationships; where to go for contraceptive, sexual health and family planning support; the joy of intimate relationships; the differences between abuse, harassment, stalking, etc.; and what consequences of various sexual behaviour is.

Relationships, Sex and Health Education (RSHE) is an umbrella term for provision and since September 2020 in England, Relationships Education is mandatory in all primary schools, Relationships and Sex Education is mandatory in all secondary schools and Health education mandatory in all state-funded schools (Department for Education (DFE) 2019). Mandatory requirements include provision in special as well as mainstream schools and guidance sets out the rights of all children, including those with special educational needs and disabilities (SEND) who may have been overlooked in previous legislation.

The DFE (2015) provides all schools with statutory guidance regarding SEND, stating schools have a requirement to ensure the needs of all pupils, including pupils with SEND, are met. Furthermore, the DFE provides schools with guidance regarding teaching of RSHE to students with SEND (DFE 2019). The DFE aims to emphasize that RSHE needs to be sensitive, age-appropriate, developmentally appropriate and in accordance with the law. However, the current education policy for RSHE and SEND is centred on a safeguarding and vulnerability approach, which may be necessary, but not at the expense of one that prioritises the rights of autistic young people to have a say in their provision. Developing provision so that it becomes more relevant and relatable; providing autistic young people with the education they need to engage in healthy and respectful relationships, and which emphasizes their strengths, needs higher priority. We contend current education policy for RSHE provision does not centre those with SEND, including autism, at the forefront of developing provision or having a say in what the provision looks like. We argue that there needs to be a shift in both policy and associated practice to address this.

RSHE for Autistic Young People from a Strengths-Based Approach

This section will consider various ways in which the needs of autistic young people could be met and developed from a strengths-based perspective of provision of RSHE. It is not the intention of this chapter to critique in detail all these approaches or to advocate for them, rather to bring together literature which has considered this. The literature thus far is limited and we argue more research in these areas is needed.

Post et al. (2014) explored how schools may respond to reports of autistic young people demonstrating, or at risk of, stalking-like behaviour. They recommend a multi-disciplinary approach because it encompasses the whole social system of the autistic young person. This multi-disciplinary approach may include law enforcement, mental health support, victim advocates, teachers, behaviour specialists and case workers. Bringing disciplines together means that a co-ordinated approach to prevention can be developed. Undertaking an assessment of the motivation for stalking and the context within which it occurs is explored, and it is suggested that this is achieved through a functional behaviour assessment or (FBA). A FBA is a process which can identify behaviours which are interfering with a young person's learning or social, emotional or behavioural development, considering behaviour within school and in other areas of the young persons' life such as community and home. A FBA can lead to appropriate interventions by the school and offers a systematic approach to intervention which can have the vantage point of a range of evidence being gathered as to the motivation of stalking-like behaviour. This means that interventions can be tailored to what the evidence suggests. FBAs can be conducted through structured interviews with the people around the autistic young person, for example, the victim (with consent and appropriate support), other students, teachers, support staff, parents, etc. FBAs can also be conducted through structured observations of the autistic young person, to determine antecedents, triggers and functions. Once the function is determined, intervention and support strategies can become more focused and the FBA can inform future case management and intervention approaches. For example, if the FBA identifies that the function of the stalking-like behaviour is to gain a romantic relationship, intervention might include support which enables relationship-seeking strategies in appropriate formats from professionals such as teachers, counsellors, psychologists and others. If the function of the stalking behaviour is identified as motivated by rejection, then coping skills might be prioritised to understand how to disengage appropriately from a relationship.

When more is understood about the stalking-like behaviour, interventions which concentrate upon perspective taking, appropriate conversation skills, or therapy such as Cognitive Behavioural Therapy (CBT)[6] can be adopted and adapted. CBT is a form of therapy which works with individuals to identify harmful or negative thoughts, leading to self-regulation. Post et al. (2014) note CBT can be used where persistent preoccupation with an object, concept or person is at the route of stalking, and CBT coping strategies may be taught to individuals to interrupt these. Padesky and Mooney (2012) discuss how CBT can be adopted and adapted to a strengths-based approach within a four-step model: (1) search, (2) construct, (3) apply, (4) practice. This involves introducing obstacles and identifying strengths, turning strengths into strategies using the client's words, identifying problem areas and then planning which strategies to utilise. A final stage in this approach is to co-design behavioural experiments to practice using the various strengths identified in the model. Padesky and Mooney (2012, 285) refer to this as a 'many pathways', approach. This 'many pathways' four-step model could be applied when working with autistic young people. For example, Perihan et al. (2020) and French (2021) note that specific modifications to the approach of CBT when interacting with autistic young people might include the use of social stories, visuals and the opportunity to practice alternative response behaviours in real-life settings. Applying this to Padesky and Mooney's (2012) four-stage model could be done by working with the autistic young person to co-design social stories which incorporate their personal strengths and use their own words to narrate and practice various outcomes in safe surroundings. In terms of perpetration of stalking, CBT may enable the autistic young person to recognise their own behaviour as such and de-escalate this. In terms of being a victim of stalking, CBT may enable the autistic young person to recognise the unhealthy nature of a relationship and to develop skills to avoid or remove themselves from this. The following is an example given by Post et al. (2014) reviewing a study by Myles and Simpson (2001) where CBT was used for the prevention and de-escalation of stalking-like behaviour perpetration. Myles and Simpson (2001) presented a case of an autistic young person who was conducting stalking-like behaviour through demonstration of a preoccupation with female peers at school. This manifested in the autistic young person following female peers and continuing to sit with them despite having negative reactions from the female peers. The school used video feedback or (VFB) to demonstrate to the autistic young person that his behaviour was not welcome. They also adopted a self-monitoring system for the autistic young person to use and record his recollections of contact with peers. A self-reinforcement activity was also integrated, whereby positive interactions with peers were discussed as alternative behaviour patterns. In this case self-reinforcement was identified as spending time with peers, who welcomed this, at lunch and walking to class with them. This is a time-consuming approach and relies upon the autistic young person identifying negative reactions from peers. It might also be difficult to capture the behaviours in ways which can be evidenced, such as through video. This also has the potential to be intrusive upon those that are experiencing victimisation within given scenarios. It can also tend toward a medicalised intervention model which centres the autistic young person as the problem.

Strengths-based approaches can also be adopted within social skills group settings. Stokes et al. (2007) found autistic young people learn social skills through their families, but this did not apply in the same way when in the context of learning about romantic functioning. Additionally, autistic young people tended to acquire fewer social skills through their peer groups. Therefore, it is important that:

> Non-disabled peers also need to be part of sex education instruction. A significant predictor of successful romantic interaction in the Stokes, Newton and Kaur (2007) study was the extent to which social skills were learned from nondisabled peers. (Post et al. 2014, 2699)

Post et al. (2014) explore social skills group intervention. This includes group work with 'appropriate peers' defined as those who are present and participate in the autistic young person's life in competent and positive ways. The social skills group consists of instruction in natural settings where possible, such as lunchtime scenarios, or friendship settings. Opportunities can be taken in the group settings to pause and describe behaviours, give rationale for behaviours and divide skills into small steps which can be practised through role play and feedback. Utilising an approach throughout social skills group intervention, which seeks to prioritise the strengths of autistic young people, would require training in specialist skills for the 'appropriate peers' to enable this.

McCann et al. (2019) reviewed provision of RSHE for people with intellectual disabilities noting that use of 'peer educators' was found in one study (Frawley and Bigby 2014) to have potential use. This study indicated that those with intellectual disabilities could be supported to deliver programmes, benefitting both their peers and the individuals themselves. This could build strengths of both the peer educators and those they work with. The programme revolved around respectful relationships and used stories developed by and about people with intellectual disabilities across four sessions: (1) Talking about sex and relationships, (2) Having rights and being safe, (3) Respectful relationships and (4) Men and respectful relationships (Frawley and Bigby 2014, 169). The programme was described 'as being able to "stand in their shoes"' (Frawley and Bigby 2014, 175) and advocates for peers with experience of intellectual disability running sessions, as they have more empathy for others with intellectual disability. As such, the programme aligns with the 'double-empathy theory' (Milton 2012, 2018) and it could be adopted and adapted for peer education by and for autistic young people. Though the peer education programme described by Frawley and Bigby (2014) offered early indications of success for both those in receipt of and those delivering the programme, it was hampered by gatekeepers not fully on board with the programme.

Post et al. (2014) group work with 'appropriate peers' and Frawley and Bigby's (2014) 'peer educator' approach could be delivered from a strengths-based approach that aligns with 'double-empathy theory' (Milton 2012, 2018). Allowing this work to take place with peers chosen by, and in a medium of, the autistic young person's choosing; rather than having these imposed, is indicative of a strengths-based approach. The important aspect here is the people and the medium are chosen by the autistic young person giving ownership and empowering them in decisions regarding their life. The use of 'high interest' artefacts to run the lessons is also encouraged, and this will be individual to the needs of different autistic young people and require that educators understand what the individuals hold in 'high interest'. For example, it has been found that autistic girls can favour interests in media celebrities (Eaton 2021) so instances where media celebrities have overcome stalking-like scenarios may be useful here within peer education approaches.

Another potential intervention is Rule-Governed Behaviour or (RGB) which is noted by Post et al. (2014) as useful to prevent stalking-like behaviours. For example, establishing rules with antecedent behaviour, such as walking with someone when invited to do so. These rules can be written, pictorial or recorded jointly with the autistic young person, who may need to express rules out loud to begin with, gradually incorporating them into internal self-statements. Alongside these strategies, Post et al. (2014) discuss the need for counselling to be incorporated with intervention strategies. RGB could be adapted for autistic young people to help them understand the rules of healthy intimate relationships from the vantage point of avoiding perpetrating stalking-like behaviour and to help them be less likely to be a victim of stalking-like behaviour. For example, rules such as phones and computers are private so if I demand access to a partner's password that is harmful; likewise, if a partner demands this from me it is unhealthy and should be a warning sign of an inappropriate relationship. From a strengths-based perspective, this would encompass finding and incorporating the autistic young person's strengths into the RGB, and working together to use the words of the autistic person to express these rules.

The National Autistic Society (n.d.) offers information which can be viewed from a strengths-based approach. It has a guide for parents which goes beyond the basics of puberty and sex education in that it begins to consider relationship development and discusses reasoning for inappropriate behaviour, for example:

> If an autistic person kisses someone unexpectedly, this could be because: They have seen two people kissing on the television and think the other person will react the way the person they saw being kissed did... They think the other person wants to kiss, because they themselves want to kiss. (National Autistic Society n.d., 6)

Guides could be extended to include other scenarios and consider developing information with autistic young people to be adopted as prevention or de-escalation strategies and which capitalises on identified strengths. Guides could be offered as starting points for conversations with autistic young people which could also include non-autistic young people so that empathy may develop. The National Autistic Society (n.d.) also considers ways to mitigate harmful behaviour through the use of social stories and behaviour diaries. Behaviour diaries could be used by autistic young people to record behaviour before, during and after events which can be discussed with the autistic young person at a later point. The National Autistic Society (n.d.) resource also suggests working through an activity called 'it's alright' where you work with the autistic young person to put together a table with different activities, like kissing or holding hands and place ticks/crosses or yes/no against the activities with different people and in varying contexts. Behaviour diaries and the activity 'it's alright' could be adapted in both situations of perpetration or victimisation of stalking-like behaviour. For example, in cases of stalking-like victimisation such as intimate partnership boundaries around sharing passwords for phones, or sharing images online, you could work with the autistic young person to identify which behaviour is appropriate or inappropriate within scenarios such as this. This could be an activity that is developed with autistic young people whether or not they are currently experiencing or perpetrating this behaviour, as it may enable them to be more likely to recognise negative or harmful behaviour if it presents in the future. These are also activities that could be conducted with both autistic young people alongside their non-autistic peers as advocated by (Post et al. 2014; Stokes et al. 2007). This kind of activity is more likely to be successful if it is repeated with a range of scenarios that have been identified as relevant to young people. It is potentially time consuming and would also be reliant upon the skills of parents, teachers or of peer educators (Frawley and Bigby 2014; Post et al. 2014).

In conclusion, we contend the approaches and provisions discussed are all useful strategies if enacted together with the autistic young person who is enabled to feel a sense of ownership. The approaches also need to be adapted and developed with a keen knowledge of the autistic young person's particular needs and strengths. Therefore, some approaches would be more or less valid. RSHE for autistic young people which considers how to prevent, or to protect from, stalking-like behaviour should come from an approach which recognises autistic young people as sexual beings who may desire intimate relationships just as other young people may. It should also recognise their strengths rather than their deficits. Understanding that provision of useful, relatable and relevant RSHE is multifaceted and complex, just as for other young people, is critical. Autistic young people will need guidance in becoming mature, sexual people, just as their non-autistic peers will. Therefore, adopting a neurodivergent paradigm and a strengths-based approach to provision of supportive resources is useful in the following ways:

1. It helps to recognise both similarities and differences in the need to improve provision of RSHE for young people with and without autism.
2. It seeks to validate the strengths of autistic young people and empower them to be in control of their provision.

3. It recognises both the multiple ways that autism may present and the intersectionality at play in the life of an autistic young person who is many things aside from their autism.

Conclusions and Recommendations

The authors of the chapter make a case that a neurodivergent paradigm (Kapp 2019; McGee 2021; Robison 2017; Singer 2017) to provision of RSHE for autistic young people may offer a step forward towards more positive programmes of RSHE that are relevant to young people and take account of their needs. We consider the value of a strengths-based approach (Lai and Szatmari 2019; Varjas et al. 2009; Weiss and Fardella 2018) and have considered approaches that can be adopted and adapted to this (for example Frawley and Bigby 2014; Post et al. 2014). We have noted that whilst Department for Education (2019) guidance strengthens the right for young people with SEND (including autism) to have provision of RSHE; the area of stalking-like behaviour, either from the vantage point of perpetrator or victim, is not adequately covered. Department for Education guidance (2015, 2019, 2020) emanates from a position of protection, safeguarding and vulnerability. Though this positioning is important, it should not overshadow empowering autistic young people to have access to and a say in the information and knowledge they need to enable healthy intimate relationships. We have demonstrated that the young population in general has a lack of understanding of stalking-like behaviour (Allen and Kay 2020; Roberts et al. 2016; Ybarra et al. 2016) and both autistic young people and their non-autistic peers would benefit from more education in the areas of stalking-like behaviour. Additionally, if this is conducted together outcomes are suggested to be more positive (Post et al. 2014; Stokes et al. 2007). The consequences of inadequate educational provision within the realms of RSHE for autistic young people are demonstrated in the literature as having the impact of isolating autistic young people from their non-autistic peers, contributing to misunderstanding autistic behaviour as stalking-like and leaving autistic young people ill-equipped to develop healthy intimate relationships. We have also noted in this chapter the ways this can impact negatively on autistic young people, for example the recent report by the National Autistic Association (2022b) which note that young autistic people are at greater risk of entering the CJS. Within the recommendations of this report are 'better support at school' and 'better social understanding support at school' (National Autistic Association 2022b). The report noted 'that a major factor for autistic young people being involved in the criminal justice system is that they can be easily led or influenced by others. This can stem from a need to be accepted and fit in' (28). The report makes recommendations around specific teaching to meet the needs of autistic young people:

> What was repeatedly emphasised to us was that poor understanding of social interaction, relationships and sex education can all contribute to autistic young people committing crimes. Providing specialist support in all of these areas is essential. Specific teaching needs to be undertaken around:

- the steps to building a friendship or relationship
- recognising and understanding other people's emotions
- specialist sex education around understanding sexual boundaries and consent (and putting this into context). (National Autistic Society 2022b).

If RSHE provision is to be improved clear, unambiguous guidance from policy is needed so that the professionals delivering this feel supported, confident and comfortable to develop and deliver effective provision. This needs to work towards developing shared understandings of what effective provision is, led by autistic young people, alongside educators and policymakers.

Provision should first and foremost be empowerment-led, enabling autistic young people to demand provision and have a say in its development (McCann, Marsh and Brown 2019; Michielsen and Brockshmidt 2021). Provision should also reject a one-size-fits-all approach and work with the autistic young people to best suit their individual needs. As such, though we have discussed types of provision such as Functional Behaviour Assessments (FBA), adapting Cognitive Behavioural Therapy (CBT), use of social stories, video-modelling, group work, Rule-Governed Behaviour (RGB), behaviour diaries, peer group work and peer educators (Frawley and Bigby 2014; French 2021; Perihan et al. 2020; 2014; National Autistic Society, n.d.; Post et al. 2014) we are not necessarily advocating for any one of these approaches. These were the types of approaches discussed thus far in literature and they may have utility. We feel that a strengths-based approach (Lai and Szatmari 2019; Varjas et al. 2009; Weiss and Fardella 2018) which works with the assets rather than the deficits of autistic young people, shows promise and needs research. We also understand there are resource implications to operate from a strengths-based approach for educators, who are already under-resourced and seek more training and support in the current system of provision (Michielsen and Brockshmidt 2021). When a stronger and shared understanding of what provision might look like is developed, then it is likely that this should be delivered in a multi-disciplinary approach (Post et al. 2014) which includes autistic young people, educators, counsellors, social workers and allied professionals. This multi-disciplinary approach would ideally work to instigate structural change in delivery; such as smaller groups, individualised approaches and working with autistic and non-autistic young people together so that each is enabled to recognise strengths of one another and appreciate different perspectives and reactions in relationships. Particularly, adopting a RSHE approach that works in empathetic ways; which understands empathy to be a two-way street between young people with and without autism, is considered a valuable approach to take (Milton 2012, 2018).

A final recommendation from this chapter, therefore, is participatory research, where autistic young people are involved as either equal partners or leaders of research (Kapps 2019; Nicolaidis et al. 2019; Pelicano et al. 2021). We contend that autistic young people need to be the generators of new knowledge so that the outcomes of this knowledge are more likely to be relevant and relatable to their lived experiences.

Discussion Questions

- We have emphasised that a more bespoke approach to Relationships, Sex and Health Education for autistic young people is required. What are the challenges in implementing this?
- We have included some research which highlights the issues that parents face in supporting their autistic young people to develop healthy intimate relationships. How could schools and other agencies work with parents/families/carers to better support autistic young people?
- Including non-autistic peers in education alongside their autistic peers has been emphasised. What are the benefits and challenges of this approach?
- Including autistic young people in research about Relationships, Sex and Health Education has been emphasised. How could this be put into practice and what would be the benefits of this?

Notes

1. We use the term stalking-like throughout rather than stalking. This term is used by others, e.g., Ybarra et al. (2016). The authors of this chapter preference stalking-like as a term rather than stalking as it is considered by the authors to be less deterministic. Autistic young people may not understand that behaviour conducted or experienced is potentially stalking-like in nature and often what might be perceived as stalking-like behaviour is not intended as such by autistic young people.
2. We use the term autistic young people 'In keeping with other autistic self-advocates' rather than 'people with autism' (Milton 2012, 883).
3. Gaslighting is a deliberate and systematic form of manipulation and control where the intent is to use false information leading to a questioning of truth.
4. Strengths-based (or asset-based) approaches focus on individuals' strengths (including personal strengths and social and community networks) and not on their deficits. Strengths-based practice is holistic and multidisciplinary and works with the individual to promote their wellbeing. It is outcomes led and not services led (Social Care Institute for excellence, n.d., 1).
5. RSHE is an acronym for compulsory Relationships, Sex and Health Education (Department for Education, 2019) which is sometimes referred to as Personal, Social and Health Education (PSHE) or Sex and Relationship Education (SRE)

within the United Kingdom. It refers to the various policy of provision within schools in the United Kingdom in recent years. We use the term RSHE throughout.

6. Cognitive Behavioural Therapy or CBT is a form of therapy which can help manage feelings and behaviours. It is based in the premise that thoughts, actions, feelings and physical reactions are part of an interconnected process. Overwhelming or negative feelings can result in negative cycles of behaviour. CBT seeks to deal with current problems. It seeks to turn negative feelings and behaviours into positive feelings and behaviours through identifying practical ways to deal with problems (National Health Service 2019).

Bibliography

Adams, C.A. and May, T. 2021. Diagnosis of Autism in Older Women: Reflections of a Psychologist and a Client. *Good Autism Practice.* 22 (7) 59–65.

Allely, C. and Creaby-Attwood, A. 2016. Sexual Offending and Autism Spectrum Disorders. *Journal of Intellectual Disabilities and Offending Behaviour.* 7 (1) 35–51.

Allen, R. and Kay, E. 2020. Raising Awareness of Stalking within Schools. *The Alice Ruggles Trust. PSHE Association. Durham Constabulary.* Available at https://slidetodoc.com/raising-awareness-of-stalking-within-schools-virtual-conference/ (Accessed 23 August 2022).

Alvares, G.A., Bebbington, K., Cleary, D., Evans, K., Glasson, E.J., Maybery, M.T., Pillar, S., Uljarević, M., Varcin, K., Wray, J., and Whitehouse, A.J. 2020. The Misnomer of 'High Functioning Autism': Intelligence Is an Imprecise Predictor of Functional Abilities at Diagnosis. *Autism.* 24 (1) 221–232.

American Psychiatric Association. (2013*) Diagnostic and Statistical Manual of Mental Disorders, 5th ed.* American Psychiatric Association, Washington, DC.

Artesani-Blanks, J. 2017. Using Social Media on the Autistic Spectrum. *PsychCentral.* Available from https://psychcentral.com/lib/using-social-media-on-the-autism-spectrum#4 (Accessed 27 April 2022). https://doi.org/10.1177/136236131985283

Autism Advocacy Network. 2022. *Autism: Medical vs Social Models.* Available from https://autismadvocacynetwork.org/neurodiversity/autism-medical-vs-social-models/ (Accessed November 2 2022).

Autism Awareness Centre Inc. 2022. *ASDs and Involvement in the Criminal Justice System.* Available from https://autismawarenesscentre.com/asds-involvement-criminal-justice-system/ (Accessed August 18 2022).

Autism Research Institute 2021. *What Is Autism?* Available from https://www.autism.org/what-is-autism/ (Accessed 23 August 2022).

Ballan, M.S. 2012. Parental Perspectives of Communication About Sexuality in Families of Children with Autism Spectrum Disorders. *Journal of Autism Developmental Disorders.* 42, 676–684. https://doi.org/10.1007/s10803-011-1293-y.

Blackmore, C.E., Woodhouse, E.L., Gillan, N., Wilson, E., Ashwood, K.L., Stoencheva, V., NolanA., McAlonan, G.M., Robertson, D.M., Whitwell, S., Deeley, Q., Craig, M.C., Zinkstok, J., Wichers, R., Spain, D., Roberts, G., Murphy, D.G.M., Murphy, C.M. and Daly, E. 2022. Adults with Autism Spectrum Disorder and the Criminal Justice System: An Investigation of Prevalence of Contact with the Criminal Justice System, Risk Factors and Sex Differences in a Specialist Assessment Service. *Autism.* 1–10. https://doi.org/10.1177/13623613221081343

Cage, E. and Troxell-Whitman, Z. 2019. Understanding the Reasons, Contexts and Costs of Camouflaging for Autistic Adults. *Journal of Autism and Developmental Disorders.* 49, 1899–1911.

Chaplin, E. and McCarthy, J. 2022. Autism and Offending Behaviour. In Nichola Tyler and Anne Sheeran (Eds). *Working with Autistic People in the Criminal Justice and Forensic Mental Health Systems: A Handbook for Practitioners*. London: Routledge. Chapter 4.

Collins, J., Horton, K., Gale-St. Ives, E., Murphy, F. and Barnoux, M. 2022. A Systematic Review of Autistic People and the Criminal Justice System: An Update of King and Murphy 2014. *Journal of Austism and Developmental Disorders*. 1–29. https://link.springer.com/article/10.1007/s10803-022-05590-3.

Dabner, L. and Newman-Clark, A. 2021. The Importance of RSHE for Disabled and NeurodiveRSHE Young People. *Brook Blog*. Available from https://brookblog.health.blog/2021/04/23/the-importance-of-RSHE-for-disabled-and-neurodiveRSHE-young-people/ (Accessed 16 May 2022).

Department for Education. 2015. *Special Educational Needs and Disability Code of Practice: 0 to 25 Years Statutory Guidance for Organisations Which Work with and Support Children and Young People Who Have Special Educational Needs or Disabilities*. Department for Education.

Department for Education. 2019. *Relationships Education, Relationships and Sex Education (RSHE) and Health Education: Statutory Guidance for Governing Bodies, Proprietors, Head Teachers, Principals, Senior Leadership Teams, Teachers*. Department for Education.

Department for Education. 2020. *Guidance: Teaching about Relationships, Sex and Health Support and Training Materials for Schools to Help Train Teachers on Relationships, Sex and Health Education. The Training Module on Teaching RSHE to Pupils with SEND (MS Powerpoint Presentation)*. Department for Education.

Eaton, J. 2021. Autism in Girls. *Autistic Girls Network Blog*. Available from https://autisticgirlsnetwork.org/autism-in-girls/ (Accessed 23 August 2022).

Frawley. P., and Bigby, C. 2014. 'I'm in Their Shoes': Experiences of Peer Educators in Sexuality and Relationship Education. *Journal of Intellectual and Developmental Disability*. 39 (2), 157–176.

French, D. 2021. Cognitive Behavioural Therapy. *Autism Parenting Magazine*. June 9. Available from https://www.autismparentingmagazine.com/cognitive-behavioral-therapy/ (Accessed 16 May 2022).

Green, R.M., Travers, A.M., Howe, Y. and McDougle, C. 2019. Women and Autism Spectrum Disorder: Diagnosis and Implications for Treatment of Adolescents and Adults. *Curentr Psychiatry Reports*. 21, 1–8. https://doi.org/10.1007/s11920-019-1006-3.

Hannah, L. A., and Stagg. S.D. 2016. Experiences of sex education and sexual awareness in young adults with autism spectrum disorder. *Journal of Autism and Developmental Disorders*. 46 (12) 3678–3687. https://doi.org/10.1007/s10803-016-2906-2

Haskins, B.G. and Silva, J.A. 2006. Asperger's disorder and criminal behaviour: Forensic psychiatric considerations. *The Journal of the American Academy of Psychiatry and the Law*. 34, 374–384.

Haque, O.S. and Waytz, A. 2012. Dehumanization in Medicine: Causes, Solutions, and Functions. *Perspectives on Psychological Science: A Journal of the Association for Psychological Science*. 7(2) 176–186. https://doi.org/10.1177/1745691611429706.

Hingsburger, D., Griffiths, D., and Quinsey, V. 1991. Detecting Counterfeit Deviance. *The Habilitative Mental Healthcare Newsletter*. 10 (9), 51–54.

Holliday Willey, L. 2015. *Pretending to be Normal: Living with Asperger's syndrome* (Expanded ed.). London: Jessica Kingsley Publishers.

Hull, L., Petrides, K.V. and Mandy, W. 2020. The Female Autism Phenolike and Camouflaging: A Narrative Review. *Review Journal of Autism and Developmental Disorders*. 7, 306–317. https://doi.org/10.1007/s40489-020-00197-9.

Kapp, S. 2019. How Social Deficit Models Exacerbate the Medical Model: Autism as Case in Point. *Autism Policy and Practice*. 2 (1) 3–28.

Lai, M.C., Lombardo, M. V., Ruigrok, A. N. V., Chakrabarti, B., Auyeung, B., Szatmari, P., et al. 2017. Quantifying and Exploring Camouflaging in Men and Women with Autism. *Autism*. 21 (6) 690–702. https://doi.org/10.1177/1362361316671012.

Lai, M.C. and Szatmari, P. 2019. Resilience in Autism: Research and Practice Prospects. *Autism.* 23 (3) 539–541.

Lord, C. and Jones, R.M. 2012. Annual Research Review: Re-thinking the Classification of Autism Spectrum Disorders. *Journal of Child Psychology and Psychiatry.* 53 (5) 490–509. https://doi.org/10.1111/j.1469-7610.2012.02547.x.

Mackin, L.M., Loew, N., Gonzalez, A., Tykol, H., and Christensen, T. 2016. Parent Perceptions of Sexual Education Needs for Their Children with Autism. *Journal of Pediatric Nurses.* Nov–Dec; 31(6) 608–618. https://doi.org/10.1016/j.pedn.2016.07.003. Epub 2016 Aug 21. PMID: 27554640.

McCann, E., Marsh, L. and Brown, M. 2019. People with Intellectual Disabilities, Relationship and Sex Education Programmes: A Systematic Review. *Health Education Journal.* 78 (8) 885–900. https://doi.org/10.1177/0017896919856047

McDaniels, B., and Fleming, A. 2016. Sexuality Education and Intellectual Disability: Time to Address the Challenge. *Sexuality and Disability* 34 (2) 215–225. https://doi.org/10.1007/s11195-016-9427-y.

McGee, M. 2021. Neurodiversity. *Contexts.* 11 (3) 12–13.

Mercer, J.E. and Allely, C.S. 2020. Autism Spectrum Disorders and Stalking. *Journal of Criminal Psychology.* 10 (3) 201–208. https://doi.org/10.1108/JCP-01-2020-0003.

Michielsen, K. and Brockschmidt, L. 2021. Barriers to Sexuality Education for Children and Young People with Disabilities in the WHO European Region: A Scoping Review. *Sex Education.* 21 (6) 674–692. https://doi.org/10.1080/14681811.2020.1851181.

Milton, D. 2012. On the Ontological Status of Autism: The 'Double Empathy Problem'. *Disability and Society.* 27 (6) 883–887. https://doi.org/10.1080/09687599.2012.710008.

Myles, B. S., and R. L. Simpson. 2001. Understanding the Hidden Curriculum: An Essential Social Skill for Children and Youth with Asperger Syndrome. *Intervention in School and Clinic.* 36, 279–286.

Milton. D. 2018. The Double Empathy Problem. *National Autistic Society.* Available from https://www.autism.org.uk/advice-and-guidance/professional-practice/double-empathy (Accessed 22 August 2022).

National Autistic Society. (n.d.). *Sex Education: A Guide for Parents.* Available from https://www.autism.org.uk/advice-and-guidance/topics/family-life-and-relationships/sex-education/parents-and-carers#H2_10 (Accessed 16 May 2022a).

National Autistic Society. 2022a. *What Is Autism?* Available from https://autism.org.uk/advice-and-guidance/what-is-autism (Accessed 15 August 2022b).

National Autistic Society. 2022b. *"My Life could be so Different". Experiences of Autistic Young People in the Youth Justice System.* London: National Autistic Society. Available at https://nas.chorus.thirdlight.com/link/n4bhhjjwhbxk-as0nu1/@/preview/1?o (Accessed 2 November 2022c).

National Health Service. 2019. *Overview—Cognitive Behavioural Therapy (CBT).* Available from https://www.nhs.uk/mental-health/talking-therapies-medicine-treatments/talking-therapies-and-counselling/cognitive-behavioural-therapy-cbt/overview/ (Accessed 2 November 2022).

Nichols, S. and Blakeley-Smith, A. 2009. "I'm Not Sure We're Ready for This …": Working with Families Toward Facilitating Healthy Sexuality for Individuals with Autism Spectrum Disorders. *Social Work in Mental Health.* 8 (1) 72–91. https://doi.org/10.1080/15332980902932383

Nicolaidis, C., Raymaker, D., Kapp, S.K., Baggs, A., Ashkenazy, E., McDonald, K., Weiner, M., Maslak, J. and Hunter, R. 2019. Practice-Based Guidelines for the Inclusion of Autistic Adults in Research as Coresearchers and Study Participants. *Autism, preprint online.* https://doi.org/10.1177/1362361319830523.

Nguyen, W., Ownsworth, T., Nicol, C. and Zimmerman, D. 2020. How I See and Feel About Myself: Domain-Specific Self-Concept and Self-Esteem in Autistic Adults. *Frontiers in Psychology.* 11 (913) 1–12

Oishi, S., Kesebir, S. and Snyder, B.H. 2009. Sociology: A Lost Connection in Social Psychology. *Personality and Social Psychology Review.* 13(4) 334–353. https://doi.org/10.1177/1088868309347835.

Oliver, M. 2013. The Social Model of Disability: Thirty Years On. *Disability and Society.* 28 (7) 1024–1026. https://doi.org/10.1080/09687599.2013.818773.

Padesky, C.A., and Mooney, K.A. 2012. Strengths-Based Cognitive-Behavioural Therapy: A Four-Step Model to Build Resilience. *Clinical Psychology and Psychotherapy.* (19) 283–290.

Pearson, A., Rees, J. and Forster, F. 2022. "This Was Just How This Friendship Worked": Experiences of Interpersonal Victimisation Among Autistic Adults. *Autism in Adulthood.* 4 (2) 141–150. https://doi.org/10.1089/aut.2021.0035.

Pellicano, E., Lawson, W., Hall, G., Mahony, J., Lilley, R., Heyworth, M., Clapham, J., and Yudell, M. 2021. "I Knew She'd Get It, and Get Me": Participants' Perspectives of a Participatory Autism Research Project. *Autism and Adulthood.* 4 (2) 120–120. https://doi.org/10.1089/aut.2021.0039.

Perihan, C., Burke, M., Bowman-Perrott, L., Bicer, A., Gallup, J., Thompson, J., and Sallese, M. 2020. Effects of Cognitive Behavioral Therapy for Reducing Anxiety in Children with High Functioning ASD: A Systematic Review and Meta-Analysis. *Journal of Autism and Developmental Disorders.* 50, 1958–1972. https://doi.org/10.1007/s10803-019-03949-7.

Post, M., Haymes, L., Storey, K., Loughrey, T. and Campbell, C. 2014 Understanding Stalking Behaviors by Individuals with Autism Spectrum Disorders and Recommended Prevention Strategies for School Settings. *Journal of Autism and Developmental Disorders.* 44 (11) 2698–2706. https://doi.org/10.1007/s10803-012-1712-8.

Psychology Today. 2022. *Neurodiversity and the Benefits of Autism.* Available from https://www.psychologytoday.com/us/basics/autism/neurodiversity-and-the-benefits-autism (Accessed 15 August 2022).

Roberts, K., Tolou-Shams, M., and Madera, K. 2016. Adolescent Versus Adult Stalking: A Brief Review. *Journal of Forensic Psychology Research and Practice.* 16 (4) 236–252. https://doi.org/10.1080/15228932.2016.1192334.

Robison, J. 2017. The Controversy Around Autism and Neurodiversity. *Psychology Today Blog.* Available from https://www.psychologytoday.com/gb/blog/my-life-aspergers/201704/the-controversy-around-autism-and-neurodiversity (Accessed 23 August 2022).

Singer, J. 2017. *Neurodiversity: The Birth of an Idea.* Judy Singer. 9780648154709 (ISBN10: 064815470X).

Social Care Institute for Excellence. (n.d.). *Strengths-Base Approaches.* Available from https://www.scie.org.uk/strengthss-based-approaches (Accessed 2 November 2022).

Stokes, M., and Newton, N. 2004. Autism Spectrum Disorders and Stalking. *The International Journal of Research and Practice.* 8 (3) 337–339.

Stokes, M., Newton, N., and Kaur, A. 2007. Stalking, and Social and Romantic Functioning Among Adolescents and Adults with Autism Spectrum Disorder. *Journal of Autism Developmental Disorders.* 37, 1969–1986.

Varjas, K., Meyers, J., Meyers, B., Kim, S., Henrich, C.C., and Tenebaum, L.S. 2009. Positive Psychology and the Prevention of School-Based Victimisation. In R. Gilman, E. S. Huebner and M. J. Furlong. (Eds.), *Handbook of Positive Psychology in Schools* (pp. 323–338). New York, NY: Routledge/Taylor and Francis.

Warrier, V., Greenberg, D.M., Weir, E., Buckingham, C., Smith, P., Lai, M.C., Allison. C. and Baron-Cohen. S. 2020. Elevated Rates of Autism, Other Neurodevelopmental and Psychiatric Diagnoses, and Autistic Traits in Transgender and Gender-Diverse Individuals. *Nature Communications.* 11 (1) 1–12 3959. https://doi.org/10.1038/s41467-020-17794-1. PMID: 32770077; PMCID: PMC7415151.

Weiss, J., and Fardella, M. 2018. Victimisation and Perpetration Experiences of Adults with Autism. *Frontiers in Psychiatry.* 9 (203) 1–10. https://doi.org/10.3389/fpsyt.2018.00203.

Ybarra, M.L., Langhinrichsen-Rohling, J., and Mitchell, K.J. 2016. Stalking-Like Behavior in Adolescence: Prevalence, Intent, and Associated Characteristics. *Psychology of Violence* 7 (2) 192–202. https://doi.org/10.1037/a0040145.

13 Improving Public Awareness of Stalking and Domestic Abuse in Young People

Maria Mellins and Clive Ruggles

Key Points

- A summary of findings from each chapter about how young people are impacted by stalking and domestic abuse.
- A reframing of the major themes that have emerged, which relate to the criminal justice system; victim support services; employment; the education system; and the media and gaps that exist in these areas.
- The Alice Ruggles Trust outline their recommendations for future work.

By Maria Mellins

The pages of this book provide accounts from varied perspectives concerning how young people are impacted by stalking and domestic abuse. Sadly, there is still a great deal of work to do. Whilst in recent years, stalking has received growing attention from the criminal justice system, support services, charities, researchers, and trainers who aim to educate others on its catastrophic impact, it is still a crime that all too often goes unidentified, is under-reported, and is misunderstood. Improving societal identification of stalking is vital to affect fundamental, long-term change. Under Key Finding 20 of Alice's *Domestic Homicide Review*, the authors outline the need for the general public to have a more detailed understanding of stalking behaviour and particularly the risk attached to incidents that

M. Mellins (✉)
St Mary's University, Twickenham, UK
e-mail: maria.mellins@stmarys.ac.uk

C. Ruggles
The Alice Ruggles Trust, Leicester, UK
e-mail: clive@alicerugglestrust.org

M. Mellins et al. (eds.), *Young People, Stalking Awareness and Domestic Abuse*,
https://doi.org/10.1007/978-3-031-32379-9_13

may appear innocent, noting that the '[p]ublic are generally unaware of stalking behaviours and associated risks'. The small acts of leaving gifts, or relentless communications may appear innocuous, they may even make people feel as though they are overacting, being dramatic, or wasting police time, but it is precisely 'within this context that greater public awareness of the risk posed by stalking needs to take place to empower both victims and bystanders' (DHR 2018, 79).

We wanted this book to focus specifically on young people as the likelihood of a young person being stalked is even higher than other age groups, whilst at the same time recognising stalking and abuse, and particularly the more emotional and psychological forms of abuse such as coercive control, is unfortunately even more challenging. After their review of sexual abuse in schools and colleges, Ofsted outlined, '[t]his rapid thematic review has revealed how prevalent sexual harassment and online sexual abuse are for children and young people' (Gov.uk 2021). The Higher Education sector paints a similarly bleak picture. Back in 2010, the National Union of Students (NUS) research, 'Hidden Marks: A study of women students of harassment, stalking, violence and sexual assault', found that students were at a higher risk of experiencing stalking and sexual violence, but that there was little awareness of this amongst them. The study stated that, '[w]e decided to undertake this research because women aged 16–24 have a higher risk of experiencing domestic violence, but there appeared to be little awareness of this amongst students' (Bailey 2010). Over a decade later, the recent Statement of Expectations released by the Office for Students (OfS) continues to call for the implementation of more 'effective systems, policies and processes to prevent and respond to incidents of harassment and sexual misconduct' (OfS 2021), demonstrating the urgent need to address safety and young people.

The reasons that stalking, and forms of relationship abuse, are not easily identified by young people (nor by their families, friends, schools, universities, workplaces, GPs, or even law enforcement) are numerous and have been discussed throughout the pages of this book, but a central theme that keeps emerging is that there appears to be some confusion about what stalking even is. Many cases of stalking don't start off using the word 'stalking', indeed sometimes that word is never found. Instead, the behaviours are thought to be strange, uncomfortable, threatening, hard to pin down, and insidious, but often cause the young person to significantly change aspects of their life and feel intense fear. Without a clear idea of what is happening to them, feeling as though they have no options, they may normalise or play down the abuse, and simply 'put up with it'. Perhaps this confusion is partly due to the framing of stalking within our society. The term 'stalking' is often minimised or used in conversation as a bit of a joke: phrases like 'I stalked them on social media' are common in modern life. We can note one recent example of stalking being presented as 'funny' from Valentine's Day. Valentine's cards are available that depict the character of Joe from the Netflix series *You*—who is shown to stalk, kidnap, and murder—accompanying the image of Joe is a strapline 'Stalker is a strong word, I prefer Valentine' and 'From your stalker'. 'Romantic' narratives of stalking are also plentiful in popular culture. Stalking is also often associated with celebrity. As Lowney and Best (1995) assert, stalking became much more visible in media of the late 1980s when it was framed as a news story of obsessed fans who engage in 'star-stalking'. Such links to celebrity can lead people to believe that stars are the main target of stalking behaviours, or that it is a crime that is rare and largely involves strangers lurking behind bushes as opposed to the much more likely scenario—*it is someone you know*.

As the chapter by Paladin National Stalking Advocacy Service demonstrates, not only are there challenges to recognising stalking, but once this behaviour is recognised, there are also many barriers for young people to gain access to essential support and advice. Firstly, the young person may not want or feel it is possible to reach out. They may be too afraid to report or seek further advice. This may be out of fear that the person stalking them may find out; it may be due to fear that their families, social networks, or colleagues will find out and 'everyone will know'; or it may be a result of intersectional factors that have led to a distrust of, or lack of access to, authority (including race, LGBTQ +, and factors relating to those with no recourse to public funds). Asking adults for help, especially adults they don't know and trust, can be a very difficult, daunting task for any young person: they have grown up in school environment where they are conditioned by peers to not 'tell on' people and 'snitches get stitches'. Added to this, even if a young person does make a disclosure to a friend, a family member, or a professional, there are challenges in ensuring they receive the right response. The advice that a young person may receive in response to the question, 'I think I am being stalked, what do I do next?' is, in today's climate, unfortunately really rather hit and miss.

Urgent attention must be given to heightening public awareness of stalking. The stakes are high, and everyone has a role to play in understanding and identifying this crime, to ensure the correct support is accessed by family, friends, acquaintances, and colleagues. As we shall see in the following section, one of the central ways that we can address societal awareness of stalking and domestic abuse is by developing safer, better-informed institutions and public services, so they have an improved response and encourage young victims and survivors to access them. Over the following pages, you will read some overarching themes that have emerged throughout this book, arranged into 'institution and public service contexts', namely the , victim support services, employment, the education system, and the media. Whilst there are certainly examples of good practice within these contexts, this book has also revealed the need to make essential changes and address gaps across key institutions in the UK and Ireland. Good work is already being done, but these environments also offer vital opportunities to significantly change the landscape and improve outcomes for young people.

Having summarised the research within this book, the final section of this chapter will turn to our partner, The Alice Ruggles Trust, who outlines how we can work together to bring about sustainable change and 'a vision for the future'.

Development of Safer Institutions

Criminal Justice System

The central question for Alice's family, and for the Alice Ruggles Trust (since its inception in 2017) is: 'if another Alice presented herself to the police today, would the outcome be very different?' (Alice Ruggles Trust Website https://alicerugglestrust.org). Encouragingly, over the past six years, since the Alice Ruggles Trust was founded, significant progress has been made. Whilst this chapter cannot capture all developments it is important to underline examples of this progress. In 2017, His Majesty's Inspectorate of Constabulary (HMIC) and HM Crown Prosecution Service Inspectorate (HMCPSI) carried out an inspection into how police and the Crown Prosecution Service (CPS) responded to harassment and stalking. This was published in a report entitled 'Living in Fear', as well as a research report on victim experience. In 2018, the CPS together with the National Police Chiefs' Council (NPCC) released a new Protocol on the appropriate handling of stalking or harassment offences as part of a package of measures to improve the Criminal Justice System response. Stalking sentences have been extended to acknowledge the seriousness and high risk of this crime, and several specialist multi-agency stalking units have been developed and set up. These include the Stalking Threat Assessment Centre (STAC), a partnership between the Metropolitan Police Service, the National Probation Service (NPS), Barnet, Enfield and Haringey NHS Trust, and the Suzy Lamplugh Trust; the Harm Reduction Unit (HRU) led by Cheshire Constabulary working alongside the NPS and local NHS services; and similar units in Hampshire and Cambridgeshire. The SPOC (Single Point of Contact) system has been introduced across all 43 police forces in England and Wales. Stalking Protection Orders (SPOs) were introduced in 2019 which carries a criminal conviction for any breach. These orders also impose positive restrictions that can be helpful to safeguard those who are being stalked, as well as providing therapies and intervention work. Stalking was also made a criminal offence in Northern Ireland under the *Protections from Stalking Act* in 2022. In terms of services, there has been an establishment of roles such as Independent Stalking Advocacy Caseworkers (ISACs), although it is acknowledged that whilst these roles are vital, they are under-resourced.

The *Domestic Abuse Act* (2021) has also included some very important changes. These include creating a legal, statutory definition for domestic abuse that recognises emotional and psychological forms of abuse, such as control, coercion, and economic abuse, and that children can be victims in their own right. The *Domestic Abuse Act* also establishes the appointment of a Domestic Abuse Commissioner who will stand up for victims and their vital support services; the Act places a duty on local authorities to provide accommodation-based support and also includes changes to family and civil court proceedings. It has introduced new criminal offences, such as non-fatal strangulation or suffocation; *threats* to disclose private sexual photographs, or 'revenge porn'; and coercive or controlling behaviour after a relationship has ended. It has also introduced measures to prevent abusers from using the 'rough sex defence'. The Act does have gaps in some areas, particularly with regard to support for migrant women and the management of serial perpetrators of domestic abuse and stalking. A full list of the key changes within the *Domestic Abuse Act* is available in Fig. 13.1.

Whilst such developments to the Criminal Justice System are certainly an important step forward, there are still many areas to work on. Much of this work is at an institutional level. Chapters have outlined that conviction rates are very low for stalking and other related crimes such as rape and sexual assault. There are serious issues with Family Courts being used as a method to continue abuse and secondary victimisation of those who report domestic abuse. As Clive Ruggles discusses later in the chapter, early indications suggest that Stalking Protection Orders (SPOs) need more research into their effectiveness and require a more embedded approach. There is also a need to expand essential training of frontline police and call handling staff to ensure they correctly identify stalking and use stalking legislation.

Further police training is a point that has been examined in Chapter 5 by O'Sullivan and Staunton during their general population study with those who have been stalked or harassed—the first survey of its kind to be conducted in Ireland. Advocates Una Ring and Eve McDowell, supported initially by the Sexual Violence Centre Cork, have successfully campaigned for the inclusion of a new stalking offence in the *Criminal Justice (Miscellaneous Provisions) Bill 2022* which will be enacted in 2023. However, the authors point out, echoing other voices within this book, that there are challenges ahead for law enforcement. An Garda Síochána and police forces in other jurisdictions need to be suitably trained and informed about the core behaviours and patterns so that they can recognise stalking and implement the law effectively. The chapter also outlines the importance of sharing information amongst agencies, and ensuring investigators avoid traps of responding to separate 'incidents' and instead investigate the history of offences and consider the wider patterns of behaviour.

Enhanced police training is also discussed in Chapter 6 in relation to technology-facilitated stalking and abuse. Banks and Andersson address the need for an improved criminal justice response to technology-facilitated coercive control and stalking behaviour. They provide a thorough discussion of how technology is used within stalking and abuse cases, including (but not limited to) smartphones with applications, computers, and—to a lesser extent—GPS devices and smart systems with video and/or audio (e.g., baby monitors, security systems) (Rogers et al. 2022). Whilst legal frameworks are in place to prosecute perpetrators of technology-facilitated abuse, evidence indicates that police officers and court officials may fail to recognise abuse and potential risks, and even if this is recognised it may be trivialised, which has serious impacts on victims and survivors and the outcomes of the case.

In terms of perpetrator-focused work, as Michael Lewis and Rachael Wheatley outline in Chapter 2, and Rachael Worthington addresses in Chapter 3, in order to find solutions to stalking we need to continue to get to the core of the

- create a statutory definition of domestic abuse, emphasising that domestic abuse is not just physical violence, but can also be emotional, controlling or coercive, and economic abuse
- establish in law the office of Domestic Abuse Commissioner and set out the Commissioner's functions and powers
- provide for a new Domestic Abuse Protection Notice and Domestic Abuse Protection Order

  place a duty on local authorities in England to provide accommodation based support to victims of domestic abuse and their children in refuges and other safe accommodation
- prohibit perpetrators of abuse from cross-examining their victims in person in the civil and family courts in England and Wales
- create a statutory presumption that victims of domestic abuse are eligible for special measures in the criminal, civil and family courts
- clarify the circumstances in which a court may make a barring order under section 91(14) of the Children Act 1989 to prevent family proceedings that can further traumatise victims
- extend the controlling or coercive behaviour offence to cover post-separation abuse.
- extend the offence of disclosing private sexual photographs and films with intent to cause distress
- create a new offence of non-fatal strangulation or suffocation of another person.
- (known as the "revenge porn" offence) to cover threats to disclose such material
- clarify by restating in statute law the general proposition that a person may not consent to the infliction of serious harm and, by extension, is unable to consent to their own death
- extend the extraterritorial jurisdiction of the criminal courts in England and Wales, Scotland and Northern Ireland to further violent and sexual offences
- provide for a statutory domestic abuse perpetrator strategy
- enable domestic abuse offenders to be subject to polygraph testing as a condition of their licence following their release from custody
- place the guidance supporting the Domestic Violence Disclosure Scheme ("Clare's law") on a statutory footing.
- provide that all eligible homeless victims of domestic abuse automatically have 'priority need' for homelessness assistance
- ensure that where a local authority, for reasons connected with domestic abuse, grants a new secure tenancy to a social tenant who had or has a secure lifetime or assured tenancy (other than an assured shorthold tenancy) this must be a secure lifetime tenancy
- prohibit GPs and other health professionals in general practice from charging a victim of domestic abuse for a letter to support an application for legal aid
- provide for a statutory code of practice relating to the processing of domestic abuse data for immigration purposes

Fig. 13.1 The Domestic Abuse Act 2021

issue concerning what makes someone vulnerable to stalking behaviours. Important perpetrator-focused initiatives are already occurring in the sector, which seek to understand, assess, interrupt, and provide therapies. For example, the recent British Psychological Society (BPS) publication *Working with individuals who have engaged in stalking: a resource for psychologists* (Wheatley et al. 2022) aims to help harmful behaviour, improve wellbeing, and encourage desistance. But whilst these valuable forensic resources are available, further initiatives need to be wholeheartedly supported and funded.

Chapter 2 also calls for further empirical studies that consider the motivations for stalking behaviours specifically within *adolescent* cases. The authors acknowledge that adolescent stalking shares motivational commonalities with adult stalking, but also draws on the study by Purcell et al. (2009) to outline one key motivational and contextual difference that relates to bullying-motivated stalking. Further research is required in order to unpick how these behaviours overlap and whether stalking is being misidentified as bullying—when do bullying behaviours meet the threshold of stalking? The need for further research on the links between bullying and stalking, and the potential to build interventions to address bullying-motivated stalking, is an area that has also been highlighted by education professionals during The Alice Ruggles Trust's SAfEE (Stalking and Abuse Awareness for Education Environments) training.

In a similar way, Chapters 7 and 8 also identify further gaps in the current research available on stalking, domestic abuse, and young people. During the 'Public and Policy Discourses' section of Chapter 7, Sadiq Bhanbhro outlines the need for further empirical research to identify the underlying narratives and assumptions behind so-called 'Honour'-Based Abuse (HBA) and how these intersect with domestic abuse and stalking. Bhanbhro explains the additional complexities that need to be considered in order to meaningfully tackle and *prevent* HBA, domestic abuse, and stalking, necessitating approaches that go even further than the common ones used to address violence against women and girls. Efforts that include introducing strict laws, training police, cultural competency-building of prosecutors, and more shelter homes for victims are all necessary but will not be sufficient to prevent these crimes. Bhanbhro argues that there is a need to bring change from within, 'to alter the social structures and narratives that create a viable environment for perpetrators of HBA'. Work is needed to engage communities in order to change the attitudes held about notions of honour and uplift young people's skills to report.

Victim-Survivor Services and Public Health

Several chapters within this book highlight the need for victim services and wider health agencies to develop their provision to ensure they are accessible to all users. For example, in Chapter 9, Paladin National Stalking Advocacy Service provides rich detail concerning their challenge to encourage younger clients to access their service. Authors Mayat and Neville explain that after their own realisation that young people were not accessing their service in the numbers they would expect, Paladin realised they had to do more to support young people referrals to their service. They highlight in their chapter that an absence of referrals from marginalised groups does not equate to a lack of need. Instead, a service must recognise their role in producing a service *with* young people. They outline that support services and the criminal justice agencies are complex and difficult to navigate for people of all ages, so to expect a young person to be able to navigate this in the same way as an adult is unrealistic. The authors outline that engaging young-person ambassadors was key to their growth in young clients, as was their commitment to developing a greater understanding of online social media use. The authors discuss the need to avoid narratives that advise young people to 'come off' social media, and instead embrace these technologies that are an embedded, interwoven aspect of young people's lives. This warning is also put forward by Banks and Andersson in Chapter 6, who states that service professionals, like their criminal justice counterparts, must not simply advocate for young people to disengage with technology, but instead should support them to optimise the technology-related safeguards available. Paladin suggests including social media champions within the service and enhancing the online provision to ensure it appears more accessible to young people.

In addition to attending to the details of their service so that it is accessible to young people, Chapter 8 reflects on the need for practitioners to think carefully about the full, lived experience of their clients to ensure that potential harms are not missed. Within this chapter, authors Mohammad Mazher Idriss and Rahmanara Chowdhury also look at the links between stalking and honour-based abuse. The chapter outlines the details of these cases and how HBA includes 'honour' killings 'where women are harmed or even killed for allegedly violating cultural norms relating to sexuality and who are seen to have 'tarnished' their family's good name and reputation'. The authors explore three pivotal case studies of HBA in relation to the 'web model of DVA' (domestic violence and abuse) that was initially developed from research conducted within UK Muslim communities. They explain the web model as a method that focuses on placing the victim at the heart of interventions and supports practitioners to understand a more holistic picture when working with clients. This picture includes consideration of intersectionality and cultural nuances. It is very useful in detecting potential harms across four different levels of a person's life, allowing practitioners to identify patterns of abusive behaviours from a variety of sources. The chapter advocates for wider engagement with the model and outlines its benefits that encourage 'a more comprehensive manner of working *with* clients rather than being limited by the confines of a risk assessment tool'. Risk assessment tools do rely heavily on the skills of the practitioner to ensure that all risk is being considered. It is therefore vital to ensure that professionals who work with people who are experiencing trauma—including those who work in criminal justice agencies, frontline victim services, mental health, and within medical contexts such as GP surgeries and hospitals—have specific awareness training so they can identify behaviours associated with stalking and HBA. This will limit the likelihood that stalking and HBA will be misidentified as other offences.

Employment

In Chapter 10, authors Laura Scarr and Morag Kennedy outline their pilot study in collaboration with the Hollie Gazzard Trust, which highlights the experience of stalking within hands-on occupations, including beauticians, tattooists, masseuses, and spa therapists. These occupations often draw young people, especially young women, to the workforce. During interviews, respondents explain how they are regularly put in risky situations within the workplace. They often work alone, and in confined spaces that restrict their movement and exit routes. In response to feelings of unsafety, discourses emerged that employees engaged with their own form of 'safety work' to find alternative ways to cope with difficult situations and keep themselves safe. These included avoidance strategies such as parking further away from work or in different streets or areas from those where clients park; not attending certain physical spaces of the business or sending colleagues on their behalf; and not wearing make-up and putting their hair up to try and avoid being noticed. Such strategies align with Vera-Gray (2018)'s and Kelly (2012)'s belief that women's 'safety work' is cultivated by the unsafety of femininity (Vera-Gray and Kelly 2020, 217).

Scarr and Kennedy also outline another important discourse concerning 'lack of employee worth'. They identify this as an area in need of further research. During this discourse, respondents articulate their frustrations with the level of safety training undertaken by senior managers and whether there was a sufficient consideration of potential risks within their workplace. Sadly for some, this is linked to a prioritisation of business needs over employee needs—money before safety. This is expanded by Nick Gazzard in the final section of the chapter. Nick Gazzard is the father of Hollie Gazzard and co-founder and CEO of the Hollie Gazzard Trust. Hollie was tragically murdered by her ex-partner in her place of work, a hair salon in Gloucester, in 2014. In this chapter, Nick Gazzard calls for improved training and safety measures within hands-on workplaces to ensure employees are sufficiently prepared for situations they may encounter. Gazzard concludes, 'more research needs to be undertaken to fully identify the impact of stalking in hands-on occupations, and what can be done to fill the gaps in education and training of both employers and employees and protect victims and potential victims by early identification of associated risks. Putting 'money' before 'safety' is never acceptable'.

When people are subjected to stalking and abuse, this will inevitably impact their work life—either directly, because the person who is stalking them may use their workspace to track, access, undermine, or humiliate them, or indirectly, as the young person struggles to work at their usual performance rate, whilst going through such trauma. It is therefore paramount that young people's workplaces, just like their education environments (which will be discussed in the next section) are equipped with suitable awareness training, and develop specific domestic abuse and stalking policies and procedures. This includes a consideration of how to keep people safe at work and how to prevent risk escalating, as well as having an understanding of the support and signposting that staff members need.

Education

As Part three of this book, *Stalking Support Services and Healthy Relationship Education*, has underlined, the education system is a vital way to inform younger members of the public about stalking and domestic abuse, especially behaviours linked to healthy relationship training and coercive control. In Chapter 11 Fiona Drouet and Poppy Gerrard-Abbott address the prevalence of Gender-Based Violence (GBV) in universities. During the chapter, Gerrard-Abbott's Ph.D. findings are discussed and links are drawn to wider research in the field concerning the specific, unique manifestations and challenges of GBV within universities. However, Gerrard-Abbott also notes that the existing body of research has gaps in fully grasping how GBV manifests in universities, and how 'community structures are uniquely enabling'. During the discussion of 'Universities as Island Living', Gerrard-Abbott notes the language that students use to describe the university setting, often likening universities to a 'bubble' and describing it as 'a world of its own' and 'out in the sticks'. The tight-knit, social networks of education contexts show them to be 'a multiplex, hosting students' academic, economic, occupational, social, and political life together, giving rise to unique challenges'. In this way, universities are both structurally interconnected and involve many areas of a young personal life, but they are also secluded, which extends possibilities for surveillance, targeting, and bullying behaviours.

As Drouet and Gerrard-Abbott outline, stalking and domestic abuse is widespread within universities and the education system more generally. Tackling these behaviours within education is, indeed, one of the central aims of the Alice Ruggles Trust who have already collaborated with the PSHE Association to introduce relationship safety resources in schools. These lessons include 'Identifying Healthy Relationships', 'Managing Unwanted Attention', and 'Reducing Inappropriate Behaviours' (https://alicerugglestrust.org/relationship-safety-resource).

Similarly, Chapter 12 by Helen Bovill, Sarah Chicken, Julie Buckland, and Kieran McCartan continues the discussion of ensuring stalking awareness within education. Bovill, Chicken, Buckland, and McCartan make important recommendations to specifically consider neurodiversity when planning and delivering education on healthy relationships and related RSHE topics. They outline the need for improvements to guidance and policy and ensuring the provision is not 'one size fits all': that it, is first and foremost empowerment-led, enabling autistic young people to demand provision, and have a say in its development (McCann et al. 2019; Michielsen and Brockschmidt 2021). This emphasis on involving young people in the development of this work is echoed in a number of chapters within this book, mirroring the approach outlined previously by Paladin.

Media

Given the myths and misunderstandings of stalking and the prevalence of this crime amongst all age groups, but particularly young people, this book has highlighted the need for increased societal awareness of stalking and more specifically the requirement for education and other key institutions in the UK and Ireland to tackle this public health issue. This education should come in many forms, including formal education in schools, colleges and universities, training within our criminal justice system, and support services and workplaces, but should also place an emphasis on the role of the media to shed light on this important topic. Thoughtfully produced, well-informed media that draw on partnerships with people with lived experience and research in these areas is vital to support us all to recognise stalking behaviour and to find much-needed support.

Collaboration between media content providers and those who have been personally affected by stalking or work in the field provides rich opportunities for public education. As Lowney and Best (1995) argue in their article, the media has shaped public understanding of stalking in the past, and these outlets have the potential to raise public awareness of stalking in a meaningful way in the future. We can note these possibilities during programming about stalking, including the recent coverage of stalking cases in *Stacey Dooley: Stalkers*, a two-part documentary series that aired on BBC in 2022, and episodes from Wondery's *Real Crime Profile* Podcast (by Jim Clemente, Laura Richards and Lisa Zambetti). These media examples have the ability to function both as educators and awareness raisers, who can signpost viewers and listeners to help and support.

In contrast, ill-informed media can have detrimental impacts on how young people within our society understand stalking and domestic abuse. We do not need to look very far to find examples of media output that does little to help the victim and survivors of domestic abuse, with even popular programming glamourising and minimising sexual violence. In Chapter 11 Fiona Drouet points out examples of damaging media narratives concerning intimate partner violence during her discussion of EmilyTest. EmilyTest is a Scottish charity that was set up in 2016 following the death of undergraduate student Emily Drouet, after she was subjected to a campaign of gender-based violence from a fellow student. During Chapter 11, Emily's mother, Fiona, outlines the role of the charity and its GBV charter, which is 'a flexible framework, based on evidence, student and survivor voices and co-creation with staff, to help institutions start or improve their work in tackling GBV' (EmilyTest website). Fiona Drouet discusses how increasingly the lines between healthy and unhealthy relationships become blurred, with pornography and more mainstream examples of films and media promoting breath play, strangulation and torture as aspects of relationships to aspire to, normalising and condoning the behaviour on a daily basis. Fiona Drouet continues by outlining the need to raise awareness of strangulation and the escalated risk that is attached to this, including a significantly higher risk of death, as well as the hidden internal injuries, long-term neurological damage, and devasting psychological injury. Fiona Drouet's discussion aligns with Tine Munk and Rachel Austin in Chapter 4, who also examines the role of adolescents' use of popular media to understand and learn about relationships and the dangers of representations of stalking that are positively framed in movies.

As this book has addressed, the media can contribute to unhelpful, narrow, and even dangerous representations of strangulation, stalking, and domestic abuse that can minimise and normalise crimes and romanticise violence, especially against women and girls. But equally, this book has also found that the media have the potential to lead the way in moulding public understanding of sexual violence. As Helen Benedict (2005) points out in her analysis of media language of rape, '[t]he media reflects public opinion, to be sure, but it also shapes it, for it is through the media that the public receives all its news and most of its information' (2005, 127). The media are a powerful institution and one that can be used to change attitudes and opinions. Therefore, further comprehensive, well-informed, and researched media that take up collaborative opportunities with experts and those with lived experience of domestic abuse and stalking is key to enhance public identification and response.

Looking Forward

By Clive Ruggles

The 2022 'Super-Complaint' and Recommendations

The Alice Ruggles Trust is one of 21 charities and partners who, as members of the National Stalking Consortium, are signatories to a 'super-complaint' on the police response to stalking that was registered on 25 November 2022, the tenth anniversary of the day when stalking first became a criminal offence in England and Wales (Suzy Lamplugh Trust, 2022a). The purpose of a super-complaint is to raise concerns that will be considered and investigated by His Majesty's Inspectorate of Constabulary and Fire and Rescue Services (HMICFRS), the College of Policing, and the Independent Office for Police Conduct (IOPC) (UK Government 2022).

Some of the specific points of concern identified in the super-complaint are:

- Only 5% of reports of stalking to the police in the year ending March 2022 resulted in a charge by the Crown Prosecution Service (CPS), a percentage that is on the decrease.
- In too many cases there is a failure to identify a course of conduct that constitutes stalking.
- In too many cases there is a failure to investigate the crime appropriately, including erroneously dropping cases due to a perceived lack of evidence.

By Clive Ruggles
Alice Ruggles Trust, Leicester, UK

- Stalking Protection Orders (SPOs), introduced in 2020 and designed to protect victims whilst evidence is collated for a prosecution, are often not being put in place by officers.
- Breaches of SPOs are too often not being followed up promptly and properly, resulting in increased danger to many victims.

The Consortium puts forward several recommendations to implement systemic change to improve the police response to stalking, including much more specialist training, greater investment in improving digital evidence retrieval for cyberstalking, and a unified recording system amongst the various criminal justice agencies to improve the tracking of stalking cases. There is also an urgent need to address why SPOs are being underused, and in particular why breaches—which indicate a high level of risk (Monckton-Smith et al. 2017; Monckton-Smith 2018)—are too often being ignored despite constituting a criminal offence in themselves. The Alice Ruggles Trust's annual conference in 2021 passed a resolution calling for an urgent and comprehensive independent review of SPOs, something that is still needed at the time of writing.

Working Together: A Vision for the Future

The Alice Ruggles Trust argues that improving the police response to stalking is just one aspect of an integrated approach involving a range of organisations which is essential in order to bring about sustainable change. We have proposed a five-point 'plan of action' based on the need for

- better 'joining of the dots' (better recognition of stalking cases in the first place);
- a better criminal justice response in dealing with cases;
- better multi-agency working to identify and manage the risk;
- better public awareness of the stalking, so that victims become known to professional services sooner; and
- more specialist stalking advocates (Alice Ruggles Trust 2023).

Whilst the first two of these relate particularly to points raised in the super-complaint and focus upon the criminal justice response to stalking cases, the third is also essential because a criminal justice response is not generally adequate in itself and does not address risks going forward. The MASIP model, for example, has been shown to work well in practice and needs to be resourced not only so that can it be emulated in other police force areas but also to ensure its sustainability.

The fourth point relates most strongly to the Trust's own plans. These include:

- Expanding and developing our stalking and relationship awareness provision within schools, both within the PSHE curriculum and via school assemblies. This means facilitating wider delivery by teachers, police community support officers, and where possible in person by representatives of the charity, and reaching younger age groups.
- Expanding our SAfEE programme of short courses for professionals working with young people, with tailored provision following on from pilot projects focusing on support staff in universities and NHS staff.

We also focus strongly on early perpetrator intervention projects to help prevent stalking behaviours developing in the first place, including (in partnership with the University of Derby) the development of a Stalking Tool for Adolescents at Risk of Stalking (STARS) to provide targeted support for teenagers at high risk of experiencing or perpetrating abuse.

Finally, the importance of specialist advocates for stalking (Independent Stalking Advisory Caseworkers, ISACs), who play a critical role in supporting the victims' safety and wellbeing, has been highlighted by research by the Suzy Lamplugh Trust (2022b) as well as personal campaigns by the parents of Gracie Spinks and Alice Ruggles (Alice Ruggles Trust 2022). A focus for campaigners has been the need for earmarked funding to ensure the availability of stalking advocates in every part of the country. Whilst the government intends to significantly increase the number of Independent Domestic Violence Advisors (IDVAs) and Independent Sexual Violence Advisors (ISVAs) by 2024/2025 (UK Government 2023), there remains a lack of recognition that stalking cases do not always involve domestic or sexual violence, and that stalking represents a huge and serious problem in its own right.

Discussion Questions

- Why is stalking so often not recognised within our society? How might we improve public awareness of stalking?
- What is a stalking advocate and how do they support victims-survivors of stalking?
- Are there specific ways that victim support services can tailor their service to provide better access for young clients?
- How important is an awareness of stalking and domestic abuse to young people's employers? What role do employers play in staff safety?
- Why are universities so 'uniquely enabling' when it comes to stalking and domestic abuse? How might they meaningfully tackle this to help safeguard their community?

Bibliography

Alice Ruggles Trust. 2020. *Relationship Safety Resource*. https://www.alicerugglestrust.org/relationship-safety-resource. Accessed 3rd January 2023.

Alice Ruggles Trust. 2022. Supporting Gracie. https://alicerugglestrust.org/post/supporting-gracie. Accessed 26th January 2023.

Alice Ruggles Trust. 2023. Improving the Police Response to Stalking. https://alicerugglestrust.org/post/improving-police-response-stalking. Accessed 26th January 2023.

Bailey, O. 2010. Hidden Marks. A Study of Women Students' Experiences of Harassment, Stalking, Violence and Sexual Assault. NUS. UK.

Benedict, H. 2005. The Language of Rape. In E. Buchwald, P. Fletcher, P.R. Fletcher, M. Roth (Eds.), *Transforming a Rape Culture*. Minnesota: Milkweed Editions.

Domestic Abuse Bill. 2019–2021.—UK Parliament. 2020. Services.Parliament.UK. https://services.parliament.uk/bills/2019-21/domesticabuse.html. Accessed 1st June 2020.

Douglass, S. (Independent Chair), Reed, D., and Adam L. 2018. Domestic Homicide Review into the Death of Alice Ruggles. Gateshead Council. Gateshead.Gov.Uk. https://www.gateshead.gov.uk/article/11258/Domestic-homicide-review-into-death-of-Alice-Ruggles. Accessed 26th April 2020.

EmilyTest. 2023. http://emilytest.co.uk. Accessed 19th January 2023.

Fissel, E.R., Reyns, B.W. and Fisher, B.S. 2020. Stalking and Cyberstalking Victimization Research: Taking Stock of Key Conceptual, Definitional, Prevalence, and Theoretical Issues. In H. Chan and L. Sheridan (eds.), *Psycho-Criminological Approaches To Stalking Behavior*. London: John Wiley and Sons.

HMIC and HMCPSI. 2017. Living in Fear–The Police and CPS Response to Harassment and Stalking: A Joint Inspection by HMIC and HMCPSI. HMIC 2017. Available from: https://www.justiceinspectorates.gov.uk/hmicfrs/publications/living-in-fear-thepolice-and-cps-response-to-harassment-and-stalking/. Accessed 1st June 2020.

Hollie Gazzard Trust. 2023. https://holliegazzard.org. Accessed 19th January 2023.

Humphreys, C.J., and J Towl, G.J. 2020. *Addressing Student Sexual Violence In Higher Education*. Bingley: Emerald Publishing.

Kelly, Liz. 2012. Standing the Test of Time? Reflections on the Concept of the Continuum of Sexual Violence. In J. Brown and S. Walklate (Eds.), *Handbook on Sexual Violence*, xvii–xxvi. London: Routledge.

Lowney, K. & Best, J. 1995. Stalking Strangers and Lovers: Changing Media Typifications of a New Crime Problem. In J. Best (Ed.), *Images of Issues. Typifying Contemporary Social Issues*. London and New York: Routledge.

McCann, E., Marsh, L. & Brown, M. (2019) People with Intellectual Disabilities, Relationship and Sex Education Programmes: A Systematic Review. *Health Education Journal*. 78 (8) 885–900 https://doi.org/10.1177/0017896919856047.

Michielsen, K. & Brockschmidt, L. (2021) Barriers to Sexuality Education for Children and Young People with Disabilities in the WHO European Region: A Scoping Review. *Sex Education*. 21 (6) 674–692. https://doi.org/10.1080/14681811.2020.1851181.

Monckton-Smith, J., Szymanska, K. & Haile, S. 2017. *Exploring the Relationship between Stalking and Homicide*. NSAW Report 04–17. https://eprints.glos.ac.uk/4553/1/NSAW%20Report%2004.17%20-%20finalsmall.pdf. Accessed 28th January 2023.

Monckton-Smith, J. 2018. *Intimate Partner Femicide Timeline*. https://eprints.glos.ac.uk/6273/1/Intimate%20Partner%20Femicide%20Timeline.pdf. Accessed 28th January 2023.

Office for National Statistics. 2019. Stalking: Findings from the Crime Survey for England and Wales. London. Retrieved from: https://www.ons.gov.uk/peoplepopulationandcommunity/crimeandjustice/datasets/stalkingfindingsfromthecrimesurveyforenglandandwales. Accessed 30th August 2020.

Office for Students. 2021. Statement of Expectations. https://www.officeforstudents.org.uk/advice-and-guidance/student-wellbeing-and-protection/prevent-and-address-harassment-and-sexual-misconduct/statement-of-expectations. Accessed 30th January 2023.

Ofsted. Gov.UK. 2021. Review of Sexual Abuse in Schools and Colleges. https://www.gov.uk/government/publications/review-of-sexual-abuse-in-schools-and-colleges/review-of-sexual-abuse-in-schools-and-colleges. Accessed 23rd January. 2023.

Paladin National Stalking Advocacy Service. 2023. https://www.paladinservice.co.uk/. Accessed 3rd January 2023.

Phipps, A. 2010. *Hidden Marks: A Study of Women Students' Experiences of Harassment, Stalking, Violence and Sexual Assault*. London: National Union of Students. Accessed 6th May 2020.

Purcell, R., Moller, B., Flower, T. & Mullen, P.E. 2009. Stalking Among Juveniles. *The British Journal of Psychiatry*. 194 451–455.

Real Crime Profile. 2018. https://wondery.com/shows/real-crime-profile/. Accessed 19th January. 2023.

Rogers, M.M., Fisher, C., Ali, P., Allmark, P. & Fontes, L. 2022. Technology-Facilitated Abuse in Intimate Relationships: A Scoping Review. *Trauma, Violence, and Abuse.*

Suzy Lamplugh Trust. 2020. https://www.suzylamplugh.org/. Accessed 3rd January 2023.

Suzy Lamplugh Trust. 2022a. Super-Complaint on the Police Response to Stalking. https://www.suzylamplugh.org/Handlers/Download.ashx?IDMF=cf3fdc8b-f958-4cc0-9fc7-9ce6de3e9137. Accessed 26th January 2023.

Suzy Lamplugh Trust. 2022b. Bridging the Gap: A Stalking Advocate for Every Victim. https://www.suzylamplugh.org/Handlers/Download.ashx?IDMF=36e87aea-15ba-437a-97f6-d5966360878f. Accessed 26th January 2023.

UK Government. 2022. https://www.gov.uk/government/collections/police-super-complaints. Accessed 26th January 2023.

UK Government. 2023. Press Release: Law to Recognise Children Born as a Result of Rape as Victims for the First Time. https://www.gov.uk/government/news/law-to-recognise-children-born-as-a-result-of-rape-as-victims-for-the-first-time. Accessed 26th January 2023.

Vera-Gray, Fiona. 2018. *The Right Amount of Panic: How Women Trade Freedom for Safety*. Bristol: Policy Press.

Vera-Gray, F. & Kelly, L. 2020. Contested Gendered Space: Public Sexual Harassment and Women's Safety Work. *International Journal of Comparative and Applied Criminal Justice* 44 (4) 265–275.

Wheatley, R., Henley, S. & Underwood, A. (Eds.). 2022. *Working with Individuals Who Have Engaged in Stalking: A Resource for Psychologists*. Leicester: British Psychological Society.

Glossary

Adolescents: The period of life between childhood and adulthood. Typically associated with 10- to 19-year-olds.

AirTag: This is a small tracking device produced by Apple and linked to their 'Find My' application for products such as the iPhone, iPad, and iPod.

Asperger's Syndrome: Often used to define someone on the autism spectrum, characterised by stronger verbal skills and sometimes high intellectual ability, was a separate definition to autism before the 2011 Diagnostic and Statistical Manual of Mental Disorders (DSM-5).

Autism Spectrum Disorder (ASD): A range of conditions characterised by challenges with social skills and restricted, repetitive behaviours within speech and non-verbal communication. Recognised by the 2011 Diagnostic and Statistical Manual of Mental Disorders (DSM-5) and in most cases replacing a diagnosis of Asperger's Syndrome.

Axis 1 and Axis 2 disorder: Axis I disorder includes clinical conditions that are psychological in nature, Axis II includes personality and developmental disorders.

Coercive control: Coercive control is defined as an act or a pattern of acts of assault, threats, humiliation, and intimidation or other abuse that is used to harm, punish, or frighten their victim.

Cognitive Behavioural Therapy (CBT): CBT is a talking therapy that can help to manage problem feelings and behaviours by changing the way the individual thinks and behaves through practical ways. It is typically used to treat mental health conditions such as anxiety and depression, but can also be useful for a range of mental and physical health problems. The underlying principle of CBT is the notion that mental disorders and problematic behaviour are maintained by cognitive factors. CBT aims to address unhelpful cognitions and behaviours. Engaging in CBT encourages individuals to identify the dysfunctional thinking and behavioural patterns, replacing them with helpful and adaptive ones. The premise of CBT is that it is how the individual perceives an event which influences their emotional reaction and behavioural response. Through the process of therapy, the individual develops healthy alternative beliefs and practices applying

M. Mellins et al. (eds.), *Young People, Stalking Awareness and Domestic Abuse*, https://doi.org/10.1007/978-3-031-32379-9

these. CBT advocates that early life experiences shape the beliefs we hold about ourselves, others, and the world.

Cyberstalking: The repeated use of electronic communications to threaten, harass, or frighten someone.

DASH: (Domestic Abuse, Stalking, Harassment, and Honour-Based Violence Assessment) risk assessment tool: The DASH is a standardised risk assessment tool to help professionals assess the risk level for the victim and risk of serious harm. It has been implemented across most UK police forces.

Diagnostic and Statistical Manual of Mental Disorders (DSM-5): The DSM-5 is the standard classification of mental disorders used by mental health professionals.

Direct Stalking: A clear link of stalking as a crime shown in the media.

Domestic abuse: The UK government's definition of domestic abuse is 'any incident or pattern of incidents of controlling, coercive, threatening behaviour, violence or abuse between those aged 16 or over who are, or have been, intimate partners or family members regardless of gender or sexuality'.

Emily Test: A Scottish Government-funded charity in Scotland working to improve gender-based violence (GBV) prevention, intervention, and support in further and higher education.

Emotional dysregulation: A term used to refer to having emotions that are overly intense in comparison to the situation that triggered them. In other words, the emotion is poorly regulated and does not fall within the traditionally accepted range of emotional reaction.

Erotomania: A delusional conviction of being loved despite the supposed lover having done nothing to encourage or sustain that belief.

Fandom: A subculture composed of fans who share a common interest (e.g., a band; musician; or TV show).

Forced Marriage Protection Orders (FMPOs): Injunctions that aim to prevent an existing or former partner from harming a victim and/or children, including physical violence, harassment, intimidation, and psychological abuse.

Functional Behaviour Assessment (FBA): A process to identify behaviours leading to appropriate interventions.

Functional magnetic resonance imaging (fMRI): A technique for measuring brain activity.

Gaslighting: A deliberate and systematic form of manipulation and control where the intent is to use false information leading to a questioning of truth.

Gender-Based Violence: Refers to harmful acts directed at an individual based on their gender. It is rooted in gender inequality, the abuse of power, and harmful norms. Gender-based violence (GBV) is a serious violation of human rights and a life-threatening health and protection issue.

Harassment: In the United Kingdom, the terms 'harassment', 'intimidation', and 'abuse' are often used interchangeably as the experience of victims can overlap. The terms 'stalking' and 'harassment' are often used interchangeably with the meanings causing misunderstanding. Stalking and harassment are not separate behaviours, but patterns of interconnected behaviours driven by diverse motivations and functions.

Health and Safety at Work Act (HASWA): Legislation introduced to apply some broad duties and best practices for employers in regards to the health and safety of their workforce. This includes a duty of care for employees, casual workers, self-employed workers, clients, visitors, and the general public.

High Functioning Autism: Largely rejected within the autistic community and neither a medical or a diagnostic term but which is often used to describe autistic individuals without intellectual impairment.

Honour-based abuse: HBA concerns male violence against women, including so-called 'honour' killings, where women are harmed or killed for allegedly violating cultural norms relating to sexuality and who are perceived to have 'tarnished' their family's good name and reputation.

Independent Domestic Violence Advisor (IDVA): An IDVA's role is to support victims of domestic violence or abuse. These victims may be at high risk of harm from intimate partners, ex-partners, or family members.

Indirect Stalking*:* An unclear link of stalking as a crime shown in the media.

Information Communication Technology: The technological infrastructure, tools, and resources that are used to transmit, store, create, share, or exchange information.

Institutional Betrayal: A concept described by psychologist Jennifer Freyd and refers to wrongdoings perpetrated by an institution upon individuals dependent on that institution, including failure to prevent or respond supportively to wrongdoings by individuals committed within the context of the institution.

Internet Movie Database (IMDb): A global online database of information related to films, television series, home videos, video games, and streaming content online. This database includes information about the cast, production crew, biographies, plot summaries, trivia, ratings, fans, and critical reviews.

Interpersonal Victimisation: The process of being victimised or becoming a victim in interpersonal relationships.

Interpersonal Violence: Interpersonal violence is often referred to as intimate partner violence, domestic violence, or battering, is a pattern of behaviour used to establish power and control over another person through fear and intimidation, often including the threat or use of violence.

Intimate Partner or Familial Abuse: Behaviours within an intimate or family relationship that causes physical, sexual, and/or psychological harm.

Intimate Relationships: Interpersonal relationships which involve physical and/or emotional intimacy.

Jurisdictions: The legal authority that governs and protects a set-out area.

Learned Behaviour: Mannerisms and behaviours which are the result of observation.

Mass Media: Numerous types of media outlets which reach a vast amount of the popular via different communications.

Meta-analysis: A quantitative statistical analysis of separate independent studies of the same subject, in order to determine overall trends.

Narcissistic tendencies (narcissistic personality): Narcissistic personality disorder is a mental health condition in which people have an unreasonably high sense of their own importance. They need and seek too much attention and want people to admire them. People with this disorder may lack the ability to understand or care about the feelings of others. But behind this mask of extreme confidence, they are not sure of their self-worth and are easily upset by the slightest criticism. A narcissistic personality disorder causes problems in many areas of life.

Non-Molestation Orders (NMOs): Designed to protect victims from abuse, threats, and harassment. This order is an injunction which means that certain actions/behaviours are not allowed. They aim to prevent an existing or former partner from harming a victim and/or children, including physical violence, harassment, intimidation, and psychological abuse.

Online Streaming Services: A provider, found online which delivers content through the subscriber's technology, e.g., laptop; mobile phone; or other handheld devices.

Para-social relationships: A one-sided relationship whereby one party of the relationship invests time and emotional energy into the other party without them knowing. Para-social relationships are commonly with musicians, music bands, bands, or celebrities.

Persistent pursuit: A constant activity which someone engages in.

Personality disorder: An individual with a personality disorder thinks, feels behaviours or relates to others differently than the average person. There are several types of personality disorder. Personality disorder is characterised by a pattern of problematic behaviour (which is outside the norm). Personality disorders are chronic conditions, which means they emerge in adolescence/early adulthood and persist into adulthood. They result in distress or impaired functioning across several contexts. For example, offending, intimate, social and family relationships, and employment.

Polyvictimisation: The process of being victimised or becoming a victim from multiple sources. This can include, but not limited to, sexual abuse, physical abuse, bullying, and exposure to family violence.

Popular Media: A method of media and its content being easily accessible to a wide audience, spanning geographic and socioeconomic realms.

Post-relationship stalking (PRS): A pattern of targeted, repeated, and unwanted intrusive acts which occurs after a romantic relationship has dissolved that can be reasonably expected to cause apprehension, distress, or fear in the person stalked.

Post-traumatic stress disorder: Individuals presenting with PTSD have experienced or witnessed an event involving actual or threatened death or serious injury that causes them to respond with intense fear and feelings of helplessness. These traumatic events are often experienced through dreams, nightmares, or flashbacks, causing severe distress and anxiety.

Protection from Harassment Act 1997: The Protection from Harassment Act 1997 was the first legislation in the United Kingdom to view stalking as a criminal offence. Although the Act was a significant move forward, there were pitfalls in its ability to effectively address the complex issue of stalking behaviour.

Protection of Freedoms Act 2012: Fifteen years from the introduction of the Protection from Harassment Act 1997, on 25 November 2012, stalking was recognised as a specific criminal offence in England and Wales, with the enactment of the Protection of Freedoms Act 2012. This was outlined as: 'Stalking (Sect. 2A) which is pursuing a course of conduct which amounts to harassment and which also amounts to stalking, and stalking (Sect. 4A) involving fear or violence or serious alarm or distress' (Strickland, 2018, p.3). This legislation attempted to address the weaknesses of the Protection from Harassment Act, by making explicit reference to stalking behaviour.

Psychopathology: The study of psychological and behavioural dysfunction occurring in mental illness and disorders.

Psychosis: Refers to when people lose some contact with reality. This may include seeing or hearing things that other people cannot see or hear (hallucinations) or believing things that are not actually true (delusions).

Qualitative: A method using non-numerical data.

Quantitative: A method that uses data in the form of numbers.

Recidivism: Recidivism is the return to criminal behaviour (such as stalking behaviour) after a period of cessation.

Relationships, Sex, and Health Education (RSHE): The various policy of provision within schools adopted in the United Kingdom.

Romance Movies: Romantic love stories that are broadcasted which focus on the passion, emotion, and affectionate involvement of the main characters.

Rule Governed Behaviour (RGB): Behaviour which is influenced by antecedents and which uses this to follow instructions.

Schizophrenia: A mental disorder characterised by delusions, hallucinations, disorganised thoughts, speech, and behaviour.

Sexual Media Practice Model: A model of how adolescents choose, interpret, and interact with the mass media is relation to sexual development.

Sexual violence: Sexual violence is defined as 'actual, attempted, or threatened sexual contact with another person that is non-consensual. Sexual contact may be construed broadly to include acts such as sexual battery (e.g., rape, sexual touching), communications of a sexual nature (e.g., exhibitionism, obscene letters or phone calls), and violating property rights for sexual purposes (e.g., voyeurism, theft or fetish objects)'. Most acts of sexual violence will constitute a breach of criminal law. The definition includes all acts of sexual violence; however, not just those that result in criminal arrest, charge, or conviction.

Social Learning Theories: The study of learned behaviours through the observation, modelling, and imitation of behaviours which are reinforced by others.

Social Masking or Camouflaging: When an autistic person copies behaviour with a view to fit in.

Social Media: Websites and applications that enable users to engage in social networking and create and share content.

Social Stories: A social learning tool to support safe, meaningful exchanges of information between an autistic person and peers, friends, family, or professionals.

Socially Awkward Stalker Typology: Desiring a relationship but lacking the social skills to appropriately achieve this.

Stalking Assessment and Management (SAM): The SAM is a set of guidelines for the assessment and management of risk for stalking. The factors in the SAM are divided into three domains. Nature of stalking, perpetrator risk factors, and victim vulnerability factors. The SAM is intended for use by criminal justice, security, and mental health professionals working in a variety of contexts where complaints of stalking arise. The SAM is intended for use in cases when there is a known or suspected history of stalking. It may be used in cases where the primary perpetrator is aged 18 years and older, regardless of the perpetrator's gender or sexual orientation.

Stalking classification systems: Classification develops an understanding of a psychological phenomenon and is central to developing theoretical explanations. This is a way of categorising stalking behaviour and classifying this into clusters of homogenous groups based on characteristics, motivations, and behaviour.

Stalking Protection Order (SPO): SPOs came into force in January 2020. The Suzy Lamplugh Trust defines SPOs as follows: 'A Stalking Protection Order (SPO) is a civil order, the aim of which is to protect victims of stalking. It can be applied for by the police and is free of charge for the victim. The order can include prohibitions for the perpetrator, such as: entering certain locations or defined areas where the victim resides or frequently visits; contacting the victim by any means, including via telephone, post, email, SMS text message or social media; or contacting the victim through a third party. The order is particular because it can also include positive requirements, such as: attend an appropriate perpetrator intervention programme; a mental health assessment; a drugs and alcohol programme; surrender devices; provide the police with access to social media accounts, mobile phones, computers, tablets, and passwords/codes; and/or sign on at a police station'. Breaching an SPO is a criminal offence.

Stalking Risk Profile (SRP): A set of structured guidelines to assess a range of risks that are present in a given stalking situation, including the risk of the stalking recurring, or involving future physical violence. It also focuses practitioners on guidance for clinical management and potential treatment. The SRP provides clinicians with guidelines for estimating the potential for stalking violence, persistence, recurrence, and psychosocial damage to the perpetrator. It is intended to allow clinicians to tailor the assessment to the individual and their unique circumstances, and to help develop a comprehensive risk management plan, including specific treatment targets. The SRP is specific to the particular stalking situation by providing an understanding of what the risks are in this situation.

Strengths-Based Approach: An approach which focuses on individual's strengths rather than their deficits and in a holistic manner to promote well-being.

Survey: A flexible method of data collection that can be used in many different types of research.

Thematic analysis: A qualitative method that aims to find, analyse, and interpret patterns of meaning (i.e., themes) in qualitative data.

Thriller Movies: Movies that evoke feelings of suspense and excitement in their audience.

Typology: Since the emergence of stalking legislation in the 1990s, several typologies have been developed in an attempt to classify stalking behaviour to aid the clinical management of this population. There are numerous widely cited and influential stalking typologies which have been proposed based on the psychological characteristics of the perpetrator, motivations, and stalker–victim relationship. The most commonly used and recognised classification system is Mullen, et al. (1999) five stalker typology system. This typology is typically cited within the academic literature and has been applied within clinical practice across different settings. It is the underpinning framework for the Stalking Risk Profile (SRP) clinical assessment tool. Within this classification system, five different stalking subtypes have been identified based on different underpinning motives, personality traits, and relationships with the victim.

Web model of domestic violence: The web model of DVA was developed specifically with research conducted within UK Muslim communities. It aimed to increase the understanding of domestic abuse within Muslim communities at an academic and practitioner level, in direct response to the lack of representation within the field at present. It visually demonstrates how domestic abuse occurs within UK Muslim communities at four levels. These are the individual psycho-social-spiritual level, the stakeholder level, at the level of intersectionality, and finally, the macro level.

Index

M. Mellins et al. (eds.), *Young People, Stalking Awareness and Domestic Abuse*, https://doi.org/10.1007/978-3-031-32379-9

www.ingramcontent.com/pod-product-compliance
Ingram Content Group UK Ltd.
Pitfield, Milton Keynes, MK11 3LW, UK
UKHW020314020626
471728UK00004B/197
9783031323782